N. Brady

A New Version of the Psalms of David

Fitted to the Tunes Used in Churches

N. Brady

A New Version of the Psalms of David
Fitted to the Tunes Used in Churches

ISBN/EAN: 9783744784887

Printed in Europe, USA, Canada, Australia, Japan

Cover: Foto ©Lupo / pixelio.de

More available books at **www.hansebooks.com**

A New Version

OF THE

PSALMS

OF

DAVID,

FITTED TO

THE TUNES USED IN CHURCHES.

BY N. BRADY, D. D. CHAPLAIN IN ORDINARY,

AND

N. TATE, ESQ. POET-LAUREAT, TO HIS MAJESTY.

London:

PRINTED BY JOHN JARVIS, 1791.

Price One Shilling and Six Pence, unbound.

Shewing how to find each Psalm by its Beginning.

A 2

3 But thou, O Lord, art my defence; on thee my hopes rely;
Thou art my glory, and shall yet lift up my head on high.
4 Since, whensoe'er in like distress to God I make my pray'r,
He heard me from his holy hill, why should I now despair?

5 Guarded by him, I laid me down my sweet repose to take:
For I through him securely sleep, through him in safety wake.
6 No force nor fury of my foes my courage shall confound,
Were they as many hosts as men, that have beset me round.

7 Arise and save me, O my God, who oft hast own'd my cause,
And scatter'd oft these foes to me and to thy righteous laws.
8 Salvation to the Lord belongs, he only can defend;
His blessing he extends to all that on his pow'r depend.

PSALM IV.

1 O LORD, that art my righteous judge, to my complaint give ear;
Thou still redeems't me from distress, have mercy, Lord, and hear.
2 How long will ye, O sons of men, to blot my fame devise?
How long your vain designs pursue, and spread malicious lies?

3 Consider, that the righteous man is God's peculiar choice;
And when to him I make my pray'r, he always hears my voice.
4 Then stand in awe of his commands, flee ev'ry thing that's ill;
Commune in private with your hearts, and bend them to his will.

5 The place of other sacrifice let righteousness supply;
And let your hope, securely fixt, on God alone rely.
6 While worldly minds impatient grow more prosp'rous times to see,
Still let the glories of thy face shine brightly, Lord, on me.

7 So shall my heart o'erflow with joy more lasting and more true,
Than theirs, who stores of corn and wine successively renew.
8 Then down in peace I'll lay my head, and take my needful rest;
No other guard, O Lord, I crave, of thy defence possest.

PSALM V.

1 LORD, hear the voice of my complaint, accept my secret pray'r;
2 To thee alone, my King, my God, will I for help repair.
3 Thou in the morn my voice shalt hear; and with the dawning day
To thee devoutly I'll look up, to thee devoutly pray.

4 For thou the wrongs that I sustain canst never, Lord, approve;
Who from thy sacred dwelling-place all evil dost remove.
5 Not long shall stubborn fools remain unpunish'd in thy view:
All such as act unrighteous things thy vengeance shall pursue.

6 The sland'ring tongue, O God of Truth, by thee shall be destroy'd,
Who hat'st alike the man in blood and in deceit employ'd.
7 But when thy boundless grace shall me to thy lov'd courts restore,
On thee I'll fix my longing eyes, and humbly there adore.

8 Conduct me by thy righteous laws, for watchful is my foe:
Therefore, O Lord, make plain the way wherein I ought to go.
9 Their mouth vents nothing but deceit, their heart is set on wrong;
Their throat is a devouring grave, they flatter with their tongue.

10 By their own counsels let them fall, oppress'd with loads of sin;
For they against thy righteous laws have harden'd rebels been.
11 But let all those that trust in thee, with shouts their joy proclaim;
Let them rejoice whom thou preserv'st, and all that love thy name.

12 To righteous men the righteous Lord his blessing will extend,
And with his favour all his saints as with a shield defend.

PSALM VI.

1 THY dreadful anger, Lord, restrain, and spare a wretch forlorn;
Correct me not in thy fierce wrath, too heavy to be borne.
2 Have mercy, Lord, for I grow faint, unable to endure
The anguish of my aching bones, which thou alone canst cure.

3 My tortur'd flesh distracts my mind, and fills my soul with grief;
But, Lord, how long wilt thou delay to grant me thy relief!
4 Thy wonted goodness, Lord, repeat, and ease my troubled soul;
Lord, for thy wondrous mercy's sake, vouchsafe to make me whole.

5 For after death no more can I thy glorious acts proclaim;
No pris'ner of the silent grave can magnify thy name.
6 Quite tir'd with pain, of groaning faint, no hope of ease I see;
The night, that quiets common griefs, is spent in tears by me.

7 My beauty fades, my sight grows dim, my eyes with weakness close;
Old age o'ertakes me, whilst I think on my insulting foes.
8 Depart, ye wicked; in my wrongs ye shall no more rejoice;
For God, I find, accepts my tears, and listens to my voice.

9, 10 He hears, and grants my humble pray'r and they that wish my fall,
Shall blush and rage to see that God protects me from them all.

PSALM VII

1 O LORD, my God, since I have plac'd my trust alone in thee,
From all my persecutors' rage do thou deliver me.
2 To save me from my threat'ning foe, Lord, interpose thy pow'r;
Lest, like a savage lion, he my helpless soul devour.

3, 4 If I am guilty, or did e'er against his peace combine;
Nay, if I have not spar'd his life, who sought unjustly mine;
5 Let then to persecuting foes my soul become a prey;
Let them to earth tread down my life, in dust my honour lay.

6 Arise, and let thine anger, Lord, in my defence engage;
Exalt thyself above my foes, and their insulting rage:
Awake, awake, in my behalf, the judgment to dispense,
Which thou hast righteously ordain'd for injur'd innocence.

7 So to thy throne adoring crowds shall still for justice fly;
O! therefore for their sake resume thy judgment-seat on high.
8 Impartial judge of all the world, I trust my cause to thee;
According to my just deserts, so let thy sentence be.

9 Let wicked arts and wicked men together be o'erthrown;
But guard the just, thou God, to whom the hearts of both are known.
10, 11 God me protects, not only me, but all of upright heart;
And daily lays up wrath for those who from his laws depart.

12 If they persist, he whets his sword, his bow stands ready bent;
13 Ev'n now with swift destruction wing'd, his pointed shafts are sent.
14 The plots are fruitless which my foe unjustly did conceive:
15 The pit he digg'd for me has prov'd his own untimely grave.

16 On his own head his spite returns, whilst I from harm am free;
On him the violence is fall'n, which he design'd for me.
17 Therefore will I the righteous ways of Providence proclaim;
I'll sing the praise of God most High and celebrate his name.

PSALM VIII.

1 O Thou, to whom all creatures bow, within this earthly frame,
Thro' all the world how great art thou! how glorious is thy name!
In heav'n thy wondrous acts are sung, nor fully reckon'd there;
2 And yet thou mak'st the infant tongue thy boundless praise declare:

Thro' thee the weak confound the strong, and crush their haughty foes;
And so thou quell'st the wicked throng, that thee and thine oppose.
3 When heav'n, thy beauteous work on high, employs my wond'ring sight;
The moon, that nightly rules the sky, with stars of feebler light;

4 What's man (say I) that, Lord, thou lov'st to keep him in thy mind?
Or what his offspring, that thou prov'st to them so wondrous kind?
5 Him next in pow'r thou didst create to thy celestial train;
6 Ordain'd with dignity and state, o'er all thy works to reign.

7 They jointly own his pow'rful sway the beasts that prey or graze;
8 The bird that wings its airy way; the fish that cuts the seas.
9 O thou to whom all creatures bow within this earthly frame,
Thro' all the world how great art thou! how glorious is thy name!

PSALM IX.

1 TO celebrate thy praise, O Lord, I will my heart prepare;
To all the list'ning world thy works, thy wondrous works declare.
2 The thought of them shall to my soul exalted pleasure bring;
Whilst to thy name, O thou most High, triumphant praise I sing.

3 Thou mad'st my haughty foes to turn their backs in shameful flight;
Struck with thy presence, down they fell, they perish'd at thy sight.
4 Against insulting foes advanc'd thou didst my cause maintain;
My right asserting from thy throne, where truth and justice reign.

5 The insolence of heathen pride thou hast reduc'd to shame;
Their wicked offspring quite destroy'd, and blotted out their name.
6 Mistaken foes! your haughty threats are to a period come:
Our city stands, which you design'd to make our common tomb.

7 8 The Lord for ever lives, who has his righteous throne prepar'd,
Impartial justice to dispense, to punish or reward.
9 God is a constant sure defence against oppressing rage;
As troubles rise, his needful aids in our behalf engage.

10 All those who have his goodness prov'd will in his truth confide;
Whose mercy ne'er forsook the man that on his help rely'd.
11 Sing praises therefore to the Lord; from Sion his abode,
Proclaim his deeds, till all the world confess no other God

PART II.

12 When he enquiry makes for blood, he'll call the poor to mind:
The injur'd humble man's complaint relief from him shall find.
13 Take pity on my troubles, Lord, which spiteful foes create,
Thou that hast rescu'd me so oft from death's devouring gate.

14 In Sion then I'll sing thy praise, to all that love thy name;
And with loud shouts of grateful joy thy saving pow'r proclaim.
15 Deep in the pit they digg'd for me the heathen pride is laid;
Their guilty feet to their own snare are heedlessly betray'd:

16 Thus by the just returns he makes the mighty Lord is known;
While wicked men by their own plots are shamefully o'erthrown.
17 No single sinner shall escape by privacy obscur'd;
Nor nation from his just revenge by numbers be secur'd.

18 His suff'ring saints, when most distrest, he ne'er forgets to aid;
Their expectation shall be crown'd, though for a time delay'd.
19 Arise, O Lord, assert thy pow'r, and let not man o'ercome;
Descend to judgment, and pronounce the guilty heathen's doom.

20 Strike terror through the nations round, till, by consenting fear,
They, to each other, and themselves, but mortal men appear.

PSALM X.

1 THY presence why withdraw'st thou, Lord? why hid'st thou now thy face,
When dismal times of deep distress call for thy wonted grace?
2 The wicked, swell'd with lawless pride, have made the poor their prey,
O let them fall by those designs which they for others lay.

3 For straight they triumph, if success their thriving crimes attend:
And sordid wretches, whom God hates, perversely they commend.
4 To own a pow'r above themselves their haughty pride disdains;
And therefore in their stubborn mind no thought of God remains.

5 Oppressive methods they pursue, and all their foes they slight;
Because thy judgments unobserv'd are far above their sight.
6 They fondly think their prosp'rous state shall unmolested be;
They think their vain designs shall thrive, from all misfortune free.

7 Vain and deceitful is their speech, with curses fill'd and lies;
By which the mischief of their heart they study to disguise.
8 Near public roads they lie conceal'd, and all their art employ,
The innocent and poor at once to rifle and destroy.

9 Not lions, couching in their dens, surprise their heedless prey
With greater cunning, or express more savage rage than they.
10 Sometimes they act the harmless man, and modest looks they wear;
That, so deceiv'd, the poor may less their sudden onset fear.

PART II.

11 For God, they think, no notice takes of their unrighteous deeds;
He never minds the suff'ring poor, nor their oppression heeds.
12 But thou, O Lord, at length arise; stretch forth thy mighty arm;
And, by the greatness of thy pow'r, defend the poor from harm.

13 No longer let the wicked vaunt, and proudly boasting say,
" Tush, God regards not what we do, he never will repay."
14 But sure thou seest, and all their deeds impartially dost try;
The orphan therefore and the poor on thee for aid rely.

15 Defenceless let the wicked fall, of all their strength bereft;
Confound, O God, their dark designs, till no remains are left.
16 Assert thy just dominion, Lord, which shall for ever stand;
Thou who the heathen didst expel from this thy chosen land.

17 Thou hear'st the humble supplicants, that to thy throne repair;
Thou first prepar'st their hearts to pray, and then accept'st their pray'r.
18 Thou in thy righteous judgment weigh'st the fatherless and poor;
That so the tyrants of the earth may persecute no more.

PSALM XI.

1 SINCE I have plac'd my trust in God, a refuge always nigh,
Why should I, like a tim'rous bird, to distant mountains fly?
2 Behold, the wicked bend their bow, and ready fix their dart:
Lurking in ambush to destroy the man of upright heart.

3 When once the firm assurance fails which public faith imparts,
'Tis time for innocence to fly from such deceitful arts.
4 The Lord hath both a temple here, and righteous throne above;
Where he surveys the sons of men, and how their counsels move.

5 If God, the righteous, whom he loves, for trial does correct;
What must the sons of violence, whom he abhors, expect?
6 Snares, fire, and brimstone on their heads shall in one tempest show'r;
This dreadful mixture his revenge into their cup shall pour.

7 The righteous Lord will righteous deeds with signal favour grace;
And to the upright man disclose the brightness of his face.

PSALM XII.

1 SINCE godly men decay, O Lord, do thou my cause defend;
For scarce these wretched times afford one just and faithful friend.
2 One neighbour now can scarce believe what t'other doth impart;
With flatt'ring lips they all deceive, and with a double heart.

3 But lips that with deceit abound can never prosper long;
God's righteous vengeance will confound the proud blaspheming tongue.
4 In vain those foolish boasters say, " our tongues are sure our own;
" With doubtful words we'll still betray, and be controul'd by none."

5 For God, who hears the suff'ring poor, and their oppression knows,
Will soon arise and give them rest, in spite of all their foes.
6 The word of God shall still abide, and void of falshood be:
As is the silver seven times try'd, from drossy mixture free.

7 The promise of his aiding grace shall reach its purpos'd end;
His servants from this faithless race he ever shall defend.
8 Then shall the wicked be perplex'd, nor know which way to fly;
When those, whom they despis'd and vex'd, shall be advanc'd on high.

PSALM XIII.

1 HOW long wilt thou forget me, Lord? must I for ever mourn?
How long wilt thou withdraw from me; oh! never to return?
2 How long shall anxious thoughts my soul, and grief my heart oppress;
How long my enemies insult, and I have no redress?

3 O hear! and to my longing eyes restore thy wonted light;
And suddenly, or I shall sleep in everlasting night.
4 Restore me, lest they proudly boast 'twas their own strength o'ercame;
Permit not them that vex my soul to triumph in my shame.

5 Since I have always plac'd my trust, beneath thy mercy's wing;
Thy saving health will come, and then my heart with joy shall spring:
6 Then shall my song, with praise inspir'd, to thee my God ascend;
Who to thy servant in distress such bounty didst extend.

PSALM XIV.

1 SURE, wicked fools must needs suppose that God is nothing but a name;
Corrupt and lewd their practice grows, no breast is warm'd with holy flame.
2 The Lord look'd down from heav'n's high tow'r and all the sons of men did view,
To see if any own'd his pow'r, if any truth or justice knew.

3 But all, he saw, were gone aside, all were degen'rate grown and base,
None took religion for their guide, not one of all the sinful race.
4 But can these workers of deceit be all so dull and senseless grown;
That they, like bread, my people eat, and God's Almighty pow'r disown?

5 How will they tremble then for fear, when his just wrath shall them o'ertake!
For, to the righteous, God is near, and never will their cause forsake.
6 Ill men in vain with scorn expose those methods which the good pursue;
Since God a refuge is for those whom his just eyes with favour view.

7 Would he his saving pow'r employ, to break his people's servile band!
Then shouts of universal joy should loudly echo thro' the land.

PSALM XV.

1 LORD, who's the happy man that may to thy blest courts repair?
Not, stranger-like, to visit them, but to inhabit there?
2 'Tis he, whose ev'ry thought and deed by rules of virtue moves;
Whose gen'rous tongue disdains to speak the thing his heart disproves.

3 Who never did a slander forge his neighbour's fame to wound;
Or hearken to a false report, by malice whisper'd round.
4 Who Vice, in all its pomp and pow'r, can treat with just neglect;
And Piety, tho' cloth'd in rags, religiously respect.

5 Who to his plighted vows and trust has ever firmly stood;
And, though he promise to his loss, he makes his promise good.
6 Whose soul in usury disdains his treasure to employ;
Whom no rewards can ever bribe, the guiltless to destroy.

7 The man, who by his steady course has happiness insur'd,
When earth's foundation shakes, shall stand, by providence secur'd.

PSALM XVI.

1 PROTECT me from my cruel foes, and shield me, Lord, from harm;
Because my trust I still repose on thy almighty arm.
2 My soul all help but thine does slight, all gods but thee disown;
Yet can no deeds of mine requite the goodness thou hast shown.

3 But those that strictly virtuous are, and love the thing that's right,
To favour always and prefer shall be my chief delight.
4 How shall their sorrows be increas'd, who other gods adore!
Their bloody offspring I detest, their very names abhor.

5 My lot is fall'n in that blest land where God is truly known;
He fills my cup with lib'ral hand; 'tis he supports my throne.
6 In nature's most delightful scene my happy portion lies;
The place of my appointed reign all other lands outvies.

7 Therefore my soul shall bless the Lord, whose precepts give me light,
And private counsel still afford in sorrow's dismal night.
8 I strive each action to approve to his all-seeing eye;
No danger shall my hopes remove, because he still is nigh.

9 Therefore my heart all grief defies, my glory does rejoice;
My flesh shall rest, in hope to rise, wak'd by his powerful voice.
10 Thou, Lord, when I resign my breath, my soul from hell shalt free;
Nor let thy holy one in death the least corruption see.

11 Thou shalt the paths of life display, which to thy presence lead;
Where pleasures dwell without allay, and joys that never fade.

PSALM XVII.

1 TO my just plea, and sad complaint, attend, O righteous Lord,
And to my pray'r, as 'tis unfeign'd, a gracious ear afford.
2 As in thy sight I am approv'd, so let my sentence be;
And with impartial eyes, O Lord, my upright dealing see.

3 For thou hast search'd my heart by day, and visited by night;
And on the strictest trial found its secret motions right.
Nor shall thy justice, Lord, alone my heart's designs acquit:
For I have purpos'd that my tongue shall no offence commit.

4 I know what wicked men would do their safety to maintain;
But me thy just and mild commands from bloody paths restrain.
5 That I may still, in spite of wrongs, my innocence secure;
O guide me in thy righteous ways, and make my footsteps sure.

6 Since heretofore I ne'er in vain to thee my pray'r addrest;
O now, my God, incline thine ear to this my just request.
7 The wonders of thy truth and love in my defence engage,
Thou whose right hand preserves thy saints from their oppressors' rage.

PART II.

8, 9 O! keep me in thy tend'rest care; thy shelt'ring wings stretch out,
To guard me safe from savage foes, that compass me about.
10 O'ergrown with luxury, enclos'd in their own fat they lie;
And with a proud blaspheming mouth both God and man defy.

11 Well may they boast; for they have now my paths encompass'd round;
Their eyes at watch, their bodies bow'd, and couching on the ground.
12 In posture of a lion set, when greedy of his prey;
Or a young lion, when he lurks within a covert way.

13 Arise, O Lord, defeat their plots, their swelling rage control;
From wicked men, who are thy sword, deliver thou my soul.
14 From worldly men, thy sharpest scourge, whose portion's here below;
Who, fill'd with earthly stores, aspire no other bliss to know;

15 Their race is num'rous, that partake their substance while they live:
Their heirs survive, to whom they may the vast remainder give.
16 But I, in uprighrness, thy face shall view without control:
And, waking, shall its image find reflecting in my soul.

PSALM XVIII.

1, 2 NO change of times shall ever shock my firm affection, Lord, to thee;
For thou hast always been a rock, a fortress and defence to me.
Thou my deliverer art, my God; my trust is in thy mighty pow'r:
Thou art my shield from foes abroad, at home my safe-guard and my tow'r.

3 To thee I will address my pray'r, (to whom all praise we justly owe);
So shall I, by thy watchful care, be guarded from my treach'rous foe.
4, 5 By floods of wicked men distress'd, with seas of sorrow compass'd round,
With dire infernal pangs oppress'd, in Death's unwieldy fetters bound.

6 To heav'n I made my mournful pray'r, to God address'd my humble moan;
Who graciously inclin'd his ear, and heard me from his holy throne.

PART II.

7 When God arose, my part to take, the conscious earth was struck with fear;
The hills did at his presence shake, nor could his dreadful fury bear.
8 Thick clouds of smoke dispers'd abroad, ensigns of wrath before him came;
Devouring fire around him glow'd, that coals were kindled at its flame.

9 He left the beauteous realms of light, whilst heav'n bow'd down its awful head;
Beneath his feet substantial night was like a sable carpet spread.
10 The chariot of the King of kings, which active troops of angels drew,
On a strong tempest's rapid wings, with most amazing swiftness flew.

11, 12 Black wat'ry mists and clouds conspir'd with thickest shades his face to veil;
But at his brightness soon retir'd, and fell in show'rs of fire and hail.
13 Thro' heav'n's wide arch a thund'ring peal God's angry voice did loudly roar:
While earth's sad face with heaps of hail, and flakes of fire, was cover'd o'er.

14 His sharpen'd arrows round he threw, which made his scatter'd foes retreat:
Like darts his nimble lightnings flew, and quickly finish'd their defeat.
15 The deep its secret stores disclos'd; the world's foundations naked lay,
By his avenging wrath expos'd, which fiercely rag'd that dreadful day.

PART III.

16 The Lord did on my side engage; from heav'n, his throne, my cause upheld;
And snatch'd me from the furious rage of threat'ning waves, that proudly swell'd
17 God his resistless pow'r employ'd my strongest foes' attempts to break;
Who else with ease had soon destroy'd the weak defence that I could make

18 Their subtle rage had near prevail'd, when I distress'd and friendless lay;
But still, when other succours fail'd, God was my firm support and stay.
19 From dangers that enclos'd me round he brought me forth, and set me free;
For some just cause his goodness found, that mov'd him to delight in me.

20 Because in me no guilt remains, God does his gracious help extend:
My hands are free from bloody stains; therefore the Lord is still my friend.
21, 22 For I his judgments kept in sight, in his just paths I always trod;
I never did his statutes slight, nor loosely wander'd from my God.

23, 24 But still my soul, sincere and pure, did ev'n from darling sins refrain;
His favours therefore yet endure, because my heart and hands are clean.

PART IV.

25, 26 Thou suit'st, O Lord, thy righteous ways to various paths of human-kind:
They, who for mercy merit praise, with thee shall wondrous mercy find.
Thou to the just shall justice show; the pure thy purity shall see:
Such as perversely choose to go, shall meet with due returns from thee.

27, 28 That he the humble soul will save, and crush the haughty's boasted might,
In me the Lord an instance gave, whose darkness he has turn'd to light.
29 On his firm succour I rely'd, and did o'er num'rous foes prevail;
Nor fear'd, whilst he was on my side, the best defended walls to scale.

30 For God's designs shall still succeed; his word will bear the utmost test;
He's a strong shield to all that need, and on his sure protection rest.
31 Who then deserves to be ador'd, but God, on whom my hopes depend,
Or who, except the mighty Lord, can with resistless pow'r defend?

PART V.

32, 33 'Tis God that girts my armour on, and all my just designs fulfils;
Thro' him my feet can swiftly run, and nimbly climb the steepest hills.
34 Lessons of war from him I take, and manly weapons learn to wield:
Strong bows of steel with ease I break, forc'd by my stronger arms to yield.

35 The buckler of his saving health protects me from assaulting foes:
His hand sustains me still; my wealth and greatness from his bounty flows.
36 My goings he enlarg'd abroad, till then to narrow paths confin'd;
And when in slipp'ry ways I trod, the method of my steps design'd.

37 Thro' him I num'rous hosts defeat, and flying squadrons captive take;
Nor from my fierce pursuit retreat, till I a final conquest make.
38 Cover'd with wounds, in vain they try their vanquish'd heads again to rear;
Spite of their boasted strength they lie beneath my feet, and grovel there.

39 God, when fresh armies take the field, recruits my strength, my courage warms;
He makes my strong opposers yield, subdu'd by my prevailing arms.
40 Thro' him the necks of prostrate foes my conqu'ring feet in triumph press;
Aided by him I root out those who hate and envy my success.

41 With loud complaints all friends they try'd; but none was able to defend:
At length to God for help they cry'd; but God would no assistance lend.
42 Like flying dust, which winds pursue, their broken troops I scatter'd round;
Their slaughter'd bodies forth I threw, like loathsome dirt that clogs the ground.

PART VI.

43 Our factious tribes, at strife till now, by God's appointment we obey:
The heathen to my sceptre bow, and foreign nations own my sway.
44 Remotest realms their homage send, when my successful name they hear;
Strangers for my commands attend, charm'd with respect, or aw'd by fear.

45 All to my summons tamely yield, or soon in battle are dismay'd:
For stronger holds they quit the field, and still in strongest holds afraid.
46 Let the eternal Lord be prais'd, the rock on whose defence I rest!
To highest heav'ns his name be rais'd, who me with his salvation bless'd!

47 'Tis God that still supports my right; his just revenge my foes pursues;
'Tis he that, with resistless might, fierce nations to my yoke subdues.
48 My universal safeguard he! from whom my lasting honours flow;
He made me great, and set me free from my remorseless bloody foe.

49 Therefore, to celebrate his fame, my grateful voice to heav'n I'll raise;
And nations, strangers to his name, shall thus be taught to sing his praise:
50 "God to his King deliv'rance sends; "shews his anointed signal grace:
"His mercy evermore extends "to David and his promis'd race."

PSALM XIX.

1 THE heav'ns declare thy glory, Lord, which that alone can fill,
The firmament and stars express their great Creator's skill.
2 The dawn of each returning day fresh beams of knowledge brings;
And from the dark returns of night divine instruction springs.

3 Their pow'rful language to no realm or region is confin'd;
'Tis nature's voice, and understood alike by all mankind.
4 Their doctrine does its sacred sense thro' earth's extent display;
Whose bright contents the circling sun does round the world convey.

5 No bridegroom, on his nuptial day, has such a cheerful face:
No giant does like him rejoice, to run his glorious race.
6 From east to west, from west to east, his restless course he goes;
And thro' his progress cheerful light and vital warmth bestows.

PART II.

7 God's perfect law converts the soul; reclaims from false desires;
With sacred wisdom his sure word the ignorant inspires.
8 The statutes of the Lord are just, and bring sincere delight:
His pure commands in search of truth assist the feeblest sight.

9 His perfect worship here is fix'd, on sure foundations laid;
His equal laws are in the scales of truth and justice weigh'd:
10 Of more esteem than golden mines, or gold refin'd with skill:
More sweet than honey, or the drops that from the comb distil.

11 My trusty counsellors they are, and friendly warnings give;
Divine rewards attend on those who by thy precepts live.
12 But what frail man observes how oft he does from virtue fall?
O cleanse me from my secret faults, thou God, that know'st them all!

13 Let no presumptuous sin, O Lord, dominion have o'er me;
That, by thy grace preserv'd, I may the great transgression flee

14 So shall my pray'r and praises be with thy acceptance blest;
And I secure on thy defence, my strength and saviour, rest.

PSALM XX.

1 THE Lord to thy request attend, and hear thee in distress;
The name of Jacob's God defend, and grant thy arms success.
2 To aid thee from on high repair, and strength from Sion give;
3 Remember all thy off'rings there, thy sacrifice receive.

4 To compass thy own heart's desire thy counsels still direct;
Make kindly all events conspire to bring them to effect.
5 To thy salvation, Lord, for aid we cheerfully repair,
With banners in thy name display'd; "the Lord accept thy pray'r."

6 Our hopes are fix'd, that now the Lord our sov'reign will defend;
From heav'n resistless aid afford, and to his pray'r attend.
7 Some trust in steeds for war design'd; on chariots some rely:
Against them all we'll call to mind the pow'r of God most high.

8 But from their steeds and chariots thrown, behold them thro' the plain,
Disorder'd, broke, and trampled down, whilst firm our troops remain.
9 Still save us, Lord, and still proceed our rightful cause to bless:
Hear, King of heav'n, in times of need, the pray'rs that we address.

PSALM XXI.

1 THE king, O Lord, with songs of praise, shall in thy strength rejoice;
With thy salvation crown'd, shall raise to heav'n his cheerful voice.
2 For thou, whate'er his lips request, not only dost impart;
But hast with thy acceptance blest, the wishes of his heart.

3 Thy goodness and thy tender care have all his hopes outgone;
A crown of gold thou mad'st him wear, and sett'st it firmly on.
4 He pray'd for life; and thou, O Lord, didst to his pray'r attend,
And graciously to him afford a life that ne'er shall end.

5 Thy sure defence thro' nations round has spread his glorious name;
And his successful actions crown'd with majesty and fame.
6 Eternal blessings thou bestow'st, and mak'st his joys increase;
Whilst thou to him unclouded show'st the brightness of thy face.

PART II.

7 Because the king on God alone for timely aid relies;
His mercy still supports his throne, and all his wants supplies.
8 But, righteous Lord, thy stubborn foes shall feel thy heavy hand;
Thy vengeful arm shall find out those that hate thy mild command.

9 When thou against them dost engage, thy just but dreadful doom
Shall, like a glowing oven's rage, their hopes and them consume.
10 Nor shall thy furious anger cease, or with their ruin end;
But root out all their guilty race, and to their seed extend.

11 For all their thoughts were set on ill, their hearts on malice bent;
But thou with watchful care didst still the ill effect prevent.
12 While they their swift retreat shall make to 'scape thy dreadful might,
Thy swifter arrows shall o'ertake, and gall them in their flight.

13 Thus, Lord, thy wondrous strength disclose, and thus exalt thy fame;
Whilst we glad songs of praise compose to thy almighty name.

PSALM XXII.

1 MY God, my God, why leav'st thou me, when I with anguish faint?
O! why so far from me remov'd, and from my loud complaint?
2 All day, but all the day unheard, to thee do I complain;
With cries implore relief all night, but cry all night in vain.

3 Yet thou art still the righteous judge of innocence oppress'd;
And therefore Israel's praises are of right to thee address'd.
4, 5 On thee our ancestors rely'd, and thy deliv'rance found;
With pious confidence they pray'd, and with success were crown'd.

6 But I am treated like a worm; like none of human birth;
Not only by the great revil'd, but made the rabble's mirth.
7 With laughter all the gazing crowd my agonies survey;
They shoot the lip, they shake the head, and thus deriding say:

8 "In God he trusted, boasting oft that he was heav'ns delight:
"Let God come down to save him now and own his favourite."

PART II

9 Thou mad'st my mother's teeming womb a living offspring bear;
When but a suckling at the breast, I was thy early care.
10 Thou guardian-like, didst shield from wrongs my helpless infant days;
And since hast been my God and guide through life's bewilder'd ways.

11 Withdraw not then so far from me, when trouble is so nigh;
O, send me help! thy help! on which I only can rely.
12 High-pamper'd bulls, a frowning herd, from Basan's forest met,
With strength proportion'd to their rage, have me around beset.

13 They gape on me, and ev'ry mouth a yawning grave appears;
The desert lion's savage roar less dreadful is than theirs.

PART III.

14 My blood's like water spil'd, my joints are rack'd and out of frame;
My heart dissolves within my breast, like wax before the flame.
15 My strength like potter's earth is parch'd, my tongue cleaves to my jaws;
And to the silent shades of death my fainting soul withdraws.

16 Like blood-hounds, to surround me, they in pack'd assemblies meet:
They pierc'd my inoffensive hands; they pierc'd my harmless feet.
17 My body's rack'd, till all my bones distinctly may be told;
Yet such a spectacle of woe as pastime they behold.

18 As spoil, my garments they divide, lots for my vesture cast:
19 Therefore approach, O Lord, my strength, and to my succour haste.
20 From their sharp swords protect thou me, of all but life bereft!
Nor let thy darling in the pow'r of cruel dogs be left.

21 To save me from the lion's jaws, thy present succour send;
As once from goring unicorns thou didst my life defend.
22 Then to my brethren I'll declare the triumphs of thy name;
In presence of assembled saints thy glory thus proclaim,

23 "Ye worshippers of Jacob's God, all you of Israel's line,
"O praise the Lord, and to your praise sincere obedience join.
24 "He ne'er disdain'd on low distress to cast a gracious eye;
"Nor turn'd from poverty his face, but hears its humble cry."

PART IV.

25 Thus in thy sacred courts will I my cheerful thanks express;
In presence of thy saints perform the vows of my distress.
26 The meek companions of my grief shall find my table spread;
And all that seek the Lord shall be with joys immortal fed.

27 Then shall the glad converted world to God their homage pay;
And scatter'd nations of the earth one sov'reign Lord obey.
28 'Tis his supreme prerogative o'er subject kings to reign:
'Tis just that he should rule the world, who does the world sustain.

29 The rich, who are with plenty fed, his bounty must confess:
The sons of want, by him reliev'd, their gen'rous patron bless.
With humble worship to his throne they all for aid resort:
That pow'r, which first their beings gave, can only them support.

30, 31 Then shall a chosen spotless race, devoted to his name,
To their admiring heirs his truth, and glorious acts proclaim.

PSALM XXIII.

1 THE Lord himself, the mighty Lord, vouchsafes to be my guide,
The shepherd by whose constant care my wants are all supply'd.
2 In tender grass he makes me feed, and gently there repose;
Then leads me to cool shades, and where refreshing water flows.

3 He does my wand'ring soul reclaim, and to his endless praise,
Instruct with humble zeal to walk in his most righteous ways.
4 I pass the gloomy vale of death, from fear and danger free:
For there his aiding rod and staff defend and comfort me.

5 In presence of my spiteful foes he does my table spread:
He crowns my cup with cheerful wine, with oil anoints my head.
6 Since God doth thus his wondrous love through all my life extend,
That life to him I will devote, and in his temple spend.

PSALM XXIV.

1 THIS spacious earth is all the Lord's, the Lord's her fullness is:
The world, and they that dwell therein, by sov'reign right are his.
2 He fram'd and fix'd it on the seas; and his almighty hand
Upon inconstant floods has made the stable fabric stand.

3 But for himself this Lord of all one chosen seat design'd:
O! who shall to that sacred hill desir'd admittance find?
4 The man whose hands and heart are pure, whose thoughts from pride are free;
Who honest poverty prefers to gainful perjury.

5 This, this is he, on whom the Lord shall show'r his blessings down:
Whom God his saviour shall vouchsafe with righteousness to crown.
6 Such is the race of saints, by whom the sacred courts are trod;
And such the proselytes that seek the face of Jacob's God.

7 Erect your heads eternal gates; unfold, to entertain
The king of glory: see! he comes with his celestial train.
8 Who is the king of glory? who! the Lord for strength renown'd;
In battle mighty; o'er his foes eternal victor crown'd.

9 Erect your heads, ye gates unfold in state to entertain
The king of glory: see! he comes with all his shining train.
10 Who is this king of glory? who! the Lord of hosts renown'd:
Of glory he alone is king, who is with glory crown'd.

PSALM XXV.

1, 2 TO God, in whom I trust, I lift my heart and voice;
O! let me not be put to shame, nor let my foes rejoice.
3 Those who on thee rely let no disgrace attend:
Be that the shameful lot of such who wilfully offend.

4, 5 To me thy truth impart, and lead me in thy way:
For thou art he that brings me help; on thee I wait all day.
6 Thy mercies and thy love, O Lord, recal to mind;
And graciously continue still as thou wert ever, kind.

7 Let all my youthful crimes be blotted out by thee;
And for thy wondrous goodness' sake, in mercy think on me.
8 His mercy and his truth, the righteous Lord displays,
In bringing wand'ring sinners home, and teaching them his ways.

9 He those in justice guides, who his direction seek;
And in his sacred paths shall lead the humble and the meek.
10 Thro' all the ways of God both truth and mercy shine,
To such as, with religious hearts, to his blest will incline.

PART II.

11 Since mercy is the grace that most exalts thy fame,
Forgive my heinous sin, O Lord, and so advance thy name.
12 Whoe'er with humble fear, to God his duty pays,
Shall find the Lord a faithful guide in all his righteous ways.

13 His quiet soul with peace shall be for ever blest;
And by his num'rous race the land successively possest.
14 For God to all his saints his secret will imparts,
And does his gracious cov'nant write in their obedient hearts.

15 To him I lift my eyes, and wait his timely aid,
Who breaks the strong and treach'rous snare which for my feet was laid.
16 O! turn, and all my griefs, in mercy, Lord, redress;
For I am compass'd round with woes, and plung'd in deep distress.

17 The sorrows of my heart to mighty sums increase!
O! from this dark and dismal state my troubled soul release!
18 Do thou with tender eyes my sad affliction see;
Acquit me, Lord, and from my guilt entirely set me free.

19 Consider, Lord, my foes, how vast their numbers grow!
What lawless force and rage they use, what boundless hate they show!
20 Protect, and set my soul from their fierce malice free;
Nor let me be asham'd, who place my stedfast trust in thee.

21 Let all my righteous acts to full perfection rise;
Because my firm and constant hope on thee alone relies.
22 To Israel's chosen race continue ever kind,
And, in the midst of all their wants, let them thy succour find.

PSALM XXVI.

1 JUDGE me, O Lord, for I the paths of righteousness have trod:
I cannot fail, who all my trust repose on thee, my God.
2, 3 Search thou my heart, whose innocence will shine the more 'tis try'd;
For I have kept thy grace in view, and made thy truth my guide.

4 I never for companions took the idle or profane;
No hypocrite, with all his arts, could e'er my friendship gain.
5 I hate the busy plotting crew, who make distracted times;
And shun their wicked company, as I avoid their crimes.

6 I'll wash my hands in innocence, and bring a heart so pure,
That when thy altar I approach, my welcome shall secure.
7, 8 My thanks I'll publish there, and tell how thy renown excels:
That seat affords me most delight in which thy honour dwells.

9 Pass not on me the sinners' doom, who murder make their trade;
10 Who others' rights, by secret bribes, or open force, invade.
11 But I will walk in paths of truth, and innocence pursue:
Protect me, therefore, and to me thy mercies, Lord, renew.

12 In spite of all assaulting foes, I still maintain my ground;
And shall survive among thy saints, thy praises to resound.

PSALM XXVII.

1 WHOM should I fear, since God to me is saving health and light?
Since strongly he my life supports, what can my soul affright?
2 With fierce intent my flesh to tear, when foes beset me round,
They stumbled, and their haughty crests were made to strike the ground.

3 Thro' him my heart, undaunted, dares with mighty hosts to cope:
Thro' him, in doubtful straits of war, for good success I hope.
4 Henceforth, within this house to dwell, I earnestly desire;
His wondrous beauty there to view, and of his will enquire.

5 For there I may with comfort rest, in times of deep distress;
And safe, as on a rock, abide in that secure recess;
6 Whilst God o'er all my haughty foes my lofty head shall raise;
And I my joyful tribute bring, with grateful songs of praise.

PART II.

7 Continue, Lord, to hear my voice, whene'er to thee I cry;
In mercy my complaints receive, nor my request deny.
8 When us to seek thy glorious face thou kindly dost advise,
"Thy glorious face I'll always seek," my grateful heart replies.

9 Then hide not thou thy face, O Lord, nor me in wrath reject:
My God, and Saviour, leave not him thou didst so oft protect.
10 Tho' all my friends, and kindred too, their helpless charge forsake;
Yet thou, whose love excels them all, wilt care and pity take.

11 Instruct me in thy paths, O Lord; my ways directly guide;
Lest envious men, who watch my steps, should see me tread aside.
12 Lord, disappoint my cruel foes; defeat their ill desire,
Whose lying lips, and bloody hands, against my peace conspire.

13 I trusted that my future life should with thy love be crown'd;
Or else my fainting soul had sunk, with sorrow compass'd round
14 God's time with patient faith expect, who will inspire thy breast
With inward strength: do thou thy part, and leave to him the rest.

PSALM XXVIII.

1 O LORD, my rock, to thee I cry, in sighs consume my breath:
O answer; or I shall become like those that sleep in death.
2 Regard my supplication, Lord, the cries that I repeat,
With weeping eyes, and lifted hands, before thy mercy-seat.

3 Let me escape the sinners' doom, who make a trade of ill;
And ever speak the person fair, whose blood they mean to spill.
4 According to their crimes' extent, let justice have its course:
Relentless be to them, as they have sinn'd without remorse.

5 Since they the works of God despise, nor will his Grace adore;
His wrath shall utterly destroy, and build them up no more.
6 But I, with due acknowledgment, his praises will resound,
From whom the cries of my distress a gracious answer found.

7 My heart its confidence repos'd in God, my strength and shield;
In him I trusted, and return'd triumphant from the field:
As he hath made my joys complete, 'tis just that I should raise
The cheerful tribute of my thanks, and thus resound his praise:

8 "His aiding pow'r supports the troops, that my just cause maintain;
"'Twas he advanc'd me to the throne, "'tis he secures my reign:"
9 Preserve thy chosen, and proceed thine heritage to bless;
With plenty prosper them, in peace; in battle, with success.

PSALM XXIX.

1 YE princes, that in might excel, your grateful sacrifice prepare;
God's glorious actions loudly tell, his wondrous pow'r to all declare.
To his great name fresh altars raise; devoutly due respect afford;
Him in his holy temple praise, where he's with solemn state ador'd.

3 'Tis he that, with amazing noise, the wat'ry clouds in sunder breaks:
The ocean trembles at his voice, when he from heav'n in thunder speaks.
4, 5 How full of pow'r his voice appears! with what majestic terror crown'd!
Which from their roots tall cedars tears, and strews their scatter'd branches round.

6 They, and the hills on which they grow, are sometimes hurry'd far away;
And leap like hinds that bounding go, or unicorns in youthful play.
7, 8 When God in thunder loudly speaks, and scatter'd flames of lightning sends,
The forest nods, the desert quakes, and stubborn Kadesh lowly bends.

9 He makes the hinds to cast their young, and lays the beasts' dark covers bare;
While those that to his courts belong, securely sing his praises there.
10, 11 God rules the angry floods on high; his boundless sway shall never cease:
His saints with strength he will supply, and bless his own with constant peace.

PSALM XXX.

I'LL celebrate thy praises, Lord, who didst thy pow'r employ
To raise my drooping head, and check my foes' insulting joy.
3 In my distress I cry'd to thee, who kindly didst relieve,
And from the grave's expecting jaws my hopeless life retrieve.

Thus to his courts, ye saints of his, with songs of praise repair;
With me commemorate his truth, and providential care.
His wrath has but a moment's reign, his favour no decay;
Your night of grief is recompens'd with joy's returning day.

But I, in prosp'rous days, presum'd; no sudden change I fear'd,
Whilst in my sunshine of success no low'ring cloud appear'd.
But soon I found thy favour, Lord, my empire's only trust;
For when thou hidst thy face, I saw my honour laid in dust.

8 Then, as I vainly had presum'd, my error I confess'd:
And thus with supplicating voice thy mercy's throne address'd:
9 "What profit is there in my blood, "congeal'd by death's cold night?
"Can silent ashes speak thy praise, "thy wondrous truth recite?

10 "Hear me, O Lord; in mercy hear; "thy wonted aid extend:
"Do thou send help, on whom alone "I can for help depend."
11 'Tis done! Thou hast my mournful scene to songs and dances turn'd;
Invested me with robes of state, who late in sackcloth mourn'd.

12 Exalted thus, I'll gladly sing thy praise in grateful verse;
And as thy favours endless are, thy endless praise rehearse.

PSALM XXXI.

1 DEFEND, me, Lord, from shame, for still I trust in thee:
As just and righteous is thy name, from danger set me free.
2 Bow down thy gracious ear, and speedy succour send:
Do thou my stedfast rock appear, to shelter and defend.

3 Since thou, when foes oppress, my rock and fortress art,
To guide me forth from this distress, thy wonted help impart.
4 Release me from the snare which they have closely laid;
Since I, O God, my strength, repair to thee alone for aid.

5 To thee, the God of truth, my life, and all that's mine,
(For thou preserv'dst me from my youth) I willingly resign.
6 All vain designs I hate of those that trust in lies;
And still my soul, in ev'ry state, to God, for succour flies.

PART II.

7 Those mercies thou hast shown, I'll cheerfully express;
For thou hast seen my straits, and known my soul in deep distress.
8 When Keilah's treach'rous race did all my strength inclose,
Thou gav'st my feet a larger space, to shun my watchful foes.

9 Thy mercy, Lord, display, and hear my just complaint;
For both my soul and flesh decay, with grief and hunger faint.
10 Sad thoughts my life oppress; my years are spent in groans
My sins have made my strength decrease, and ev'n consum'd my bones.

11 My foes my suff'rings mock'd; my neighbours did upbraid;
My friends, at sight of me, were shock'd and fled, as men dismay'd.
12 Forsook by all am I, as dead, and out of mind;
And like a shatter'd vessel lie, whose parts can ne'er be join'd.

13 Yet sland'rous words they speak, and seem my pow'r to dread;
Whilst they together counsel take, my guiltless blood to shed.
14 But still my stedfast trust I on thy help repose:
That thou, my God, art good and just, my soul with comfort knows.

PART III.

15 Whate'er events betide, thy wisdom times them all:
Then, Lord, thy servant safely hide from those that seek his fall.
16 The brightness of thy face to me, O Lord, disclose;
And as thy mercies still increase, preserve me from my foes.

17 Me from dishonour save, who still have call'd on thee;
Let that, and silence in the grave, the sinner's portion be.
18 Do thou their tongues restrain, whose breath in lies are spent;
Who false reports, with proud disdain, against the righteous vent.

19 How great thy mercies are to such as fear thy name,
Which thou, for those that trust thy care, dost to the world proclaim!
20 Thou keep'st them in thy sight, from proud oppressors free:
From tongues that do in strife delight, they are preserv'd by thee.

21 With glory and renown God's name be ever bless'd:
Whose love, in Keilah's well fenc'd town, was wond'rously express'd!
22 I said, in hasty flight, "I'm banish'd from thy eyes!"
Yet still thou kept'st me in thy sight, and heard'st my earnest cries.

23 O! all ye saints, the Lord with eager love pursue;
Who to the just will help afford, and give the proud their due.
24 Ye that on God rely, courageously proceed:
For he will still your hearts supply with strength, in time of need.

PSALM XXXII.

1 HE's blest, whose sins have pardon gain'd no more in judgment to appear;
2 Whose guilt remission has obtain'd, and whose repentance is sincere.
3 While I conceal'd the fretting sore, my bones consum'd without relief;
All day did I with anguish roar; but no complaints asswag'd my grief.

4 Heavy on me thy hand remain'd, by day and night alike distrest,
Till quite of vital moisture drain'd, like land with summer's drought opprest.
5 No sooner I my wound disclos'd, the guilt that tortur'd me within,
But thy forgiveness interpos'd, and mercy's healing balm pour'd in.

6 True penitents shall thus succeed, who seek thee whilst thou may'st be found
And from the common deluge freed, shall see remorseless sinners drown'd.
7 Thy favour, Lord, in all distress, my tow'r of refuge I must own:
Thou shalt my haughty foes suppress, and me with songs of triumph crown.

8 In my instruction then confide, you that would truth's safe path descry,
Your progress I'll securely guide, and keep you in my watchful eye.
9 Submit yourselves to wisdom's rule, like men that reason have attain'd;
Not like th' ungovern'd horse or mule, whose fury must be curb'd and rein'd.

o Sorrows on sorrows multiply'd, the harden'd sinner shall confound:
But them who in his truth confide, blessings of mercy shall surround.
1 His saints, that have perform'd his laws their life in triumph shall employ:
Let them (as they alone have cause) in grateful raptures shout for joy.

PSALM XXXIII.

LET all the just to God, with joy, their chearful voices raise;
For well the righteous it becomes to sing glad songs of praise.
, 3 Let harps, and psalteries, and lute, in joyful consort meet;
And new-made songs of loud applause the harmony complete.

, 5 For faithful is the word of God; his works with truth abound;
He justice loves; and all the earth, is with his goodness crown'd.
By his almighty word, at first, the heav'nly arch was rear'd;
And all the beauteous hosts of light at his command appear'd.

The swelling floods, together roll'd, he makes in heaps to lie;
And lays as in a storehouse safe, the wat'ry treasures by.
, 9, Let earth, and all that dwell therein, before him trembling stand;
For, when he spake the word, 'twas made; 'twas fix'd at his command.

o He, when the heathen closely plot, their counsels undermines:
His wisdom ineffectual makes the people's rash designs.
1 Whate'er the mighty Lord decrees shall stand for ever sure;
The settled purpose of his heart to ages shall endure.

PART II.

2 How happy then are they, to whom the Lord for God is known!
Whom he, from all the world besides, has chosen for his own.
3, 14, 15 He all the nations of the earth, from heav'n, his throne, survey'd;
He saw their works, and view'd their thoughts, by him their hearts were made.

6, 17 No king is safe by num'rous hosts; their strength the strong deceives;
No manag'd horse, by force or speed, his warlike rider saves.
8, 19 'Tis God, who those that trust in him, beholds with gracious eyes:
He frees their soul from death; their want, in time of dearth, supplies.

0, 21 Our soul on God with patience waits; our help and shield is he:
Then, Lord, let still our hearts rejoice, because we trust in thee.
2 The riches of thy mercy, Lord, do thou to us extend;
Since we, for all we want or wish, on thee alone depend.

PSALM XXXIV.

THRO' all the changing scenes of life, in trouble and in joy,
The praises of my God shall still my heart and tongue employ.
Of his deliv'rance I will boast, till all that are distrest,
From my example comfort take, and charm their griefs to rest.

O! magnify the Lord with me, with me exalt his name:
When in distress to him I call'd, he to my rescue came.
Their drooping hearts were soon refresh'd who look'd to him for aid;
Desir'd success in ev'ry face a chearful air display'd.

"Behold, (say they) behold the man whom providence reliev'd;
"The man so dang'rously beset, so wond'rously retriev'd!"

7 The hosts of God encamp around the dwellings of the just:
Deliv'rance he affords to all who on his succour trust.

8 O! make but trial of his love, experience will decide
How blest they are, and only they, who in his truth confide.
9 Fear him ye saints; and you will then have nothing else to fear:
Make you his service your delight, your wants shall be his care.

10 While hungry lions lack their prey, the Lord will food provide
For such as put their trust in in him, and see their needs supply'd.

PART II.

11 Approach, ye piously dispos'd, and my instruction hear:
I'll teach you the true discipline of his religious fear.
12 Let him who length of life desires, and prosp'rous days would see,
13 From sland'ring language keep his tongue, his lips from falsehood free.

14 The crooked paths of vice decline, and virtue's ways pursue;
Establish peace, where 'tis begun; and where 'tis lost, renew.
15 The Lord from heav'n beholds the just with favourable eyes;
And, when distress'd, his gracious ear is open to their cries;

16 But turns his wrathful look on those whom mercy can't reclaim,
To cut them off, and from the earth blot out their hated name.
17 Deliv'rance to his saints he gives, when his relief they crave:
18 He's nigh to heal the broken heart, and contrite spirit save.

19 The wicked oft, but still in vain, against the just conspire;
20 For under their affliction's weight he keeps their bones intire.
21 The wicked from their wicked arts, their ruin shall derive;
Whilst righteous men, whom they detest, shall them and theirs survive.

22 For God preserves the souls of those who on his truth depend;
To them, and their posterity, his blessings shall descend.

PSALM XXXV.

1 AGAINST all those that strive with me, O Lord, assert my right;
With such as war unjustly wage, do thou my battles fight.
2 Thy buckler take, and bind thy shield upon my warlike arm:
Stand up, O God, in my defence; and keep me safe from harm.

3 Bring forth thy spear; and stop their course, that haste my blood to spill;
Say to my soul, "I am thy health, and will preserve thee still."
4 Let them with shame be cover'd o'er, who my destruction sought;
And such as did my harm devise, be to confusion brought.

5 Then shall they fly, dispers'd like chaff before the driving wind:
God's vengeful minister of wrath shall follow close behind.
6 And when thro' dark and slipp'ry ways, they strive his rage to shun,
His vengeful ministers of wrath shall goad them as they run.

7 Since, unprovok'd by any wrong, they hid their treach'rous snare;
And for my harmless soul, a pit did without cause prepare;
8 Surpris'd by mischiefs unforeseen, by their own arts betray'd,
Their feet shall fall into the net, which they for me had laid;

9 Whilst my glad soul shall God's great name for this deliv'rance bless,
And by his saving health secur'd, its grateful joy express;
10 My very bones shall say, "O Lord, who can compare with thee?
"Who sets the poor and helpless man from strong oppressors free."

PART II.

11 False witnesses, with forg'd complaints, against my truth combin'd;
And to my charge such things they laid as I had ne'er design'd.
12 The good which I to them had done, with evil they repaid;
And did by malice undeserv'd, my harmless life invade.

13 But as for me, when they were sick, I still in sackcloth mourn'd;
I pray'd and fasted, and my pray'r to my own breast return'd.
14 Had they my friends or brethren been, I could have done no more;
Nor with more decent signs of grief, a mother's loss deplore.

15 How different did their carriage prove, in times of my distress;
When they in crowds together met, did savage joy express.
The rabble too, in num'rous throngs, by their example came;
And ceas'd not, with reviling words, to wound my spotless fame.

16 Scoffers, that noble tables haunt, and earn their bread with lies,
Did gnash their teeth, and sland'ring jests maliciously devise.
17 But, Lord, how long wilt thou look on? on my behalf appear;
And save my guiltless soul, which they, like rav'ning beasts, would tear.

PART III.

18 So I, before the list'ning world, shall grateful thanks express;
And, where the great assembly meets, thy name with praises bless.
19 Lord, suffer not my causeless foes, who me unjustly hate,
With open joy, or secret signs, to mock my sad estate.

20 For they, with hearts averse to peace, industriously devise,
Against the men of quiet minds, to forge malicious lies.
21 Nor with these private arts content, aloud they vent their spight;
And say, "At last we found him out, he did it in our sight."

22 But thou, who dost both them and me with righteous eyes survey,
Assert my innocence, O Lord, and keep not far away.
23 Stir up thyself in my behalf; to judgment, Lord, awake;
Thy righteous servant's cause, O God, to thy decision take.

24 Lord, as my heart has upright been, let me thy justice find:
Nor let my cruel foes obtain the triumphs they design'd.
25 O let them not amongst themselves in boasting language say,
"At length our wishes are complete; at last he's made our prey."

26 Let such as in my harm rejoic'd, for shame their faces hide;
And foul dishonour wait on those that proudly me defy'd.
27 Whilst they with chearful voices shout, who my just cause befriend;
And bless the Lord, who loves to make success his saints attend.

28 So shall my tongue thy judgments sing, inspir'd with grateful joy;
And chearful hymns in praise of thee shall all my days employ.

PSALM XXXVI.

1 MY crafty foe with flatt'ring art, his wicked purpose would disguise,
But reason whispers to my heart, he ne'er sets God before his eyes.
2 He sooths himself, retir'd from sight, secure he thinks his treach'rous game;
Till his dark plots, expos'd to light, their false contriver brand with shame.

3 In deeds he is my foe confest, whilst with his tongue he speaks me fair;
True wisdom's banish'd from his breast, and vice has sole dominion there.
4 His wakeful malice spends the night in forging his accurs'd designs;
His obstinate ungen'rous spite no execrable means declines.

5 But, Lord, thy mercy, my sure hope, above the heav'nly orb ascends;
Thy sacred truth's unmeasur'd scope beyond the spreading sky extends:
6 Thy justice, like the hills, remains; unfathom'd depths thy judgments are;
Thy providence the world sustains; the whole creation is thy care.

7 Since of thy goodness all partake, with what assurance should the just
Thy shelt'ring wings their refuge make, and saints to thy protection trust!
8 Such guests shall to thy courts be led, to banquet on thy love's repast;
And drink, as from a fountain's head, of joys that shall for ever last.

9 With thee the springs of life remain; thy presence i. eternal day:
10 O! let thy saints thy favour gain; to upright hearts thy truth display.
11 Whilst pride's insulting foot would spurn, and wicked hands my life surprise;
12 Their mischiefs on themselves return; down, down they're fall'n no more to rise.

PSALM XXXVII.

1 THO' wicked men grow rich or great
Yet let not their successful state
Thy anger or thy envy raise:
2 For they, cut down, like tender grass,
Or, like young flow'rs, away shall pass,
Whose blooming beauty soon decays.

3 Depend on God, and him obey;
So thou within the land shalt stay,
Secure from danger, and from want:
4 Make his commands thy chief delight;
And he, thy duty to requite,
Shall all thy earnest wishes grant.

5 In all thy ways trust thou the Lord,
And he will needful help afford,
To perfect ev'ry just design:
6 He'll make, like light, serene and clear,
Thy clouded innocence appear,
And as a mid-day sun to shine.

7 With quiet mind on God depend,
And patiently for him attend;
Nor let thy anger fondly rise,
Tho' wicked men with wealth abound
And with success their plots are crown'd
Which they maliciously devise.

8 From anger cease, and wrath forsake;
Let no ungovern'd passion make
Thy wav'ring heart espouse their crime
9 For God shall sinful men destroy;
Whilst only they the land enjoy,
Who trust on him, and wait his time.

10 How soon shall wicked men decay!
Their place shall vanish quite away,
Nor by the strictest search be found.
11 Whilst humble souls possess the earth,
Rejoicing still with godly mirth,
With peace and plenty always crown'd.

PART II.

12 While sinful crouds, with false design,
Against the righteous few combine,
And gnash their teeth and threat'ning stand;

13 God shall their empty plots deride,
And laugh at their defeated pride:
He sees their ruin near at hand.

14 They draw the sword, and bend the bow,
The poor and needy to o'erthrow,
And men of upright lives to slay:
15 But their strong bow shall soon be broke
Their sharpen'd weapons' mortal stroke
Thro' their own hearts shall force its way,

16 A little with God's favour bless'd,
That's by one righteous man possess'd,
The wealth of many bad excels:
17 For God supports the just man's cause,
But as for those that break his laws,
Their unsuccessful pow'r he quells.

18 His constant care the upright guides,
And over all their life presides;
Their portion shall for ever last:
19 They, when distress o'erwhelms the earth
Shall be unmov'd, and ev'n in dearth
The happy fruits of plenty taste.

20 Not so the wicked man, and those
Who proudly dare God's will oppose;
Destruction is their hapless share:
Like fat of lambs, their hopes and they,
Shall in an instant melt away,
And vanish into smoke and air.

PART III,

21 Whilst sinners, brought to sad decay,
Still borrow on, and never pay,
The just have will and pow'r to give:
22 For such as God vouchsafes to bless,
Shall peaceably the earth possess,
And those he curses shall not live.

23 The good man's way is God's delight;
He orders all the steps aright
Of him that moves by his command;
24 Tho' he sometimes may be distress'd,
Yet shall he ne'er be quite oppress'd;
For God upholds him with his hand.

25 From my first youth, till age prevail'd,
I never saw the righteous fail'd,
Or want o'ertake his num'rous race;

26 Because compassion fill'd his heart,
And he did chearfully impart,
God made his offspring's wealth increase
27 With caution shun each wicked deed;
In virtue's ways with zeal proceed,
And so prolong your happy days:

28 For God, who judgment loves, does still
Preserve his saints secure from ill,
While soon the wicked race decays.
29, 30-1 The upright shall possess the land
His portion shall for ages stand;
His mouth with wisdom is supply'd;

His tongue by rules of judgment moves;
His heart the law of God approves;
Therefore his footsteps never slide.

PART IV.

32 In wait the watchful sinner lies,
In vain the righteous to surprize,
In vain his ruin does decree:
33 God will not him defenceless leave,
To his revenge expos'd, but save;
And, when he's sentenc'd, set him free

34 Wait still on God; keep his command;
And thou, exalted in the land,
Thy blest possessions ne'er shall quit;
The wicked soon destroy'd shall be,
And at his dismal tragedy,
Thou shalt a safe spectator sit.

35 The wicked I in power have seen
And, like a bay-tree, fresh and green,
That spreads its pleasant branches round

36 But he was gone as swift as thought;
And tho' in ev'ry place I sought,
No sign or track of him I found.
37 Observe the perfect man with care,
And mark all such as upright are;
Their roughest days in peace shall end:

38 While on the latter end of those,
Who dare God's sacred will oppose,
A common ruin shall attend.
39 God to the just will aid afford;
Their only safeguard is the Lord;
Their strength in time of need is he:

40 Because on him they still depend,
The Lord will timely succour send,
And from the wicked set them free.

PSALM XXXVIII.

THY chast'ning wrath, O Lord, restrain, | tho' I deserve it all;
Nor let at once on me the storm | of thy displeasure fall.
2 In ev'ry wretched part of me | thy arrows deep remain;
Thy heavy hand's afflicting weight, | I can no more sustain.

3 My flesh is one continued wound, | thy wrath so fiercely glows;
Betwixt my punishment and guilt, | my bones have no repose.
4 My sins, which to a deluge swell, | my sinking head o'erflow;
And for my feeble strength to bear | too vast a burthen grow.

5 Stench and corruption fill my wounds; | my folly's just return:
6 With trouble I am warp'd and bow'd, | and all day long I mourn.
7 A loath'd disease afflicts my loins, | infecting ev'ry part;
8 With sickness worn I groan and roar, | through anguish of my heart.

PART II.

9 But, Lord, before thy searching eyes | all my desires appear:
And sure my groans have been too loud, | not to have reach'd thine ear.
10 My heart's oppress'd, my strength decay'd, | my eyes depriv'd of light:
11 Friends, lovers, kinsmen, gaze aloof | on such a dismal sight.

12 Meanwhile the foes that seek my life, | their snares to take me set;
Vent slanders, and contrive all day | to forge some new deceit.
13 But I, as if both deaf and dumb, | nor heard, nor once reply'd;
14 Quite deaf and dumb, like one whose tongue | with conscious guilt is ty'd.

15 For, Lord, to thee I do appeal, | my innocence to clear;
Assur'd that thou, the righteous God, | my injur'd cause wilt hear.
16 "Hear me, said I, lest my proud foes | "a spiteful joy display:
"Insulting, if they see my foot | "but once to go astray."

17 And with continual grief oppress'd, | to sing I now begin:
18 To thee, O Lord, I will confess, | to thee bewail my sin.
19 But, whilst I languish, my proud foes | their strength and vigour boast;
And they that hate me without cause | are grown a dreadful host.

20 Ev'n they whom I oblig'd, return | my kindness with despite;
And are my enemies, because | I chuse the path that's right.
21 Forsake me not, O Lord, my God, | nor far from me depart;
22 Make haste to my relief, O thou | who my salvation art.

PSALM XXXIX.

1 RESOLV'D to watch o'er all my ways, | I kept my tongue in awe;
I curb'd my hasty words, when I | the wicked prosp'rous saw.
2 Like one that's dumb, I silent stood | and did my tongue refrain
From good discourse, but that restraint | increas'd my inward pain.

3 My heart did glow with working thoughts, | and no repose could take;
Till strong reflection fann'd the fire, | and thus at length I spake:
4 Lord, let me know my term of days, | how soon my life will end:
The num'rous train of ills disclose, | which this frail state attend.

5 My life, thou know'st, is but a span, | a cypher sums my years;
And ev'ry man, in best estate, | but vanity appears.

Man, like a shadow, vainly walks, with fruitless cares oppress'd :
He heaps up wealth, but cannot tell by whom 'twill be possess'd

Why then should I on worthless toys with anxious cares attend ?
On thee alone my stedfast hope shall ever, Lord, depend.
9 Forgive my sins ; nor let me scorn'd by foolish sinners be ;
For I was dumb, and murmur'd not, because 'twas done by thee.

0 The dreadful burthen of thy wrath in mercy soon remove ;
Lest my frail flesh too weak to bear the heavy load should prove.
1 For when thou chast'nest man for sin, thou mak'st his beauty fade.
(So vain a thing is he !) like cloth by fretting moths decay'd.

2 Lord, hear my cry, accept my tears, and listen to my pray'r,
Who sojourn like a stranger here, as all my fathers were.
3 O ! spare me yet a little time ; my wasted strength restore,
Before I vanish quite from hence, and shall be seen no more.

PSALM XL.

I WAITED meekly for the Lord, till he vouchsaf'd a kind reply ;
Who did his gracious ear afford, and heard from heav'n my humble cry.
He took me from the dismal pit, when founder'd deep in miry clay ;
On solid ground he plac'd my feet, and suffer'd not my steps to stray.

The wonders he for me has wrought, shall fill my mouth with songs of praise ;
And others, to his worship brought, to hopes of like deliv'rance raise.
For blessings shall that man reward, who on th' almighty Lord relies ;
Who treats the proud with disregard, and hates the hypocrite's disguise.

Who can the wondrous works recount, which thou, O God, for us hast wrought :
The treasures of thy love surmount the pow'r of numbers, speech and thought.
I've learnt, that thou hast not desir'd off'rings and sacrifice alone ;
Nor blood of guiltless beasts requir'd, for man's transgressions to atone.

I therefore come---come to fulfil the oracles thy books impart ;
'Tis my delight to do thy will ; thy law is written in my heart.

PART II.

In full assemblies I have told thy truth and righteousness at large ;
Nor did, thou know'st, my lips withhold from utt'ring what thou gav'st in charge.
0 Nor kept within my breast confin'd thy faithfulness and saving grace :
But preach'd thy love, for all design'd that all might that and truth embrace.

1 Then let those mercies I declar'd to others, Lord, extend to me :
Thy loving-kindness my reward, thy truth my safe protection be.
2 For I with troubles am distress'd, too numberless for me to bear ;
Nor less with loads of guilt oppress'd, that plunge and sink me to despair.

As soon, alas ! may I recount the hairs on this afflicted head ;
My vanquish'd courage they surmount, and fill my drooping soul with dread.

PART III.

3 But, Lord, to my relief draw near ; for never was more pressing need :
In my deliv'rance, Lord, appear, and add to that deliv'rance, speed.
4 Confusion on their heads return, who to destroy my soul combine ;
Let them, defeated, blush and mourn, insnar'd in their own vile design.

15 Their doom let desolation be, with shame their malice be repaid,
Who mock'd my confidence in thee, and sport of my affliction made:
16 While those who humbly seek thy face, to joyful triumphs shall be rais'd;
And all who prize thy saving grace, with me resound, the Lord be prais'd.

17 Thus, wretched tho' I am and poor, of me th' almighty Lord takes care;
Thou, God, who only canst restore, to my relief with speed repair.

PSALM XLI.

1 HAPPY the man, whose tender care relieves the poor distress'd!
When troubles compass him around, the Lord shall give him rest.
2 The Lord his life, with blessings crown'd, in safety shall prolong;
And disappoint the will of those that seek to do him wrong.

3 If he in languishing estate, oppress'd with sickness, lie;
The Lord will easy make his bed, and inward strength supply.
4 Secure of this, to thee, my God, I thus my pray'r address'd;
"Lord, for thy mercy, heal my soul, tho' I have much transgress'd."

5 My cruel foes, with sland'rous words, attempt to wound my fame;
"When shall he die," say they, "and men forget his very name?"
6 Suppose they formal visits make, 'tis all but empty show:
They gather mischief in their hearts, and vent it where they go.

7, 8 With private whispers, such as these, to hurt me they devise,
"A sore disease afflicts him now, he's fall'n no more to rise:"
9 My own familiar bosom friend, on whom I most rely'd,
Has me, whose daily guest he was, with open scorn defy'd.

10 But thou, my sad and wretched state, in mercy, Lord, regard;
And raise me up, that all their crimes may meet their just reward.
11 By this, I know, thy gracious ear is open when I call;
Because thou suffer'st not my foes to triumph in my fall.

12 Thy tender care secures my life from danger and disgrace;
And thou vouchsaf'st to set me still before thy glorious face.
13 Let therefore Israel's Lord and God from age to age be bless'd;
And all the people's glad applause with loud amens express'd.

PSALM XLII

1 AS pants the hart for cooling streams, when heated in the chace;
So longs my soul, O God, for thee, and thy refreshing grace.
2 For thee, my God, the living God, my thirsty soul doth pine;
O! when shall I behold thy face, thou Majesty divine?

3 Tears are my constant food, while thus insulting foes upbraid:
"Deluded wretch! where's now thy God? and where his promis'd aid?"
4 I sigh whene'er my musing thoughts those happy days present,
When I with troops of pious friends thy temple did frequent:

When I advanc'd with songs of praise my solemn vows to pay,
And led the joyful sacred throng that keep the festal day.
5 Why restless, why cast down, my soul? trust God; who will employ
His aid for thee, and change these sighs to thankful hymns of joy.

6 My soul's cast down, O God; but thinks on thee and Sion still;
From Jordan's bank, from Hermon's heights, and Missar's humbler hill,

7 One trouble calls another on; and gath'ring o'er my head,
Fall spouting down, till round my soul a roaring sea is spread.

8 But when thy presence, Lord of life, has once dispell'd this storm,
To thee I'll midnight anthems sing, and all my vows perform.
9 God of my strength, how long shall I, like one forgotten, mourn,
Forlorn, forsaken, and expos'd to my oppressor's scorn?

10 My heart is pierc'd, as with a sword, while thus my foes upbraid:
"Vain boaster, where is now thy God? and where his promis'd aid?"
11 Why restless, why cast down, my soul? hope still; and thou shalt sing
The praise of him who is thy God, thy health's eternal spring.

PSALM XLIII.

1 JUST Judge of heav'n, against my foes, do thou assert my injur'd right;
O! set me free, my God, from those that in deceit and wrong delight.
2 Since thou art still my only stay, why leav'st thou me in deep distress?
Why go I mourning all the day whilst me insulting foes oppress?

3 Let me with light and truth be bless'd; be these my guides to lead the way,
Till on thy holy hill I rest, and in thy sacred temple pray.
4 Then will I there fresh altars raise to God, who is my only joy;
And well-tun'd harps, with songs of praise, shall all my grateful hours employ.

5 Why then cast down, my soul? and why so much oppress'd with anxious care?
On God, thy God, for aid rely, who will thy ruin'd state repair.

PSALM XLIV.

1 O LORD, our fathers oft have told, in our attentive ears,
Thy wonders in their days perform'd, and elder times than theirs;
2 How thou, to plant them here, didst drive the heathen from this land,
Dispeopled by repeated strokes of thy aveng ng hand.

3 For not their courage, nor their sword, to them possession gave;
Nor strength, that from unequal force their fainting troops could save;
But thy right hand, and pow'rful arm, whose succour they implor'd;
Thy presence with the chosen race, who thy great name ador'd.

4 As thee their God our fathers own'd, thou art our sov'reign king:
O! therefore, as thou didst to them, to us deliv'rance bring.
5 Through thy victorious name our arms the proudest foes shall quell;
And crush them with repeated strokes, as oft as they rebel.

6 I'll neither trust my bow nor sword, when I in fight engage;
7 But thee, who hast our foes subdu'd, and sham'd their spiteful rage.
8 To thee the triumph we ascribe, from whom the conquest came;
In God we will rejoice all day, and ever bless his name.

PART II.

9 But thou hast cast us off; and now most shamefully we yield;
For thou no more vouchsaf'st to lead our armies to the field.
10 Since when, to ev'ry upstart foe we turn our backs in fight;
And with our spoil their malice feast, who bear us ancient spite.

11 To slaughter doom'd, we fall like sheep, into their butch'ring hands;
Or (what's more wretched yet) survive, dispers'd thro' heathen lands.

12 Thy people thou hast sold for slaves, and set their price so low,
That not thy treasure by the sale, but their disgrace may grow.

13, 14 Reproach'd by all the nations round, the heathen's by-word grown;
Whose scorn of us is both in speech and mocking gesture, shown.
15 Confusion strikes me blind; my face in conscious shame I hide,
16 While we are scoff'd, and God blasphem'd, by their licentious pride.

PART III.

17 On us this heap of woe is fall'n; all this we have endur'd;
Yet, have not, Lord, renounc'd thy name, or faith to thee abjur'd;
18 But in thy righteous paths have kept our hearts and steps with care;
19 Tho' thou hast broken all our strength, and we almost despair.

20 Could we, forgetting thy great name, on other gods rely,
21 And not the searcher of all hearts, the treach'rous crime descry?
22 Thou see'st what suff'rings for thy sake, we ev'ry day sustain;
All slaughter'd, or reserv'd like sheep appointed to be slain.

23 Awake, arise; let seeming sleep no longer thee detain;
Nor let us, Lord, who sue to thee, for ever sue in vain.
24 O! wherefore hidest thou thy face from our afflicted state,
25 Whose soul and bodies sink to earth, with grief's oppressive weight?

26 Arise, O Lord, and timely haste to our deliv'rance make;
Redeem us, Lord:---if not for ours, yet for thy mercy's sake.

PSALM XLV.

1 WHILE I the King's loud praise rehearse, indited by my heart,
My tongue is like the pen of him that writes with ready art,
2 How matchless is thy form, O King? thy mouth with grace o'erflows;
Because fresh blessings God on thee, eternally bestows.

3 Gird on thy sword, most mighty Prince; and, clad in rich array,
With glorious ornaments of pow'r majestic pomp display.
4 Ride on in state, and still protect the meek, the just, and true;
Whilst thy right hand, with swift revenge, does all thy foes pursue.

5 How sharp thy weapons are to them that dare thy power despise!
Down, down they fall, while through their heart the feather'd arrow flies.
6 But thy firm throne, O God, is fix'd, for ever to endure:
Thy sceptre's sway shall always last, by righteous laws secure.

7 Because thy heart by justice led, did upright ways approve,
And hated still the crooked paths, where wand'ring sinners rove;
Therefore did God, thy God, on thee the oil of gladness shed;
And has, above thy fellows round, advanc'd thy lofty head.

8 With cassia, aloes, and myrrh, thy royal robes abound;
Which from the stately wardrobe brought spread grateful odours round.
9 Among the honourable train, did princely virgins wait;
The Queen was plac'd at thy right hand, in golden robes of state.

PART II.

10 But thou, O royal bride, give ear, and to my words attend,
Forget thy native country now, and every former friend.

11 So shall thy beauty charm the king; nor shall his love decay:
For he is now become thy Lord; to him due rev'rence pay.
12 The Tyrian matrons, rich and proud, shall humble presents make;
And all the wealthy nations sue, thy favour to partake.

13 The king's fair daughter's fairer soul all inward graces fill:
Her raiment is of purest gold, adorn'd with costly skill.
14 She in her nuptial garments dress'd, with needles richly wrought,
Attended by her virgin train, shall to the king be brought.

15 With all the state of solemn joy the triumph moves along,
Till, with wide gates, the royal court receives the pompous throng.
16 Thou in thy royal Father's room, must princely sons expect;
Whom thou to diff'rent realms may'st send to govern and protect:

17 Whilst this my song to future times transmits thy glorious name;
And makes the world with one consent, thy lasting praise proclaim.

PSALM XLVI.

1 GOD is our refuge in distress,
A present help when dangers press;
In him, undaunted we'll confide;
2, 3 Tho' earth were from her center tost,
And mountains in the ocean lost,
Torn piece-meal by the roaring tide.

4 A gentler stream with gladness still
The city of our Lord shall fill,
The royal state of God most high.
5 God dwells in Sion, whose fair tow'rs
Shall mock th'assaults of earthly pow'rs;
While his almighty aid is nigh.

6 In tumults when the heathen rag'd,
And kingdoms war against us wag'd,
He thunder'd and dispers'd their pow'rs

7 The Lord of Hosts conducts our arms,
Our tow'r of refuge in alarms,
Our father's Guardian-God, and ours.
8 Come, see the wonders he hath wrought,
On earth what desolation brought;
How he has calm'd the jarring world:

9 He broke the warlike spear and bow:
With them their thund'ring chariots too
Into devouring flames were hurl'd.
10 Submit to God's almighty sway;
For him the heathen shall obey,
And earth her sov'reign Lord confess:

11 The God of Hosts conducts our arms,
Our tow'r of refuge in alarms,
As to our fathers in distress.

PSALM XLVII.

1, 2 O ALL ye people, clap your hands and with triumphant voices sing:
No force the mighty power withstands of God the universal King,
3, 4 He shall opposing nations quell, and with success our battles fight;
Shall fix the place where we must dwell, the pride of Jacob, his delight.

5, 6 God is gone up, our Lord and King, with shouts of joy, and trumpets sound;
To him repeated praises sing, and let the chearful song rebound.
7, 8 Your utmost skill in praise be shown, for him, who all the world commands,
Who sits upon his righteous throne, and spreads his sway o'er heathen lands.

9 Our chiefs and tribes, that far from hence to serve the God of Abr'ham came,
Found him their constant sure defence, how great and glorious is his name.

PSALM XLVIII.

1 THE Lord, the only God, is great, and greatly to be prais'd;
In Sion, on whose happy mount his sacred throne is rais'd.

2 Her tow'rs, the joy of all the earth, with beauteous prospects rise;
On the north side th' almighty King's imperial city lies.

3 God in her palaces is known; his presence is her guard:
4 Confederate kings withdrew their siege, and of success despair'd.
5 They view'd her walls, admir'd and fled, with grief and terror struck;
6 Like women whom the sudden pangs of travail had o'ertook.

7 No wretched crew of mariners appear like them forlorn,
When fleets from Tarshish' wealthy coasts by eastern winds are torn.
8 In Sion we have seen perform'd a work that was foretold,
In pledge that God, for times to come, his city will uphold.

9 Not in our fortresses and walls, did we, O God, confide;
But on the temple fix'd our hopes, in which thou dost reside.
10 According to thy sov'reign name, thy praise thro' earth extends;
Thy pow'rful arm as justice guides, chastises or defends.

11 Let Sion's mount with joy resound; her daughters all be taught
In songs his judgments to extol, who this deliv'rance wrought.
12 Compass her walls in solemn pomp your eyes quite round her cast;
Count all her tow'rs, and see if there you find one stone misplac'd.

13 Her forts and palaces survey, observe their order well;
That, with assurance, to your heirs his wonders you may tell.
14 This God is ours, and will be ours, whilst we in him confide;
Who, as he has preserv'd us now, till death will be our guide.

PSALM XLIX.

1, 2 LET all the list'ning world attend, and my instruction hear:
Let high and low, and rich and poor, with joint consent give ear.
3 My mouth, with sacred wisdom fill'd, shall good advice impart,
The sound result of prudent thoughts, digested in my heart.

4 To parables of weighty sense I will my ear incline;
Whilst to my tuneful harp I sing dark words of deep design.
5 Why should my courage fail in times of danger and of doubt,
When sinners, that would me supplant, have compass'd me about?

6 Those men, that all their hope and trust in heaps of treasure place,
And boast in triumph, when they see their ill-got wealth increase,
7 Are yet unable from the grave their dearest friend to free;
Nor can, by force of bribes, reverse th' almighty Lord's decree.

8, 9 Their vain endeavours they must quit the price is held too high:
No sums can purchase such a grant, that man should never die.
10 Not wisdom can the wise exempt, nor fools their folly save;
But both must perish, and, in death, their wealth to others leave.

11 For tho' they think their stately seats shall ne'er to ruin fall;
But their remembrance last in lands which by their names they call;
12 Yet shall their fame be soon forgot, how great soe'er their state:
With beasts their memory, and they, shall share one common fate.

PART II.

13 How great their folly is, who thus absurd conclusions make!
And yet their children, unreclaim'd, repeat the gross mistake.

14 They all, like sheep to slaughter led, the prey of death are made;
Their beauty while, the just rejoice, within the grave shall fade.

15 But God will yet redeem my soul; and from the greedy grave
His greater pow'r shall set me free, and to himself receive.
16 Then fear not thou, when worldly men in envy'd wealth abound;
Nor tho' their prosp'rous house increase, with state and honour crown'd.

17 For when they're summon'd hence by death, they leave all this behind;
No shadow of their former pomp within the grave they find:
18 And yet they thought their state was blest, caught in the flatt'rers' snare,
Who with their vanity comply'd, and prais'd their worldly care.

19 In their forefathers' steps they tread; and when, like them, they die,
Their wretched ancestors and they in endless darkness lie.
20 For man, how great soe'er his state, unless he's truly wise,
As like a sensual beast he lives, so like a beast he dies.

PSALM L.

1, 2 THE Lord hath spoke, the mighty God
Hath sent his summons all abroad,
From dawning light, till day declines,
The list'ning earth his voice hath heard,
And he from Sion hath appear'd,
Where beauty in perfection shines.

3, 4 Our God shall come, and keep no more
Misconstru'd silence, as before;
But wasting flames before him send:
Around shall tempests fiercely rage,
Whilst he does heav'n and earth engage,
His just tribunal to attend.

5, 6 Assemble all my saints to me,
(Thus runs the great divine decree)
That in my lasting cov'nant live;
And off'rings bring with constant care;
The heav'ns his justice shall declare;
For God himself shall sentence give.

7, 8 Attend, my people; Israel, hear
Thy strong accuser I'll appear;
Thy God, thy only God, am I:
'Tis not of off'rings I complain,
Which, daily in my temple slain,
My sacred altar did supply.

9 Will this alone atonement make?
No bullock from thy stall I'll take,
Nor he-goat from thy fold accept:
10 The forest beasts, that range alone,
The cattle too, are all my own,
That on a thousand hills are kept.

11 I know the fowls, that build their nests
In craggy rocks; and savage beasts
That loosely haunt the open fields;
12 If seiz'd with hunger I could be,
I need not seek relief from thee,
Since the world's mine, and all it yields.

13 Think'st thou that I have any need
On slaughter'd bulls and goats to feed,
To eat their flesh and drink their blood?
14 The sacrifices I require,
Are hearts which love and zeal inspire,
And vows with strictest care made good.

15 In time of trouble call on me,
And I will set thee safe and free;
And thou returns of praise shalt make
16 But to the wicked, thus saith God:
How dar'st thou teach my laws abroad,
Or in thy mouth my cov'nant take?

17 For stubborn thou, confirm'd in sin,
Hast proof against instruction been,
And of my word didst lightly speak:
18 When thou a subtle thief didst see,
Thou gladly with him didst agree,
And with adult'rers didst partake.

19 Vile slander is thy chief delight;
Thy tongue, by envy mov'd, and spite,
Deceitful tales does hourly spread:
20 Thou dost with hateful scandals wound
Thy brother, and with lies confound
The offspring of thy mother's bed.

21 These things didst thou, whom still I strove
To gain with silence and with love
Till thou didst wickedly surmise,
That I was such a one as thou:
But I'll reprove and shame thee now,
And set thy sins before thine eyes.

22 Mark this, ye wicked fools, lest I
Let all my bolts of vengeance fly,
Whilst none shall dare your cause to own:
23 Who praises me, due honour gives,
And to the man that justly lives,
My strong salvation shall be shown.

PSALM LI.

1 HAVE mercy, Lord, on me, as thou wert ever kind;
Let me, oppress'd with loads of guilt, thy wonted mercy find.
2, 3 Wash off my foul offence, and cleanse me from my sin;
For I confess my crime and see how great my guilt has been.

4 Against thee, Lord, alone, and only in thy sight,
Have I transgress'd, and tho' condemn'd, must own thy judgments right.
5 In guilt each part was form'd of all this sinful frame;
In guilt I was conceiv'd and born the heir of sin and shame.

6 Yet thou, whose searching eye does inward truth require,
In secret didst with wisdom's laws, my tender soul inspire.
7 With hyssop purge me, Lord; and so I clean shall be:
I shall with snow in whiteness vie, when purify'd by thee.

8 Make me to hear with joy, thy kind forgiving voice,
That so the bones which thou hast broke, may with fresh strength rejoice.
9, 10 Blot out my crying sins, nor me in anger view;
Create in me a heart that's clean, an upright mind renew:

PART II.

11 Withdraw not thou thy help, nor cast me from thy sight:
Nor let thy holy spirit take it's everlasting flight.
12 The joy thy favour gives let me again obtain;
And thy free spirit's firm support my fainting soul sustain.

13 So I thy righteous ways to sinners will impart;
Whilst my advice shall wicked men to thy just laws convert.
14 My guilt of blood remove, my Saviour and my God;
And my glad tongue shall loudly tell thy righteous acts abroad.

15 Do thou unlock my lips, with sorrow clos'd and shame;
So shall my mouth thy wond'rous praise to all the world proclaim.
16 Could sacrifice atone, whole flocks and herds should die
But on such off'rings thou disdain'st to cast a gracious eye.

17 A broken spirit is by God most highly priz'd;
By him a broken contrite heart shall never be despis'd.
18 Let Sion favour find, of thy good will assur'd;
And thy own city flourish long, by lofty walls secur'd.

19 The just shall then attend, and pleasing tribute pay;
And sacrifice of choicest kind upon thy altar lay.

PSALM LII.

1 IN vain, O man of lawless might, thou boast'st thyself in ill;
Since God, the God in whom I trust, vouchsafes his favour still.

2 Thy wicked tongues doth sland'rous tales
maliciously devise:
And sharper than a razor set,
it wounds with treach'rous lies.

3, 4 Thy thoughts are more on ill than good,
on lies than truth employ'd;
Thy tongue delights in words, by which
the guiltless are destroy'd.
5 God shall for ever blast thy hopes,
and snatch thee soon away;
Nor in thy dwelling-place permit,
nor in the world to stay.

6 The just, with pious fear, shall see
the downfall of thy pride;
And at thy sudden ruin laugh,
and thus thy fall deride
7 "See there the man that haughty was,
who proudly God defy'd,
"Who trusted in his wealth, and still
on wicked arts rely'd."

8 But I am like those olive plants,
that shade God's temple round;
And hope with his indulgent grace
to be for ever crown'd.
9 So shall my soul, with praise, O God,
extol thy wondrous love;
And on thy name with patience wait;
for this thy saints approve.

PSALM LIII.

THE wicked fools must sure suppose,
that God is but a name:
This gross mistake their practice shows,
since virtue all disclaim.
The Lord look'd down from heav'ns high tow'r,
the sons of men to view,
To see if any own'd his pow'r,
or truth or justice knew.

3 But all he saw were backwards gone,
degen'rate grown and base;
None for religion car'd, not one
of all the sinful race.
But are those workers of deceit
so dull and senseless grown,
That they like bread my people eat,
and God's just pow'r disown?

Their causeless fears shall strangely grow;
and they, despis'd of God,
Shall soon be foil'd: his hand shall throw
their shatter'd bones abroad.
Would he his saving pow'r employ
to break our servile band,
Loud shouts of universal joy
should echo thro' the land.

PSALM LIV.

LORD, save me, for thy glorious name;
and in thy strength appear,
To judge my cause; accept my pray'r,
and to my words give ear.
Mere strangers, whom I never wrong'd,
to ruin me design'd;
And cruel men that fear'd not God,
against my soul combin'd.

4, 5 But God takes part with all my friends;
and he's the surest guard:
The God of truth shall give my foes
their falsehood's due reward;
While I my grateful off'rings bring,
and sacrifice with joy;
And in his praise my time to come
delightfully employ.

From dreadful danger and distress
the Lord hath set me free:
Through him shall I of all my foes
the just destruction see.

PSALM LV.

GIVE ear thou judge of all the earth,
and listen when I pray;
Nor from thy humble suppliant turn
thy glorious face away.
Attend to this my sad complaint,
and hear my grievous moans;
While I my mournful case declare
with artless sighs and groans.

Hark how the foe insults aloud!
how fierce oppressors rage!
Whose slandrous tongues, with wrathful hate,
against my fame engage.

4, 5 My heart is wrack'd with pain; with deadly frights distress'd;
With fear and trembling compass'd round, with horror quite oppress'd.

6 How often wish'd I then, that I the dove's swift wings could get;
That I might take my speedy flight, and seek a safe retreat!
7, 8 Then would I wander far from hence, and in wild deserts stray,
Till all this furious storm were spent, this tempest pass'd away.

PART II.

9 Destroy, O Lord, their ill designs, their counsels soon divide;
For through the city my griev'd eyes have strife and rapine spy'd.
10 By day and night, on ev'ry wall, they walk their constant round;
And in the midst of all her strength are grief and mischief found.

11 Whoe'er through ev'ry part shall roam, will fresh disorders meet:
Deceit and guile their constant posts maintain in ev'ry street.
12 For 'twas not any open foe, that false reflections made;
For then I could with ease have borne the bitter things he said;

'Twas none who hatred had profess'd, that did against me rise;
For then I had withdrawn myself from his malicious eyes.
13, 14 But 'twas e'en thou, my guide, my friend, whom tend'rest love did join;
Whose sweet advice I valu'd most, whose pray'rs were mix'd with mine.

15 Sure vengeance, equal to the crimes, such traitors must surprise;
And sudden death requite those ills they wickedly devise.
16, 17 But I will call on God, who still shall in my aid appear:
At morn, at noon, and night I'll pray; and he my voice shall hear.

PART III.

18 God has releas'd my soul from those that did with me contend;
And made a num'rous host of friends my righteous cause defend.
19 For he, who was my help of old, shall now his suppliant hear;
And punish them, whose prosp'rous state makes them no God to fear.

20 Whom can I trust, if faithless men perfidiously devise
To ruin me, their peaceful friend, and break the strongest ties?
21 Though soft and melting are their words, their hearts with war abound:
Their speeches are more smooth than oil, and yet like swords they wound.

22 Do thou, my soul, on God depend, and he shall thee sustain:
He aids the just, whom to supplant the wicked strive in vain.
23 My foes, that trade in lies and blood, shall all untimely die;
Whilst I, for health and length of days, on thee, my God, rely.

PSALM LVI.

1 DO thou, O God, in mercy help; for man my life pursues;
To crush me with repeated wrongs, he daily strife renews.
2 Continually my spiteful foes to ruin me combine;
Thou seest, who sitt'st enthron'd on high, what mighty numbers join.

3 But though sometimes surpriz'd by fear, (on danger's first alarm)
Yet still for succour I depend on thy almighty arm.
4 God's faithful promise I shall praise, on which I now rely:
In God I trust, and, trusting him, the arm of flesh defy.

5 They wrest my words, and make them speak a sense they never meant:
Their thoughts are all, with restless spite, on my destruction bent.
6 In close assemblies they combine, and wicked projects lay;
They watch my steps and lie in wait to make my soul their prey.

7 Shall such injustice still escape? O righteous God, arise:
Let thy just wrath (too long provok'd) this impious race chastise.
8 Thou number'st all my steps, since first I was compell'd to flee:
My very tears are treasur'd up, and register'd by thee.

9 When therefore I invoke thy aid, my foes shall be o'erthrown:
For I am well assur'd that God my righteous cause will own.
10, 11 I'll trust God's word, and so despise the force that man can raise;
12 To thee, O God, my vows are due; to thee I'll render praise.

13 Thou hast retriev'd my soul from death? and thou wilt still secure
The life thou hast so oft preserv'd, and make my footsteps sure:
14 That thus protected by thy pow'r, I may this light enjoy;
And in the service of my God my lengthen'd days employ.

PSALM LVII.

1 THY mercy, Lord, to me extend:
On thy protection I depend;
And to thy wing for shelter haste,
Till this outrageous storm is past.

2 To thy tribunal, Lord, I fly,
Thou Sov'reign Judge, and God most high,
Who wonders hast for me begun,
And wilt not leave thy work undone.

3 From heav'n protect me by thine arm,
And shame all those who seek my harm:
To my relief thy mercy send,
And truth, on which my hopes depend.

4 For I with savage men converse,
Like hungry lions wild and fierce;
With men whose teeth are spears, their words
Invenom'd darts and two-edg'd swords.

5 Be thou, O God, exalted high;
And as thy glory fills the sky,
So let it be on earth display'd,
Till thou art here as there obey'd.

6 To take me they their net prepar'd,
And had almost my soul ensnar'd;
But fell themselves, by just decree,
Into the pit they made for me.

7 O God, my heart is fix'd, 'tis bent,
Its thankful tribute to present;
And, with my heart, my voice I'll raise
To thee, my God, in songs of praise.

8 Awake my glory, harp, and lute,
No longer let your strings be mute:
And I, my tuneful part to take,
Will with the early dawn awake.

9 Thy praises, Lord, I will resound
To all the list'ning nations round:
10 Thy mercy highest heav'n transcends;
Thy truth beyond the clouds extends.

11 Be thou, O God, exalted high;
And as thy glory fills the sky,
So let it be on earth display'd,
Till thou art here as there obey'd.

PSALM LVIII.

1 SPEAK, O ye judges of the earth, if just your sentence be;
Or must not innocence appeal to heav'n from your decree?
2 Your wicked hearts and judgments are alike by malice sway'd;
Your griping hands, by weighty bribes, to violence betray'd.

3 To virtue strangers from the womb, their infant steps went wrong:
They prattled slander, and in lies employ'd their lisping tongue.

4 No serpent of parch'd Afric's breed does ranker poison bear;
The drowsy adder will as soon unlock his sullen ear.

5 Unmov'd by good advice, and deaf as adders they remain;
From whom the skilful charmer's voice can no attention gain.
6 Defeat, O God, their threat'ning rage, and timely break their pow'r;
Disarm these growling lions' jaws, ere practis'd to devour.

7 Let now their insolence, at height, like ebbing tides be spent:
Their shiver'd darts deceive their aim, when they their bows have bent.
8 Like snails let them dissolve to slime; like hasty births become
Unworthy to behold the sun, and dead within the womb.

9 Ere thorns can make the flesh-pots boil, tempestuous wrath shall come
From God, and snatch them hence alive to their eternal doom.
10 The righteous shall rejoice to see their crimes with vengeance meet!
And saints in persecutors' blood shall dip their harmless feet.

11 Transgressors then with grief shall see just men rewards obtain;
And own a God, whose justice will the guilty earth arraign.

PSALM LIX.

1 DELIVER me, O Lord, my God, from all my spiteful foes;
In my defence oppose thy pow'r to theirs who me oppose.
2 Preserve me from a wicked race, who make a trade of ill;
Protect me from remorseless men, who seek my blood to spill.

3 They lie in wait, and mighty pow'rs against my life combine,
Implacable; yet, Lord, thou know'st for no offence of mine.
4 In haste they run about, and watch my guiltless life to take:
Look down, O Lord, on my distress, and to my help awake.

5 Thou Lord of Hosts and Israel's God, their heathen rage suppress;
Relentless vengeance take on those who stubbornly transgress.
6 At evening, to beset mine house, like growling dogs they meet;
While others through the city range, and ransack ev'ry street.

7 Their thoughts invenom'd slander breathe: their tongues are sharpen'd swords:
"Who hears? (say they) or, hearing, dares reprove our lawless words?"
8 But from thy throne thou shalt, O Lord, their baffled plots deride,
And soon to scorn and shame expose their boasted heathen pride.

9 On thee I wait: 'tis on thy strength for succour I depend;
'Tis thou, O God, art my defence, who only can defend.
10 Thy mercy, Lord, which has so oft from danger set me free,
Shall crown my wishes, and subdue my haughty foes to me.

11 Destroy them not, O Lord, at once; restrain thy vengeful blow:
Lest we, ungratefully, too soon forget their overthrow.
Disperse them through the nations round, by thy avenging pow'r:
Do thou bring down their haughty pride, O Lord, our shield and tow'r.

12 Now in the height of all their hopes, their arrogance chastise:
Whose tongues have sinn'd without restraint, and curses join'd with lies.
13 Nor shalt thou, whilst their rage endures, thine anger, Lord, suppress;
That distant lands, by thy just doom, may Israel's God confess.

14 At ev'ning let them still persist like growling dogs to meet;
Still wander all the city round, and traverse ev'ry street.
15 Then, as for malice now they do, for hunger let them stray;
And yell their vain complaints aloud, defeated of their prey.

16 Whilst early I thy mercy sing, thy wondrous pow'r confess;
For thou hast been my sure defence, my refuge in distress.
17 To thee with never-ceasing praise, O God, my strength, I'll sing:
Thou art my God, the rock from whence my health and safety spring.

PSALM LX.

1 O GOD, who hast our troops dispers'd,
Forsaking those who left thee first;
As we thy just displeasure mourn,
To us in mercy, Lord, return.

2 Our strength, that firm as earth did stand,
Is rent by thy avenging hand;
O! heal the breaches thou hast made;
We shake, we fall, without thy aid!

3 Our folly's sad effects we feel!
For, drunk with discord's cup, we reel;
4 But now, for them who thee rever'd,
Thou hast thy truth's bright banner rear'd.

5 Let thy right hand thy saints protect:
Lord, hear the pray'rs that we direct.
6 The holy God has spoke; and I,
O'erjoy'd, on his firm word rely.

To thee in portions I'll divide
Fair Sichem's soil, Samaria's pride;
To Sichem, Succoth next I'll join,
And measure out her vale by line.

7 Manasseh, Gilead, both subscribe
To my command, with Ephraim's tribe:
Ephraim by arms supports my cause,
And Judah by religious laws.

8 Moab my slave and drudge shall be,
Nor Edom from my yoke get free:
Proud Palestine's imperious state
Shall humbly on our triumph wait.

8 But who shall quell these mighty pow'rs,
And clear my way to Edom's tow'rs?
Or thro' her guarded frontiers tread
The path that doth to conquest lead?

10 Ev'n thou, O God, who hast dispers'd
Our troops (for we forsook thee first;)
Those whom thou didst in wrath forsake,
Aton'd, thou wilt victorious make.

11 Do thou our fainting cause sustain:
For human succours are but vain.
12 Fresh strength and courage God bestows;
'Tis he treads down our proudest foes.

PSALM LXI.

1 LORD, hear my cry, regard my pray'r, which I, oppress'd with grief,
2 From earth's remotest parts address to thee for kind relief.
O, lodge me safe, beyond the reach of persecuting pow'r;
3 Thou who so oft from spiteful foes hast been my shelt'ring tow'r.

4 So shall I in thy sacred courts secure from danger lie;
Beneath the covert of thy wings all future storms defy.
5 In sign my vows are heard, once more I o'er thy chosen reign:
6 O, bless with long and prosp'rous life the king thou didst ordain.

7 Confirm his throne, and make his reign accepted in thy sight;
And let thy truth and mercy both in his defence unite.
8 So shall I ever sing thy praise, thy name for ever bless;
Devote my prosp'rous days to pay the vows of my distress.

PSALM LXII

1, 2 MY soul for help on God relies; from him alone my safety flows:
My rock, my health, that strength supplies to bear the shock of all my foes.

3 How long will ye contrive my fall,
which will but hasten on your own?
You'll totter like a bending wall,
or fence of uncemented stone.

4 To make my envy'd honours less
they strive with lies, their chief delight;
For they, tho' with their mouths they bless,
in private curse with inward spite.
5, 6 But thou, my soul, on God rely;
on him alone thy trust repose:
My rock and health with strength supply
to bear the shock of all my foes.

7 God does his saving health dispense,
and flowing blessings daily send:
He is my fortress and defence;
on him my soul shall still depend.
8 In him, ye people, always trust;
before his throne pour out your hearts:
For God, the merciful and just,
his timely aid to us imparts.

9 The vulgar fickle are and frail;
the great dissemble and betray;
And, laid in truth's impartial scale,
the lightest things will both outweigh.
10 Then trust not in oppressive ways;
by spoil and rapine grow not vain;
Nor let your hearts, if wealth increase,
be set too much upon your gain.

11 For God has oft his will express'd,
and I this truth have fully known;
To be of boundless pow'r possess'd,
belongs, of right, to God alone.
12 Though mercy is his darling grace,
in which he chiefly takes delight;
Yet will he all the human race
according to their works requite.

PSALM LXIII.

1 O God, my gracious God, to thee
My morning pray'rs shall offer'd be:
For thee my thirsty soul does pant:
My fainting flesh implores thy grace,
Within this dry and barren place,
Where I refreshing waters want.

2 O, to my longing eyes, once more
That view of glorious pow'r restore,
Which thy majestic house displays;
3 Because to me thy wondrous love
Than life itself does dearer prove,
My lips shall always speak thy praise.

4 My life, while I that life enjoy,
In blessing God I will employ;
With lifted hands adore his name:
5 My soul's consent shall be as great
As theirs who choicest dainties eat,
While I with joy his praise proclaim.

6 When down I lie, sweet sleep to find,
Thou, Lord, art present to my mind;
And when I wake in dead of night:
7 Because thou still dost succour bring,
Beneath the shadow of thy wing
I rest with safety and delight.

8 My soul, when foes would me devour,
Cleaves fast to thee, whose matchless pow'r
In her support is daily shown:
9 But those the righteous Lord shall slay,
That my destruction wish, and they
That seek my life shall lose their own.

10 They by untimely ends shall die,
Their flesh a prey to foxes lie;
But God shall fill the king with joy:
11 Who thee confess shall still rejoice;
Whilst the false tongue, and lying voice,
Thou, Lord, shalt silence and destroy.

PSALM LXIV.

1 LORD, hear the voice of my complaint;
to my request give ear;
Preserve my life from cruel foes,
and free my soul from fear.
2 O, hide me with thy tend'rest care,
in some secure retreat,
From sinners that against me rise;
and all their plots defeat.

3 See how, intent to work my harm,
they whet their tongues like swords,
And bend their bows to shoot like darts,
sharp lies, and bitter words.
4 Lurking in private at the just,
they take their secret aim;
And suddenly at them they shoot,
quite void of fear and shame.

To carry on their ill designs they mutually agree;
They speak of laying private snares, and think that none shall see.
With utmost diligence and care their wicked plots they lay;
The deep designs of all their hearts are only to betray.

But God, to anger justly mov'd, his dreadful bow shall bend,
And on his flying arrow's point shall swift destruction send.
Those slanders, which their mouth did vent, upon themselves shall fall:
Their crimes, disclos'd, shall make them be despis'd and shunn'd by all.

The world shall then God's power confess, and nations trembling stand,
Convinc'd that 'tis the mighty work of his avenging hand:
0 Whilst righteous men, whom God secures, in him shall gladly trust;
And all the list'ning earth shall hear loud triumphs of the just.

PSALM LXV.

FOR thee, O God, our constant praise in Sion waits, thy chosen seat:
Our promis'd altars there we'll raise, and all our zealous vows complete.
O thou, who to my humble pray'r didst always bend thy list'ning ear,
To thee shall all mankind repair, and at thy gracious throne appear.

Our sins (though numberless) in vain to stop thy flowing mercy try;
Whilst thou o'erlook'st the guilty stain, and washest out the crimson dye.
Blest is the man who, near thee plac'd, within thy sacred dwelling lives!
Whilst we at humbler distance taste the vast delight thy temple gives.

By wondrous acts, O God, most just, have we thy gracious answer found:
In thee remotest nations trust, and those whom stormy waves surround.
7 God, by his strength sets fast the hills, and does his matchless pow'r engage:
With which the sea's loud waves he stills, and angry crowd's tumultuous rage.

PART II.

Thou, Lord, dost barb'rous lands dismay, when they thy dreadful tokens view:
With joy they see the night and day, each other's track by turns pursue.
From out thy unexhausted store thy rain relieves the thirsty ground;
Makes lands, that barren were before, with corn and useful fruits abound.

0 On rising ridges down it pours, and ev'ry furrow'd valley fills:
Thou mak'st them soft with gentle show'rs, in which a blest increase distils.
1 Thy goodness does the circling year with fresh returns of plenty crown;
And when thy glorious paths appear, thy fruitful clouds drop fatness down.

2 They drop on barren forests, chang'd by them to pastures fresh and green:
The hills about in order rang'd, in beauteous robes of joy are seen.
3 Large flocks with fleecy wool adorn the cheerful downs; the vallies bring
A plenteous crop of full-ear'd corn, and seem for joy to shout and sing.

PSALM LXVI.

2 LET all the lands, with shouts of joy, to God their voices raise;
Sing psalms, in honour of his name, and spread his glorious praise.
And let them say, how dreadful, Lord, in all thy works art thou!
To thy great pow'r thy stubborn foes shall all be forc'd to bow.

Through all the earth the nations round shall thee their God confess;
And, with glad hymns, their aweful dread of thy great name express.

5 O! come, behold the works of God; and then with me you'll own,
That he to all the sons of men has wondrous judgments shown.

6 He made the sea become dry land, thro' which our fathers walk'd;
Whilst to each other of his might with joy his people talk'd.
7 He, by his pow'r, for ever rules; his eyes the world survey:
Let no presumptuous man rebel against his sov'reign sway.

PART II.

8, 9 O, all ye nations, bless our God, and loudly speak his praise;
Who keeps our souls alive, and still confirms our stedfast ways.
10 For thou hast try'd us, Lord, as fire does try the precious ore:
11 Thou brought'st us into straits, where we oppressing burdens bore.

12 Insulting foes did us, their slaves, through fire and water chase;
But yet, at last, thou brought'st us forth into a wealthy place.
13 Burnt off'rings to thy house I'll bring and there my vows will pay;
14 Which I with solemn zeal did make in trouble's dismal day.

15 Then shall the richest incense smoke, the fattest rams shall fall,
The choicest goats from out the fold, and bullocks from the stall.
16 O come, all ye that fear the Lord; attend with heedful care,
Whilst I what God for me has done with grateful joy declare.

17, 18 As I before his aid implor'd, so now I praise his name;
Who, if my heart had harbour'd sin, would all my pray'rs disclaim,
19 But God to me, whene'er I cry'd, his gracious ear did bend,
And to the voice of my request, with constant love attend.

20 Then bless'd for ever be my God, who never, when I pray,
Withholds his mercy from my soul, nor turns his face away,

PSALM LXVII.

1 TO bless thy chosen race, in mercy, Lord, incline;
And cause the brightness of thy face on all thy saints to shine:
2 That so thy wond'rous way may through the world be known;
Whilst distant lands their tribute pay, and thy salvation own.

3 Let diff'ring nations join to celebrate thy fame;
Let all the world, O Lord, combine to praise thy glorious name.
4 O let them shout and sing with joy and pious mirth;
For thou the righteous Judge and King, shall govern all the earth.

5 Let diff'ring nations join to celebrate thy fame;
Let all the world, O Lord, combine to praise thy glorious name.
6 Then shall the teeming ground a large increase disclose;
And we with plenty shall be crown'd, which God, our God, bestows,

7 Then God upon our land shall constant blessings show'r;
And all the world in awe shall stand of his resistless pow'r.

PSALM LXVIII.

1 LET God, the God of battle, rise, and scatter his presumptuous foes;
Let shameful rout their host surprise, who spitefully his pow'r oppose.
2 As smoke in tempest's rage is lost, or wax into the furnace cast;
So let their sacrilegious host before his wrathful presence waste.

3 But let the servants of his will his favour's gentle beams enjoy;
Their upright hearts let gladness fill, and chearful songs their tongues employ
4 To him your voice in anthems raise: Jehovah's awful name he bears:
In him rejoice, extol his praise, who rides upon high-rolling spheres.

5 Him, from his empire of the skies, to this low world compassion draws,
The orphan's claim to patronize, and judge the injur'd widow's cause.
6 'Tis God, who from a foreign soil restores poor exiles to their home;
Makes captives free; and fruitless toil their proud oppressors' righteous doom.

7 'Twas so of old, when thou didst lead, in person, lord, our armies forth;
Strange terrors through the desart spread, convulsions shook th' astonish'd earth.
8 The breaking clouds did rain distil, and heav'n's high arches shook with fear
How then should Sinai's humble hill, of Israel's God the presence bear?

9 Thy hand, at famish'd earth's complaint, reliev'd her from celestial stores:
And when thy heritage was faint, assuag'd the drought with plenteous show'rs.

10 Where savages had rang'd before, at ease thou mad'st our tribes reside;
And, in the desart, for the poor thy gen'rous bounty did provide

PART II.

11 Thou gav'st the word; we sally'd forth and in that pow'ful word o'ercame;
While virgin-troops, with songs of mirth, in state our conquest did proclaim.
12 Vast armies, by such gen'rals led, as yet had ne'er receiv'd a foil,
Forsook their camp with sudden dread, and to our women left the spoil.

13 Tho' Egypt's drudges you have been, your army's wings shall shine as bright
As doves in golden sunshine seen, or silver'd o'er with paler light.
14 'Twas so, when God's almighty hand o'er scatter'd kings the conquest won;
Our troops drawn up on Jordan's strand, high Salmon's glitt'ring snow outshone.

15 From thence to Jordan's farther coast and Bashan's hill we did advance:
No more her height shall Bashan boast but that she's God's inheritance.
16 But wherefore tho' the honour's great should this, O mountain, swell your pride
For Sion is his chosen seat, where he for ever will reside.

17 His chariots numberless; his pow'rs are heav'nly hosts that wait his will;
His presence now fills Sion tow'rs, as once it honour'd Sinai's hill.
18 Ascending high, in triumph thou captivity hast captive led;
And on thy people didst bestow the spoil of armies once their dread.

Ev'n rebels shall partake thy grace, and humble proselytes repair
To worship at thy dwelling place, and all the world pay homage there.
19 For benefits each day bestow'd, be daily his great name ador'd;
20 Who is our Saviour and our God, of life and death the sov'reign Lord.

21 But justice for his harden'd foes proportion'd vengeance hath decreed
To wound the hoary head of those who in presumptuous crimes proceed.
22 The Lord hath thus in thunder spoke "as I subdu'd proud Bashan's king,
"Once more I'll break my people's yoke and from the deep my servants bring.

23 "Their feet shall with a crimson flood of slaughter'd foes be cover'd o'er;
"Nor earth receive such impious blood but leave for dogs th' unhallow'd gore.*

PSALM LXIX.

PART III.

24 When marching to thy blest abode,
the wond'ring multitude survey'd
The pompous state of thee, our God,
in robes of majesty array'd:
25 Sweet-singing Levites led the van,
loud instruments brought up the rear;
Between both troops a virgin train
with voice and timbrel charm'd the ear.

26 This was the burden of their song:
" In full assemblies bless the Lord;
" All, who to Israel's tribes belong,
the God of Israel's praise record."
27 Nor little Benjamin alone,
from neighb'ring bounds did there attend
Nor only Judah's nearer throne,
her counsellors did send:

But Zebulon's remoter seat,
and Napthali's more distant coast,
(The grand procession to complete)
sent up their tribes, a princely host.
28 Thus God to strength and union brought
our tribes at strife till that blest hour:
This work which thou, O God, hast wrought
confirm with fresh recruits of pow'r.

29 To visit Salem, Lord, descend,
and Sion, thy terrestrial throne;
Where kings with presents shall attend,
and thee with offer'd crowns atone.
30 Break down the spearmen's ranks, who threat
like pamper'd herds of savage might;
Their silver armour'd chiefs defeat,
who in destructive war delight.

31 Egypt shall then to God stretch forth
her hands, and Afric homage bring:
32 The scatter'd kingdoms of the earth
their common sov'reign's praises sing.
33 Who mounted on the loftiest sphere
of ancient heav'n, sublimely rides;
From whence his dreadful voice we hear
like that of warring winds and tides.

34 Ascribe ye pow'r to God most high:
of humble Israel he takes care;
Whose strength from out the dusky sky,
darts shining terrors through the air.
35 How dreadful are the sacred courts,
where God has fix'd his earthly throne!
His strength his feeble saints supports,
to give God praise, and him alone.

PSALM LXIX.

1 SAVE me, O God, from waves that roll
And press to overwhelm my soul.
2 With painful steps in mire I tread,
And deluges o'erflow my head.
3 With restless cries my spirits faint,
My voice is hoarse with long complaint;
My sight decays with tedious pain,
Whilst for my God I wait in vain.

4 My hairs, tho' numerous, are but few
Compar'd with foes that me pursue
With groundless hate, grown now of might,
To execute their lawless spite:
They force me, guiltless, to resign,
As rapine, what by right was mine.
5 Thou, Lord, my innocence doth see,
Nor are my sins conceal'd from thee.

6 Lord God of Hosts, take timely care,
Lest, for thy sake, thy saints despair:
7 Since I have suffer'd for thy name
Reproach, and hid my face in shame
8 A stranger to my country grown,
Nor to my nearest kindred known;
A foreigner, expos'd to scorn
By brethren of my mother born.

9 For zeal to thy lov'd house and name,
Consumes me like devouring flame;
Concern'd at their affronts to thee,
More than at slanders cast on me.
10 My very tears and abstinence
They construe in a spiteful sense.
11 When cloath'd with sackcloth for their sake,
They me their common proverb make.

12 Their judges at my wrongs do jest,
Those wrongs they ought to have redress'd;
How should I then expect to be
From libels of lewd drunkards free?

13 But, Lord, to thee I will repair
For help, with humble, timely pray'r.
Relieve me from thy mercy's store:
Display thy truth's deserving pow'r.

14 From threat'ning dangers me relieve,
And from the mire my feet retrieve;
From spiteful foes in safety keep,
And snatch me from the raging deep.
15 Controul the deluge, ere it spread,
And roll its waves above my head;
Nor deep destruction's open pit
To close her jaws on me permit.

16 Lord, hear the humble pray'r I make,
For thy transcending goodness' sake;
Relieve thy supplicant once more
From thy abounding mercy's store.
17 Nor from thy servant hide thy face:
Make haste, for desp'rate is my case:
18 Thy timely succour interpose,
And shield me from remorseless foes.

19 Thou know'st what infamy and scorn
I from my enemies have borne;
Nor can their close dissembled spite,
Or darkest plots, escape my sight.
20 Reproach and grief have broke my heart:
I look'd for some to take my part,
To pity or relieve my pain!
But look'd, alas! for both in vain.

21 With hunger pin'd for food I call:
Instead of food, they give me gall;
And when with thirst my spirits sink,
They give me vinegar to drink.
22 Their tables, therefore, to their health
Shall prove a snare, a trap their wealth:
23 Perpetual darkness seize their eyes,
And sudden blasts their hopes surprise;

24 On them thou shalt thy fury pour,
Till thy fierce wrath their race devour;
25 And make their house a dismal cell,
Where none will e'er vouchsafe to dwell.
26 For new afflictions they procur'd,
For him who had thy stripes endur'd;
And made the wounds thy scourge had torn,
To bleed afresh, with sharper scorn.

27 Sin shall to sin their steps betray,
Till they to truth have lost the way.
28 From life thou shalt exclude their soul;
Nor with the just their names inroll.
29 But me, howe'er distress'd and poor,
Thy strong salvation shall restore:
30 Thy pow'r with songs I'll then proclaim,
And celebrate with thanks thy name.

31 Our God shall this more highly prize
Than herds or flocks in sacrifice:
32 Which humble saints with joy shall see
And hope for like redress with me.
33 For God regards the poor's complaint;
Sets pris'ners free from close restraint.
34 Let heav'n,earth,sea, their voices raise,
And all the world resound his praise.

35 For God will Sion's walls erect;
Fair Judah's cities he'll protect;
Till all her scatter'd sons repair
To undisturb'd possession there.
36 This blessing they shall at their death,
To their religious heirs bequeath;
And they to endless ages more,
Of such as his blest name adore.

PSALM LXX.

1 O LORD, to my relief draw near,
For my deliv'rance, Lord, appear,
for never was more pressing need:
and add to that deliv'rance, speed.
2 Confusion on their heads return,
Let them, defeated, blush and mourn,
who to destroy my soul combine;
ensnar'd in their own vile design.

3 Their doom let desolation be;
Who mock'd my confidence in thee,
with shame their malice be repaid,
and sport of my afflictions made.
4 While those who humbly seek thy face,
And all who prize thy saving grace,
to joyful triumphs shall be rais'd;
with me shall sing, the Lord be prais'd.

5 Thus, wretched though I am, and poor,
Thou, God, who only canst restore,
the mighty Lord of me takes care;
to my relief with speed repair.

PSALM LXXI.

1, 2 IN thee I put my stedfast trust; defend me, Lord, from shame;
Incline thine ear, and save my soul, for righteous is thy name.
3 Be thou my strong abiding place, to which I may resort:
'Tis thy decree that keeps me safe; thou art my rock and fort.

4, 5 From cruel and ungodly men, protect and set me free;
For, from my earliest youth till now, my hope has been in thee.
6 Thy constant care did safely guard my tender infant-days;
Thou took'st me from my mother's womb, to sing thy constant praise,

7, 8 While some on me with wonder gaze, thy hand supports me still:
Thy honour therefore, and thy praise, my mouth shall always fill.
9 Reject not then thy servant, Lord, when I with age decay;
Forsake me not, when worn with years, my vigour fades away.

10 My foes against my fame and me with crafty malice speak;
Against my soul they lay their snares and mutual counsel take.
11 " His God, say they, forsakes him now, on whom he did rely:
" Pursue and take him, whilst no hope of timely aid is nigh."

12 But thou, my God, withdraw not far, for speedy help I call;
13 To shame and ruin bring my foes, that seek to work my fall.
14 But as for me, my stedfast hope shall on thy pow'r depend;
And I in grateful songs of praise my time to come will spend.

PART II.

15 Thy righteous acts, and saving health, my mouth shall still declare;
Unable yet to count them all, though summ'd with utmost care
16 While God vouchsafes me his support, I'll in his strength go on;
All other righteousness disclaim, and mention his alone.

17 Thou, Lord, hast taught me from my youth to praise thy glorious name;
And, ever since, thy wondrous works have been my constant theme.
18 Then now forsake me not, when I am grey and feeble grown;
Till I to these and future times thy strength and pow'r have shown

19 How high thy justice soars, O God! how great and wond'rous are
The mighty works which thou hast done, who may with thee compare?
20 Me, whom thy hand has sorely press'd, thy grace shall yet relieve;
And from the lowest depths of woe, with tender care retrieve.

21 Through thee, my time to come shall be with pow'r and greatness crown'd;
And me, who dismal years have pass'd, thy comforts shall surround.
22 Then I, with psaltery and harp, thy truth, O Lord, will praise;
To thee, the God of Jacob's race, my voice in anthems raise.

23 Then joy shall fill my mouth, and songs employ my chearful voice;
My grateful soul by thee redeem'd, shall in thy strength rejoice.
24 My tongue thy just and righteous acts shall all the day proclaim;
Because thou didst confound my foes, and brought'st them all to shame

PSALM LXXII.

1 LORD, let thy just decrees the king in all his ways direct;
And let his son, throughout his reign, thy righteous laws respect.

2 So shall he still thy people judge with pure and upright mind,
Whilst all the helpless poor shall him their just protector find.
3 Then hills and mountains shall bring forth the happy fruits of peace;
Which all the land shall own to be the work of righteousness:

4 Whilst he the poor and needy race shall rule with gentle sway,
And from their humble necks shall take oppressive yokes away.
5 In ev'ry heart thy awful fear shall then be rooted fast,
As long as sun and moon endure, or time itself shall last.

6 He shall descend like rain, that chears the meadow's second birth;
Or like warm show'rs, whose gentle drops refresh the thirsty earth.
7 In his blest days the just and good shall be with favour crown'd;
The happy land shall ev'ry where with endless peace abound.

8 His uncontrol'd dominion shall from sea to sea extend;
Begin at Proud Euphrates' streams, at Nature's limits end.
9 To him the savage nations round shall bow their servile heads;
His vanquish'd foes shall lick the dust, where he his conquests spreads.

10 The Kings of Tarshish, and the Isles, shall costly presents bring;
From spicy Sheba gifts shall come, and wealthy Saba's king.
11 To him shall ev'ry king on earth his humble homage pay,
And diff'ring nations gladly join to own his righteous sway.

12 For he shall set the needy free, when they for succour cry;
Shall save the helpless and the poor, and all their wants supply.

PART II.

13 His providence for needy souls shall due supplies prepare;
And over their defenceless lives shall watch with tender care.
14 He shall preserve and keep their souls from fraud and rapine free;
And, in his sight, their guiltless blood of mighty price shall be.

15 Therefore shall God his life and reign to many years extend;
While eastern princes tribute pay, and golden presents send.
For him shall constant pray'rs be made, through all his prosp'rous days:
His just dominion shall afford a lasting theme of praise.

16 Of useful grain, through all the land, great plenty shall appear
A handful sown on mountain tops a mighty crop shall bear:
It's fruit, like cedars shook by winds, a rattling noise shall yield;
The city too shall thrive and vie for plenty with the field.

17 The mem'ry of his glorious name through endless years shall run;
His spotless fame shall shine as bright and lasting as the sun.
In him the nations of the world shall be completely bless'd,
And his unbounded happiness by every tongue confess'd.

18 Then bless'd be God, the mighty Lord, the God whom Israel fears;
Who only wondrous in his works, beyond compare, appears.
19 Let earth be with his glory fill'd; for ever bless his name;
Whilst to his praise the list'ning world their glad assent proclaim.

PSALM LXXIII.

PSALM LXXIII.

1 AT length, by certain proofs 'tis plain, that God will to his saints be kind,
That all whose hearts are pure and clean; shall his protecting favour find.

2, 3 Till this sustaining truth I knew, my stagg'ring feet had almost fail'd:
I griev'd the sinner's wealth to view, and envy'd when the fools prevail'd.

4, 5 They to the grave in peace descend, and, whilst they live, are hale and strong
No plagues or troubles them offend, which oft to other men belong.
6, 7 With pride, as with a chain, they're held, and rapine seems their robe of state;
Their eyes stand out with fatness swell'd; they grow, beyond their wishes, great.

8, 9 With hearts corrupt, and lofty talk, oppressive methods they defend;
Their tongue thro' all the earth does walk, their blasphemies to heav'n ascend.
10 And yet admiring crouds are found, who servile visits duly make;
Because with plenty they abound, of which their flatt'ring slaves partake.

11 Their fond opinions these pursue, till they with them profanely cry,
"How should the Lord our actions view, can he perceive who dwells so high?"
12 Behold the wicked! these are they who openly their sins profess:
And yet their wealth's increas'd each day, and all their actions meet success.

13, 14 Then have I cleans'd my heart, said I, and wash'd my hands from guilt in vain,
If all the day oppress'd I lie, and ev'ry morning suffer pain.
15 Thus did I once to speak intend: but, if such things I rashly say,
Thy children, Lord, I must offend, and basely should their cause betray.

PART II.

16, 17 To fathom this my thoughts I bent, but found the case too hard for me;
Till to the house of God I went: then I their end did plainly see.
18 How high soe'er advanc'd, they all on slipp'ry places loosely stand;
Thence into ruin headlong fall, cast down by thy avenging hand.

19, 20 How dreadful and how quick their fate! despis'd by thee, when they're destroy'd;
As waking men with scorn do treat the fancies that their dreams employ'd.
21, 22 Thus was my heart with grief oppress'd, my reins were rack'd with restless pains;
So stupid was I, like a beast who no reflecting thought retains.

23, 24 Yet still thy presence me supply'd, and thy right hand assistance gave;
Thou first shalt with thy counsel guide, and then to glory me receive.
25 Whom then in heav'n but thee alone, have I, whose favour I require?
Throughout the spacious earth there's none that I besides thee can desire.

26 My trembling flesh, and aching heart, may often fail to succour me;
But God shall inward strength impart, and my eternal portion be.
27 For they that far from thee remove, shall into sudden ruin fall:
If after other Gods they rove, thy vengeance shall destroy them all.

28 But as for me, 'tis good and just that I should still to God repair:
In him I always put my trust, and will his wondrous works declare.

PSALM LXXIV.

1 WHY hast thou cast us off, O God wilt thou no more return?
O, why against thy chosen flock, does thy fierce anger burn?
2 Think on thy ancient purchase, Lord, the land that is thy own,
By thee redeem'd; and Sion's Mount, where once thy glory shone.

3 O, come and view our ruin'd state! how long our troubles last.
See how the foe, with wicked rage, has laid thy temple waste!
4 Thy foes blaspheme thy name: where late thy zealous servants pray'd,
The heathen there with haughty pomp, their banners have display'd.

5, 6 Those curious carvings, which did once advance the artist's fame,
With ax and hammer they destroy, like works of vulgar frame.
7 Thy holy temple they have burn'd; and what escap'd the flame,
Has been profan'd, and quite defac'd, though sacred to thy name.

8 Thy worship wholly to destroy maliciously they aim'd;
And all the sacred places burn'd, where we thy praise proclaim'd.
9 Yet of thy presence thou vouchsaf'st no tender signs to send:
We have no prophet now, that knows when this sad state shall end.

PART II.

10 But, Lord, how long wilt thou permit th' insulting foe to boast?
Shall all the honour of thy name for evermore be lost?
11 Why hold'st thou back thy strong right hand, and on thy patient breast,
When vengeance calls to stretch it forth, so calmly let'st it rest.

12 Thou heretofore, with kingly pow'r, in our defence hast fought;
For us, throughout the wond'ring world, hast great salvation wrought.
13 'Twas thou, O God, that didst the sea by thy own strength divide:
Thou break'st the wat'ry monster's head; the waves o'erwhelm'd their pride.

14 The greatest, fiercest of them all, that seem'd the deep to sway,
Was by thy pow'r destroy'd, and made to savage beasts a prey.
15 Thou cleav'st the solid rock, and mad'st the waters largely flow:
Again, thou mad'st through parted streams thy wand'ring people go.

16 Thine is the cheerful day, and thine the black return of night;
Thou hast prepar'd the glorious sun, and ev'ry feebler light.
17 By thee the borders of the earth in perfect order stand:
The summer's warmth the winter's cold attend on thy command.

PART III.

18 Remember, Lord, how scornful foes have daily urg'd our shame;
And how the foolish people have blasphem'd thy holy name.
19 O, free thy mourning turtle-dove, by sinful crowds beset:
Nor the assembly of thy poor for evermore forget.

20 Thy ancient cov'nant, Lord, regard, and make thy promise good:
For now each corner of the land is fill'd with men of blood.
21 O, let not the oppress'd return with sorrow cloath'd and shame;
But let the helpless and the poor for ever praise thy name.

22 Arise, O God, in our behalf; thy cause and ours maintain;
Remember how insulting fools each day thy name profane.
23 Make thou the boasting of thy foes for evermore to cease;
Whose insolence, if unchastis'd, will more and more increase.

PSALM LXXV.

1 TO thee, O God, we render praise, to thee with thanks repair;
For that thy name to us is nigh, thy wondrous works declare.
2 In Israel, when my throne is fix'd, with me shall justice reign,
3 The land with discord shakes; but I the sinking frame sustain.

4 Deluded wretches I advis'd their errors to redress;
And warn'd bold sinners, that they should their swelling pride suppress.
5 Bear not yourselves so high, as if no pow'r could yours restrain;
Submit your stubborn necks, and learn to speak with less disdain.

6 For that promotion, which to gain your vain ambition strives,
From neither east nor west, nor yet from southern climes arrives.
7 For God the great disposer is, and sov'reign judge alone;
Who casts the proud to earth, and lifts the humble to a throne.

8 His hand holds forth a dreadful cup! with purple wine 'tis crown'd;
The deadly mixture, which his wrath deals out to nations round.
9 Of this his saints sometimes may taste; but wicked men shall squeeze
The bitter dregs, and be condemn'd to drink the very lees.

10 His prophet, I to all the world this message will relate;
The justice then of Jacob's God my song shall celebrate.
11 The wicked's pride I will reduce, their cruelty disarm;
Exalt the just, and seat him high, above the reach of harm.

PSALM LXXVI.

1 IN Judah the Almighty's known,
(Almighty there by wonders shown)
His name in Jacob does excel:
2 His sanctuary in Salem stands:
The majesty that heav'n commands
In Sion condescends to dwell.

3 He brake the bow and arrows there,
The shield, the temper'd sword, and spear;
There slain the mighty army lay:
4 Whence Sion's fame through earth is spread,
Of greater glory, greater dread,
Than hills where robbers lodge their prey.

5 Their valiant chiefs, who came for spoil,
Themselves met there a shameful foil:
Securely down to sleep they lay:
But wak'd no more; their stoutest band
Ne'er lifted one resisting hand
'Gainst him that did their legions slay.

6 When Jacob's God began to frown,
Both horse and charioteers, o'erthrown,
Together slept in endless night.
7 When thou, whom heav'n and earth revere,
Dost once with wrathful look appear,
What mortal pow'r can stand thy sight?

8 Pronounc'd from heav'n, earth heard its doom;
9 Grew hush'd with fear, when thou didst come,
The meek with justice to restore.
10 The wrath of man shall yield thee praise,
Its last attempts but serve to raise
The triumphs of almighty pow'r.

11 Bow to the Lord, ye nations; bring
Vow'd presents to the Eternal King:
Thus to his name due rev'rence pay,
12 Who proudest potentates can quell;
To earthly kings more terrible,
Than to their trembling subjects they.

PSALM LXXVII.

1 TO God I cry'd, who to my help did graciously repair:
2 In trouble's dismal day I sought my God with humble pray'r.
All night my fest'ring wounds did run; no med'cine gave relief:
My soul no comfort would admit; my soul indulg'd her grief.

3 I thought on God, and favours past; but that increas'd my pain;
I found my spirit more oppress'd, the more I did complain.
4 Through ev'ry watch of tedious night, thou keep'st my eyes awake;
My grief is swell'd to that excess, I sigh, but cannot speak.

5 I call'd to mind the days of old, with signal mercy crown'd;
Those famous years, of ancient times, for miracles renown'd.
6 By night I recollect my songs, on former triumphs made;
Then search, consult, and ask my heart, where's now that wondrous aid?

7 Has God for ever cast us off? withdrawn his favour quite?
8 Are both his mercy and his truth retir'd to endless night?
9 Can his long-practis'd love forget its wonted aids to bring?
Has he in wrath shut up and seal'd his mercy's healing spring?

10 I said, my weakness hints these fears; but I'll my fears disband;
I'll yet remember the Most High, and years of his right hand.
11 I'll call to mind his works of old, the wonders of his might;
12 On them my heart shall meditate, my tongue shall them recite.

13 Safe lodg'd from human search on high, O God, thy counsels are!
Who is so great a God as ours? who can with him compare?
14 Long since a God of wonders thee thy rescu'd people found:
15 Long since hast thou thy chosen seed with strong deliv'rance crown'd.

16 When thou, O God, the waters saw, the frighted billows shrunk;
The troubled depths themselves, for fear, beneath their channels sunk.
17 The clouds pour'd down, while rending skies did with their noise conspire:
Thy arrows all abroad were sent, wing'd with avenging fire.

18 Heav'n with thy thunder's voice was torn, whilst all the lower world
With lightnings blaz'd; earth shook and seem'd from her foundations hurl'd.
19 Through rolling streams thou find'st thy way, thy paths in waters lie;
Thy wondrous passage, where no sight thy footsteps can descry.

20 Thou led'st thy people like a flock, safe through the desert land,
By Moses their meek skilful guide, and Aaron's sacred hand.

PSALM LXXVIII.

1 HEAR, O my people, to my law devout attention lend;
Let the instruction of my mouth deep in your hearts descend.
2 My tongue, by inspiration taught, shall parables unfold,
Dark oracles, but understood, and own'd for truths of old:

3 Which we from sacred registers of ancient times have known,
And our forefathers' pious care to us has handed down.
4 We will not hide them from our sons our offspring shall be taught
The praises of the Lord, whose strength has works of wonder wrought.

5 For Jacob he this law ordain'd, this league with Israel made;
With charge, to be from age to age, from race to race, convey'd.
6 That generations yet to come should to their unborn heirs
Religiously transmit the same, and they again to theirs.

7 To teach them that in God alone their hope securely stands;
That they should ne'er his works forget but keep his just commands.
8 Lest, like their fathers, they might prove a stiff rebellious race,
False-hearted, fickle to their God, unstedfast in his grace.

9 Such were revolting Ephraim's sons, who, though to warfare bred,
And skilful archers, arm'd with bows, from field ignobly fled.
10, 11 They falsify'd their league with God, his orders disobey'd,
Forgot his works and miracles, before their eyes display'd.

12 Nor wonders, which their fathers saw, did they in mind retain;
Prodigious things in Egypt done, and Zoan's fertile plain.
13 He cut the seas to let them pass, restrain'd the pressing flood;
While pil'd in heaps, on either side, the solid waters stood.

14 A wondrous pillar led them on, compos'd of shade and light:
A shelt'ring cloud it prov'd by day, a leading fire by night,
15 When drought oppress'd them, where no stream the wilderness supply'd,
He cleft the rock, whose flinty breast dissolv'd into a tide.

16 Streams from the solid rock he brought, which down in rivers fell,
That, trav'ling with their camp, each day renew'd the miracle.
17 Yet there they sinn'd against him more, provoking the Most High,
In that same desert, where he did their fainting souls supply.

18 They first incens'd him in their hearts, that did his pow'r distrust,
And long'd for meat, not urg'd by want, but to indulge their lust.
19 Then utter'd their blaspheming doubts can God (say they) prepare
" A table in the wilderness, set out with various fare?

20 " He smote the flinty rock, 'tis true, and gushing streams ensu'd;
" But can he corn and flesh provide for such a multitude?"
21 The Lord with indignation heard: from heav'n avenging flame
On Jacob fell, consuming wrath on thankless Israel came.

22 Because their unbelieving herd in God would not confide,
Nor trust his care, who had from heav'n their wants so oft supply'd.
23 Though he had made his clouds discharge provisions down in show'rs;
And, when earth fail'd, reliev'd their needs from his celestial stores.

24 Though tasteful manna was rain'd down, their hunger to relieve:
Though from the stores of heav'n they did sustaining corn receive.
25 Thus man with angels' sacred food, ungrateful man, was fed;
Not sparingly, for still they found a plenteous table spread.

26 From heav'n he made an east wind blow, that did the south command,
27 To rain down flesh like dust, and fowls like seas' unnumber'd sand.
28 Within their trenches he let fall the luscious easy prey,
And all around their spreading camp the ready booty lay.

29 They fed, were fill'd; he gave them leave their appetites to feast;
30, 31 Yet still their wanton lust crav'd on, nor with their hunger ceas'd;
But whilst in their luxurious mouths they did their dainties chew,
The wrath of God smote down their chiefs and Israel's chosen slew.

PART II.

32 Yet still they sinn'd nor would afford his miracles belief;
33 Therefore through fruitless travels he consum'd their lives in grief.
34 When some were slain, the rest return'd to God with early cry;
35 Own'd him the rock of their defence, their Saviour, God most high.

36 But this was feign'd submission all; their heart their tongue bely'd;
37 Their heart was still perverse, nor would firm in his leagues abide.
38 Yet, full of mercy, he forgave, nor did with death chastise;
But turn'd his kindled wrath aside, or would not let it rise.

39 For he remember'd they were flesh, that could not long remain;
A murm'ring wind, that's quickly past, and ne'er returns again.
40 How oft did they provoke him there, how oft his patience grieve,
In that same desert where he did their fainting souls relieve.

41 They tempted him by turning back, and wickedly repin'd,
When Israel's God refus'd to be by their desires confin'd.
42 Nor call'd to mind the hand and day that their redemption brought;
43 His signs in Egypt wondrous works in Zoan's valley wrought.

44 He turn'd their rivers into blood, that man and beast forbore,
And rather chose to die for thirst than drink the putrid gore.
45 He sent devouring swarms of flies; hoarse frogs annoy'd their soil;
46 Locusts and caterpillars reap'd the harvest of their toil.

47 Their vines with batt'ring hail were broke; with frost the fig tree dies!
48 Lightning and hail made flocks and herds one gen'ral sacrifice.
49 He turn'd his anger loose, and set no time for it to cease;
And, with their plagues, ill angels sent their torments to increase.

50 He clear'd a passage for his wrath to ravage uncontrol'd;
The murrain on their firstlings seiz'd in ev'ry field and fold.
51 The deadly pest from beast to man, from field to city, came;
It slew their heirs, their eldest hopes, through all the tents of Ham.

52 But his own tribe, like folded sheep, he brought from their distress;
And them conducted like a flock, throughout the wilderness.
53 He led them on, and in their way no cause of fear they found;
But march'd securely through those deeps, in which their foes were drown'd.

54 Nor ceas'd his care, till them he brought safe to his promis'd land,
And to his holy mount, the prize of his victorious hand.
55 To them the outcast heathen's land, he did by lot divide;
And in their foes' abandon'd tents made Israel's tribes reside.

PART III.

56 Yet still they tempted, still provok'd the wrath of God most high;
Nor would to practise his commands their stubborn hearts apply;
57 But in their faithless fathers' steps perversely choose to go;
They turn'd aside, like arrows shot from some deceitful bow.

58 For him to fury they provok'd with altars set on high;
And with their graven images inflam'd his jealousy.
59 When God heard this, on Israel's tribes his wrath and hatred fell;
60 He quitted Shiloh, and the tents where once he chose to dwell.

61 To vile captivity his ark, his glory to disdain,
62 His people to the sword he gave, nor would his wrath restrain.
63 Destructive war their ablest youth untimely did confound;
No virgin was to th' altar led, with nuptial garlands crown'd.

64 In fight the sacrificer fell, the priest a victim bled;
And widows, who their death should mourn, themselves of grief were dead.

65 Then, as a giant rous'd from sleep, whom wine had thoroughly warm'd
Shouts out aloud, the Lord awak'd, and his proud foe alarm'd.

66 He smote their host, that from the field a scatter'd remnant came,
With wounds imprinted on their backs of everlasting shame.
67 With conquest crown'd he Joseph's tents, and Ephraim's tribe forsook;
68 But Judah chose, and Sion's mount for his lov'd dwelling took.

69 His temple he erected there, with spires exalted high:
While deep, and fix'd, as those of earth, the strong foundations lie.
70 His faithful servant David too he for his choice did own,
And from the sheepfolds him advanc'd to sit on Judah's throne.

71 From tending on the teeming ewes, he brought him forth to feed
His own inheritance, the tribes of Israel's chosen seed.
72 Exalted thus, the monarch prov'd a faithful shepherd still;
He fed them with an upright heart, and guided them with skill.

PSALM LXXIX.

1 BEHOLD, O God, how heathen hosts have thy possession seiz'd!
Thy sacred house they have defil'd, thy holy city raz'd.
2 The mangled bodies of thy saints abroad unbury'd lay;
Their flesh expos'd to savage beasts, and rav'nous birds of prey.

3 Quite through Jer'salem was their blood like common water shed;
And none were left alive to pay last duties to the dead.
4 The neighb'ring lands our small remains with loud reproaches wound;
And we a laughing stock are made to all the nations round.

5 How long wilt thou be angry, Lord? must we for ever mourn?
Shall thy devouring jealous rage, like fire, for ever burn?
6 On foreign lands, that know not thee, thy heavy vengeance show'r;
Those sinful kingdoms let it crush, that have not own'd thy power.

7 For their devouring jaws have prey'd on Jacob's chosen race;
And to a barren desert turn'd their fruitful dwelling-place.
8 O think not on our former sins, but speedily prevent
The utter ruin of thy saints, almost with sorrow spent.

9 Thou God of our salvation, help, and free our souls from blame;
So shall our pardon and defence exalt thy glorious name.
10 Let infidels, that scoffing say, "Where is the God they boast?"
In vengeance for thy slaughter'd saints, perceive thee to their cost.

11 Lord, hear the sighing pris'ner's moans, thy saving pow'r extend;
Preserve the wretches doom'd to die, from that untimely end.
12 On them, who us oppress, let all our suff'rings be repaid;
Make their confusion seven times more than what on us they laid.

13 So we, thy people and thy flock, shall ever praise thy name:
And with glad hearts our grateful thanks from age to age proclaim.

PSALM LXXX.

1 O ISRAEL's shepherd, Joseph's guide, our pray'rs to thee vouchsafe to hear;
Thou that dost on the cherubs ride, again in solemn state appear.
2 Behold how Benjamin expects, with Ephraim and Manasseh join'd,
In our deliv'rance the effects of thy resistless strength to find.

3 Do thou convert us, Lord, do thou the lustre of thy face display;
And all the ills we suffer now, like scatter'd clouds shall pass away.
4 O thou, whom heav'nly hosts obey, how long shall thy fierce anger burn?
How long thy suffering people pray, and to their pray'rs have no return?

5 When hungry, we are forc'd to drench, our scanty food in floods of woe;
When dry, our raging thirst we quench with streams of tears that largely flow.
6 For us the heathen nations round as for a common prey, contest
Our foes with spiteful joys abound, and at our lost condition jest.

7 Do thou convert us, Lord, do thou the lustre of thy face display;
And all the ills we suffer now, like scatter'd clouds shall pass away.

PART II.

8 Thou brought'st a vine from Egypt's land; and, casting out the heathen race,
Didst plant it with thine own right hand, and firmly fix'd it in their place.
9 Before it thou prepard'st the way, and mad'st it take a lasting root,
Which bless'd with thy indulgent ray, o'er all the land did widely shoot.

10, 11 The hills were cover'd with its shade, its goodly bows did cedars seem:
Its branches to the sea were spread, and reach'd to proud Euphrates' stream.
12 Why then hast thou its edge o'er-thrown, which thou hadst made so firm and strong;
Whilst all its grapes, defenceless grown, are pluck'd by those that pass along.

13 See how the bristling forest boar, with dreadful fury lays it waste;
Hark how the savage monsters roar, and to their helpless prey make haste.

PART III.

14 To thee, O God of hosts, we pray; thy wonted goodness, Lord, renew:
From heav'n thy throne this vine survey, and her sad state with pity view.
15 Behold the vineyard made by thee which thy right hand did guard so long;
And keep that branch from danger free, which for thyself thou mad'st so strong.

16 To wasting flames 'tis made a prey, and all its spreading boughs cut down;
At thy rebuke they soon decay, and perish at thy dreadful frown.
17 Crown thou the king with good success, by thy right hand secur'd from wrong:
The Son of Man in mercy bless, whom for thyself thou mad'st so strong,

18 So shall we still continue free from whatso'er deserves thy blame;
And if once more reviv'd by thee, will always praise thy holy name.
19 Do thou convert us, Lord, do thou the lustre of thy face display;
And all the ills we suffer now, like scatter'd clouds shall pass away.

PSALM LXXXI.

1 TO God, our never-failing strength, with loud applauses sing:
And jointly make a chearful noise to Jacob's awful King.
2 Compose a hymn of praise, and touch your instruments of joy!
Let psalteries and pleasant harps your grateful skill employ.

3 Let trumpets, at the great new moon, their joyful voices raise,
To celebrate th' appointed time, the solemn day of praise.
4 For this a statute was of old, which Jacob's God decreed,
To be with pious care observ'd by Israel's chosen seed.

5 This he for a memorial fix'd, when freed from Egypt's land;
Strange nations' barb'rous speech we heard but could not understand.

6 Your burden'd shoulders I reliev'd, (thus seems our God to say;)
Your servile hands by me were freed from lab'ring in the clay.

7 Your ancestors, with wrongs oppress'd, to me for aid did call:
With pity I their suff'rings saw, and set them free from all.
They sought for me, and from the cloud in thunder I reply'd;
At Meribah's contentious stream their faith and duty try'd.

PART II.

8 Whilst I my solemn will declare; my chosen people hear:
If thou, O Israel, to my words wilt lend thy list'ning ear,
9 Then shall no God besides myself within thy coasts be found;
Nor shall thou worship any God of all the nations round.

10 The Lord thy God, am I, who thee brought forth from Egypt's land;
'Tis I that all thy just desires supply with lib'ral hand.
11 But they, my chosen race, refus'd to hearken to my voice;
Nor would rebellious Israel's sons make me their happy choice.

12 So I, provok'd, resign'd them up to ev'ry lust a prey;
And in their own perverse designs permitted them to stray.
13 O that my people wisely would my just commandments heed!
And Israel in my righteous ways with pious care proceed!

14 Then should my heavy judgments fall on all that them oppose,
And my avenging hand be turn'd against their num'rous foes,
15 Their enemies and mine should all before my footstool bend:
But as for them, their happy state should never know an end.

16 All parts with plenty should abound: with finest wheat their field:
The barren rocks, to please their taste, should richest honey yield.

PSALM LXXXII.

1 GOD in the great assembly stands, where his impartial eye,
In state surveys the earthly gods, and does their judgments try.
2, 3 How dare ye then unjustly judge, or be to sinners kind?
Defend the orphans and the poor; let such your justice find.

4 Protect the humble helpless man, reduc'd to keep distress,
And let not him become a prey to such as would oppress.
5 They neither know, nor will they learn, but blindly rove and stray:
Justice and truth, the world supports, through all the land decay.

6 Well then might God in anger say, I've call'd you by my name:
" I've said y'are God's, and all ally'd to the most high in fame.
7 " But ne'ertheless your unjust deeds to strict account I'll call:
" You all shall die like common men, like other tyrants fall."

8 Arise, and thy just judgments, Lord, throughout the earth display;
And all the nations of the world shall own thy righteous way.

PSALM LXXXIII.

1 HOLD not thy peace, O Lord our God, no longer silent be;
Nor with consenting quiet looks our ruin calmly see:
2 For lo! the tumults of thy foes o'er all the land are spread;
And those who hate thy saints and thee, lift up their threat'ning head.

3 Against thy zealous people, Lord, they craftily combine;
And to destroy thy chosen saints have laid their close design;
"Come, let us cut them off (say they) their nation quite deface;
"That no remembrance may remain of Israel's hated race."

Thus they against thy people's peace consult with one consent;
And diff'rent nations, jointly leagu'd, the common malice vent.
The Ishmaelites that dwell in tents, with warlike Edom join'd,
And Moab's sons our ruin vow, with Hagar's race combin'd.

Proud Ammon's offspring, Gebel too with Ameleck conspire;
The Lords of Palestine, and all the wealthy sons of Tyre.
All these the strong Assyrian king their firm ally have got:
Who with a pow'rful army aids th' incestuous race of Lot.

PART II.

But let such vengeance come to them, as once to Midian came;
To Jabin and proud Sisera, at Kishon's fatal stream.
9 When thy right hand their num'rous hosts near Endor did confound,
And left their carcases for dung, to feed the hungry ground.

11 Let all the mighty men the fate of Zeb and Oreb share:
As Zeba and Zalmuna, so let all their princes fare.
12 Who, with the same design inspir'd, thus vainly boasting spake,
"In firm possession for ourselves let us God's houses take."

13 To ruin let them haste, like wheels which downwards swiftly move;
Like chaff before the wind, let all their scatter'd forces prove.
14, 15 As flames consume dry wood, or heath that on parch'd mountains grows,
So let thy fierce pursuing wrath, with terrors strike thy foes.

16, 17 Lord, shroud their faces with disgrace, that they may own thy name:
Or them confound, whose harden'd hearts thy gentler means disclaim.
18 So shall the wond'ring world confess, that thou, who claim'st alone
Jehovah's name, o'er all the earth hast rais'd thy lofty throne.

PSALM LXXXIV.

O GOD of Hosts, the mighty Lord, how lovely is the place,
Where thou, inthron'd in glory, shew'st the brightness of thy face!
My longing soul faints with desire to view thy blest abode:
My panting heart and flesh cry out for thee the living God.

The birds, more happy far than I, around thy temple throng;
Securely there they build, and there securely hatch their young.
O Lord of Hosts, my King and God, how highly blest are they,
Who in thy temple always dwell, and there thy praise display!

Thrice happy they, whose choice has thee their sure protection made;
Who long to tread the sacred ways that to thy dwelling lead!
Who pass through Baca's thirsty vale, yet no refreshments want:
Their pools are fill'd with rain, which thou at their request dost grant.

Thus they proceed from strength to strength, and still approach more near,
Till all on Sion's holy mount before their God appear.
O Lord, the mighty God of Hosts, my just request regard:
Thou God of Jacob, let my pray'r be still with favour heard.

9 Behold, O God, for thou alone
canst timely aid dispense:
On thy anointed servant look,
be thou his strong defence.
10 For in thy courts one single day
'tis better to attend,
Than, Lord, in any place besides
a thousand days to spend.

Much rather in God's house will I
the meanest office take,
Than in the wealthy tents of sin
my pompous dwelling make.
11 For God, who is our sun and shield,
will grace and glory give;
And no good thing will he withhold
from them that justly live.

12 Thou God, whom heav'nly hosts obey,
how highly bless'd is he,
Whose hope and trust, securely plac'd,
is still repos'd on thee!

PSALM LXXXV.

1 LORD, thou hast granted to thy land
the favours we implor'd,
And faithful Jacob's captive race
hast graciously restor'd.
2, 3 Thy people's sins hast thou forgiv'n,
and all their guilt defac'd:
Thou hast not let thy wrath flame on,
nor thy fierce anger last.

4 O God our Saviour, all our hearts
to thy obedience turn;
That, quench'd with our repenting tears,
thy wrath no more may burn.
5, 6 For why should'st thou be angry still,
and wrath so long retain?
Revive us, Lord, and let thy saints
thy wonted comfort gain.

7 Thy gracious favour, Lord, display,
which we have long implor'd;
And, for thy wondrous mercy's sake,
thy wonted aid afford.
8 God's answer patiently I'll wait;
for he, with glad success,
(If they no more to folly turn)
his mourning saints will bless.

9 To all that fear his holy name,
his sure salvation's near;
And in its former happy state
our nation shall appear.
10 For mercy now with truth is join'd,
and righteousness with peace;
Like kind companions, absent long,
with friendly arms embrace.

11, 12 Truth from the earth shall spring, whilst heav'n
shall streams of justice pour:
And God, from whom all goodness flows,
shall endless plenty show'r.
13 Before him righteousness shall march,
and his just paths prepare;
Whilst we his holy steps pursue
with constant zeal and care.

PSALM LXXXVI.

1 TO my complaint, O Lord, my God,
thy gracious ear incline;
Hear me, distress'd, and destitute
of all relief but thine.
2 Do thou, O God, preserve my soul,
that does thy name adore;
Thy servant keep, and him, whose trust
relies on thee, restore.

3 To me, who daily thee invoke,
thy mercy, Lord, extend;
4 Refresh thy servant's soul, whose hopes
on thee alone depend.
5 Thou, Lord, art good, not only good,
but prompt to pardon too;
Of plenteous mercy to all those
who for thy mercy sue.

6 To my repeated humble pray'r,
O Lord, attentive be:
7 When troubled, I on thee will call,
for thou wilt answer me.
8 Among the gods there's none like thee,
O Lord, alone divine!
To thee as much inferior they
as are their works to thine.

Therefore their great Creator thee the nations shall adore;
Their long misguided pray'rs and praise to thy blest name restore.
All shall confess thee great, and great the wonders thou hast done;
Confess thee God, the God supreme confess thee God alone.

PART II.

Teach me thy way, O Lord, and I from truth shall ne'er depart;
In rev'rence to thy sacred name devoutly fix my heart.
Thee will I praise, O Lord my God, praise thee with heart sincere;
And to thy everlasting name eternal trophies rear.

Thy boundless mercy shewn to me transcends my pow'r to tell;
For thou hast oft redeem'd my soul from lowest depths of hell.
O God, the sons of pride and strife have my destruction sought;
Regardless of thy pow'r, that oft has my deliv'rance wrought.

But thou thy constant goodness didst to my assistance bring;
Of patience, mercy, and of truth, thou everlasting spring!
O bounteous Lord, thy grace and strength to me thy servant show;
Thy kind protection, Lord, on me, thine handmaid's son bestow.

Some signal give, which my proud foes may see with shame and rage,
When thou, O Lord, for my relief and comfort dost engage.

PSALM LXXXVII.

GOD's temple crowns thy holy mount;
The Lord there condescends to dwell:
His Sion's gates, in his account,
Our Israel's fairest tents excel.
Fame glorious things of thee shall sing,
O city of the almighty King!

I'll mention Rahab with due praise,
In Babylon's applauses join,
The fame of Ethiopia raise,
With that of Tyre and Palestine;
And grant that some, amongst them born
Their age and country did adorn.

5 But still of Sion I'll aver,
That many such from her proceed;
Th' Almighty shall establish her,
6 His gen'ral list shall shew, when read,
That such a person there was born,
And such did such an age adorn.

7 He'll Sion find with numbers fill'd
Of such as merit high renown;
For hand and voice musicians skill'd;
And (her transcending fame to crown)
Of such he shall successions bring,
Like waters from a living spring.

PSALM LXXXVIII.

TO thee, my God and Saviour, I by day and and night address my cry:
2 Vouchsafe my mournful voice to hear; to my distress incline thine ear:
For seas of trouble me invade, my soul draws nigh to death's cold shade.

Like one whose strength and hopes are fled, they number me among the dead.
Like those who, shrouded in the grave, from thee no more remembrance have;
Cast off from thy sustaining care, down to the confines of despair.
Thy wrath has hard upon me lain, afflicting me with restless pain:
Me all thy mountain waves have prest, too weak, alas! to bear the least.

Remov'd from friends, I sigh alone in a loath'd dungeon laid, where none
A visit will vouchsafe to me, confin'd, past hopes of liberty.

9 My eyes from weeping never cease, they waste, but still my griefs increase;
Yet daily, Lord, to thee I pray'd, with out-stretch'd hands invoke thy aid.

10 Wilt thou by miracle revive the dead, whom thou forsook'st alive?
From death restore, thy praise to sing, whom thou from prison would'st not bring?
11 Shall the mute grave thy love confess? a mould'ring tomb thy faithfulness?
12 Thy truth and pow'r renown obtain, where darkness and oblivion reign?

13 To thee, O Lord, I cry, forlorn; my pray'r prevents the early morn.
14 Why hast thou, Lord, my soul forsook, not once vouchsaf'd a gracious look?
15 Preparing sorrows bear me down, which from my youth with me have grown?
Thy terrors past distract my mind, and fears of blacker days behind.

16 Thy wrath hast burst upon my head, thy terrors fill my soul with dread;
17 Environ'd as with waves combin'd, and for a gen'ral deluge join'd.
18 My lovers, friends, familiars, all remov'd from sight, and out of call;
To dark oblivion all retir'd dead, or at least to me expir'd.

PSALM LXXXIX.

1 THY mercies, Lord, shall be my song; my song on them shall ever dwell;
To ages yet unborn my tongue thy never-failing truth shall tell.
2 I have affirm'd, and still maintain, thy mercy shall for ever last;
Thy truth that does the heav'ns sustain, like them, shall stand for ever fast.

3 Thus spak'st thou by thy prophet's voice; "With David I a league had made;
"To him, my servant, and my choice, by solemn oath this grant convey'd:
4 "While earth, and seas, and skies endure, thy seed shall in thy sight remain:
"To them thy throne I will insure; they shall to endless ages reign."

5 For such stupendous truth and love, both heav'n and earth just praises owe,
By choirs of angels sung above, and by assembled saints below.
6 What seraph of celestial birth to vie with Israel's God shall dare?
Or who among the gods of earth with our almighty Lord compare?

7 With rev'rence and religious dread his saints should to his temple press;
His fear through all their hearts should spread, who his almighty name confess.
8 Lord God of armies, who can boast of strength or pow'r like thine renown'd?
Of such a num'rous faithful host, as that which does thy throne surround:

9 Thou dost the lawless sea control, and change the prospect of the deep;
Thou mak'st the sleeping billows roll: thou mak'st the rolling billows sleep.
10 Thou brak'st in pieces Rahab's pride, and didst oppressing pow'r disarm:
Thy scatter'd foes have dearly try'd the force of thy resistless arm.

11 In thee the sov'reign right remains, of earth, and heav'n; thee, Lord, alone
The world, and all that it contains, their maker and preserver own.
12 The poles on which the globe does rest were form'd by thy creating voice;
Tabor and Hermon, east and west, in thy sustaining pow'r rejoice.

13 Thy arm is mighty, strong thy hand, yet, Lord, thou dost with justice reign
14 Possess'd of absolute command, thou truth and mercy dost maintain.
15 Happy, thrice happy they, who hear thy sacred trumpet's joyful sound;
Who may at festivals appear, with thy most glorious presence crown'd.

16 Thy saints shall always be o'erjoy'd who on thy sacred name rely;
And, in thy righteousness employ'd, above their foes be rais'd on high.

For in thy strength they shall advance, whose conquests from thy favour spring;
The Lord of Hosts is our defence, and Israel's God our Israel's King.

Thus spak'st thou by thy prophet's voice "A mighty champion I will send:
"From Judah's tribe have I made choice of one who shall the rest defend.
"My servant David I have found, with holy oil anointed him;
"Him shall the hand support that crown'd, and guard that gave the diadem.

"No prince from him shall tribute force, no son of strife shall him annoy:
"His spiteful foes I will disperse, and them before his face destroy.
"My truth and grace shall him sustain: his armies, in well-order'd ranks,
"Shall conquer, from the Tyrian main to Tygris and Euphrates' banks.

"Me for his father he shall take, his God and rock of safety call;
"Him I my first-born son will make and earthly kings his subjects all.
"To him my mercy I'll secure, my cov'nant make for ever fast.
"His seed for ever shall endure! his throne, 'till heav'n dissolves, shall last.

PART II.

"But if his heirs my law forsake, and from my sacred precepts stray;
"If they my righteous statutes break, nor strictly my commands obey;
"Their sins I'll visit with a rod, and for their folly make them smart;
"Yet will not cease to be their God, nor from my truth, like them, depart.

"My cov'nant I will ne'er revoke, but in remembrance fast retain:
"The thing that once my lips have spoke shall in eternal force remain.
"Once have I sworn, but once for all, and made my holiness the tie,
"That I my grant will ne'er recall, nor to my servant David lie.

"Whose throne and race the constant sun shall, like his course, establish'd see:
"Of this my oath, thou conscious moon in heav'n my faithful witness be."
Such was thy gracious promise, Lord, but thou hast now our tribes forsook;
Thy own anointed hast abhor'd, and turn'd on him thy wrathful look,

Thou seemest to have render'd void the cov'nant with thy servant made:
Thou hast his dignity destroy'd and in the dust his honour laid.
Of strong holds thou hast him bereft, and brought his bulwarks to decay;
His frontier coasts defenceless left, a public scorn and common prey.

His ruin does glad tidings yield to foes advanc'd by thee to might;
Thou hast his conqu'ring sword unsteel'd his valour turn'd to shameful flight.
His glory is to darkness fled, his throne is levell'd with the ground;
His youth to wretched bondage led, with shame o'erwhelm'd and sorrow drown'd.

How long shall we thy absence mourn? wilt thou for ever, Lord, retire?
Shall thy consuming anger burn, till that and we at once expire?
Consider, Lord, how short a space thou dost for mortal life ordain:
No method to prolong the race, but loading it with grief and pain.

What man is he that can controul death's strict unalterable doom?
Or rescue from the grave his soul, the grave that must mankind intomb?
Lord, where's thy love, thy boundless grace, the oath to which thy truth did seal,
Consign'd to David and his race, the grant which time should ne'er repeal?

50 See how thy servants treated are with infamy, reproach, and spite;
Which in my silent breast I bear from nations of licentious might,
51 How they, reproaching thy great name have made thy servant's hope their jest:
52 Yet thy just praises we'll proclaim, and ever sing, the Lord be blest.
Amen, Amen.

PSALM XC.

1 O LORD, the saviour and defence of us thy chosen race,
From age to age thou still hast been our sure abiding-place.
2 Before thou brought'st the mountains forth, or th' earth and world didst frame
Thou always wert the mighty God, and ever art the same.

3 Thou turnest Man, O Lord, to dust, of which he first was made:
And when thou speak'st the word, return, 'tis instantly obey'd.
4 For in thy sight a thousand years are like a day that's past,
Or like a watch in dead of night, whose hours unminded waste.

5 Thou sweep'st us off as with a flood, we vanish hence like dreams;
At first we grow like grass, that feels the sun's reviving beams;
6 But howsoever fresh and fair its morning beauty shows;
'Tis all cut down and wither'd quite, before the evening close,

7, 8 We by thine anger are consum'd, and by thy wrath dismay'd:
Our public crimes and secret sins before thy sight are laid.
9 Beneath thy anger's sad effects our drooping days we spend:
Our unregarded years break off, like tales that quickly end.

10 Our term of time is seventy years, an age that few survive:
But if, with more than common strength, to eighty we arrive;
Yet then our boasted strength decays, to sorrow turn'd and pain:
So soon the slender thread is cut, and we no more remain.

PART II.

11 But who thy anger's dread effects does as he ought revere?
And yet thy wrath does fall or rise, as more or less we fear.
12 So teach us, Lord, th' uncertain sum of our short days to mind,
That to true wisdom all our hearts may ever be inclin'd.

13 O to thy servant, Lord, return, and speedily relent!
As we forsake our sins, do thou revoke our punishment.
14 To satisfy and chear our souls, thy early mercy send;
That we may all our days to come in joy and comfort spend.

15 Let happy times with large amends, dry up our former tears,
Or equal at the least the term of our afflicted years,
16 To all thy servants, Lord, let this thy wond'rous works be known,
And to our offspring yet unborn thy glorious pow'r be shown.

17 Let thy bright rays upon us shine, give thou our work success;
The glorious work we have in hand do thou vouchsafe to bless.

PSALM XCI.

1 HE that has God his guardian made
Shall under the Almighty's shade,
Secure and undisturb'd abide.

2 Thus to my soul of him I'll say,
He is my fortress and my stay,
My God, in whom I will confide.

His tender love and watchful care,
Shall free thee from the fowler's snare,
And from the noisome pestilence:
He over thee his wings shall spread.
And cover thy unguarded head;
His truth shall be thy strong defence.

No terrors that surprise by night,
Shall thy undaunted courage fright,
Nor deadly shafts that fly by day;
Nor plague, of unknown rise, that kills
In darkness, nor infectious ills
That in the hottest season slay.

A thousand at thy side shall die,
At thy right hand ten thousand lie,
While thy firm health untouch'd remains:
Thou only shalt look on to see
The wicked's dismal tragedy,
And count the sinner's mournful gains

Because (with well-plac'd confidence)
Thou mak'st the Lord thy sure defence
And on the highest dost rely;

10 Therefore no ill shall thee befall,
Nor to thy healthful dwelling shall
Any infectious plagues draw nigh.

11 For he, throughout the happy days,
To keep thee safe in all thy ways,
Shall give his angels strict commands:
12 And they, lest thou should'st chance to meet
With some rough stone to wound thy feet
Shall bear thee safely in their hands.

13 Dragons and asps that thirst for blood,
And lions roaring for their food,
Beneath his conqu'ring feet shall lie:
14 Because he lov'd and honour'd me,
Therefore, says God, I'll set him free,
And fix his glorious throne on high.

15 He'll call; I'll answer when he calls,
And rescue him when ill befalls:
Increase his honour and his wealth:
16 And when, with undisturb'd content
His long and happy life is spent,
His end I'll crown with saving health.

PSALM XCII.

1 HOW good and pleasant must it be to thank the Lord most high;
And with repeated hymns of praise his name to magnify!
2 With ev'ry morning's early dawn his goodness to relate!
And of his constant truth, each night the glad effects repeat!

3 To ten-stringed instruments we'll sing, with tuneful psalt'ries join'd;
And to the harp with solemn sounds, for sacred use design'd.
4 For through thy wondrous works, O Lord, thou mak'st my heart rejoice:
The thoughts of them shall make me glad, and shout with chearful voice.

5, 6 How wondrous are thy works, O Lord! how deep are thy decrees!
Whose winding tracks, in secret laid, no stupid sinner sees.
7 He little thinks, when wicked men, like grass look fresh and gay,
How soon their short-liv'd splendor must for ever pass away,

8, 9 But thou, my God, art still most high; and all thy lofty foes,
Who thought they might securely sin, shall be o'erwhelm'd with woes.
10 Whilst thou exalt'st my sov'reign pow'r, and mak'st it largely spread;
And with refreshing oil anoint'st My consecrated head.

11 I soon shall see my stubborn foes to utter ruin brought;
And hear the dismal end of those who have against me fought.
12 But righteous men, like fruitful palms, shall make a glorious show;
As cedars, that on Lebanon in stately order grow.

13, 14 These planted in the house of God, within his courts shall thrive;
Their vigour and their lustre both shall in old age revive.
15 Thus will the Lord his justice show; and God, my strong defence,
Shall due rewards to all the world impartially dispense.

PSALM XCIII.

1 WITH glory clad, with strength array'd, the Lord, that o'er all nature reigns,
The world's foundation strongly laid, and the vast fabric still sustains.
2 How surely 'stablish'd is thy throne! which shall no change or period see;
For thou, O Lord, and thou alone, art God from all eternity.

3, 4 The floods, O Lord, lift up their voice and toss the troubled waves on high;
But God above can still their noise, and make the angry sea comply.
5 Thy promise, Lord, is ever sure; and they that in thy house would dwell,
That happy station to secure, must still in holiness excel.

PSALM XCIV.

1, 2 O GOD, to whom revenge belongs, thy vengeance now disclose:
Arise, thou Judge of all the earth, and crush thy haughty foes,
3, 4 How long, O Lord, shall sinful men their solemn triumphs make;
How long their wicked actions boast, and insolently speak?

5, 6 Not only they thy saints oppress, but, unprovok'd, they spill
The widow's and the stranger's blood, and helpless orphans kill.
7 "And yet the Lord shall ne'er perceive, (profanely thus they speak)
"Nor any notice of our deeds the God of Jacob take."

8 At length, ye stupid fools, your wants endeavour to discern;
In folly will you still proceed, and wisdom never learn?
9, 10 Can he be deaf who form'd the ear? or blind who fram'd the eye?
Shall earth's great Judge not punish those, who his known will defy?

11 He fathoms all the thoughts of men, to him their hearts lie bare;
His eyes surveys them all, and sees how vain their counsels are.

PART II.

12 Bless'd is the man whom thou, O Lord, in kindness dost chastise,
And by thy sacred rules to walk dost lovingly advise.
13 This man shall rest and safety find in seasons of distress,
Whilst God prepares a pit for those that stubbornly transgress.

14 For God will never from his saints his favour wholly take:
His own possession and his lot he will not quite forsake.
15 The world shall then confess thee just in all that thou hast done:
And those that chuse thy upright ways, shall in those paths go on.

16 Who will appear in my behalf, when wicked men invade?
Or who, when sinners would oppress, my righteous cause shall plead?
17, 18, 19 Long since had I in silence slept, but that the Lord was near,
To stay me when I slipt; when sad, my troubled heart to chear.

20 Wilt thou, who art a God most just, their sinful throne sustain,
Who make the law a fair pretence their wicked ends to gain?
21 Against the lives of righteous men they form their close design;
And blood of innocents to spill, in solemn league combine.

22 But my defence is firmly plac'd in God the Lord most High;
He is my rock, to which I may for refuge always fly.
23 The Lord shall cause their ill designs on their own heads to fall:
He in their sins shall cut them off; our God shall slay them all.

PSALM XCV.

1 O COME, loud anthems, let us sing,
Loud thanks to our almighty king
For we our voices high should raise,
When our salvation's rock we praise.

2 Into his presence let us haste,
To thank him for his favours past;
To him address, in joyful songs,
The praise that to his name belongs.

3 For God the Lord, enthron'd in state,
Is, with unrivall'd glory, great:
A king superior far to all,
Whom gods the heathen falsely call.

4 The depths of earth are in his hand,
Her secret wealth at his command;
The strength of hills that reach the skies
Subjected to his empire lies,

5 The rolling ocean's vast abyss
By the same sov'reign right is his;
'Tis mov'd by his almighty hand,
That form'd and fix'd the solid land.

6 O let us to his courts repair,
And bow with adoration there;
Down on our knees devoutly all
Before the Lord our Maker fall.

7 For he's our God, our Shepherd he,
His flock and pasture sheep are we;
If then you'll (like his flock) draw near
To-day if you his voice will hear,

8 Let not your harden'd hearts renew
Your fathers crimes and judgments too;
Nor here provoke my wrath, as they
In desert plains of Meribah.

9 When through the wilderness they mov'd,
And me with fresh temptations prov'd,
They still through unbelief rebell'd,
Whilst they my wondrous works beheld.

10, 11 They forty years my patience griev'd,
Though daily I their wants reliev'd.
Then—'tis a faithless race, I said,
Whose heart from me has always stray'd.

12 They ne'er will tread my righteous path;
Therefore to them in settled wrath,
Since they despis'd my rest, I sware,
That they should never enter there.

PSALM XCVI.

1 SING to the Lord a new-made song;
Let earth in one assembled throng
Her common patron's praise resound:

2 Sing to the Lord, and bless his name,
From day to day his praise proclaim,
Who us hath with salvation crown'd.

3 To heathen lands his fame rehearse,
His wonders to the universe.

4 He's great, and greatly to be prais'd;
In majesty and glory rais'd
Above all other deities.

5 For pageantry and idols all
Are they whom gods the heathens call:
He only rules who made the skies.

6 With majesty and honour crown'd,
Beauty and strength his throne surround.

7 Be therefore both to him restor'd
By you, who have false gods ador'd:
Ascribe due honour to his name:

8 Peace-off'rings on his altar lay,
Before his throne your homage pay,
Which he, and he alone can claim.

9 To worship at his sacred court,
Let all the trembling world resort.

10 Proclaim aloud, Jehovah reigns,
Whose pow'r the universe sustains,
And banish'd justice will restore.

11 Let therefore heav'n new joys confess,
And heav'nly mirth let earth express;
Its loud applause the ocean roar;
Its mute inhabitants rejoice,
And for this triumph find a voice.

12 For joy let fertile vallies sing,
The cheerful groves their tribute bring;
The tuneful choir of birds awake,

13 The Lord's approach to celebrate,
Who now sets out with aweful state,
His circuit through the earth to take.
From heav'n to judge the world he's come,
With justice to reward and doom.

PSALM XCVII.

1 JEHOVAH reigns, let all the earth in his just government rejoice:
Let all the isles, with sacred mirth, in his applause unite their voice.
2 Darkness and clouds of aweful shade his dazzling glory shrowd in state:
Justice and truth his guards are made, and fix'd by his pavillion wait.

3 Devouring fire, before his face, his foes around with vengeance struck:
4 His lightnings set the world on blaze; earth saw it, and with terror shook.
The proudest hills his presence felt, their height nor strength could help afford;
5 The proudest hills like wax did melt in presence of the almighty Lord.

6 The heav'ns, his righteousness to show, with storms of fire our foes pursu'd;
And all the trembling world below, have his descending glory view'd.
7 Confounded be their impious hosts, who make the gods to whom they pray;
All who of pageant idols boast, to him, ye gods, your worship pay.

8 Glad Sion of thy triumph heard, and Judah's daughters were o'erjoy'd:
Because thy righteous judgments, Lord, have pagan pride and pow'r destroy'd.
9 For thou, O God, art seated high, above earth's potentates enthron'd:
Thou, Lord, unrivall'd in the sky, supreme by all the gods art own'd.

10 You, who to serve the Lord aspire, abhor what's ill, and truth esteem;
He'll keep his servants' soul entire, and them from wicked hands redeem.
11 For seeds are sown of glorious light, a future harvest for the just:
And gladness for the heart that's right, to recompence its pious trust.

12 Rejoice, ye righteous, in the Lord; memorials of his holiness:
Deep in your faithful breasts record, and with your thankful tongues confess.

PSALM XCVIII.

1 SING to the Lord a new made song, who wondrous things has done;
With his right hand and holy arm the conquest he has won.
2 The Lord has through the astonish'd world display'd his saving might,
And made his righteous acts appear in all the heathens' sight.

3 Of Israel's house his love and truth have ever mindful been;
Wide earth's remotest parts the pow'r of Israel's God have seen.
4 Let therefore earth's inhabitants their cheerful voices raise,
And all with universal joy resound their Maker's praise.

5 With harp and hymn's soft melody, into the concert bring
6 The trumpet and shrill cornet's sound, before th' Almighty King.
7 Let the loud ocean roar her joy, with all the seas contain;
The earth and her inhabitants join concert with the main.

8 With joy let riv'lets swell to streams, to spreading torrents they;
And echoing vales from hill to hill redoubled shouts convey;
9 To welcome down the world's great judge who does with justice come,
And with impartial equity, both to reward and doom.

PSALM XCIX.

1 JEHOVAH reigns, let therefore all the guilty nations quake:
On cherub's wings he sits enthron'd; let earth's foundation shake:
2 On Sion's hill he keeps his court, his palace makes her tow'rs;
Yet thence his sov'reignty extends supreme o'er earthly pow'rs.

3 Let therefore all with praise address his great and dreadful name,
And with his unresisted might his holiness proclaim.
4 For truth and justice, in his reign, of strength and pow'r take place;
His judgments are with righteousness dispens'd to Jacob's race.

5 Therefore exalt the Lord our God, before his footstool fall;
And with his unresisted might his holiness extol.
6 Moses and Aaron thus of old among his priests ador'd;
Among his prophets Samuel thus his sacred name implor'd.

Distress'd, upon the Lord they call'd, who ne'er their suit deny'd;
But, as with rev'rence they implor'd, he graciously reply'd.
7 For with their camp, to guide their march, the cloudy pillar mov'd:
They kept his law, and to his will obedient servants prov'd.

8 He answer'd them, forgiving oft his people for their sake;
And those who rashly them oppos'd did sad examples make.
9 With worship, at his sacred courts, exalt our God and Lord;
For he, who only holy is, alone should be ador'd.

PSALM C.

1, 2 WITH one consent let all the earth to God their cheerful voices raise;
Glad homage pay with aweful mirth, and sing before him songs of praise.
3 Convinc'd that he is God alone, from whom both we and all proceed;
We, whom he chuses for his own; the flock that he vouchsafes to feed.

4 O, enter then his temple gate, thence to his courts devoutly press,
And still your grateful hymns repeat, and still his name with praises bless.
5 For he's the Lord, supremely good, his mercy is for ever sure;
His truth, which always firmly stood, to endless ages shall endure.

PSALM CI.

1 OF mercy's never-failing spring,
And stedfast judgment I will sing;
And since they both to thee belong,
To thee, O Lord, address my song.
2 When, Lord, thou shalt with me reside,
Wise discipline my reign shall guide;
With blameless life myself I'll make
A pattern for my court to take.

3 No ill design will I pursue,
Nor those my fav'rites make that do;
4 Who to reproof has no regard,
Him will I totally discard.
5 The private slanderer shall be
In public justice doom'd by me;
From haughty looks I'll turn aside,
And mortify the heart of pride.

6 But honesty, call'd from her cell,
In splendor at my court shall dwell;
Who virtue's practice make their care,
Shall have the first preferments there.
7 No politics shall recommend
His country's foe to be my friend:
None e'er shall to my favour rise
By flatt'ring or malicious lies.

8 All those who wicked courses take,
An early sacrifice I'll make;
Cut off, destroy, till none remain
God's holy city to prophane.

PSALM CII.

1 WHEN I pour out my soul in pray'r, do thou, O Lord, attend;
To thy eternal throne of grace let my sad cry ascend.
2 O hide not thou thy glorious face, in times of deep distress;
Incline thine ear, and, when I call, my sorrow soon redress.

3 Each cloudy portion of my life, like scatter'd smoke expires;
My shrivell'd bones are like a hearth parch'd with continual fires.
4 My heart, like grass that feels the blast of some infectious wind,
Does languish so with grief, that **scarce** my needful food I mind.

5 By reason of my sad estate I spend my breath in groans;
My flesh is worn away, my skin scarce hides my starting bones.
6 I'm like a pelican become, that does in deserts mourn;
Or like an owl, that sits all day on barren trees forlorn.

7 In watchings, or in restless dreams, the night by me is spent,
As by those solitary birds, that lonesome roofs frequent.
8 All day by railing foes I'm made the subject of their **scorn;**
Who all, possess'd with furious rage, have my destruction sworn.

9 When grov'ling on the ground I lie, oppress'd with grief and fears,
My bread is strew'd with ashes o'er, my drink is mix'd with **tears.**
10 Because on me with double weight thy heavy wrath doth lie;
For thou, to make my fall more great, didst lift me up on high.

11 My days, just hast'ning to their end, are like an ev'ning shade:
My beauty does, like wither'd grass, with waning lustre fade.
12 But thy eternal state, O Lord, no length of time shall waste;
The mem'ry of thy wondrous works from age to age shall last.

13 Thou shalt arise, and Sion view with an unclouded face;
For now her time is come, thy **own** appointed day of grace.
14 Her scatter'd ruins, by thy saints, with pity are survey'd;
They grieve to see her lofty spires in dust and rubbish laid.

15, 16 The name and glory of the Lord all heathen kings shall fear;
When he shall Sion build again, and in full state appear.
17, 18 When he regards the poor's request, nor slights their earnest pray'r;
Our sons, for their recorded grace, shall his just praise declare.

19 For God, from his abode on high, his gracious beams display'd;
The Lord from heav'n, his lofty throne, hath all the earth survey'd.
20 He listen'd to the captives' moans, he heard their mournful cry,
And freed by his resistless pow'r the wretches doom'd to die.

21 That they in Sion, where he dwells, might celebrate his fame,
And through the holy city sing loud praises to his name.
22 When all the tribes assembling there, their solemn vows address,
And neighb'ring lands, with glad consent, the Lord their God confess.

23 But e'er my race is run, my strength thro' his fierce wrath decays;
He has, when all my wishes bloom'd, **cut** short **my hopeful days.**
24 Lord, end not thou my life, said I, when half is scarcely past:
Thy years, from worldly changes free, **to** endless ages last.

25 The strong foundations of the earth of old by thee were laid;
Thy hands the beauteous arch of heav'n **with** wondrous skill have made.
26, 27 Whilst thou for ever shalt endure, they soon shall pass away;
And, like a garment often worn, shall tarnish and decay.

Like that, when thou ordain'st their change, to thy command they bend:
But thou continu'st still the same, nor have thy years an end.
28 Thou to the children of thy saints shall lasting quiet give;
Whose happy race, securely fix'd, shall in thy presence live.

PSALM CIII.

1, 2 MY soul inspir'd with sacred love, God's holy name for ever bless:
Of all his favours mindful prove, and still thy grateful thanks express.
3, 4 'Tis he that all thy sins forgives, and after sickness makes thee sound;
From danger he thy life retrieves, by him with grace and mercy crown'd.

5, 6 He with good things thy mouth supplies, thy vigour, eagle-like, renews:
He, when the guiltless suff'rer cries, his foe with just revenge pursues.
7 God made of old his righteous ways to Moses and our fathers known;
His works, to his eternal praise, were to the sons of Jacob shown.

8 The Lord abounds with tender love, and unexampled acts of grace:
His waken'd wrath doth slowly move, his willing mercy flies apace.
9, 10 God will not always harshly chide, but with his anger quickly part;
And loves his punishments to guide, more by his love than our desert.

11 As high as heav'n its arch extends above this little spot of clay,
So much his boundless love transcends the small respects that we can pay.
12, 13 As far as 'tis from east to west, so far has he our sins remov'd,
Who with a father's tender breast, has such as fear him always lov'd.

14, 15 For God, who all our frame surveys, considers that we are but clay;
How fresh soe'er we seem, our days like grass or flow'rs must fade away.
16, 17 Whilst they are nipt with sudden blasts, nor can we find their former place;
God's faithful mercy ever lasts, to those that fear him, and their race.

18 This shall attend on such as still proceed in his appointed way;
And who not only know his will, but to it just obedience pay.
19, 20 The Lord, the universal King, in heav'n has fix'd his lofty throne:
To him, ye angels, praises sing, in whose great strength his pow'r is shown.

21 Ye that his just commands obey, and hear and do his sacred will;
Ye hosts of his, this tribute pay, who still what he ordains fulfil.
22 Let ev'ry creature jointly bless the mighty Lord: and, thou my heart,
With grateful joy thy thanks express and in this concert bear thy part.

PSALM CIV.

1 BLESS God, my soul; thou, Lord, alone, possessest empire without bounds;
With honour thou art crown'd, thy throne eternal majesty surrounds.
2 With light thou dost thyself enrobe, and glory for a garment take;
Heav'ns curtains stretch beyond the globe, thy canopy of state to make.

3 God builds on liquid air, and forms his palace chambers in the skies;
The clouds his chariots are, and storms the swift-wing'd steed with which he flies.
4 As bright as flame, as swift as wind, his ministers heav'n's palace fill,
To have their sundry tasks assign'd; all proud to serve their sov'reign's will.

5, 6 Earth on her center fix'd, he set her face with waters overspread;
Nor proudest mountains dared as yet to lift above the waves their head.
7 But when thy awful face appear'd, th' insulting waves dispers'd; they fled,
When once thy thunder's voice they heard, and by their haste confess'd their dread.

8 Thence up by secret tracks they creep, and, gushing from the mountain's side,
Through vallies travel to the deep, appointed to receive their tide.

9 There hast thou fix'd the ocean's bounds the threat'ning surges to repel;
That they no more o'erpass their mounds nor to a second deluge swell:

PART II.

10 Yet thence in smaller parties drawn, the sea recovers her lost hills;
And starting springs from ev'ry lawn surprise the vales with plenteous rills.
11 The fields' tame beasts are thither led, weary with labour, faint with drought:
And asses on wild mountains bred, have sense to find these currents out.

12 There shady trees, from scorching beams, yield shelter to the feather'd throng;
They drink, and to the bounteous streams return the tribute of their song.
13 His rain from heav'n parch'd hills recruit, that soon transmit the liquid store;
Till earth is burden'd with her fruit, and nature's lap can hold no more.

14 Grass, for our cattle to devour, he makes the growth of ev'ry field;
Herbs, for man's use, of various pow'r, that either food or physic yield.
15 With cluster'd grapes he crowns the vine to cheer men's hearts oppress'd with cares
Gives oil that makes his face to shine, and corn that wasted strength repairs.

PART III.

16 The trees of God, without the care or art of man, with sap are fed;
The mountain cedar looks as fair as those in royal gardens bred.
17 Safe in the lofty cedar's arms the wand'rers of the air may rest;
The hospitable pine from harms protects the stork, her pious guest.

18 Wild goats the craggy rock ascend, its tow'ring heights their fortress make,
Whose cells in labyrinths extend, where feebler creatures refuge take.
19 The moon's inconstant aspect shows, th' appointed seasons of the year;
Th' instructed sun his duty knows, his hours to rise and disappear.

20, 21 Darkness he makes the earth to shroud, when forest beasts securely stray;
Young lions roar their wants aloud to Providence that sends them prey.
22 They range all night, on slaughter bent, till summon'd by the rising morn;
To skulk in dens, with one consent, the conscious ravagers return.

23 Forth to the tillage of his soil the husbandman securely goes,
Commencing with the sun his toil, with him returns to his repose.
24 How various, Lord, thy works are found; for which thy wisdom we adore,
The earth is with thy treasure crown'd, till nature's hand can grasp no more.

PART IV.

25 But still the vast unfathom'd main, of wonders a new scene supplies,
Whose depths inhabitants contain of ev'ry form and ev'ry size.
26 Full freighted ships from ev'ry port there cut their unmolested way:
Leviathan, whom there to sport thou mad'st, has compass there to play.

27 These various troops of sea and land, in sense of common wants agree:
All wait on thy dispensing hand, and have their daily alms from thee,
28 They gather what thy stores disperse, without their trouble to provide:
Thou op'st thy hand, the universe, the craving world is all supply'd.

29 Thou for a moment hid'st thy face, the num'rous ranks of creatures mourn
Thou tak'st their breath, all nature's race forthwith to mother earth return.

30 Again thou send'st thy spirit forth t' inspire the mass with vital seed;
Nature's restor'd, and parent earth smiles on her new-created breed.

31 Thus through successive ages stands firm fix'd thy providential care;
Pleas'd with the work of thy own hands, thou dost the waste of time repair.
32 One look of thine, one wrathful look, earth's panting breast with terror fills:
One touch from thee with clouds of smoke in darkness shrowds the proudest hills.

33 In praising God, while he prolongs my breath, I will that breath employ;
34 And join devotion to my songs, sincere, as in him is my joy.
35 While sinners from earth's face are hurl'd, my soul, praise thou his holy name,
Till with my song the list'ning world join concert, and his praise proclaim.

PSALM CV.

1 O RENDER thanks, and bless the Lord: invoke his sacred name;
Acquaint the nations with his deeds, his matchless deeds proclaim.
2 Sing to his praise, in lofty hymns, his wondrous works rehearse;
Make them the theme of your discourse, and subject of your verse.

3 Rejoice in his almighty name, alone to be ador'd;
And let their hearts o'erflow with joy, that humbly seek the Lord.
4 Seek ye the Lord, his saving strength devoutly still implore;
And, where he's ever present, seek his face for evermore.

5 The wonders that his hands have wrought keep thankfully in mind:
The righteous statutes of his mouth, and laws to us assign'd.
6 Know ye his servant Abr'am's seed, and Jacob's chosen race:
7 He's still our God, his judgments still throughout the earth take place.

8 His cov'nant he hath kept in mind for num'rous ages past;
Which yet for thousand ages more, in equal force shall last.
9 First sign'd to Abr'am, next, by oath, to Isaac made secure;
10 To Jacob and his heirs at law for ever to endure:

11 That Canaan's land should be their lot, when yet but few there were;
12 But few in number, and those few all friendless strangers there.
13 In pilgrimage from realm to realm securely they remov'd:
14 While proudest monarchs, for their sakes, severely he reprov'd.

15 "These mine anointed are (said he), let none my servants wrong;
"Nor treat the poorest prophet ill, that does to me belong."
16 A dearth at last, by his command, did through the land prevail;
Till corn, the chief support of life, sustaining corn did fail.

17 But his indulgent providence had pious Joseph sent,
Sold into Egypt, but their death who sold him to prevent,
18 His feet with heavy chains were crush'd, with calumny his fame;
19 Till God's appointed time and word to his deliv'rance came.

20 The king his sov'reign order sent, and rescu'd him with speed;
Whom private malice had confin'd, the people's ruler freed.
21 His court, revenues, realms were all subjected to his will;
22 His greatest princes to control and teach his statesmen skill.

PSALM CVI.

PART II.

23 To Egypt then, invited guests, half-famish'd Israel came,
And Jacob held, by royal grant, the fertile soil of Ham.
24 Th' Almighty there with such increase his people multiply'd,
Till with their proud oppressors they in strength and number vy'd.

25 Their vast increase th' Egyptians' hearts with jealous anger fir'd,
Till they his servants to destroy by treach'rous arts conspir'd.
26 His servant Moses then he sent, his chosen Aaron too:
27 Empower'd with signs and miracles, to prove their mission true.

28 He call'd for darkness, darkness came, Nature his summons knew;
29 Each stream and lake, transform'd to blood, the wand'ring fishes slew.
30 In putrid floods, throughout the land, the pest of frogs was bred;
From noisome fens sent up to croak at Pharaoh's board and bed.

31 He gave the sign, and swarms of flies came down in cloudy hosts,
Whilst earth's enliven'd dust below, bred lice through all their coasts.
32 He sent them batt'ring hail for rain, and fire for cooling dew:
33 He smote their vines and forest plants, and garden's pride o'erthrew.

34 He spake the word, and locusts came, and caterpillars join'd
They prey'd upon the poor remains the storm had left behind.
35 From trees to herbage they descend, no verdant thing they spare;
But, like the naked fallow field, leave all the pastures bare.

36 From fields to villages and towns, commission'd vengeance flew:
One fatal stroke their eldest hopes and strength of Egypt slew.
37 He brought his servants forth, enrich'd with Egypt's borrow'd wealth;
And, what transcends all treasures else, enrich'd with vig'rous health.

38 Egypt rejoic'd, in hopes to find her plagues with them remov'd;
Taught dearly now to fear worse ills by those already prov'd.
39 Their shrouding canopy by day, a journeying cloud was spread:
A fiery pillar all the night their desert marches led.

40 They long'd for flesh; with ev'ning quails he furnish'd ev'ry tent:
From heav'n's high granary, each morn, the bread of angels sent.
41 He smote the rock, whose flinty breast pour'd forth a gushing tide;
Whose flowing stream where'er they march'd, the desert's drought supply'd.

42 For still he did on Abr'am's faith and ancient league reflect:
43 He brought his people forth with joy, with triumph his elect.
44 Quite rooting out their heathen foes from Canaan's fertile soil,
To them in cheap possession gave the fruit of others' toil.

45 That they his statutes might observe, his sacred laws obey.
For benefits so vast, let us our songs of praise repay.

PSALM CVI.

1 O RENDER thanks to God above
The fountain of eternal love;
Whose mercy firm through ages past
Has stood, and shall for ever last.
2 Who can his mighty deeds express,
Not only vast, but numberless?
What mortal eloquence can raise
His tribute of immortal praise?
3 Happy are they, and only they,
Who from thy judgments never stray;
Who know what's right, not only so,
But always practise what they know.

Extend to me that favour Lord,
Thou to thy chosen dost afford:
When thou return'st to set them free,
Let thy salvation visit me,
O may I worthy prove to see
Thy saints in full prosperity;
That I the joyful choir may join,
And count thy people's triumph mine.

But ah! can we expect such grace,
Of parents vile, the viler race?
Who their misdeeds have acted o'er,
And with new crimes increas'd the score
Ungrateful, they no longer thought
On all his works in Egypt wrought:
The Red Sea they no sooner view'd,
But they their base distrust renew'd.

8 Yet he, to vindicate his name,
Once more to their deliv'rance came,
To make his sov'reign pow'r known,
That he is God, and he alone.
9 To right and left, at his command,
The parting deep disclos'd her sand;
Where firm and dry the passage lay,
As through some parch'd and desert way:

10 Thus rescu'd from their foes they were
Who closely press'd upon their rear;
11 Whose rage pursu'd them to those waves
That prov'd the rash pursuers' graves.
12 The wat'ry mountains sudden fall,
O'erwhelm'd proud Pharoah, host and all
This proof did stupid Israel move
To own God's truth, and praise his love.

PART II.

But soon these wonders they forgot,
And for his counsel waited not;
But lusting in the wilderness,
Did him with fresh temptations press.
Strong food at their request he sent,
But made their sin their punishment.
Yet still his saints they did oppose,
The priest and prophet whom he chose.

But earth the quarrel to decide,
Her vengeful jaws extending wide,
Rash Dathan to her centre drew,
With proud Abiram's factious crew.
The rest of those who did conspire
To kindle wild Sedition's fire,
With all their impious train, became
A prey to Heav'n's devouring flame.

Near Horeb's mount a calf they made,
And to the molten image pray'd;
Adoring what their hands did frame,
They chang'd their glory to their shame.

21 Their God and Saviour they forgot,
And all his works in Egypt wrought;
22 His signs in Ham's astonish'd coast,
And where proud Pharaoh's troops were lost.

23 Thus urg'd, his vengeful hand he rear'd,
But Moses in the breach appear'd;
The saint did for the rebels pray,
And turn'd Heav'n's kindled wrath away.
24 Yet they his pleasant land despis'd,
Nor his repeated promise priz'd,
25 Nor did th' Almighty's voice obey:
But when God said, Go up, would stay.

26 This seal'd their doom, without redress,
To perish in the wilderness;
27 Or else to be by heathens' hands
O'erthrown, and scatter'd through the lands.

PART III.

Yet unreclaim'd, this stubborn race
Baal Peor's worship did embrace;
Became his impious guests, and fed
On sacrifices to the dead.
Thus they persisted to provoke
God's vengeance to the final stroke;
'Tis come;—the deadly pest is come
To execute their gen'ral doom.

But Phineas, fir'd with holy rage,
(Th' Almighty Vengeance to assuage)
Did, by two bold offenders' fall,
Th' atonement make that ransom'd all.
31 As him a heav'nly zeal had mov'd,
So Heav'n the zealous act approv'd;
To him confirming, and his race,
The priesthood he so well did grace.
32 At Meribah God's wrath they mov'd,
Who Moses for their sakes reprov'd;
33 Whose patient soul they did provoke,
Till rashly the meek prophet spoke.

34 Nor, when possess'd of Canaan's land,
Did they perform their Lord's command
Nor his commission'd sword employ,
The guilty nations to destroy.

35 Not only spar'd the Pagan crew,
But mingling learnt their vices too;

36 And worship to those idols paid,
Which them to fatal snares betray'd.

37, 38 To Devils they did sacrifice
Their children with relentless eyes;
Approach'd their altars through a flood
Of their own sons' and daughters' blood.
No cheaper victims would appease
Canaan's remorseless deities;
No blood her idols reconcile,
But that which did the land defile.

PART IV.

39 Nor did these savage cruelties
The harden'd reprobates suffice;
For after their hearts' lust they went,
And daily did new crimes invent.

40 But sins of such infernal hue
God's wrath against his people drew,
Till he, their once indulgent Lord,
His own inheritance abhorr'd.

41 He then defenceless did expose
To their insulting heathen foes:
And made them on the triumph wait
Of those who bore them greatest hate.

42 Nor thus his indignation ceas'd:
Their list of tyrants still increas'd,
Till they, who God's mild sway declin'd,
Were made the vassals of mankind.

43 Yet, when distress'd, they did repent,
His anger did as oft relent:
But freed, they did his wrath provoke,
Renew'd their sins, and he their yoke.

44 Nor yet implacable he prov'd,
Nor heard their wretched cries unmov'd;

45 But did to mind his promise bring,
And Mercy's inexhausted spring.

46 Compassion too he did impart
Ev'n to their foes' obdurate heart,
And pity for their suff'rings bred
In those who them to bondage led.

47 Still save us, Lord, and Israel's bands
Together bring from heathen lands;
So to thy name our thanks we'll raise,
And ever triumph in thy praise.

48 Let Israel's God be ever bless'd,
His name eternally confess'd:
Let all his saints, with full accord,
Sing loud Amens—Praise ye the Lord.

PSALM CVII.

1 TO God your grateful voices raise, who does your daily patron prove:
And let your never-ceasing praise attend to his eternal love.

2, 3 Let those give thanks whom he from bands of proud oppressing foes releas'd;
And brought them back from distant lands, from North and South, and West and East.

4, 5 Through lonely desart ways they went, nor could a peopled city find;
Till quite with thirst and hunger spent, their fainting souls within them pin'd.

6 Then soon to God's indulgent ear did they their mournful cry address;
Who graciously vouchsaf'd to hear, and freed them from their deep distress.

7 From crooked paths he led them forth, and in the certain way did guide
To wealthy towns of great resort, where all their wants were well supply'd.

8 O then, that all the earth with me would God for this his goodness praise,
And for the mighty works which he throughout the wond'ring word displays.

9 For he, from heaven, the sad estate of longing souls with pity views;
To hungry souls that pant for meat, his goodness daily food renews.

PSALM CVII.

PART II.

10 Some lie, with darkness compass'd round,
in death's uncomfortable shade,
And with unweildy fetters bound,
by pressing cares more heavy made,
11, 12 Because God's counsels they defy'd,
and lightly priz'd his holy word,
With these afflictions they were try'd:
they fell, and none could help afford.

13 Then soon to God's indulgent ear
did they their mournful cry address;
Who graciously vouchsaf'd to hear,
and freed them from their deep distress.
14 From dismal dungeons, dark as night,
and shades as black as death's abode,
He brought them forth to chearful light,
and welcome liberty bestow'd.

15 O then that all the earth with me,
would God for this his goodness praise,
And for the mighty works which he
throughout the wondrous world displays!
16 For he with his almighty hand
the gates of brass in pieces broke:
Nor could the massy bars withstand,
or temper'd steel resist his stroke.

PART III.

17 Remorseless wretches, void of sense,
with bold transgressions God defy;
And for their multiply'd offence,
oppress'd with sore diseases lie.
18 Their soul a prey to pain and fear,
abhors to taste the choicest meats;
And they by faint degrees draw near
to death's inhospitable gates.

19 Then straight to God's indulgent ear
do they their mournful cry address,
Who graciously vouchsafes to hear,
and frees them from their deep distress.
20 He all their sad distempers heals,
his word both health and safety gives;
And, when all human succour fails,
from near destruction them retrieves.

21 O then that all the earth with me
would God for this his goodness praise,
And for the mighty works which he
throughout the wond'ring world displays.
22 With off'rings let his altar flame,
whilst they their grateful thanks express,
And with loud joy his holy name
for all his acts of wonder bless!

PART IV.

23, 24 They that in ships with courage bold,
o'er swelling waves their trade pursue,
Do God's amazing works behold,
and in the deep his wonders view.
25 No sooner his command is past,
but forth the dreadful tempest flies,
Which sweeps the sea with rapid haste,
and makes the stormy billows rise.

26 Sometimes the ships, toss'd up to heav'n,
on tops of mountain waves appear;
Then down the steep abyss are driv'n,
whilst ev'ry soul dissolves with fear.
27 They reel and stagger to and fro,
like men with fumes of wine oppress'd;
Nor do the skilful seamen know
which way to steer, what course is best.

28 Then straight to God's indulgent ear,
they do their mournful cry address;
Who graciously vouchsafes to hear,
and frees them from their deep distress.
29, 30 He does the raging storm appease,
and makes the billows calm and still;
With joy they see their fury cease,
and their intended course fulfil.

31 O then that all the earth with me
would God for this his goodness praise,
And for the mighty works which he
throughout the wond'ring world displays!
32 Let them, where all the tribes resort,
advance to heav'n his glorious name,
And in the elders' sovereign court,
with one consent his praise proclaim.

PSALM CVII.

PART V.

33, 34 **A** fruitful land, where **streams** abound,
God's just revenge, if people sin,
Will turn to dry and barren ground,
to punish those that dwell therein.
35 36 The parch'd and desart heath he makes
to flow with streams and springing wells,
Which for his lot the hungry takes,
and in strong cities safely dwells.

37 38 He sows the field, **the vineyard** plants,
which gratefully his toil repay;
Nor can whilst God his blessings grants,
his fruitful seed or stock decay.
39 But when his sins Heav'n's wrath provoke,
his health and substance fade away;
He feels th' oppressors' galling yoke,
and is of grief the wretched prey.

40 **The** prince that slights what God commands,
expos'd to scorn, must quit the throne;
And over wild and desart lands,
where no path offers, stray alone.
41 Whilst God, from all afflicting cares,
sets up the humble man on high,
And makes in time his num'rous **heirs**
with his increasing flocks to vie.

42, 43 Then sinners **shall** have nought to say,
the just a decent joy shall show;
The wise these strange events shall weigh,
and thence God's goodness fully know.

PSALM CVIII.

O GOD, my heart is fully bent
to magnify thy name;
My tongue with cheerful songs of praise
shall celebrate thy fame.
2 Awake, my lute; nor thou, my harp,
thy warbling notes delay;
Whilst I with early hymns of joy
prevent the dawning day.

3 To all the list'ning tribes, O Lord,
thy wonders I will tell;
And to those nations sing thy praise
that round about us dwell.
4 Because thy mercy's boundless height
the highest heav'n transcends,
And far beyond th' aspiring clouds
thy faithful truth extends.

5 Be thou, **O God,** exalted high
above the starry frame:
And let **the world,** with one consent,
confess thy glorious name.
6 That all my chosen people thee
their Saviour may declare;
Let thy right hand protect me still,
and answer thou my pray'r.

7 Since God himself has said the word,
whose promise cannot fail,
With joy I Sechem shall divide,
and measure Succoth's vale.
8 Gilead is mine, Manasseh too,
and Ephraim owns my cause;
Their strength my regal pow'r supports,
and Judah gives my laws.

9 Moab I'll make my servile drudge,
on vanquish'd Edom tread;
And through the proud Philistine lands
my conqu'ring banners spread.
10 By whose support and aid shall I
their well-fenc'd city gain?
Who will my troops securely lead
through Edom's guarded plain?

67 **Lord,** wilt not thou assist our arms,
which late thou didst forsake?
And wilt not thou of these our hosts
once more the guidance take?
12, O, **to** thy servant in distress
thy speedy succour send;
For vain it is on human aid
for safety to depend.

3 Then valiant acts shall we perform, if thou thy pow'r disclose;
For God it is, and God alone, that treads down all our foes.

PSALM CIX.

O GOD, whose former mercies make my constant praise thy due,
Hold not thy peace, but my sad state with wonted favour view.
For sinful men, with lying lips, deceitful speeches frame,
And with their study'd slanders seek to wound my spotless fame.

Their restless hatred prompts them still malicious lies to spread;
And all against my life combine, by causeless fury led.
Those, whom with tend'rest love I us'd, my chief opposers are:
Whilst I, of other friends bereft, resort to thee by pray'r.

Since mischief, for the good I did, their strange reward does prove,
And hatred's the return they make for undissembled love:
Their guilty leader shall be made to some ill man a slave;
And, when he's try'd, his mortal foe for his accuser have.

His guilt, when sentence is pronounc'd, shall meet a dreadful fate,
Whilst his rejected pray'r but serves his crimes to aggravate.
He, snatch'd by some untimely fate, sha'n't live out half his days;
Another, by divine decree, shall on his office seize.

10 His seed shall orphans be, his wife a widow plung'd in grief;
His vagrant children beg their bread, where none can give relief.
1 His ill-got riches shall be made to usurers a prey;
The fruit of all his toil shall be by strangers borne away.

2 None shall be found that to his want their mercy will extend,
Or to his helpless orphan seed the least assistance lend.
3 A swift destruction soon shall seize on his unhappy race;
And the next age his hated name shall utterly deface.

4 The vengeance of his father's sins upon his head shall fall;
God on his mother's crimes shall think, and punish him for all.
5 All these, in horrid order rank'd, before the Lord shall stand,
Till his fierce anger quite cuts off their mem'ry from the land.

PART II.

6 Because he never mercy show'd, but still the poor oppress'd;
And sought to slay the helpless man, with heavy woes distress'd:
7 Therefore the curse he lov'd to vent shall his own portion prove;
And blessing, which he still abhorr'd, shall far from him remove.

8 Since he in cursing took such pride, like water it shall spread,
Through all his veins, and stick like oil, with which his bones are fed.
9 This, like a poison'd robe, shall still his constant cov'ring be,
Or an envenom'd belt, from which he shall be never free.

0 Thus shall the Lord reward all those that ill to me design,
That with malicious false reports against my life combine.
11 But for thy glorious name, O God, do thou deliver me;
And for thy gracious mercy's sake, preserve and set me free.

12 For I, to utmost straits reduc'd, am void of all relief;
My heart is wounded with distress, and quite pierc'd thro' with grief.

23 I, like an ev'ning shade, decline which vanishes apace:
Like locusts, up and down I'm toss'd, and have no certain place.

24, 25 My knees with fasting are grown weak, my body lank and lean;
All that behold me shake their heads, and treat me with disdain.
26, 27 But for thy mercy's sake, O Lord, do thou my foes withstand;
That all may see 'tis thy own act, the work of thy right hand.

28 Then let them curse, so thou but bless: let shame the portion be
Of all that my destruction seek, while I rejoice in thee.
29 My foe shall with disgrace be cloath'd, and, spite of all his pride,
His own confusion, like a cloke, the guilty wretch shall hide.

30 But I to God, in grateful thanks, my cheerful voice will raise;
And where the great assembly meets, set forth his noble praise.
31 For him the poor shall always find their sure and constant friend:
And he shall from unrighteous dooms their guiltless souls defend.

PSALM CX.

1 THE Lord unto my Lord thus spake,
"Till I thy foes thy footstool make,
"Sit thou, in state, at my right hand:
2 "Supreme in Sion thou shalt be,
"And all thy proud opposers see
"Subjected to thy just command.

3 "Thee, in thy pow'r's triumphant day,
"The willing nations shall obey:
"And, when thy rising beams they view,
"Shall all (redeem'd from Error's night)
"Appear as numberless and bright
"As crystal drops and morning dew."

4 The Lord hath sworn, nor sworn in vain,
That, like Melchisedech's, thy reign
And priesthood shall no period know:
5 No proud competitor to sit
At thy right hand will he permit,
But in his wrath crown'd heads o'erthrow.

5 The sentenc'd heathen he shall slay,
And fill with carcasses his way,
Till he hath struck earth's tyrants dead;
7 But in the high-way brooks shall first,
Like a poor pilgrim, slake his thirst,
And then in triumph raise his head.

PSALM CXI.

1 PRAISE ye the Lord; our God to praise
My soul her utmost pow'rs shall raise
With private friends, and in the throng
Of saints, his praise shall be my song.

2 His works for greatness though renown'd,
His wondrous works with ease are found
By those who seek for them aright,
And in the pious search delight.

3 His works are all of matchless fame,
And universal glory claim;
His truth, confirm'd through ages past,
Shall to eternal ages last.

4 By precepts he has us enjoin'd,
To keep his wondrous works in mind;
And to posterity record,
That good and gracious is our Lord.

5 His bounty, like a flowing tide,
Has all his servants' wants supply'd;
And he will ever keep in mind
His cov'nant with our fathers sign'd.

6 At once astonish'd and o'erjoy'd,
They saw his matchless pow'r employ'd;
Whereby the heathen were suppress'd,
And we their heritage possess'd.

7 Just are the dealings of his hands;
Immutable are his commands:
8 By truth and equity sustain'd,
And for eternal rules ordain'd.

9 He set his saints from bondage free,
And then establish'd his decree,
For ever to remain the same;
Holy and rev'rend is his name.

10 Who Wisdom's sacred prize would win
Must with the fear of God begin;
Immortal praise and heav'nly skill
Have they, who know and do his will.

PSALM CXII.

HALLELUJAH.

1 THAT man is bless'd, who stands in awe
Of God, and loves his sacred law:
2 His seed on earth shall be renown'd,
And with successive honours crown'd.

3 His house, the seat of wealth, shall be
An inexhausted treasury;
His justice, free from all decay,
Shall blessings to his heirs convey.

4 The soul that's fill'd with Virtue's light
Shines brightest in Affliction's night;
To pity the distress'd inclin'd,
As well as just to all mankind.

5 His lib'ral favours he extends,
To some he gives, to others lends;
Yet, what his charity impairs,
He saves by prudence in affairs.

6 Beset with threat'ning dangers round,
Unmov'd shall he maintain his ground:
The sweet remembrance of the just
Shall flourish, when he sleeps in dust.

7 Ill tidings never can surprise
His heart that fix'd, on God relies:
8 On Safety's rock he sits and sees
The shipwreck of his enemies.

9 His hands, while they his alms bestow'd,
His glory's future harvest sow'd,
Whence he shall reap wealth, fame, renown,
A temp'ral and eternal crown.

10 The wicked shall his triumph see,
And gnash their teeth in agony;
While their unrighteous hopes decay,
And vanish with themselves away.

PSALM CXIII.

1 YE saints and servants of the Lord,
The triumphs of his name record;
2 His sacred name for ever bless.
3 Where'er the circling sun displays
His rising beams or setting rays,
Due praise to his great name address.

4 God thro' the world extends his sway:
The regions of eternal day
But shadows of his glory are.
5 With him, whose majesty excels,
Who made the heav'n in which he dwells,
Let no created pow'r compare.

6 Though 'tis beneath his state to view
In highest heav'n what angels do,
Yet he to earth vouchsafes his care:
He takes the needy from his cell,
Advancing him in courts to dwell,
Companion to the greatest there.

7 When childless families despair,
He sends the blessing of an heir,
To rescue their expiring name;
Makes her that barren was to bear,
And joyfully her fruit to rear:
O then extol his matchless fame!

PSALM CXIV.

1 WHEN Israel, by the Almighty led
From Egypt march'd, and Jacob's seed
(enrich'd with their oppressors' spoil)
from bondage in a foreign soil;

2 Jehovah, for his residence,
His mansion royal, and from thence
chose out imperial Judah's tent,
through Israel's camp his orders sent.

3 The distant sea with terror saw,
Old Jordan's streams, surpris'd with awe,
and from th' Almighty's presence fled;
retreated to their fountain's head.
4 The taller mountains skipp'd like rams,
The hills skipp'd after them like lambs,
when danger near the fold they hear;
affrighted by their leader's fear.

5 O sea! what made your tide withdraw,
Why, Jordan, against nature's law,
and naked leave your oozy bed?
recoil'dst thou to thy fountain's head?

6 Why, mountains, did ye skip like rams, when danger does approach the fold?
Why after you the hills like lambs, when they their leader's flight behold?

7 Earth, tremble on; well may'st thou fear thy Lord and maker's face to see:
When Jacob's aweful God draws near, 'tis time for earth and seas to flee.
8 To flee from God, who nature's law confirms and cancels at his will;
Who springs from flinty rocks can draw, and thirsty vales with water fill.

PSALM CXV.

1 LORD, not to us, we claim no share, but to thy sacred name
Give glory, for thy mercy's sake, and truth's eternal fame.
2 Why should the heathen cry, Where's now the God whom we adore?
3 Convince them that in heav'n thou art, and uncontroul'd thy pow'r.

4 Their gods but gold and silver are, the works of mortal hands;
5 With speechless mouth and sightless eyes the molten idol stands.
6 The pageant has both ears and nose, but neither hears nor smells;
7 Its hands and feet nor feel nor move, no life within it dwells

8 Such senseless stocks they are, that we can nothing like them find,
But those who on their help rely, and them for gods design'd.
9 O Israel, make the Lord your trust, who is your help and shield:
10 Priests, Levites, trust in him alone, who only help can yield.

11 Let all, who truly fear the Lord, on him their fear rely;
Who them in danger can defend, and all their wants supply.
12, 13 Of us he oft has mindful been, and Israel's house will bless;
Priests, Levites, Proselytes, e'en all who his great name confess.

14 On you and on your heirs, he will increase of blessings bring;
15 Thrice happy you, who fav'rites are of this almighty king!
16 Heav'ns highest orb of glory he his empire's seat design'd!
And gave this lower globe of earth a portion to mankind

17 They who in death and silence sleep, to him no praise afford;
18 But we will bless for evermore our ever-living Lord.

PSALM CXVI.

1 MY soul with grateful thoughts of love intirely is possest,
Because the Lord vouchsaf'd to hear the voice of my request.
2 Since he has now his ear inclin'd, I never will despair;
But still in all the straits of life to him address my pray'r.

3 With deadly sorrows compass'd round, with pains of hell oppress'd,
When troubles seiz'd my aching heart, and anguish rack'd my breast;
4 On God's almighty name I call'd, and thus to him I pray'd:
"Lord, I beseech thee, save my soul, with sorrow quite dismay'd."

5, 6 How just and merciful is God; how gracious is the Lord!
Who saves the harmless, and to me does timely help afford.
7 Then, free from pensive cares, my soul, resume thy wonted rest;
For God has wondrously to thee his bounteous love exprest.

8 When death alarm'd me, he remov'd my dangers and my fears:
My feet from falling he secur'd, and dry'd my eyes from tears.
9 Therefore my life's remaining years, which God to me shall lend,
Will I in praises to his name, and in his service spend.

10, 11 In God I trusted, and of him in greatest straits did boast;
(For in my flight all hopes of aid from faithless men were lost,)
12, 13 Then what return to him shall I for all his goodness make?
I'll praise his name, and with glad zeal the cup of blessing take.

14, 15 I'll pay my vows amongst his saints, whose blood (howe'er despis'd
By wicked men) in God's account is always highly priz'd:
16 By various ties. O Lord, must I to thy dominion bow;
Thy humble handmaid's son before, thy ransom'd captive now!

17, 18 To thee I'll off'rings bring of praise; and, whilst I bless thy name,
The just performance of my vows to all thy saints proclaim.
19 They in Jerusalem shall meet, and in thy house shall join,
To bless thy name with one consent and mix their songs with mine.

PSALM CXVII.

1 WITH chearful notes let all the earth to heav'n their voices raise:
Let all, inspir'd with godly mirth, sing solemn hymns of praise.
2 God's tender mercy knows no bound, his truth shall ne'er decay:
Then let the willing nations round their grateful tribute pay.

PSALM CXVIII.

1, 2 O PRAISE the Lord, for he is good, his mercies ne'er decay:
That his kind favours ever last, let thankful Israel say.
3, 4 Their sense of his eternal love let Aaron's house express;
And that it never fails, let all that fear the Lord confess.

5 To God I made my humble moan, with troubles quite opprest;
And he releas'd me from my straits, and granted my request.
6 Since therefore God does on my side, so graciously appear,
Why should the vain attempts of men possess my soul with fear?

7 Since God with those that aid my cause, vouchsafes my part to take,
To all my foes I need not doubt a just return to make.
8, 9 For better 'tis to trust in God, and have the Lord our friend,
Than on the greatest human pow'r for safety to depend.

10, 11 Though many nations, closely leagu'd, did oft beset me round;
Yet, by his boundless pow'r sustain'd, I did their strength confound.
12 They swarm'd like bees, and yet their rage was but a short-liv'd blaze;
For whilst on God I still rely'd, I vanquish'd them with ease.

13 When all united press'd me hard, in hopes to make me fall,
The Lord vouchsaf'd to take my part, and sav'd me from them all.
14 The honour of my strange escape to him alone belongs;
He is my saviour and my strength; he only claims my songs.

15 Joy fills the dwelling of the just, whom God has sav'd from harm;
For wondrous things are brought to pass by his almighty arm.
16 He, by his own resistless pow'r, has endless honour won;
The saving strength of his right hand amazing works has done.

16 God will not suffer me to fall, but still prolongs my days;
That, by declaring all his works, I may advance his praise.
18 When God had sorely me chastis'd, till quite of hopes bereav'd,
His mercy from the gates of death my fainting life repriev'd.

19 Then open wide the temple gates to which the just repair,
That I may enter in and praise, my great deliv'rer there.
20. 21 Within those gates of God's abode to which the righteous press,
Since thou hast heard, and set me safe, thy holy name I'll bless.

22, 23 That which the builders once refus'd, is now the corner-stone:
This is the wondrous work of God, the work of God alone.
24. 25 This day is God's; let all the land exalt their chearful voice:
Lord, we beseech thee, save us now, and make us still rejoice.

26 Him that approaches in God's name let all th' assembly bless;
"We that belong to God's own house have wish'd you good success."
27 God is the Lord, through whom we all both light and comfort find;
Fast to the altar's horn, with cords, the chosen victim bind.

28 Thou art my Lord, O God, and still I'll praise thy holy name;
Because thou only art my God, I'll celebrate thy fame.
29 O then, with me, give thanks to God, who still does gracious prove;
And let the tribute of our praise be endless as his love.

PSALM CXIX.

ALEPH.

1 HOW bless'd are they who always keep the pure and perfect way!
Who never from the sacred paths of God's commandments stray!
2 How bless'd! who to his righteous laws have still obedient been!
And have with fervent humble zeal his favour sought to win!

3 Such men their utmost caution use to shun each wicked deed;
But in the path which he directs with constant care proceed.
4 Thou strictly hast enjoin'd us, Lord, to learn thy sacred will;
And all our diligence employ thy statutes to fulfil.

5 O then that thy most holy will might o'er my ways preside!
And I the course of all my life by thy direction guide!
6 Then, with assurance, should I walk, from all confusion free;
Convinc'd, with joy, that all my ways with thy commands agree.

7 My upright heart shall my glad mouth with chearful praises fill;
When, by thy righteous judgments taught, I shall have learnt thy will.
8 So to thy sacred laws shall I all due observance pay:
O then forsake me not, my God, nor cast me quite away.

BETH.

9 How shall the young preserve their ways from all pollution free?
By making still their course of life with thy commands agree.
10 With hearty zeal for thee I seek, to thee for succour pray;
O suffer not my careless steps from thy right paths to stray.

11 Safe in my heart, and closely hid, thy word, my treasure, lies;
To succour me with timely aid, when sinful thoughts arise.
12 Secur'd by that, my grateful soul shall ever bless thy name;
O teach me then by thy just laws my future life to frame.

13 My lips, unlock'd by pious zeal, to others have declar'd,
How well the judgments of thy mouth deserve our best regard.

14 Whilst in the way of thy commands more solid joy I found,
Than had I been with vast increase of envy'd riches crown'd.

15 Therefore thy just and upright laws shall always fill my mind;
And those sound rules which thou prescrib'd, all due respect shall find.
16 To keep thy statutes undefac'd shall be my constant joy;
The strict remembrance of thy word shall all my thoughts employ.

GIMEL.

17 Be gracious to thy servant, Lord, do thou thy life defend,
That I, according to thy word, my future time may spend.
18 Enlighten both my eyes and mind, that so I may discern
The wondrous works which they behold, who thy just precepts learn.

19 Though like a stranger in the land, from place to place I stray,
Thy righteous judgments from my sight remove not thou away.
20 My fainting soul is almost pin'd, with earnest longing spent,
Whilst always on the eager search of thy just will intent.

21 Thy sharp rebuke shall crush the proud, whom still thy curse pursues;
Since they to walk in thy right ways presumptuously refuse.
22 But far from me do thou, O Lord, contempt and shame remove;
For I thy sacred laws affect with undissembled love.

23 Though princes oft, in council met, against thy servant spake:
Yet I thy statutes to observe my constant bus'ness make.
24 For thy commands have always been my comfort and delight;
By them I learn, with prudent care, to guide my steps aright.

DALETH.

25 My soul, oppress'd with deadly care, close to the dust does cleave;
Revive me, Lord, and let me now thy promis'd aid receive.
26 To thee I still declar'd my ways, who didst incline thine ear;
O teach me then my future life by thy just laws to steer.

27 If thou wilt make me know thy laws, and by their guidance walk,
The wondrous works which thou hast done shall be my constant talk.
28 But see, my soul within me sinks, press'd down with weighty care;
Do thou according to thy word, my wasted strength repair.

29 Far, far from me be all false ways and lying arts remov'd!
But kindly grant I still may keep the path by thee approv'd!
30 Thy faithful ways, thou God of truth, my happy choice I've made;
Thy judgments, as my rule of life, before me always laid.

31 My care has been to make my life with thy commands agree;
O then preserve thy servant, Lord, from shame and ruin free.
32 So in the way of thy commands shall I with pleasure run,
And, with a heart enlarg'd with joy, successfully go on.

HE.

33 Instruct me in thy statutes, Lord, thy righteous paths display;
And I from them, through all my life, will never go astray.
34 If thou true wisdom from above wilt graciously impart,
To keep thy perfect laws I will devote my zealous heart.

35 Direct me in the secret ways to which thy precepts lead;
Because my chief delight has been thy righteous paths to tread.
36 Do thou, to thy most just commands incline my willing heart:
Let no desire of worldly wealth from thee my thoughts divert.

37 From those vain objects turn my eyes, which this false world displays;
But give me lively pow'r and strength to keep thy righteous ways.
38 Confirm the promise which thou mad'st, and give thy servant aid,
Who to transgress thy sacred law is awfully afraid.

39 The foul disgrace I justly fear, in mercy, Lord, remove;
For all the judgments thou ordain'st are full of grace and love.
40 Thou know'st how after thy commands my longing heart does pant:
O then make haste to raise me up, and promis'd succour grant.

VAU.

41 Thy constant blessing, Lord, bestow, to chear my drooping heart;
To me, according to thy word, thy saving health impart.
42 So shall I, when my foes upbraid, this ready answer make;
"In God I trust, who never will his faithful promise break."

43 Then let not quite the word of truth be from my mouth remov'd;
Since still my ground of stedfast hope, thy just decrees hath prov'd,
44 So I to keep thy righteous laws with all my study bend;
From age to age, my time to come, in their observance spend.

45 Ere long I trust to walk at large, from all incumbrance free;
Since I resolve to make my life with thy commands agree.
46 Thy laws shall be my constant talk and princes shall attend,
Whilst I the justice of thy ways with confidence defend.

47 My longing heart and ravish'd soul shall both o'erflow with joy,
When in thy lov'd commandments I my happy hours employ.
48 Then will I to thy just decrees lift up my willing hands;
My care and bus'ness then shall be to study thy commands.

ZAIN.

49 According to thy promis'd grace, thy favour, Lord, extend;
Make good to me the word, on which thy servant's hopes depend.
50 That only comfort in distress did all my griefs controul;
Thy word, when troubles hemm'd me round, reviv'd my fainting soul.

51 Insulting foes did proudly mock, and all my hopes deride;
Yet from thy law not all their scoff could make me turn aside.
52 Thy judgments then of ancient date, I quickly call'd to mind,
Till, ravish'd with such thoughts, my soul did speedy comfort find.

53 Sometimes I stand amaz'd, like one with deadly horror struck,
To think how all my sinful foes have thy just laws forsook.
54 But I thy statutes and decrees my chearful anthems made;
Whilst through strange lands and desert wilds I like a pilgrim stray'd.

55 Thy name that chear'd my heart by day, has fill'd my thoughts by night;
I then resolv'd by thy just laws to guide my steps aright.
56 That peace of mind, which has my soul in deep distress sustain'd,
By strict obedience to thy will I happily obtain'd.

PSALM CXIX.

CHETH.

O Lord, my God, my portion thou
and sure possession art;
Thy words I stedfastly resolve
to treasure in my heart.
With all the strength of warm desire
I did thy grace implore:
Disclose, according to thy word,
thy mercy's boundless store.

With due reflection and strict care
on all my ways I thought:
And so, reclaim'd to thy just paths,
my wand'ring steps I brought.
I lost no time, but made great haste,
resolv'd, without delay,
To watch, that I might never more
from thy commandments stray.

Though num'rous troops of sinful men
to rob me have combin'd,
Yet I thy pure and righteous laws
have ever kept in mind.
In dead of night I will arise
to sing thy solemn praise;
Convinc'd how much I always ought
to love thy righteous ways.

To such as fear thy holy name
myself I closely join;
To all who their obedient wills
to thy commands resign.
O'er all the earth thy mercy, Lord,
abundantly is shed;
O make me then exactly learn
thy sacred paths to tread.

TETH.

With me, thy servant, thou hast dealt
most graciously, O Lord;
Repeated benefits bestow'd,
according to thy word.
Teach me the sacred skill, by which
right judgment is attain'd,
Who in belief of thy commands
have stedfastly remain'd.

Before affliction stopp'd my course,
my footsteps went astray:
But I have since been disciplin'd
thy precepts to obey.
8 Thou art, O Lord, supremely good,
and all thou dost is so;
On me, thy statutes to discern,
thy saving skill bestow.

The proud have forg'd malicious lies,
my spotless fame to stain;
But my fix'd heart, without reserve,
thy precepts shall retain.
While pamper'd they, with prosp'rous ills,
in sensual pleasures live,
My soul can relish no delight
but what thy precepts give.

'Tis good for me that I have felt
affliction's chast'ning rod,
That I might duly learn and keep
the statutes of my God.
The law that from thy mouth proceeds,
of more esteem I hold
Than untouch'd mines, than thousand mines
of silver and of gold.

JOD.

3 To me, who am the workmanship
of thy almighty hands,
The heav'nly understanding give
to learn thy just commands.
4 My preservation to thy saints
strong comfort will afford,
To see success attend my hopes,
who trusted in thy word.

5 That right thy judgments are, I now
by sure experience see;
And that in faithfulness, O Lord,
thou hast afflicted me.
6 O let thy tender mercy now
afford me needful aid;
According to thy promise, Lord,
to me thy servant made.

To me thy saving grace restore,
that I again may live;
[illegible]ose soul can relish no delight
but what thy precepts give.

78 Defeat the proud, who, unprovok'd, to ruin me have sought,
Who only on thy sacred laws employ my harmless thought.

79 Let those that fear thy name espouse my cause, and those alone,
Who have by strict and pious search thy sacred precepts known.
80 In thy blest statutes let my heart continue always sound;
That guilt and shame, the sinner's lot, may never me confound.

CAPH.

81 My soul with long expectance faints to see thy saving grace:
Yet still on thy unerring word my confidence I place.
82 My very eyes consume and fail with waiting for thy word;
O! when wilt thou thy kind relief and promis'd aid afford?

83 My skin like shrivel'd parchment shows, that long in smoke is set;
Yet no affliction me can force thy statutes to forget.
84 How many days must I endure of sorrow and distress?
When wilt thou judgment execute on them who me oppress?

85 The proud have digg'd a pit for me, that have no other foes
But such as are averse to thee, and thy just laws oppose,
86 With sacred truth's eternal laws all thy commands agree;
Men persecute me without cause; thou, Lord, my helper be.

87 With close designs against my life they had almost prevail'd;
But in obedience to thy will, my duty never fail'd,
88 Thy wonted kindness, Lord, restore, my drooping heart to cheer;
That by thy righteous statutes I my life's whole course may steer.

LAMED.

89 For ever, and for ever, Lord, unchang'd thou dost remain;
Thy word establish'd in the heav'ns, does all their orbs sustain.
90 Through circling ages, Lord, thy truth immoveable shall stand,
As doth the earth which thou uphold'st by thy almighty hand.

91 All things the course by thee ordain'd ev'n to this day fulfil;
They are thy faithful subjects all, and servants of thy will.
92 Unless thy sacred law had been my comfort and delight,
I must have fainted and expir'd in dark affliction's night.

93 Thy precepts, therefore, from my thoughts shall never, Lord, depart;
For thou by them hast to new life restor'd my dying heart.
94 As I am thine, intirely thine, protect me, Lord, from harm,
Who have thy precepts sought to know, and carefully perform.

95 The wicked have their ambush laid my guiltless life to take;
But in the midst of danger I thy word my study make.
96 I've seen an end of what we call perfection here below;
But thy commandments, like thyself, no change or period know.

MEM.

97 The love that to thy laws I bear, no language can display;
They with fresh wonders entertain my ravish'd thoughts all day.
98 Through thy commands I wiser grow than all my subtle foes;
For thy sure word doth me direct, and all my ways dispose.

99 From me my former teachers now may abler counsel take,
Because thy sacred precepts I my constant study make.
100 In understanding I excel the sages of our days;
Because by thy unerring rules I order all my ways,

101 My feet with care I have refrain'd from every sinful way,
That to thy sacred word I might intire obedience pay.
102 I have not from thy judgments stray'd, by vain desires misled;
For, Lord, thou hast instructed me, thy righteous paths to tread.

103 How sweet are all thy words to me! O what divine repast!
How much more grateful to my soul, than honey to my taste!
104 Taught by thy secret precepts, I with heav'nly skill am blest,
Through which the treach'rous ways of sin I utterly detest.

NUN.

105 Thy word is to my feet a lamp, the way of truth to show;
A watch-light to point out the path in which I ought to go.
106 I swear (and from my solemn oath will never start aside)
That in thy righteous judgments I will stedfastly abide.

107 Since I with griefs am so opprest, that I can bear no more,
According to thy word do thou my fainting soul restore.
108 Let still my sacrifice of praise with thee acceptance find;
And in thy righteous judgments, Lord, instruct my willing mind.

109 Though ghastly dangers me surround, my soul they cannot awe,
Nor with continual terrors keep from thinking on thy law.
110 My wicked and invet'rate foes for me their snares have laid:
Yet I have kept the upright path, nor from thy precepts stray'd.

111 Thy testimonies I have made my heritage and choice:
For they, when other comforts fail, my drooping heart rejoice:
112 My heart with early zeal began thy statutes to obey,
And till my course of life is done, shall keep thy upright way.

SAMECH.

113 Deceitful thoughts and practices I utterly detest;
But to thy law affection bear too great to be exprest
114 My hiding-place, my refuge-tow'r and shield art thou, O Lord;
I firmly anchor all my hopes on thy unerring word.

115 Hence ye that trade in wickedness, approach not my abode;
For firmly I resolve to keep the precepts of my God.
116 According to thy gracious word, from danger set me free;
Nor make me of those hopes asham'd, that I repose in thee.

117 Uphold me, so shall I be safe, and rescu'd from distress;
To thy decrees continually my just respect address.
118 The wicked thou hast trod to earth, who from thy statutes stray'd:
Their vile deceit the just reward of their own falsehood made.

119 The wicked from thy holy land thou dost like dross remove;
I therefore with such justice charm'd, thy testimonies love.
120 Yet with that love they make me dread, lest I should so offend,
When on transgressors I behold thy judgments thus descend.

PSALM CXIX.

AIN.

121 Judgment and justice I have lov'd; O therefore, Lord, engage
In my defence, nor give me up to my oppressors' rage.
122 Do thou be surety, Lord, for me, and so shall this distress
Prove good for me; nor shall the proud, my guiltless soul oppress;

123 My eyes, alas! begin to fail, in long expectance held:
Till thy salvation they behold, and righteous word fulfill'd.
124 To me, thy servant, in distress, thy wonted grace display,
And discipline my willing heart thy statutes to obey.

125 On me, devoted to thy fear, thy sacred skill bestow,
That of thy testimonies I the full extent may know.
126 'Tis time, high time, for thee, O Lord, thy vengeance to employ,
When men with open violence thy sacred law destroy.

127 Yet their contempt of thy commands but makes their value rise
In my esteem, who purest gold compar'd with them despise.
128 Thy precepts therefore I account in all respects, divine;
They teach me to discern the right, and all false ways decline.

PE.

129 The wonders which thy laws contain, no words can represent:
Therefore to learn and practise them, my zealous heart is bent.
130 The very entrance to thy word celestial light displays;
And knowledge of true happiness to simplest minds conveys.

131 With eager hopes I waiting stood, and fainting with desire,
That of thy wise commands I might the sacred skill acquire.
132 With favour, Lord, look down on me, who thy relief implore;
As thou art wont to visit those who thy blest name adore.

133 Directed by thy heavenly word let all my footsteps be;
Nor wickedness of any kind dominion have o'er me.
134 Release, intirely set me free from persecuting hands,
That, unmolested, I may learn and practise thy commands.

135 On me devoted to thy fear, Lord, make thy face to shine:
Thy statutes both to know and keep, my heart with zeal incline.
136 My eyes to weeping fountains turn, whence briny rivers flow,
To see mankind against thy laws in bold defiance go.

TSADDI.

137 Thou art the righteous Judge, in whom wrong'd innocence may trust;
And like thyself, thy judgments, Lord, in all respects are just.
138 Most just and true those statutes were, which thou didst first decree;
And all with faithfulness perform'd succeeding times shall see.

139 With zeal my flesh consumes away, my soul with anguish frets,
To see my foes contemn at once thy promises and threats.
140 Yet each neglected word of thine (howe'er by them despis'd)
Is pure, and for eternal truth by me, thy servant, priz'd.

141 Brought, for thy sake, to low estate, contempt from all I find;
Yet no affronts or wrongs can drive thy precepts from my mind.

142 Thy righteousness shall then endure, when time itself is past;
Thy law is truth itself, that truth which shall for ever last.

143 Tho' trouble, anguish, doubts, and dread, to compass me unite:
Beset with danger, still I make thy precepts my delight.
144 Eternal and unerring rules thy testimonies give:
Teach me the wisdom that will make my soul for ever live.

KOPH.

145 With my whole heart to God I call'd, Lord, hear my earnest cry;
And I thy statutes to perform will all my care apply.
146 Again more fervently I pray'd, O save me, that I may
Thy testimonies truly know, and stedfastly obey.

147 My earlier pray'r the dawning day prevented, while I cry'd
To him, on whose engaging word my hope alone rely'd.
148 With zeal have I awak'd before the midnight watch was set,
That I of thy mysterious work might perfect knowledge get.

149 Lord, hear my supplicating voice, and wonted favour shew;
O quicken me, and so approve thy judgment ever true.
150 My persecuting foes advance, and hourly nearer draw;
What treatment can I hope from them who violate thy law?

151 Though they draw nigh, my comfort is, thou, Lord, art yet more near;
Thou, whose commands are righteous all, thy promises sincere.
152 Concerning thy divine decrees, my soul has known of old,
That they were true, and shall their truth, to endless ages hold.

RESCH.

153 Consider my affliction, Lord, and me from bondage draw;
Think on thy servant in distress, who ne'er forgets thy law.
154 Plead thou my cause; to that and me thy timely aid afford;
With beams of mercy quicken me according to thy word.

155 From harden'd sinners thou remov'st salvation far away;
'Tis just thou should'st withdraw from them who from thy statutes stray.
156 Since great thy tender mercies are to all who thee adore;
According to thy judgments, Lord, my fainting hopes restore.

157 A num'rous host of spiteful foes against my life combine:
But all too few to force my soul thy statutes to decline.
158 Those bold transgressors I beheld, and was with grief oppress'd,
To see with what audacious pride thy cov'nant they transgress'd.

159 Yet while they slight, consider, Lord, how I thy precepts love:
O therefore quicken me with beams of mercy from above.
160 As from the birth of time thy truth has held through ages past,
So shall thy righteous judgments, firm, to endless ages last.

SCHIN.

161 Though mighty tyrants without cause, conspire my blood to shed,
Thy sacred word has pow'r alone to fill my heart with dread.
162 And yet that word my joyful breast with heav'nly rapture warms;
Nor conquest, nor the spoils of war, have such transporting charms.

163 Perfidious practices and lies I utterly detest;
But to thy laws affection bear, too vast to be exprest.
164 Sev'n times a day, with grateful voice, thy praises I resound,
Because I find thy judgments all with truth and justice crown'd.

165 Secure, substantial peace have they who truly love thy law:
No smiling mischief them can tempt, nor frowning danger awe.
166 For thy salvation I have hop'd, and though so long delay'd,
With chearful zeal and strictest care all thy commands obey'd.

167 Thy testimonies I have kept, and constantly obey'd;
Because the love I bore to them thy service easy made.
168 From strict observance of thy laws I never yet withdrew;
Convinc'd that my most secret ways are open to thy view.

TAU.

169 To my request and earnest cry attend, O gracious Lord;
Inspire my heart with heav'nly skill, according to thy word.
170 Let my repeated pray'r at last before thy throne appear;
According to thy plighted word, for my relief draw near.

171 Then shall my grateful lips return the tribute of their praise,
When thou thy counsels hast reveal'd, and taught me thy just ways.
172 My tongue the praises of thy word shall thankfully resound,
Because thy promises are all with Truth and Justice crown'd.

173 Let thy almighty arm appear, and bring me timely aid;
For I the laws thou hast ordain'd, my heart's free choice have made.
174 My soul has waited long to see thy saving grace restor'd,
Nor comfort knew, but what thy laws, thy heav'nly laws afford.

175 Prolong my life, that I may sing my great Restorer's praise,
Whose justice from the depths of woe my fainting soul shall raise.
176 Like some lost sheep I've stray'd, till I despair my way to find;
Thou, therefore, Lord, thy servant seek, who keeps thy laws in mind.

PSALM CXX.

1 IN deep distress I oft have cry'd
To God who never yet deny'd
To rescue me, oppress'd with wrongs:
2 Once more, O Lord, deliv'rance send,
From lying lips my soul defend,
And from the rage of sland'ring tongues:

3 What little profit can accrue,
And yet what heavy wrath is due,
O thou perfidious tongue, to thee?
4 Thy sting upon thyself shall turn:
Of lasting flames that fiercely burn,
The constant fuel thou shalt be.

5 But O! how wretched is my doom,
Who am a sojourner become
In barren Mesech's desert soil!
With Kedar's wicked tents inclos'd,
To lawless savages expos'd,
Who live on nought but theft and spoil.

5 My hapless dwelling is with those
Who peace and amity oppose,
And pleasure take in others harms!
7 Sweet peace is all I court and seek;
But when to them of peace I speak,
They straight cry out, To arms, to arms.

PSALM CXXI.

1 TO Sion's hill I lift my eyes, from thence expecting aid:
2 From Sion's hill, and Sion's God, who heav'n and earth has made.

Then thou, my soul, in safety rest, thy guardian will not sleep:
His watchful care, that Israel guards, will Israel's monarch keep.

Shelter'd beneath th' Almighty's wings thou shalt securely rest;
Where neither sun nor moon shall thee by day or night molest.
From common accidents of life his care shall guard thee still;
From the blind strokes of chance, and foes that lie in wait to kill.

At home, abroad, in peace, and war, thy God shall thee defend;
Conduct thee thro' life's pilgrimage safe to thy journey's end.

PSALM CXXII.

O 'TWAS a joyful sound to hear our tribes devoutly say,
Up, Israel, to the temple haste, and keep your festal day.
At Salem's courts we must appear with our assembled pow'rs,
In strong and beauteous order rang'd, like her united tow'rs.

'Tis thither by divine command the tribes of God repair,
Before his ark to celebrate his name with praise and pray'r.
Tribunals stand erected there, where equity takes place;
There stand the courts and palaces of royal David's race.

O, pray we then for Salem's peace, for they shall prosp'rous be,
(Thou holy city of our God!) who bear true love to thee.
May peace within thy sacred walls a constant guest be found,
With plenty and prosperity thy palaces be crown'd.

For my dear brethren's sake, and friends no less than brethren dear,
I'll pray---May peace in Salem's tow'rs a constant guest appear,
But most of all I'll seek thy good, and ever wish thee well,
For Sion and the temple's sake, where God vouchsafes to dwell.

PSALM CXXIII.

2 ON thee, who dwell'st above the skies,
For mercy wait my longing eyes
As servants watch their master's hands,
And maids their mistresses' commands.

3, 4 O then have mercy on us, Lord,
Thy gracious aid to us afford:
To us, whom cruel foes oppress,
Grown rich and proud by our distress.

PSALM CXXIV.

HAD not the Lord (may Israel say) been pleas'd to interpose,
2 Had he not then espous'd our cause, when men against us rose,
4, 5 Their wrath had swallow'd us alive and rag'd without controul;
Their spite and pride's united floods had quite o'erwhelm'd our soul.

But prais'd be our eternal Lord, who rescu'd us that day,
Nor to their savage jaws gave up our threaten'd lives a prey.
Our soul is like a bird escap'd from out the fowler's net;
The snare is broke, their hopes are cross'd, and we at freedom set.

Secure in his almighty name our confidence remains,
Who, as he made both heav'n and earth, of both sole monarch reigns.

PSALM CXXV.

WHO place on Sion's God their trust, like Sion's rock shall stand;
Like her immoveable be fix'd by his almighty hand.

2 Look how the hills on ev'ry side Jerusalem inclose;
So stands the Lord around his saints to guard them from their foes.

3 The wicked may afflict the just, but ne'er too long oppress,
Nor force him by despair to seek base means for his redress.
4 Be good, O righteous God, to those who righteous deeds affect:
The heart that innocence retains, let innocence protect.

5 All those who walk in crooked paths, the Lord shall soon destroy;
Cut off th' unjust, but crown the saints with lasting peace and joy.

PSALM CXXVI.

1 WHEN Sion's God her sons recall'd from long captivity,
It seem'd at first a pleasing dream of what we wish'd to see;
2 But soon in unaccustom'd mirth we did our voice employ;
And sung our great Restorer's praise in thankful hymns of joy.

Our heathen foes repining stood, yet were compell'd to own,
That great and wondrous was the work our God for us had done.
3 'Twas great, say they, 'twas wondrous great, much more should we confess;
The Lord has done great things, whereof we reap the glad success.

4 To us bring back the remnant, Lord, of Isr'el's captive bands,
More welcome than refreshing show'rs to parch'd and thirsty lands.
5 That we, whose work commenc'd in tears, may see our labours thrive,
Till finish'd with success, to make our drooping hearts revive.

6 Tho' he despond that sows his grain, yet doubtless he shall come
To bind his full-ear'd sheaves, and bring the joyful harvest home.

PSALM CXXVII.

1 WE build with fruitless cost, unless the Lord the pile sustain,
Unless the Lord the city keep, the watchmen wake in vain.
2 In vain we rise before the day, and late to rest repair:
Allow no respite to our toil, and eat the bread of care.

3 Supplies of life, with ease to them, he on his saints bestows;
He crowns their labour with success, their nights with sound repose.
4 Children, those comforts of our life, are presents from the Lord;
He gives a num'rous race of heirs, as Piety's reward.

5 As arrows in a giant's hand, when marching forth to war,
Ev'n so the sons of sprightly youth their parents safeguard are.
6 Happy the man whose quivers fill'd with these prevailing arms,
He needs not fear to meet his foe, at law, or war's alarms.

PSALM CXXVIII.

1 THE man is blest that fears the Lord, not only worship pays,
But keeps his steps confin'd with care to his appointed ways.
2 He shall upon the sweet returns of his own labour feed;
Without dependance, live and see his wishes all succeed.

3 His wife, like a fair fertile vine, her lovely fruit shall bring;
His children, like young olive plants, about his table spring.
4, 5 Who fears the Lord shall prosper thus; him Sion's God shall bless;
And grant him all his days to see Jerusalem's success.

6 He shall live on, till heirs from him descend with vast increase;
Much bless'd in his own prosp'rous state, and more in Israel's peace.

PSALM CXXIX.

1 FROM my youth up, may Israel say, they oft have me assail'd,
2 Reduc'd me oft to heavy straits, but never quite prevail'd.
3 They oft have plow'd my patient back with furrows deep and long:
4 But our just God has broke their chains, and rescu'd us from wrong.

5 Defeat, confusion, shameful rout be still the doom of those,
Their righteous doom, whom Sion hate, and Sion's God oppose.
6 Like corn upon our houses tops, untimely let them fade,
Which too much heat, and want of root, has blasted in the blade:

7 Which in his arms no reaper takes, but unregarded leaves;
No binder thinks it worth his pains to fold it into sheaves.
8 No traveller that passes by, vouchsafes a minute's stop,
To give it one kind look, or crave heav'n's blessing on the crop.

PSALM CXXX.

1 FROM lowest depths of woe to God I sent my cry;
2 Lord, hear my supplicating voice, and graciously reply.
3 Should'st thou severely judge, who can the trial bear?
4 But thou forgiv'st, lest we despond, and quite renounce thy fear.

5 My soul with patience waits for thee the living Lord;
My hopes are on thy promise built, thy never-failing word.
6 My longing eyes look out for thy enliv'ning ray,
More duly than the morning watch to spy the dawning day.

7 Let Israel trust in God, no bounds his mercy knows;
The plenteous source and spring from whence eternal mercy flows;
8 Whose friendly streams to us, supplies in want convey;
A healing spring, a spring to cleanse and wash our guilt away.

PSALM CXXXI.

1 O LORD, I am not proud of heart, nor cast a scornful eye;
Nor my aspiring thoughts employ in things for me to high.
2 With infant innocence thou know'st I have myself demean'd;
Compos'd to quiet, like a babe that from the breast is wean'd.

3 Like me let Israel hope in God, his aid alone implore;
Both now and ever trust in him, who lives for evermore.

PSALM CXXXII.

1 LET David, Lord, a constant place in thy remembrance find;
Let all the sorrows he endur'd be ever in thy mind.
2 Remember what a solemn oath to thee, his Lord, he swore;
How to the mighty God he vow'd, whom Jacob's sons adore:

3, 4 I will not go into my house, nor to my bed ascend;
No soft repose shall close my eyes, nor sleep my eye-lids bend;
5 Till for the Lord's design'd abode I mark the destin'd ground;
a decent place of rest for Jacob's God have found.

6 Th' appointed place with shouts of joy, at Ephrata we found,
And made the wood and neighb'ring fields our glad applause resound.
7 O with due rev'rence let us then to his abode repair;
And, prostrate at his footstool fall'n, pour out our humble pray'r.

8 Arise, O Lord, and now possess thy constant place of rest;
Be that, not only with thy ark, but with thy presence blest.
9, 10 Clothe thou thy priests with righteousness, make thou thy saints rejoice;
And, for thy servant David's sake, hear thy anointed's voice.

11 God sware to David in his truth, (nor shall his oath be vain)
One of thy offspring after thee upon thy throne shall reign.
12 And if thy seed my cov'nant keep and to my laws submit;
Their children too upon thy throne for evermore shall sit.

13, 14 For Sion does in God's esteem all other seats excel;
His place of everlasting rest where he desires to dwell.
15, 16 Her stores, says he, I will increase, her poor with plenty bless;
Her saints shall shout for joy, her priests my saving health confess.

17 There David's pow'r shall long remain in his successive line,
And my anointed servant there shall with fresh lustre shine.
18 The faces of his vanquish'd foes confusion shall o'erspread;
Whilst, with confirm'd success, his crown shall flourish on his head.

PSALM CXXXIII.

1 HOW vast must their advantage be! how great their pleasure prove!
Who live like brethren, and consent in offices of love!
2 True love is like that precious oil, which, pour'd on Aaron's head,
Ran down his beard, and o'er his robes its costly moisture shed.

3 'Tis like refreshing dew, which does on Hermon's top distil;
Or like the early drops that fall on Sion's fruitful hill.
4 For Sion is the chosen seat, where, the almighty King
The promis'd blessing has ordain'd, and life's eternal spring.

PSALM CXXXIV.

1 BLESS God, ye servants that attend upon his solemn state,
That in his temple, night by night, with humble rev'rence wait:
2, 3 Within his house lift up your hands, and bless his holy name;
From Sion, bless thy Israel, Lord, who earth and heav'n didst frame.

PSALM CXXXV.

1 O PRAISE the Lord with one consent, and magnify his name;
Let all the servants of the Lord his worthy praise proclaim.
2 Praise him all ye that in his house attend with constant care,
With those that to his utmost courts with humble zeal repair.

3 For this our truest int'rest is, glad hymns of praise to sing;
And with loud songs to bless his name, a most delightful thing.
4 For God his own peculiar choice the sons of Jacob makes;
And Israel's offspring for his own most valu'd treasure takes.

5 That God is great we often have by glad experience found;
And seen how he, with wondrous pow'r, above all gods is crown'd.

6 For he, with unresisted strength, performs his sov'reign will,
In heav'n and earth, and wat'ry stores that earth's deep caverns fill.

7 He raises vapours from the ground, which, pois'd in liquid air,
Fall down at last in show'rs, through which his dreadful lightnings glare:
8 He from his storehouse brings the wind; and he with vengeful hand
The first-born slew of man and beast through Egypt's mourning land.

9 He dreadful signs and wonders shew'd through stubborn Egypt's coasts,
Nor Pharaoh could his plagues escape, nor all his num'rous hosts.
10, 11 'Twas he that various nations smote, and mighty kings suppress'd:
Sihon and Og, and all besides, who Canaan's land possess'd.

2, 13 Their land upon his chosen race he firmly did entail;
For which his fame shall always last, his praise shall never fail.
14 For God shall soon his people's cause with pitying eyes survey;
Repent him of his wrath, and turn his kindled rage away.

5 Those idols, whose false worship spreads o'er all the heathen lands,
Are made of silver and of gold, the work of human hands.
16, 17 They move not their fictitious tongues, nor see with polish'd eyes;
Their counterfeited ears are deaf, no breath their mouth supplies.

18 As senseless as themselves are they that all their skill apply
To make them, or in dang'rous times on them for aid rely.
19 Their just returns of thanks to God let grateful Israel pay;
Nor let the priests of Aaron's race to bless the Lord delay.

20 Their sense of his unbounded love let Levi's house express;
And let all those who fear the Lord his name for ever bless.
21 Let all with thanks his wondrous works in Sion's court proclaim,
Let them in Salem, where he dwells, exalt his holy name.

PSALM CXXXVI.

1 TO God the mighty Lord your joyful thanks repeat:
To him due praise afford, as good as he is great:
For God does prove our constant friend,
His boundless love shall never end.

2, 3 To him whose wondrous pow'r all other gods obey,
Whom earthly kings adore, this grateful homage pay.
For God, &c.

4, 5 By his almighty hand amazing works are wrought;
The heav'ns by his command were to perfection brought.
For God, &c.

6 He spreads the ocean round about the spacious land;
And made the rising ground above the waters stand.
For God, &c.

7, 8, 9 Through heav'n he did display his num'rous hosts of light;
The sun to rule by day, the moon and stars by night.
For God, &c.

10, 11, 12 He struck the first-born dead of Egypt's stubborn land;
And thence his people led with his resistless hand.
For God, &c.

13, 14 By him the raging sea, as if in pieces rent,
Disclos'd a middle way, thro' which his people went,
For God, &c.

15 Where soon he overthrew proud Pharaoh and his host,
Who, daring to pursue, were in the billows lost.
For God, &c.

16, 17, 18 Thro' deserts vast and wild he led the chosen seed;
And famous princes foil'd, and made great monarchs bleed,
For God, &c.

19, 20 Sihon, whose potent hand great Ammon's sceptre sway'd;
And Og, whose stern command rich Bashan's land obey'd.
For God, &c.

21, 22 And of his wondrous grace, their lands, whom he destroy'd,
He gave to Israel's race, to be by them enjoy'd.
For God, &c.

23, 24 He, in our depth of woes, on us with favour thought,
And from our cruel foes in peace and safety brought.
For God, &c.

25, 26 He does the food supply on which all creatures live:
To God who reigns on high, eternal praises give.
For God will prove our constant friend,
His boundless love shall never end.

PSALM CXXXVII.

1 WHEN we, our weary limbs to rest, sat down by proud Euphrates' stream,
We wept, with doleful thoughts opprest, and Sion was our mournful theme.
2 Our harps, that when with joy we sung, were wont their tuneful parts to bear,
With silent strings neglected hung on willow trees that wither'd there.

3 Meanwhile our foes, who all conspir'd to triumph in our slavish wrongs,
Music and mirth of us requir'd, "Come, sing us one of Sion's songs."
4 How shall we tune our voice to sing? or touch our harps with skilful hands?
Shall hymns of joy to God, our king, be sung by slaves in foreign lands?

5 O Salem, once our happy seat! when I of thee forgetful prove,
Let then my trembling hand forget the speaking strings with art to move!
6 If I to mention thee forbear, eternal silence seize my tongue;
Or if I sing one cheerful air, till thy deliv'rance is my song.

7 Remember, Lord, how Edom's race, in thy own city's fatal day,
Cry'd out, "Her stately walls deface, and with the ground quite level lay."
8 Proud Babel's daughter, doom'd to be of grief and woe the wretched prey;
Bless'd is the man, who shall to thee the wrongs thou laid'st on us repay.

9 Thrice blest, who with just rage possest, and deaf to all the parents' moans,
Shall snatch thy infants from the breast, and dash their heads against the stones.

PSALM CXXXVIII.

WITH my whole heart, my God and king, thy praise I will proclaim;
Before the Gods with joy I'll sing, and bless thy holy name.
I'll worship at thy sacred seat; and, with thy love inspir'd,
The praises of thy truth repeat, o'er all thy works admir'd.

Thou graciously inclin'dst thine ear, when I to thee did cry;
And, when my soul was press'd with fear, didst inward strength supply.
Therefore shall ev'ry earthly prince thy name with praise pursue,
Whom these admir'd events convince that all thy works are true.

They all thy wondrous ways, O Lord, with cheerful songs shall bless;
And all thy glorious acts record, thy aweful pow'r confess.
For God, although enthron'd on high, does thence the poor respect;
The proud far off his scornful eye beholds with just neglect.

Though I with troubles am oppress'd, he shall my foes disarm,
Relieve my soul when most distress'd, and keep me safe from harm.
The Lord, whose mercies ever last, shall fix my happy state;
And, mindful of his favours past, shall his own works complete.

PSALM CXXXIX.

1 THOU, Lord, by strictest search hast known
My rising up, and lying down;
My secret thoughts are known to thee,
Known long before conceiv'd by me.

Thine eye my bed and path surveys,
My public haunts and private ways;
Thou know'st what 'tis my lips would vent,
My yet unutter'd words' intent.

Surrounded by thy pow'r I stand,
On ev'ry side I find thy hand.
O skill, for human reach too high!
Too dazzling bright for mortal eye!

O could I so perfidious be,
To think of once deserting thee,
Where, Lord, could I thy influence shun?
Or, whither from thy presence run?

If up to heav'n I take my flight,
'Tis there thou dwell'st enthron'd in light:
If down to hell's infernal plains,
'Tis there almighty vengeance reigns.

If I the morning's wings could gain,
And fly beyond the western main,
Thy swifter hand would first arrive,
And there arrest thy fugitive.

11 Or, should I try to shun thy sight
Beneath the sable wings of night;
One glance from thee, one piercing ray,
Would kindle darkness into day.

12 The veil of night is no disguise,
No skreen from thy all-searching eyes;
Thro' midnight shades thou find'st thy way,
As in the blazing noon of day.

13 Thou know'st the texture of my heart,
My reins and ev'ry vital part:
Each single thread in Nature's loom,
By thee was cover'd in the womb.

14 I'll praise thee, from whose hands I came,
A work of such a curious frame;
The wonders thou in me hast shown,
My soul with grateful joy must own.

15 Thine eyes my substance did survey
Whilst yet a lifeless mass it lay;
In secret how exactly wrought,
Ere from its dark inclosure brought.

16 Thou didst the shapeless embryo see,
Its parts were register'd by thee;
Thou saw'st the daily growth they took,
Form'd by the model of thy book:

17 Let me acknowledge too, O God,
That since this maze of life I trod,
Thy thoughts of love to me surmount
The pow'er of numbers to recount.

18 Far sooner could I reckon o'er
The sands upon the ocean's shore;
Each morn, revising what I've done,
I find th' account but new begun.

19 The wicked thou shalt slay, O God!
Depart from me, ye men of blood,
20 Whose tongues heav'n's majesty profane,
And take th' Almighty's name in vain.

21 Lord, hate not I their impious crew,
Who thee with enmity pursue?
And does not grief my heart oppress,
When reprobates thy laws transgress?

22 Who practise enmity to thee
Shall utmost hatred have from me;
Such men I utterly detest,
As if they were my foes profest.

23, 24 Search, try, O God, my thoughts and heart,
If mischief lurks in any part;
Correct me where I go astray,
And guide me in thy perfect way.

PSALM CXL.

1 PRESERVE me, Lord, from crafty foes of treacherous intent;
2 And from the sons of violence, on open mischief bent.
3 Their sland'ring tongue the serpent's sting in sharpness does exceed:
Between their lips the gall of asps and adders' venom breed.

4 Preserve me, Lord, from wicked hands, nor leave my soul forlorn,
A prey to sons of violence, who have my ruin sworn.
5 The proud for me have laid a snare, and spread their wily net;
With traps and gins, where e'er I move, I find my steps beset.

6 But thus environ'd with distress, thou art my God, I said;
Lord, hear my supplicating voice, that calls to thee for aid.
7 O Lord, the God, whose saving strength kind succour did convey,
And cover'd my advent'rous head in battle's doubtful day:

8 Permit not their unjust designs to answer their desire;
Lest they, encourag'd by success, to bolder crimes aspire.
9 Let first their chiefs the sad effects of their injustice mourn;
The blast of their envenom'd breath upon themselves return.

10 Let them who kindled first the flame, its sacrifice become;
The pit they digg'd for me, be made their own untimely tomb.
11 Tho' Slander's breath may raise a storm, it quickly will decay;
Their rage does but the torrent swell that bears themselves away.

12 God will assert the poor man's cause, and speedy succour give:
The just shall celebrate his praise, and in his presence live.

PSALM CXLI.

1 TO thee, O Lord, my cries ascend, O haste to my relief;
And with accustom'd pity hear the accents of my grief.
2 Instead of off'rings, let my pray'r like morning incense rise;
My lifted hands supply the place of ev'ning sacrifice.

3 From hasty language curb my tongue, and let a constant guard
Still keep the portal of my lips with wary silence barr'd.
4 From wicked men's designs and deeds my heart and hands restrain;
Nor let me in the booty share of their unrighteous gain.

.et upright men reprove my faults, and I shall think them kind;
.ike balm that heals a wounded head, I their reproof shall find:
\nd, in return, my fervent pray'r I shall for them address,
Vhen they are tempted and reduc'd, like me, to sore distress.

Vhen sculking in Engedi's rock, I to their chiefs appeal,
f one reproachful word I spoke, when I had pow'r to kill.
'et us they persecute to death; our scatter'd ruins lie
\s thick as from the hewer's axe the sever'd splinters fly

Jut, Lord, to thee I still direct my supplicating eyes,
) leave not destitute my soul, whose trust on thee relies.
)o thou preserve me from the snares that wicked hands have laid;
.et them in their own nets be caught, while my escape is made.

PSALM CXLII.

TO God with mournful voice, in deep distress I pray'd;
2 Made him the umpire of my cause, my wrongs before him laid.
'hou didst my steps direct, when my griev'd soul despair'd;
'or where I thought to walk secure, they had their traps prepar'd.

look'd, but found no friend to own me in distress:
\ll refuge fail'd, no man vouchsaf'd his pity or redress.
'o God at last I pray'd; thou, Lord, my refuge art,
Ay portion in the land of life, till life itself depart.

Reduc'd to greatest straits, to thee I make my moan;
) save me from oppressing foes, for me too pow'rful grown.
'hat I may praise thy name, my soul from prison bring;
Vhilst of thy kind regard to me assembled saints shall sing.

PSALM CXLIII.

LORD, hear my pray'r, and to my cry thy wonted audience lend:
In thy accustom'd faith and truth a gracious answer send.
Vor at thy strict tribunal bring thy servant to be try'd;
'or in thy sight no living man can e'er be justify'd.

'he spiteful foe pursues my life, whose comforts all are fled;
Ie drives me into caves as dark as mansions of the dead.
My spirit therefore is o'erwhelm'd, and sinks within my breast;
My mournful heart grows desolate, with heavy woes opprest.

call to mind the days of old, and wonders thou hast wrought:
My former dangers and escapes employ my musing thought.
'o thee my hands in humble pray'r I fervently stretch out;
My soul for thy refreshment thirsts, like land oppress'd with drought.

Iear me with speed; my spirit fails; thy face no longer hide,
.est I become forlorn, like them that in the grave reside.
'hy kindness early let me hear, whose trust on thee depends;
'each me the way where I should go; my soul to thee ascends.

)o thou, O Lord, from all my foes, preserve and set me free;
\ safe retreat against their rage my soul implores from thee.
Thou art my God, thy righteous will instruct me to obey;
.et thy good spirit lead and keep my soul in thy right way.

11 O! for the sake of thy great name, revive my drooping heart:
For thy truth's sake, to me distress'd, thy promis'd aid impart.
12 In pity to my suff'rings, Lord, reduce my foes to shame;
Slay them that persecute a soul devoted to thy name.

PSALM CXLIV.

1 FOR ever bless'd be God the Lord, who does his needful aid impart,
At once both strength and skill afford to wield my arms with warlike art.
2 His goodness is my fort and tow'r, my strong deliv'rance and my shield;
In him I trust, whose matchless pow'r makes to my sway fierce nations yield.

3 Lord, what's in man that thou should'st love of him such tender care to take?
What in his offspring could thee move such great account of him to make?
4 The life of man does quickly fade, his thoughts but empty are and vain,
His days are like a flying shade, of whose short stay no signs remain.

5 In solemn state, O God, descend, whilst heaven its lofty head inclines;
The smoaking hills asunder rend, of thy approach the aweful signs.
6 Discharge thy dreadful lightnings round, and make my scatter'd foes retreat;
Them with thy pointed arrows wound, and their destruction soon compleat.

7, 8 Do thou, O Lord, from heav'n engage thy boundless pow'r, my foes to quell,
And snatch me from the stormy rage of threat'ning waves that proudly swell.
Fight thou against my foreign foes, who utter speeches false and vain;
Who, tho' in solemn leagues they close, their sworn engagements ne'er maintain.

9 So I to thee, O King of Kings, in joyful hymns my voice shall raise,
And instruments of various strings shall help me thus to sing thy praise:
10 "God does to kings his aid afford, to them his sure salvation sends;
"'Tis he that from the murd'ring sword his servant David still defends."

11 Fight thou against my foreign foes, who utter speeches false and vain;
Who, tho' in solemn league they close, their sworn engagements ne'er maintain.
12 Then our young sons like trees shall grow well planted in some fruitful place;
Our daughters shall like pillars show, design'd some royal court to grace.

13 Our garners, fill'd with various store, shall us and ours with plenty feed;
Our sheep increasing more and more, shall thousands and ten thousands breed.
14 Strong shall our lab'ring oxen grow, nor in their constant labour faint;
Whilst we no war nor slav'ry know, and in our streets hear no complaint.

15 Thrice happy is that people's case, whose various blessings thus abound;
Who God's true worship still embrace, and are with his protection crown'd.

PSALM CXLV.

1, 2 THEE I'll extol, my God and King, thy endless praise proclaim:
This tribute daily I will bring, and ever bless thy name.
3 Thou, Lord, beyond compare, art great, and highly to be prais'd:
Thy majesty, with boundless height, above our knowledge rais'd.

4 Renown'd for mighty acts, thy fame to future time extends;
From age to age thy glorious name successively descends.
5, 6 Whilst I thy glory and renown, and wondrous works exprest,
The world with me thy might shall own, and thy great pow'r confess.

7 The praise that to thy love belongs, they shall with joy proclaim;
Thy truth of all their grateful songs shall be the constant theme.

The Lord is good; fresh acts of grace his pity still supplies;
His anger moves with slowest pace, his willing mercy flies.

, 10 Thy love thro' earth extends its fame, to all thy works exprest;
These shew thy praise, whilst thy great name is by thy servants blest.
1 They, with the glorious prospect fir'd, shall of thy kingdom speak;
And thy great pow'r, by all admir'd, their lofty subject make.

2 God's glorious works of ancient date shall thus to all be known;
And thus his kingdom's royal state with public splendour shown.
3 His stedfast throne, from changes free, shall stand for ever fast;
His boundless sway no end shall see, but time itself out-last.

PART II.

4. 15 The Lord does them support that fall, and makes the prostrate rise;
For his kind aid all creatures call, who timely food supplies.
6 Whate'er their various wants require, with open hand he gives;
And so fulfils the just desire of ev'ry thing that lives.

7, 18 How holy is the Lord, how just, how righteous all his ways!
How nigh to him, who with firm trust for his assistance prays!
19 He grants the full desires of those who him with fear adore;
And will their troubles soon compose, when they his aid implore.

20 The Lord preserves all those with care whom grateful love employs;
But sinners, who his vengeance dare, with furious rage destroys.
21 My time to come, in praises spent, shall still advance his fame,
And all mankind, with one consent, for ever bless his name.

PSALM CXLVI.

1, 2 O PRAISE the Lord, and thou, my soul, for ever bless his name;
His wondrous love, while life shall last my constant praise shall claim
3 On Kings, the greatest sons of men, let none for aid rely;
They cannot save in dang'rous times, nor timely help apply.

4 Depriv'd of breath, to dust they turn, and there neglected lie,
And all their thoughts and vain designs together with them die.
5 Then happy he, who Jacob's God for his protector takes;
Who still, with well-plac'd hope, the Lord his constant refuge makes.

6 The Lord, who made both heav'n and earth, and all that they contain,
Will never quit his stedfast truth, nor make his promise vain.
7 The poor opprest, from all their wrongs are eas'd by his decree;
He gives the hungry needful food, and sets the pris'ners free.

8 By him the blind receive their sight, the weak and fall'n he rears;
With kind regard and tender love he for the righteous cares.
9 The strangers he preserves from harm, the orphan kindly treats,
Defends the widow, and the wiles of wicked men defeats.

10 The God that does in Sion dwell is our eternal King:
From age to age his reign endures: let all his praises sing.

PSALM CXLVII.

1 O PRAISE the Lord with hymns of joy, and celebrate his fame!
For pleasant, good, and comely 'tis to praise his holy name.

PSALM CXLVIII.

2 His holy city God will build, though level'd with the ground;
Bring back his people, though dispers'd through all the nations round.

3, 4 He kindly heals the broken hearts, and all their wounds doth close:
He tells the number of the stars, their sev'ral names he knows.
5, 6 Great is the Lord, and great his pow'r, his wisdom has no bound;
The meek he raises, and throws down the wicked to the ground.

7 To God, the Lord, a hymn of praise with grateful voices sing:
To songs of triumph tune the harp, and strike each warbling string.
8 He covers heav'n with clouds, and thence refreshing rains bestows:
Through him, on mountain-tops, the grass with wondrous plenty grows.

9 He savage beasts, that loosely range, with timely food supplies;
He feeds the ravens' tender brood, and stops their hungry cries.
10 He values not the warlike steed, but does his strength disdain;
The nimble foot, that swiftly runs, no prize from him can gain.

11 But he to him that fears his name, his tender love extends:
To him that on his boundless grace with stedfast hope depends.
12, 13 Let Sion and Jerusalem to God their praise address:
Who fenc'd their gates with massy bars, and does their children bless.

14, 15 Through all their borders he gives peace, with finest wheat they're fed;
He speaks the word, and what he wills is done as soon as said.
16 Large flakes of snow, like fleecy wool, descend at his command;
And hoary frost, like ashes spread, is scatter'd o'er the land.

17 When, join'd to these, he does his hail in little morsels break,
Who can against his piercing cold secure defences make?
18 He sends his word, which melts the ice, he makes his wind to blow:
And soon the streams, congeal'd before, in plenteous currents flow.

19 By him his statutes and decrees to Jacob's sons were shown;
And still to Israel's chosen seed his righteous laws are known.
20 No other nations this can boast; nor did he e'er afford
To heathen lands his oracles, and knowledge of his word.
Hallelujah.

PSALM CXLVIII.

1, 2 YE boundless realms of joy,
Exalt your Maker's fame;
His praise your song employ
Above the starry frame:
Your voices raise,
Ye Cherubim
And Seraphim,
To sing his praise.

3, 4 Thou moon that rul'st the night,
And sun that guid'st the day,
Ye glitt'ring stars of light,
To him your homage pay.
His praise declare,
Ye heav'ns above,
And clouds that move
In liquid air.

5, 6 Let them adore the Lord
And praise his holy name,
By whose almighty word
They all from nothing came;
And all shall last,
From changes free:
His firm decree
Stands ever fast.

7, 8 Let earth her tribute pay;
Praise him, ye dreadful whales,
And fish that thro' the sea
Glide swift with glitt'ring scales:
Fire, hail, and snow,
And misty air,
And winds that, where
He bids them, blow.

9, 10 By hills and mountains (all
In grateful concert join'd)
By cedars stately tall,
And trees for fruit design'd;
By ev'ry beast,
And creeping thing,
And fowl of wing,
His name be blest.

11, 12 Let all of royal birth,
With those of humbler frame,
And judges of the earth,
His matchless praise proclaim.
In this design
Let youths with maids,
And hoary heads
With children join.

13 United zeal be shown,
His wondrous fame to raise,
Whose glorious name alone
Deserves our endless praise.
Earth's utmost ends
His pow'r obey:
His glorious sway
The sky transcends.

14 His chosen saints to grace,
He sets them up on high,
And favours Israel's race,
Who still to him are nigh.
O therefore raise
Your grateful voice,
And still rejoice
The Lord to praise.

PSALM CXLIX.

1, 2 O PRAISE ye the Lord,
Prepare your glad voice
His praise in the great
Assembly to sing,
In our great Creator
Let Israel rejoice;
And children of Sion
Be glad in their king.

3, 4 Let them his great name
Extol in the dance;
With timbrel and harp
His praises express,
Who always takes pleasure
His saints to advance,
And with his salvation
The humble to bless.

5, 6 With glory adorn'd
His people shall sing
To God, who their beds
With safety does shield;
Their mouths fill'd with praises
Of him their great king;
Whilst a two-edged sword
Their right hand shall wield

7, 8 Just vengeance to take
For injuries past;
To punish those lands
For ruin design'd;
With chains, as their captives,
To tie their kings fast,
With fetters of iron
Their nobles to bind.

9 Thus shall they make good,
When them they destroy,
The dreadful decree
Which God does proclaim:
Such honour and triumph
His saints shall enjoy;
O therefore for ever
Exalt his great name.

PSALM CL.

1 O PRAISE the Lord in that blest place
From whence his goodness largely flows:
Praise him in heav'n, where he his face
Unveil'd in perfect glory shows.

2 Praise him for all the mighty acts,
Which he in our behalf has done;
His kindness this return exacts
With which our praise should equal run.

3 Let the shrill trumpet's warlike voice
Make rocks and hills his praise rebound
Praise him with harp's melodious noise,
And gentle psaltry's silver sound.

4 Let virgin troops soft timbrels bring,
And some with graceful motion dance;
Let instruments of various strings,
With organs join'd, his praise advance.

5 Let them who joyful hymns compose,
To cymbals set their songs of praise;
Cymbals of common use, and those
That loudly sound on solemn days.

6 Let all that vital breath enjoy,
The breath he does to them afford,
In just returns of praise employ:
Let ev'ry creature praise the Lord.

GLORIA PATRI.

COMMON MEASURE.

1 TO Father, Son, and Holy Ghost,
the God whom we adore;
Be glory as it was, is now,
and shall be evermore.

As the 100 PSALM.

3 To Father, Son, and Holy Ghost,
the God whom earth and heav'n adore,
Be glory, as it was of old,
is now, and shall be evermore.

As PSALM 37, and last part of PSALM 119.

4 To Father, Son, and Holy Ghost,
The God whom Heav'n's triumphant host,
and suff'ring saints on earth adore,
Be glory, as in ages past,
As now it is, and so shall last
when time itself must be no more.

As PSALM 148.

5 To God the Father, Son,
And Spirit, ever bless'd,
Eternal Three in One,
All worship be address'd,
As heretofore
It was, is now,
And shall be so
For evermore.

As PSALM 149.

6 By angels in heav'n
of ev'ry degree,
And saints upon earth,
All praise be addrest
To God in three persons,
One God ever blest,
As it has been, now is,
And always shall be.

THE END.

WHOLE BOOK

OF

PSALMS

COLLECTED INTO

ENGLISH METRE.

BY THOMAS STERNHOLD, JOHN HOPKINS,

AND OTHERS.

London:

PRINTED BY JOHN JARVIS, 1791.

Price One Shilling and Six Pence, unbound.

AN ALPHABETICAL TABLE,

Shewing how to find each Psalm by its Beginning.

THE PSALMS OF DAVID.

PSALM I. T. S.

1 THE man is blest that has not lent to wicked men his ear,
Nor led his life as sinners do, nor sat in scorner's chair;
2 But in the law of God the Lord doth set his whole delight,
And in the same doth exercise himself both day and night.

3 He shall be like a tree that is planted the rivers nigh,
Which in due season bringeth forth its fruit abundantly;
4 Whose leaf shall never fade nor fall, but flourishing shall stand:
Ev'n so all things shall prosper well that this man takes in hand.

5 As for ungodly men, with them it shall be nothing so;
But as the chaff, which by the wind is driven to and fro.
6 Therefore the wicked men shall not in judgment stand upright,
Nor in th' assembly of the just shall sinners come in sight.

7 For why? the way of godly men unto the Lord is known;
Whereas the way of wicked men shall quite be overthrown.

PSALM II. T. S.

1 WHY did the Gentiles tumults raise? what rage was in their brain?
Why do the people still contrive a thing that is but vain?
2 The kings and rulers of the earth conspire and are all bent
Against the Lord, and Christ his Son, whom he among us sent.

3 Shall we be bound to them? say they, let all their bonds be broke,
And of their doctrine and their law let us reject the yoke.
4 But he that in the heav'n doth dwell their doings will deride,
And make them all as mocking-stocks throughout the world so wide.

5 For in his wrath he shall reprove their pride and scornful way,
And in his fury trouble them, and unto them shall say,
6 I have anointed him my king upon my holy hill;
I will therefore, Lord, preach thy law according to thy will;

7 The law whereof the Lord himself hath thus said unto me,
Thou art my only Son, this day have I begotten thee:
8 All people I will give to thee, as heirs at thy request;
The ends and coasts of all the earth by thee shall be possest:

9 Thou shalt them bruise, ev'n like to those that under foot are trod:
And as a potter's vessel break them with an iron rod.
10 Now ye, O kings, and rulers all, be wise therefore and learn'd,
By whom the matters of the world are judged and discern'd.

11 See that ye serve the Lord above in trembling and in fear:
See that with rev'rence ye rejoice when ye to him draw near.
12 See that ye do embrace and kiss his Son without delay,
Lest in his wrath ye suddenly perish from the right way.

13 If once his wrath (but little) shall be kindled in his breast,
Then only they that trust in him shall happy be and blest.

PSALM III. T. S.

1 O LORD, how are my foes increas'd, who vex me more and more?
They break my heart when as they say, God can him not restore.
2 But thou, O Lord, art my defence, when I am hard bestead,
My worship and my honour both, and thou hold'st up my head.

3 Then with my voice unto the Lord I did both call and cry,
And he out of his holy hill did hear me instantly.
4 I laid me down, and quietly I slept and rose again;
For why? I know assuredly the Lord did me sustain.

5 If thousands up against me rise, I will not be afraid;
For thou art still my Lord and God, my Saviour and my aid.
6 Rise up therefore, save me, my God, to thee I make my pray'r,
For thou hast broke the cheeks and teeth of all that wicked are.

7 Salvation only doth belong to thee, O Lord, above,
Who on thy people dost bestow thy blessing and thy love.

PSALM IV. T. S.

1 O GOD, that art my righteousness, Lord, hear me when I call;
Thou hast set me at liberty when I was bound in thrall:
2 Have mercy, Lord, therefore, on me, and grant me my request,
For unto thee incessantly to cry I will not rest.

3 O mortal men, how long will ye my glory thus despise?
Why wander ye in vanity, and follow after lies?
4 Know ye that good and godly men the Lord doth take and chuse!
And when to him I make complaint he doth me not refuse.

5 Sin not, but stand in awe therefore, examine well your heart,
And in your chamber quietly see ye yourselves convert.
6 Offer to God the sacrifice of righteousness and praise,
And look that in the living Lord ye put your trust always.

7 The greater sort crave worldly goods, and riches do embrace;
But, Lord, grant us thy countenance, thy favour and thy grace:
8 For thou thereby shalt make my heart more joyful and more glad,
Than they that of their corn and wine full great increase have had.

9 In peace therefore lie down will I, taking my rest and sleep;
For thou only dost me, O Lord, preserve and safely keep.

PSALM V. T. S.

1 INCLINE thine ears, O Lord, and let my words have free access
To thee who art my God and king, from whom I seek redress.
2 Hear me betimes, Lord, tarry not, for I will have respect
My supplication in the morn to thee for to direct.

3 And I will patiently still trust in thee, my God alone;
Thou art not pleas'd with wickedness, and ill with thee dwells none:
4 Such as be foolish shall not stand in sight of thee, O Lord;
Vain workers of iniquity thou hast always abhorr'd:

5 The lyars and base flatterers shall be destroy'd by thee,
Blood-thirsty and deceitful men likewise shall hated be.

6 Therefore will I come to thy house, trusting upon thy grace,
And rev'rently will worship thee towards thy holy place.

7 Lord, lead me in thy righteousness, for to confound my foes;
Also the way that I shall walk before my face disclose:
8 For in their mouths there is no truth, their inward filth is great,
Their throat an open sepulchre, and tongues full of deceit.

9 Destroy their false conspiracies, that they may come to nought;
Subvert them in their heaps of sin, who have rebellion wrought;
10 But those that put their trust in thee, let them be glad always,
And render thanks for thy defence, and give thy name the praise.

11 For thou with favour wilt encrease the just and righteous still,
And with thy grace, as with a shield, defend him from all ill.

PSALM VI. T. S.

1 LORD, in thy wrath reprove me not, tho' I deserve thine ire,
Nor yet correct me in thy rage, O Lord, I thee desire:
2 For I am weak, therefore, O Lord, of mercy me forbear,
And heal me, Lord, for why? thou know'st my bones do quake for fear.

3 My soul is troubled very sore, and vex'd exceedingly;
But, Lord, how long wilt thou delay to cure my misery?
4 Lord, turn thee to thy wonted grace, some pity on me take;
O save me, not for my deserts, but for thy mercies' sake.

5 For why? no man among the dead remembereth thee at all;
Or who shall worship thee, O Lord, that in the pit do fall?
6 So grievous is my plaint and moan, that I grow wond'rous faint,
All the night long I wash my bed with tears of my complaint.

7 My sight is dim, and waxeth old with anguish of my heart,
For fear of them that be my foes, and would my soul subvert.
8 But now depart from me, all ye that work iniquity,
Because the Lord hath heard the voice of my complaint and cry:

9 He heard not only the request and prayer of my sad heart,
But it received at my hands, and took it in good part.
10 And now my foes that vexed me the Lord will soon defame,
And suddenly confound them all with great rebuke and shame.

PSALM VII. T. S.

1 O LORD my God, I put my trust and confidence in thee;
Save me from them that me pursue, and still deliver me:
2 Lest like a lion me be tear and rend in pieces small,
While there is none to succour me, and rid me out of thrall.

3 O Lord my God, if I have done the thing that is not right,
Or else if I be found in fault, or guilty in thy sight;
4 Or to my friend rewarded ill, or left him in distress,
Who me pursu'd most cruelly, and hated me causeless:

5 Then let my foe pursue my soul, let him my life down thrust
Unto the earth, and also lay mine honour in the dust.
6 Stand up, O Lord, in wrath, because my foes do rage so fast;
Unto the judgment rise for me which thou commanded hast.

7 Then shall great nations come to thee, and know thee by this thing,
If thou declare, for love of them, thyself as Lord and king.
8 And as thou art of all men judge, O Lord, now judge thou me,
According to my righteousness, and my integrity.

PART II.

9 Lord, cease the hate of wicked men, and be the just man's guide,
By whom the secrets of all hearts are searched and descry'd.
10 I take my help to come of God in all my pain and smart,
Who doth preserve all those that be of pure and perfect heart.

11 The just man and the wicked both God judgeth by his power,
So that he feels his mighty hand ev'n every day and hour.
12 Except he change his mind, I die: for ev'n as he thinks fit,
He whets his sword, he bends his bow, aiming where he may hit;

13 And doth prepare his mortal darts, his arrows keen and sharp,
For them that do me persecute, and do on mischief harp.
14 But lo, tho' he in travail be of his dev'lish forecast;
Yet of his mischief once conceiv'd he brings foth nought at last:

15 He digs a ditch, and makes it deep, in hope to hurt his brother;
But he shall fall into the pit that he digg'd up for other.
16 Thus wrong returneth to the hurt of him in whom it bred,
And all the mischief that he wrought shall fall on his own head.

17 I will give thanks to God, therefore, that judgeth righteously,
And with my song will praise the name, of him that is most high.

PSALM VIII. T. S.

1 O GOD our Lord, how wonderful are thy works ev'ry where!
Thy fame surmounts in dignity the highest heav'ns that are.
2 E'en by the mouth of sucking babes thou wilt confound thy foes;
For in those babes thy might is seen, thy graces they disclose.

3 And when I see the heav'ns above, the works of thine own hand,
The sun, the moon, and all the stars, in order as they stand;
4 Lord, what is man, that thou of him tak'st such abundant care!
Or what the son of man, whom thou to visit dost not spare!

5 For thou hast made him little less than angels in degree,
And thou hast also crowned him with glorious dignity.
6 Thou hast prefer'd him to be lord of all thy works, and thou
Hast in subjection unto him put all things here below.

7 As sheep, and neat, and all beasts else that in the field do feed,
Fowls of the air, fish in the sea, and all that therein breed:
8 O God our Lord, how excellent is thy most glorious Name
In all the earth! therefore we do praise and adore the same.

PSALM IX. T. S.

1 WITH heart and mouth to thee, O Lord, will I sing laud and praise,
And speak of all thy wondrous works, and them declare always.
2 I will be glad, and much rejoice in thee, O God most high,
And make my songs extol thy Name above the starry sky.

3 Because my foes are driven back and turned unto flight,
They do fall down, and are destroy'd by thy great pow'r and might.
4 Thou hast avenged all my wrong, my grief and all my grudge;
Thou dost with justice hear my cause most like a righteous judge.

5 Thou dost rebuke the heathen folk, and wicked so confound,
That afterwards the memory of them cannot be found.
6 Destructions to an end are come, and cities overthrown;
With them likewise are perished their fame and great renown.

7 Know thou that he who is above for evermore shall reign,
And in the seat of equity true judgment will maintain:
8 With justice he will keep and guide the world and every wight;
And so will yield with equity to every man his right.

9 He is protector of the poor, what time they be opprest;
He is in all adversity their refuge and their rest.
10 And they that know thy holy Name therefore shall trust in thee;
For thou forsakest not their suit in their necessity.

PART II.

11 Sing psalms therefore unto the Lord, who dwells on Sion hill;
Among the people all declare his noble acts and will.
12 For he is mindful of the blood of them that be opprest,
Forgetting not the humble man who seeks to him for rest.

13 Have mercy, Lord, on me because my foes do yet remain;
Who from the gates of death are wont to raise me up again:
14 In Sion that I may set forth thy praise with heart and voice;
And that in thy salvation great my soul may still rejoice.

15 The heathen stick fast in the pit which they themselves prepar'd,
And in the net that they did hide their own feet are ensnar'd.
16 By judgments great the Lord is known, whilst wicked men are caught,
And fast intangled in the work which their own hands have wrought.

17 The wicked and deceitful men go down to hell below,
And all the people of the world that God refuse to know.
18 But sure the Lord will not forget the poor man's grief and pain;
The patient people never look for help of him in vain.

19 O Lord, arise, lest men prevail that be of worldly might;
And let the heathen folk receive their judgment in thy sight.
20 Lord, strike such terror, fear and dread into their hearts and then
They will be forced to confess themselves to be but men.

PSALM X. T. S.

1 WHAT is the cause that thou, O Lord, so far off now dost stand?
Why hidest thou thy face in time when trouble is at hand?
2 The poor do perish by the proud and wicked men's desire;
Let them be taken in the craft which they themselves conspire.

3 For in the lust of his own heart th' ungodly doth delight,
So doth the wicked praise himself and doth the Lord despite.
4 He is so proud that right and wrong he setteth all apart:
Nay, nay, there is no God, saith he, for thus he thinks in heart.

5 Because his ways do prosper still, he doth thy laws neglect;
And with a blast doth puff against such as would him correct?
6 Tush, tush, saith he, I have no dread lest my estate should change;
And why? for all adversity to him is very strange.

7 His mouth is full of cursedness, of fraud, deceit, and guile;
Under his tongue there nothing is but what is base and vile.
8 He lieth hid in ways and holes to slay the innocent;
Against the poor that pass by him his cruel eyes are bent.

9 And, like a lion, privily lies lurking in his den,
That he may snare them in his net, and spoil poor harmless men.
10 With cunning craft and subtilty he croucheth down alway:
So are great heaps of poor men made by his strong pow'r a prey.

PART II.

11 Tush, God forgetteth this, saith he, therefore I may be bold;
His countenance is cast aside, he doth it not behold.
12 Arise, O Lord our God, in whom the poor man's hope doth rest;
Lift up thy hand, do not forget the poor that be opprest.

13 Why should the proud and wicked man blaspheme God's holy name,
Whilst in his heart he crieth, Tush, God cares not for the same?
14 But thou seest all their wickedness, and well dost understand,
That friendless and poor fatherless are left into thy hand.

15 Of wicked and malicious men then break the pow'r alway,
That they with their iniquity may perish and decay.
16 The Lord shall reign for evermore as king and God alone,
And he will chase out of the land the heathen folk each one.

17 Thou hearest, Lord, the poor's complaint, their prayer and their request;
Their hearts thou wilt confirm, until thine ears to hear be prest.
18 To judge the poor and fatherless and help them to their right,
That they may be no more oppress'd by men of worldly might.

PSALM XI. T. S.

1 IN God the Lord I put my trust, why say ye to my soul,
Unto the mountains swiftly fly as doth the winged fowl?
2 Behold, the wicked bend their bows, their arrows they prepare,
To shoot in secret at those, who sincere and upright are.

3 Of worldly hope all stays were shrunk, and clearly brought to nought;
Alas! the just and upright man, what evil hath he wrought?
4 But he that in his temple is most holy and most high,
And in the highest heav'ns doth sit in royal majesty.

5 The poor and simple man's estate considers in his mind,
And searches out full narrowly the manners of mankind;
6 And with a cheerful countenance the righteous man will use,
But in his heart he doth abhor all such as mischief muse;

And on the sinners casteth snares as thick as hail or rain,
Brimstone and fire, and whirlwinds great, appointed for their pain.
7 Ye see then how a righteous God doth righteousness embrace,
And unto just and upright men, shews forth his pleasant face.

PSALM XII. T. S.

1 HELP, Lord, for good and godly men do perish and decay,
And faith and truth from worldly men is parted clean away.
2 Whoso doth with his neighbour talk, 'tis all but vanity;
For ev'ry man bethinketh how to speak deceitfully.

3 But flatt'ring and deceitful lips, and tongues that be so stout
To speak proud words and make great brags, the Lord soon cuts them out.
4 For they say still, we will prevail our lips shall us extol;
Our tongues are ours, we ought to speak, what lord shall us controul?

5 But for the great complaint and cry of those that are opprest,
I will arise now, saith the Lord, and them restore to rest.
6 God's word is like to silver pure, that from the dross is try'd,
Which hath not less than seven times in the fire been purify'd.

7 Now since thy promise is to help, Lord, keep thy promise then,
And save us now and evermore from this ill kind of men.
8 For now the wicked world is full of mischiefs manifold,
Whilst vanity with worldly men so highly is extoll'd.

PSALM XIII. T. S.

1 HOW long wilt thou forget me, Lord? shall it for ever be?
How long dost thou intend to hide thy face away from me?
2 In heart and mind how long shall I with care tormented be?
And how long shall my deadly foe thus triumph over me?

3 Behold me now, O Lord my God, and hear me sore oppress'd;
Lighten my eyes, lest I do sleep as one by death possess'd:
4 Lest that my enemy do say, behold, I do prevail;
Lest they also that hate my soul rejoice to see me fail.

5 But from thy mercy and goodness my hope shall not depart;
In thy relief and saving health right glad shall be my heart.
6 I will give thanks unto the Lord, and praises to him sing,
Because he hath heard my request for ev'ry needful thing.

PSALM XIV. T. S.

1 THERE is no God, do foolish men affirm in their mad mood;
Their drifts are all corrupt and vain, not one of them doth good.
2 The Lord beheld from heaven most high the whole race of mankind,
And saw not one that sought indeed the living God to find:

3 They went all wide and were corrupt, and truly there was none
That in the world did any good, no, not so much as one.
4 Is all their judgment so far lost, that all work mischief still,
Eating my people ev'n as bread, not one to seek God's will?

5 When they thus rage, then suddenly great fear on them shall fall,
For God doth love the righteous men, and will preserve them all.
6 Ye mock the doings of the poor, to their reproach and shame,
Because they put their trust in God, and call upon his name.

7 But who shall give thy people health? and when wilt thou fulfil
Thy promise made to Israel from out of Sion hill?

8 For when thou shalt restore again such as were captive led,
Then Jacob shall therein rejoice, and Israel be glad.

PSALM XV. T. S.

1 WITHIN thy tabernacle, Lord, who shall inhabit still?
Or whom wilt thou receive to dwell in thy most holy hill?
2 The man whose life is uncorrupt, whose works are just and straight,
Whose heart doth think the very truth, and tongue speaks no deceit;

3 That to his neighbour doth no ill in body, goods, or name,
Nor willingly doth slanders raise which might impair the same;
4 That in his heart regardeth not malicious wicked men,
But those that love and fear the Lord, he maketh much of them;

5 His oath and all his promises that keepeth faithfully,
Altho' he make his cov'nant so that he doth lose thereby;
6 That putteth not to usury his money and his coin,
Nor for to hurt the innocent doth bribe nor yet purloin.

7 Whoso doth these things faithfully and turneth not therefrom,
Shall never perish in this world, nor that which is to come.

PSALM XVI. T. S.

1 LORD, keep me, for I trust in thee, and do confess indeed,
Thou art my God, and of my goods thou hast not any need:
2 Therefore I give them to the saints that in the world do dwell;
Namely, unto the faithful flock in virtue that excel.

3 Their sorrows shall be multiply'd who run so hastily
To offer to the idol gods, that are but vanity.
4 As for their bloody sacrifice and off'rings of that sort,
I will not touch, neither thereof shall my lips make report.

5 For why? the Lord the portion is of my inheritance,
And he it is that doth preserve my lot from all mischance.
6 The place wherein my lot is fall'n in beauty doth excel,
My heritage assign'd to me doth please me wondrous well.

7 I thank the Lord that caused me to understand the right;
For by this means my secret thoughts do teach me in the night.
8 I set the Lord still in my sight, and trust him over all;
For he doth stand at my right hand, therefore I shall not fall.

9 Wherefore my heart and tongue also rejoice exceedingly,
My flesh likewise doth rest in hope to rise again; for why?
10 Thou wilt not leave my soul in hell, because thou lovest me;
Nor yet wilt give thy Holy One corruption for to see;

11 But wilt me shew the way to life, where there is joy in store,
And where at thy right hand there are pleasures for evermore.

PSALM XVII. T. S.

1 O LORD, give ear to my just cause, attend unto my cry,
And hear the prayer I offer up to thee unfeignedly;
2 And let the judgment of my cause proceed always from thee,
And let thine eyes behold and clear truth and simplicity.

3 Thou hast well try'd me in the night, and yet couldst nothing find,
That I have spoken with my tongue, that was not in my mind.
4 As for the works of wicked men, and paths perverse and ill,
For love of thy most holy name I have refrained still.

5 Then in thy paths that be most pure guide me, Lord, and preserve,
That from the way wherein I walk my steps may never swerve.
6 For I do call to thee, O Lord, surely thou wilt me aid;
Then hear my prayer, and weigh right well the words that I have said.

7 O thou the Saviour of them all that put their trust in thee,
Declare thy strength on them that spurn against thy majesty.
8 O keep me as thou wouldest keep the apple of thine eye,
And under covert of thy wings defend me secretly.

PART II.

9 From wicked men that trouble me, and daily me annoy,
And from my foes that go about my soul for to destroy;
10 Who wallow in their worldly wealth, and are so full and fat,
That in their pride they do not spare to speak they care not what.

11 They lie in wait where I should pass, with craft me to confound;
And musing mischief in their minds, to cast me to the ground:
12 Much like a lion greedily that would his prey embrace,
Or lurking like a lion's whelp within some secret place.

13 Up, Lord, in haste, prevent my foe, and cast him at my feet;
Save thou my soul from the ill man, and with thy sword him smite:
14 Deliver me, Lord, by thy pow'r, out of these tyrants' hands,
Who now so long time reigned have, and keep us in their bands;

15 I mean from worldly men, who do in worldly goods abound,
That have no hope or joy but what in this life can be found.
16 Thou of thy store their bellies fill'st with pleasure to their mind;
Their children have enough, and leave the rest to theirs behind.

17 But as for me, I will behold thy face in righteousness,
And shall be satisfy'd when I awake with thy likeness.

PSALM XVIII. T. S.

1 O GOD, my strength and fortitude, of force I must love thee;
Thou art my castle and defence in my necessity.
2 My God, my rock, in whom I trust, the worker of my wealth,
My refuge, buckler, and my shield, the horn of all my health.

3 When I sing praise unto the Lord, most worthy to be serv'd,
Then from my foes I am right sure that I shall be preserv'd.
4 The pangs of death did compass me, and bound me every where,
The flowing waves of wickedness did put me in great fear:

5 The sly and subtle snares of hell were round about me set,
And for my life there was prepar'd a deadly trapping net:
6 I thus beset with pain and grief did pray to God for grace,
And he forthwith heard my complaint out of his holy place.

7 Such is his power, that in his wrath he made the earth to quake,
Yea, the foundation of the mount of Basan for to shake:

8 Forth from his nostrils went a smoke, when kindled was his ire,
And from his mouth came burning coals of hot consuming fire.

9 The Lord descended from above, and bow'd the heav'ns most high;
And underneath his feet he cast the darkness of the sky;
10 On cherubs and on cherubims full royally he rode,
And on the wings of mighty winds came flying all abroad:

PART II.

11 And like a den most dark he made his hid and secret place,
With waters black and airy clouds encompassed he was.
12 At his bright presence did thick clouds in haste away retire,
And in the stead thereof there came hailstones and coals of fire.

13 The fiery darts and thunderbolts disperse them here and there,
And with his frequent lightnings he doth put them in great fear.
14 When thou, O Lord, with great rebuke thy anger dost declare,
The springs and the foundations of the world discover'd are.

15 And from above the Lord sent down to fetch me from below,
And pluck'd me out of waters great that would me overflow;
16 And me deliver'd from my foes that sought me to enthral,
Yea, from such foes as were too strong for me to deal withal.

17 They did prevent me evermore in time of my great grief;
But yet the Lord is my defence, my succour and relief.
18 He brought me forth in open place, that so I might be free,
And kept me safe, because he had a favour unto me.

19 According to my innocence, so did he me regard;
And to the cleanness of my hands he gave me my reward;
20 For that I walked in his ways, and in his paths have trod,
And not departed wickedly from him that is my God:

PART III.

21 But evermore I have respect to his law and decree,
His statutes and commandments I cast not away from me;
22 But pure and clean and uncorrupt appear'd before his face,
And did refrain from wickedness and sin in ev'ry case.

23 The Lord will therefore me reward as I have done aright,
And to the cleanness of my hands appearing in his sight.
24 For, Lord, with him that holy is wilt thou be holy too,
And with the good and virtuous man thou wilt uprightly do;

25 And for the loving and elect thy favour wilt reserve,
And thou wilt use the wicked men as wicked men deserve.
26 For thou dost save the simple folk in trouble when they lie,
And dost bring down the countenance of them that look full high.

27 The Lord will light my candle so, that it shall shine full bright;
The Lord my God will make also my darkness to be light.
28 For by thy help an host of men discomfit, Lord, I shall;
By thee I scale and over-leap the strength of any wall.

29 Unspotted are the ways of God, his word is purely try'd;
He is a sure defence to such as in his faith abide.

30 For who is God, except the Lord? for other there is none;
Or else who is omnipotent, saving our God alone?

PART IV.

31 The God that girdeth me with strength is he that I do mean;
That all the ways wherein I walk did evermore keep clean;
32 That made my feet like to the hart's in swiftness of my pace,
And for my safety brought me forth into an open place.

33 He did in order put my hands in battle for to fight;
To break in sunder bars of brass he gave my arms the might.
34 Thou teachest me thy saving health, thy right hand is my tow'r;
Thy love and gentleness also doth still increase my pow'r;

35 And under me thou makest plain the way where I should go,
So that my feet shall never slip, nor wander to and fro:
36 And fiercely I pursue and take my foes that me annoy'd,
And from the field do not return till they be all destroy'd.

37 So I suppress and wound my foes, that they can rise no more;
For underneath my feet they fall, I wound them all so sore.
38 For thou hast girded me with strength, unto the battle, and
Thou wilt throw down my enemies that do against me stand.

39 Lord, thou hast given me the necks of all my enemies;
That so I might destroy all those that up against me rise.
40 They call'd for help, but none gave ear, nor came to their relief;
Yea, to the Lord they call'd for aid, yet heard he not their grief.

PART V.

41 And still, like dust before the wind, I drive them under feet,
And sweep them out like filthy dirt that lieth in the street.
42 Thou keep'st me from seditious folk, that still in strife are led:
And thou dost of the heathen folk appoint me to be head:

43 A people strange, to me unknown, and yet they shall me serve,
And at the first obey my word, whereas my own will swerve.
44 I shall be irksome to my own, they will not see my light;
But wander wide out of the way, and hide them out of sight.

45 But blessed be the living Lord, most worthy of all praise,
He is my rock and saving health, praised be he always.
46 For it is he that gave me pow'r revenged for to be,
And with his holy word subdu'd the people unto me.

47 And from my foe deliver'd me, and set me over those
That cruel and ungodly were, and up against me rose.
48 And for this cause, O Lord my God, to thee give thanks I shall,
And sing out praises to thy name among the Gentiles all.

49 Deliv'rance great thou giv'st the king, and dost reserve in store
Mercy for thine anointed, and his seed for evermore.

PSALM XIX. T. S.

1 THE heav'ns and firmament on high do wondrously declare
God's glory and omnipotence, his works and what they are.
2 The wondrous works of God appear by ev'ry day's success.
The nights likewise which their race run the self-same thing express.

3 There is no language, tongue, or speech, where their sound is not heard;
In all the earth and coasts thereof their knowledge is conferr'd,
4 In them the Lord made for the sun a place of great renown,
Who like a bridegroom ready trimm'd comes from his chamber down.

5 And as a valiant champion, who would to honour rise,
With joy doth haste to take in hand some noble enterprise:
6 And all the sky from end to end he compasseth about;
Nothing can hide it from his heat, but he will find it out.

7 How perfect is the law of God! his covenant is sure,
Converting souls, and making wise the simple and obscure.
8 The Lord's commands are righteous, and rejoice the heart likewise;
His precepts are most pure, and do give light unto the eyes.

9 The fear of God is excellent, and ever doth endure;
The judgments of the Lord also most righteous are and pure;
10 And more to be desired are than much fine gold alway;
The honey and the honey-comb are not so sweet as they.

11 By them thy servant is forewarn'd to have God in regard,
And in performance of the same there shall be great reward.
12 But Lord! what earthly man doth know the errors of his life?
Then cleanse me from my secret sins, which are in me most rife:

13 And keep me, that presumptuous sins prevail not over me;
And so shall I be innocent, and great offences flee.
14 Accept my mouth and heart also, my words and thoughts each one;
For my redeemer and my strength, O Lord, thou art alone.

PSALM XX. T. S.

1 IN trouble and adversity the Lord God hear thee still;
The majesty of Jacob's God defend thee from all ill:
2 And send thee from his holy place his help at ev'ry need;
And so in Sion 'stablish thee, and make thee strong indeed.

3 Rememb'ring well the sacrifice that now to him is done,
And so receive most graciously thy offerings each one,
4 According to thy heart's desire the Lord grant unto thee,
And all thy counsel and thy mind full well perform may he.

5 We will rejoice when thou us sav'st, and banners will display
Unto the Lord, who thy requests fulfilled hath alway.
6 The Lord will his anointed save, I know well by his grace,
And send him help by his right-hand out of his holy place.

7 In chariots some put confidence, and some in horses trust;
But we remember God our Lord, who keepeth promise just.
8 They all fall down, but we do rise, and stand up stedfastly:
O save and help us, Lord and King, when we to thee do cry.

PSALM XXI. T. S.

1 O LORD, how joyful is the king in thy strength and thy power,
Exceedingly he doth rejoice in thee his Saviour.
2 For thou hast given unto him his godly heart's desire;
To him thou nothing hast deny'd of that he did require.

3 Thou didst prevent him with thy gifts and blessings manifold,
And thou hast set upon his head a crown of perfect gold.
4 And when he asked life of thee, thereof thou mad'st him sure,
To have long life, yea, such a life as ever shall endure.

5 Great is his glory by thy help, thy benefit and aid;
Great worship and great honour both thou hast upon him laid.
6 Thou wilt give him felicity that never shall decay,
And with thy cheerful countenance wilt comfort him alway.

7 Because the king doth strongly trust in God for to prevail,
Therefore his goodness and his grace to save him will not fail.
8 Thy enemies shall feel thy force, and those that thee withstand;
Find out thy foes, and let them feel the power of thy right hand.

9 And like an oven, burn them, Lord, in fiery flame and fume;
Thy anger shall destroy them all, and fire shall them consume.
10 And thou shalt root out of the earth their fruit that should increase,
And from the number of thy folk their seed shall end and cease,

11 For they much mischief did contrive against thy holy name;
Yet they did fail, and had no power for to perform the same:
12 But as a mark thou shalt them set in a most open place,
And charge thy bow-strings readily against their very face.

13 Be thou exalted, Lord, in thy own strength, which is our tower;
So shall we sing right solemnly, praising thy might and power.

PSALM XXII. T. S.

1 O GOD my God, wherefore dost thou forsake me utterly?
And helpest not when I do make my great complaint and cry?
2 To thee my God, ev'n all day long I do both cry and call;
I cease not all the night, and yet thou hearest not at all.

3 But thou that in thy holy place for evermore dost dwell,
Thou art the joy, the comfort and glory of Israel;
4 And him in whom our fathers old had all their hope and stay,
Who, when they put their trust in thee, delivered'st them all way.

5 They were preserved ever when they called on thy name;
And for the faith they had in thee they were not put to shame.
6 But I am now become more like, a worm than to a man;
An outcast whom the people scorn with all the spite they can.

7 All men despise as they behold me walking on the way,
They grin, make mouths, and nod their heads, and on this wise do say,
8 This man did glory in the Lord, his favour and his love;
Let him redeem and help him now, his power if he will prove.

9 But from the prison of the womb I was by thee releast,
Thou didst preserve me still in hope, whilst I did suck the breast,
10 I was committed from my birth with thee to have abode;
Since I came from my mother's womb thou hast been still my God.

PART II.

11 Then, Lord, depart not now from me, in this my present grief,
Since I have none to be my help, my succour and relief.

12 For many bulls do compass me that be full strong of head;
Yea, bulls so fat, as tho' they had in Basan field been fed.

13 They gape upon me greedily, as tho' they would me slay,
Ev'n like a lion roaring out and ramping for his prey.
14 But I drop down like water shed, my joints in sunder break;
My heart doth in my body melt like wax, I am so weak;

15 My strength doth like a potsherd dry, my tongue it cleaveth fast
Unto my jaws, and I am brought to dust of death at last.
16 For many dogs do compass me, in council they do meet,
Conspiring still against my life, piercing my hands and feet.

17 I was tormented so, that I might all my bones have told,
Whilst they do look and stare at me when they do me behold.
18 My garments they divided have in parts among them all,
And for my coat they did cast lots to whom it should befall.

19 Therefore I pray thee be not far from me at my great need;
But rather, since thou art my strength, to help me, Lord, make speed
20 And from the sword save thou my soul by thy might and thy pow'r,
And ever keep my darling dear from dogs that would devour;

21 And from the lion's mouth that would me all in sunder tear,
From midst the horns of unicorns, O Lord, thou didst me hear.
22 Then shall I to my brethren all thy majesty record,
And in thy church shall praise the name of thee the living Lord.

PART III.

23 All ye that fear him, praise the Lord, thou Jacob, him adore,
And all ye seed of Israel, fear him for evermore.
24 For he despiseth not the poor, he hideth not away
His countenance when they do call, but hears them when they pray.

25 Among the folk that fear the Lord I will therefore proclaim
Thy praise, and keep my promise made for setting forth thy name.
26 The poor shall eat and be suffic'd; such as their minds do give
To seek the Lord and praise his name, their hearts shall ever live.

27 The coasts of all the earth shall praise the Lord and seek his grace,
The heathen folk shall worship all before his blessed face.
28 The kingdoms of the heathen folk the Lord shall have therefore;
And he shall be their governor, and king for evermore.

29 The rich man of his goodly gifts shall taste and feed also,
And in his presence worship him, and bow their knees full low.
30 And all that shall go down to dust of life by him shall taste;
A seed shall serve and worship him, till time away shall waste:

31 They shall declare and plainly shew his truth and righteousness
Unto a people yet unborn, who shall his name confess.

PSALM XXIII. W. W.

1 THE Lord is only my support, and he that doth me feed;
How can I then lack any thing whereof I stand in need?
2 In pastures green he feedeth me, where I do safely lie,
And after leads me to the streams which run most pleasantly.

3 And when I find myself near lost, then doth he me home take,
Conducting me in his right paths, ev'n for his own name's sake.
4 And tho' I were ev'n at death's door, yet would I fear no ill;
For both thy rod and shepherd's crook afford me comfort still.

5 Thou hast my table richly spread in presence of my foe,
Thou hast my head with balm refresh'd, my cup doth overflow.
6 And finally, whilst breath doth last thy grace shall me defend;
And in the house of God will I my life for ever spend.

ANOTHER OF THE SAME BY T. S.

1 MY shepherd is the living Lord, nothing therefore I need:
In pastures fair, near pleasant streams, he setteth me to feed.
2 He shall convert and glad my soul, and bring my mind in frame,
To walk in paths of righteousness, for his most holy name.

3 Yea, though I walk in vale of death, yet will I fear no ill;
Thy rod and staff do comfort me, and thou art with me still:
4 And in the presence of my foes my table thou dost spread;
Thou dost fill full my cup, and thou anointed hast my head.

5 Thro' all my life thy favour is so frankly shew'd to me,
That in thy house for evermore my dwelling-place shall be.

PSALM XXIV. J. H.

1 THE earth is all the Lord's, with all her store and furniture;
Yea, his is all the world, and all that therein doth endure:
2 For he has fastly founded it above the seas to stand,
And plac'd below the liquid floods to flow beneath the land.

3 Who is the man, O Lord, that shall ascend unto thy hill?
Or pass into thy holy place, there to continue still?
4 Ev'n he whose hands and heart are pure, which nothing doth defile,
His soul not set on vanity, and hath not sworn to guile:

5 Him that is such a one the Lord most highly will regard,
And from his God and Saviour shall receive a just reward.
6 This is the generation of them that do seek his grace,
Ev'n them that with an upright heart, O Jacob, seek thy face.

7 Ye gates and everlasting doors, lift up your heads on high;
Then shall the king of glorious state come in triumphantly.
8 Who is the king of glorious state? the great and mighty Lord,
The mighty Lord in battle strong and trial of the sword.

9 Ye gates and everlasting doors, lift up your heads on high;
Then shall the king of glorious state come in triumphantly.
10 Who is the king of glorious state? the Lord of Hosts it is,
The kingdom and the royalty of glorious state is his.

PSALM XXV. T. S.

1 I LIFT my heart to thee, my God and guide most just,
Now suffer me to take no shame, for in thee I do trust.
2 Let not my foes rejoice, nor make a scorn of me;
And let them not be overthrown that put their trust in thee.

3 But shame shall them befal who harm them wrongfully ;
Therefore thy paths and thy right ways unto me, Lord, descry.
4 Direct me in thy truth, and teach me, I thee pray ;
Thou art my Saviour and my God, on thee I wait alway.

5 Thy mercies manifold remember, Lord, I pray ;
In pity thou art plentiful, and so hast been alway.
6 Remember not the faults and frailty of my youth,
Call not to mind how ignorant I have been of thy truth :

7 Nor after my deserts let me thy mercy find ;
But of thine own benignity, Lord, have me in thy mind.
8 His mercy is full sweet, his truth a perfect guide ;
Therefore the Lord will sinners teach, and such as go aside.

9 The humble he will teach his precepts to obey,
He will direct in all his paths the lowly man alway.
10 For all the ways of God both truth and mercy are,
To them that do his covenant and statutes keep with care.

PART II.

11 Now for thy holy name, O Lord, I thee intreat
To grant me pardon for my sin, for it is very great.
12 Whoso doth fear the Lord, by him he shall be kept
To lead his life in such a way as he doth best accept :

13 His soul shall evermore in goodness dwell and stand ;
His seed and his posterity inherit shall the land.
14 All those that fear the Lord know his secret intent,
And unto them he doth declare his will and testament.

15 My eyes and thankful heart to him I will advance,
That pluck'd my feet out of the snare of sin and ignorance.
16 With mercy me behold, to thee I make my moan ;
For I am poor and desolate, and comfortless alone.

17 The troubles of my heart are multiply'd indeed ;
Bring me out of this misery, necessity and need.
18 Behold my poverty, my anguish and my pain ;
Remit my sin and my offence, and make me clean again.

19 O Lord, behold my foes, how they do still increase,
Pursuing me with deadly hate, that fain would live in peace.
20 Preserve and keep my soul, and still deliver me ;
And let me not be overthrown, because I trust in thee.

21 Let truth and uprightness for ever wait on me,
Because my hope and confidence hath always been in thee.
22 Deliver, Lord, thy folk, and send them some relief,
I mean thy chosen Israel, from all their pain and grief.

PSALM XXVI. T. S.

1 LORD, be my judge, and thou shalt see my paths be right and plain :
I trust in God, and hope that he with strength will me sustain.
2 Prove me, my God, I thee desire my ways to search and try,
As men do prove their gold with fire, my heart and reins espy.

3 Thy loving-kindness in my sight I do behold always;
I ever walked in thy truth, and will do all my days.
4 I do not love to haunt or use with men whose deeds are vain;
To come in house I do refuse with the deceitful train.

5 I much abhor the wicked sort, their deeds I do despise;
I do not once to them resort, that hurtful things devise.
6 My hands I wash, and do proceed in works to walk upright;
Then to thy altar I make speed, to offer there in sight:

7 That I may speak and preach the praise that doth belong to thee,
And so declare how wondrous ways thou hast been good to me.
8 O God, thy house I love most dear, to me it doth excel;
My chief delight is to be near the place where thou dost dwell.

9 O shut not up my soul with them in sin that take their fill,
Nor yet my life among those men that seek much blood to spill.
10 For in their hands much mischief is, their lives therewith abound,
And nothing else in their right hand but bribes are to be found.

11 But I resolve in righteousness my time and days to spend:
Therefore, that I may not transgress, let thy grace me defend.
12 My foot is stay'd for all assays, it standeth well and right:
Wherefore to God will I give praise in all the people's sight.

PSALM XXVII. J. H.

1 THE Lord is both my health and light, shall man make me dismay'd?
Since God doth give me strength and might, why should I be afraid?
2 While that my foes with all their strength began with me to brawl,
Thinking to eat me up, at length themselves have caught the fall.

3 Tho' they encamp'd against me lie, my heart is not afraid;
And if in battle they will try, I trust in God for aid.
4 One thing of God I do require, that he will not deny;
For which I pray and will desire, till he to me apply:

5 That I within his holy place my life throughout may dwell;
To see the beauty of his face, and view his temple well.
6 In time of dread he shall me hide within his place most pure,
And keep me secret by his side, as on a rock most sure.

7 At length I know the Lord's good grace shall make me strong and stout,
My foes to foil and clean deface that compass me about.
8 Therefore within his house will I give sacrifice of praise;
With psalms and songs I will apply to laud the Lord always.

PART II.

9 Lord, hear the voice of my request, for which to thee I cry;
Have mercy, Lord, on me opprest, and help me speedily.
10 My heart confesseth unto thee, I sue to have thy grace;
Then seek my face, saidst thou to me; Lord I will seek thy face.

11 In wrath turn not thy face away, nor suffer me to slide;
My help thou hast been to this day, be still my God and guide.
12 When both my parents me forsake, and cast me off at large,
Even then the Lord himself doth take of me the care and charge.

13 Teach me, O Lord, the way to thee, and lead me on forth-right,
For fear of such as watch for me, to trap me if they might.
14 O leave me not unto the will of them that be my foes;
For they devise against me still false witness to depose.

15 I utterly should faint, but that this hope supporteth me,
That in the land wherein I live God's goodness I shall see.
16 Trust still in God, whose whole thou art, his will abide thou must;
He will support and heal thy heart, if thou in him do trust.

PSALM XXVIII. T. S.

1 THOU art, O Lord, my strength and stay, the succour which I crave;
Neglect me not, lest I be like them that are laid in grave.
2 My voice and supplications hear, when unto thee I cry,
When I lift up my hands unto thy holy ark most high.

3 Repute me not among those men in sin that take their fill,
That speak right fair unto their friends, but think in heart full ill.
4 According to those wicked deeds which they did most regard,
And after their inventions, Lord, let them receive reward.

5 Because they never mind the works of God, he will therefore,
Instead of building of them up, destroy them evermore.
6 To render thanks unto the Lord how great a cause have I,
My voice, my prayer and my complaint that heard so willingly!

7 He is my shield and fortitude, my buckler in distress;
My heart rejoiceth greatly, and my song shall him confess.
8 He is our strength and our defence, our foes for to resist,
The health and the salvation of his own elect by Christ.

9 Thy people and thy heritage, Lord, bless, guide and preserve;
Increase them, Lord, and rule their hearts, that they may never swerve.

PSALM XXIX. T. S.

1 GIVE to the Lord, ye potentates, give ye with one accord
All praise and honour, might and strength unto the living Lord:
2 Give glory to his holy Name, and honour him alone;
Give worship to his Majesty, within his holy throne.

3 His voice doth rule the waters all, as he himself doth please;
He doth prepare the thunder-claps, and governs all the seas.
4 The voice of God is of great force, and wondrous excellent;
It is most mighty in effect, and most magnificent.

5 The voice of God doth rend and break the cedar-trees so long,
The cedar-trees of Lebanon, which are both high and strong:
6 And makes them leap like as a calf, or as the unicorn;
Not only trees, but mountains great, whereon the trees are born.

7 His voice divides the flames of fire, and shakes the wilderness:
It makes the desert quake for fear, that Cades called is:
8 It makes the hinds for fear to calve, and coverts plain appear;
And in his temple every man speaks of his glory there.

9 The Lord doth sit upon the floods their fury to restrain;
And he likewise as Lord and King for evermore shall reign.

10 The Lord will give his people strength,
whereby they shall increase;
And he will bless his chosen flock
with everlasting peace.

PSALM XXX. J. H.

1 ALL laud and praise with heart and voice,
O Lord, I give to thee,
Who didst not make my foes rejoice,
but hast exalted me.
2 O Lord my God, to thee I cry'd
in all my pain and grief;
Thou gav'st an ear, and didst provide
to ease me with relief.

3 Thou, Lord, hast brought my soul from hell,
and thou the same didst save
From them that in the pit do dwell,
and kept'st me from the grave.
4 Sing praise, ye saints, that prove and see
the goodness of the Lord;
In honour of his Majesty
rejoice with one accord.

5 For why? his anger but a space
doth last, ceasing again;
But in his favour and his grace
always doth life remain.
6 Tho' heaviness and pangs full sore
abide with us all night,
The Lord to joy shall us restore,
before the day be light.

7 When I enjoy'd the world at will,
thus would I boast and say,
Tush, I am sure to feel no ill,
my wealth shall not decay;
8 For thou, O Lord, of thy good grace
didst send me strength and aid:
But when thou turn'dst away thy face,
my mind was sore dismay'd.

9 Wherefore again then did I cry
to thee, O Lord of might,
And my complaints did multiply,
praying both day and night:
10 What gain is in my blood, said I,
if death destroy my days?
Can dust declare thy Majesty,
or give thy truth its praise?

11 Wherefore, my God, some pity take,
O Lord, I thee desire;
Do not, O Lord, my soul forsake,
of thee I help require.
12 Then thou didst turn my grief and woe
into a cheerful voice;
My sackcloth didst take off also,
and mad'st me to rejoice.

13 Wherefore my soul incessantly
shall sing unto thy praise;
O Lord my God, to thee will I
give laud and thanks always.

PSALM XXXI. J. H.

1 O LORD, I put my trust in thee,
let nothing work me shame;
As thou art just, deliver me,
and set me free from blame.
2 Hear me, O Lord, and that right soon,
to help me make good speed;
Be thou my rock and house of stone,
my fence in time of need.

3 For why? as stones thy strength is try'd,
thou art my fort and tower;
For thy name's sake be thou my guide,
and lead me in thy power.
4 Pluck thou my feet out of the snare
which they for me have laid;
Thou art my strength, and all my care
is for thy mighty aid.

5 Into thy hands, Lord, I commit
my soul, which is thy due,
Because thou hast redeemed it,
O Lord my God most true.
6 I hate such folk as will not part
from things to be abhorr'd;
When they on trifles set their heart,
my trust is in the Lord.

7 For I will in thy mercy joy,
I see it doth excel;
Thou seest when aught would me annoy,
and know'st my soul full well.
8 Thou hast not left me in their hand
that would me overcharge;
But thou hast set me out of band,
to walk abroad at large.

PART II.

9 Great grief, O Lord, doth me assail, some pity on me take;
My eyes wax dim, my sight doth fail, my heart with fear doth ache;
10 My life is worn with grief and pain, my years in woe are past,
My strength is gone, and thro' disdain my bones corrupt and waste.

11 Among my foes I am a scorn, my friends are all dismay'd;
My neighbours and my kinsmen born to see me are afraid.
12 As men once dead are out of mind, so am I now forgot;
As little use of me they find, as of a broken pot.

13 I heard the brags of all the rout, their threats my mind did fray,
How they conspir'd and went about to take my life away.
14 But, Lord, I trust in thee for aid, not to be overtrod;
For I confess and still have said, thou art the Lord my God.

15 The length of all my life and age, O Lord, is in thy hand;
Defend me from the wrath and rage of them that me withstand.
16 To me thy servant, Lord, express and shew thy joyful face,
And save me, Lord, for thy goodness, thy mercy and thy grace.

PART III.

17 Lord, let me not be put to shame, because on thee I call,
But let the wicked bear the blame, and into the grave fall.
18 O Lord, make dumb their lips out-right who given are to lies,
And cruelly with pride and spite against the just devise.

19 How plentiful thy mercies be laid up for thy children,
That fear and put their trust in thee before the sons of men!
20 Thy presence shall them fence and guide from all proud brags and wrongs,
Within thy place thou shalt them hide from all the strife of tongues.

21 Thanks to the Lord that hath declar'd on me his grace so far,
Me to defend with watch and ward, as in a town of war.
22 Thus did I say both day and night, when I was sore opprest,
Lo, I am clean cast out of sight, yet heard'st thou my request.

23 Ye saints, love ye the Lord alway, the faithful he doth guide,
And to the proud he doth repay according to their pride.
24 Be of good courage, all ye just, on God your strength depend:
For those in him that put their trust he ever will defend.

PSALM XXXII. T. S.

1 THE man is blest whose wickedness the Lord forgiven hath,
And he whose sin is likewise hid, and cover'd from his wrath;
2 And blest is he to whom the Lord imputeth not his sin,
Who in his heart hath hid no guile, nor fraud is found therein.

3 For whilst that I kept close my sin in silence and constraint,
My bones did waste and wear away with daily moan and plaint.
4 Both night and day thy hand on me so grievous was and smart,
My moisture like the summer's heat to dryness did convert.

5 I did therefore confess my faults, and all my sins reveal,
Then thou, O Lord, didst me forgive, and all my sins conceal.

6 The humble man shall pray therefore, and seek thee in due time,
So that the floods of waters great shall have no power on him.

7 When trouble and adversity do compass me about,
Thou art my refuge and my joy, and thou didst rid me out.
8 Come hither, and I will thee teach how thou shalt walk aright;
I will thee guide, as I myself have learn'd by proof and sight:

9 Be not so rude and ignorant as is the horse and mule,
Whose mouth without a rein or bit from harm thou canst not rule.
10 The wicked man shall manifold sorrows and grief sustain;
But unto him that trusts in God his goodness shall remain.

11 Be joyful therefore in the Lord, ye just, lift up your voice;
And ye of pure and perfect heart, with cheerfulness rejoice.

PSALM XXXIII. J. H.

1 YE righteous, in the Lord rejoice; it is a seemly sight
That upright men with thankful voice should praise the Lord of might.
2 Praise ye the Lord with harp, and sing to him with psaltery,
With ten-string'd instrument sounding praise ye the Lord most high.

3 Sing to the Lord a song most new, with courage give him praise,
For why? his word is ever true, his works and all his ways:
4 Both judgment, equity and right he ever lov'd and will,
And with his gifts he doth delight the earth throughout to fill.

5 For by the word of God alone the heav'ns above were wrought,
Their hosts and powers ev'ry one his breath to pass has brought;
6 The waters great gather'd hath he on heaps within the shore,
And hid them in the depth to be as in a house of store.

7 Let all the earth then fear the Lord, and keep his righteous law,
And all the world with one accord dread him and stand in awe:
8 What he commanded, wrought it was at once with utmost speed;
What he doth will is brought to pass with full effect indeed.

9 The counsels of the nations rude the Lord doth bring to nought,
He doth defeat the multitude of their device and thought:
10 But his decrees continue still, they never slack nor 'swage;
The motions of his mind and will take place in ev'ry age.

PART II.

11 Blessed are they to whom the Lord as God and guide is known,
Whom he doth chuse of mere accord to take them as his own.
12 The Lord from heav'n did cast his sight on mortal men by birth,
Beholding from his seat of might the dwellers on the earth;

13 The Lord, I say, whose hand hath wrought man's heart, and doth it frame,
'Tis he alone doth know the thought and working of the same.
14 A king that trusteth in his host shall nought prevail at length,
The man that of his might doth boast shall fail for all his strength:

15 The troops of horsemen all shall fail, their sturdy steeds shall swerve;
The strength of horse shall not prevail the rider to preserve:
16 But lo, the eyes of God attend and watch to aid the just,
With such as fear him to offend, and on his goodness trust;

17 That he of death and great distress may set their souls from dread,
And if that dearth their land oppress in hunger them to feed
18 Wherefore our soul doth whole depend on God our strength and stay:
He is our shield, us to defend, and drive all darts away.

19 Our joyful souls alway proclaim his power and his might:
For why? in his most holy name we hope and much delight.
20 Therefore let thy goodness, O Lord, still present with us be,
As we always with one accord do only trust in thee.

PSALM XXXIV. T. S.

1 I WILL give laud and honour both unto the Lord always,
My mouth also for evermore shall speak unto his praise.
2 I do delight to praise the Lord, in soul, in heart, in voice,
That humble men may hear thereof, and heartily rejoice.

3 Therefore see that ye magnify with me the living Lord;
Let us exalt his holy name always with one accord.
4 For I myself besought the Lord, he answer'd me again,
And me deliver'd speedily from all my fear and pain.

5 Whoso they be that him behold, shall see his light most clear;
Their countenance shall not be dash'd, they never need to fear.
6 The poor distressed man for help unto the Lord doth call,
Who doth him hear without delay, and rids him out of thrall.

7 The angel of the Lord doth pitch his tents in ev'ry place,
To save all such as do him fear, that nothing them deface.
8 Taste and consider well therefore, that God is good and just;
O happy man, that maketh him his only stay and trust!

9 O fear the Lord, all ye his saints, who is a mighty king;
For they that fear the living Lord are sure to lack nothing.
10 The lions shall be hunger bit, and pin'd with famine much;
But as for them that fear the Lord, no lack shall be to such.

PART II.

11 Come near to me, my children, and unto my words give ear;
I will teach you the perfect way, how ye the Lord shall fear.
12 Who is the man that would live long, and lead a happy life?
See thou refrain thy tongue and lips from all deceit and strife;

13 Turn back thy face from doing ill, and do the godly deed;
Enquire for peace and quietness, and follow it with speed.
14 For why? the eyes of God above upon the just are bent,
His ears likewise to hear the cry of the poor innocent.

15 But he doth frown and bend his brows upon the wicked train,
And cuts away the memory that should of them remain.
16 But when the just do call and cry, the Lord doth hear them so,
That out of pain and misery forthwith he lets them go.

17 The Lord is ever nigh to them that broken-hearted are,
And for the contrite spirit he salvation doth prepare.
18 Full many be the miseries that righteous men endure;
But of deliv'rance from them all the Lord doth them secure

19 The Lord doth so preserve and keep their very bones alway,
That not so much as one of them doth perish or decay.
20 The sin shall slay the wicked man which he himself hath wrought,
And such as hate the righteous man shall soon be brought to nought.

21 But they that fear the living Lord are ever safe and sound;
And as for those that trust in him, nothing shall them confound.

PSALM XXXV. J. H.

1 LORD, plead my cause against my foes, confound their force and might
And take my part against all those that seek with me to fight;
2 Lay hold upon the spear and shield, thyself in armour dress,
Stand up with me to fight the field, and help me from distress:

3 Gird on thy sword and stop the way, my enemies withstand,
That thou unto my soul may'st say, I am thy help at hand.
4 Confound them with rebuke and blame, that seek my soul to spill;
Let them turn back and flee with shame, that think to work me ill.

5 Let them disperse and flee abroad, as wind doth drive the dust:
That so the angel of our God their might away may thrust.
6 Let all their ways be void of light, and slipp'ry like to fall;
And send thy angel with thy might to persecute them all.

7 For why? without my fault have they in secret set their gin,
And digg'd a pit in my path-way, to take my soul therein,
8 When they think least and have no care, O Lord, destroy them all;
Let them be caught in their own snare, and in their mischief fall.

9 But let my soul, my heart, and voice, in God have joy and wealth,
That in the Lord I may rejoice, and in his saving health:
10 Then all my bones shall speak and say (my parts shall all agree)
O thou great God of heaven and earth, what man is like to thee!

PART II.

11 Thou dost defend the weak from them that are both stout and strong,
And rid the poor from wicked men that spoil and do them wrong,
12 My cruel foes against me rise to witness things untrue,
And to accuse me they devise of things I never knew.

13 Where I to them did shew good will, they quit me with disdain:
That they should pay my good with ill my soul doth sore complain.
14 When they were sick I mourn'd therefore, myself in sackcloth clad,
With fasting I did faint full sore, and pray'd with heart most sad;

15 As they had been my brethren dear I did myself behave,
As one that mourneth heavily about his mother's grave:
16 But they in my adversity did gather in a rout;
Yea, abject slaves reproachfully at me did mock and flout.

17 The belly-gods and flatt'ring train, that all good things deride,
At me did grin with great disdain, turning their mouths aside.
18 Lord, when wilt thou for me appear? why dost thou stay and pause?
O rid my soul, my darling dear, out of these lions' claws;

19 And then will I give thanks to thee before the church always;
And where most of the people be, there will I shew thy praise.

20 Let not my foes prevail on me, which hate me for no fault;
Neither let them wink with their eyes, that causeless me assault.

PART III.

21 Of peace no word they think or say, their talk is all untrue;
They still consult how to betray all those that peace pursue.
22 With open mouth they run at me, their fury is like fire;
Well, well, say they, our eye doth see the thing that we desire.

23 But, Lord, thou seest what ways they take, and what they do intend;
Be not far off, nor me forsake, but speedy help me send.
24 Awake, arise, and stir abroad, defend me in my right;
Revenge my cause, O Lord my God, and aid me with thy might.

25 According to thy righteousness, O Lord God, set me free;
And let them not their pride express, nor triumph over me.
26 Let not their hearts rejoice, nor cry, E'en so we would it have;
Nor give them cause to say on high, He's sunk into the grave.

27 Confound them all that do rejoice when they my trouble see,
Let them be cloathed with rebuke that boast with scorn at me.
28 But let them heartily rejoice who love my upright way;
Let them all times with heart and voice still praise the Lord, and say,

29 Great is the Lord, and doth excel, and he doth much delight
To see his servants prosper well, it is his pleasant sight.
30 Wherefore my tongue I will apply thy righteousness to praise;
To thee, O Lord my God, will I give laud and thanks always.

PSALM XXXVI. J. H.

1 THE wicked by his works unjust doth thus persuade my heart,
That in the Lord he hath no trust, his fear is set apart.
2 Yet doth he joy in his estate to walk as he began,
So long till he deserve the hate of God as well as man.

3 His words are wicked, vile and naught his tongue no truth doth tell;
Yet at no hand will he be taught which way he may do well.
4 When he should sleep, then doth he muse his mischiefs to fulfil;
No wicked way doth he refuse, nor any thing that's ill.

5 But, Lord, thy goodness doth ascend above the heavens most high,
So doth thy truth itself extend unto the cloudy sky.
6 Much more than hills both high and steep thy justice is exprest;
Thy judgments like the seas most deep: thou sav'st both man and beast:

7 Thy mercy is above all things, O God, it doth excel:
In trust whereof, as in thy wings, the sons of men shall dwell.
8 Within thy house they shall be fed with plenty at their will,
Of all delights they shall be sped, and take thereof their fill;

9 Because the well of life most pure doth ever flow from thee,
And in thy light we are full sure eternal light to see.
10 From such as thee desire to know let not thy grace depart,
Thy righteousness declare and show to men of upright heart.

11 Let not the proud on me prevail, O Lord, of thy good grace;
Nor let the wicked me assail to throw me out of place.

12 But they in their device shall fall that wicked works maintain;
They shall be certainly cast down, and never rise again.

PSALM XXXVII. W. W.

1 GRUDGE not to see the wicked men in wealth to flourish still,
Nor envy such as ill to do have bent and set their will:
2 For as the grass and the green herbs do wither and decay,
So shall their great prosperity soon pass and fade away.

3 Trust thou therefore in God alone, to do well give thy mind;
So shalt thou have the land as thine, and there sure food shalt find.
4 In God set all thy heart's delight, and look what thou wouldst have,
Or else canst wish in all the world, thou need'st it not to crave.

5 Cast both thyself and thy affairs on God with perfect trust,
And then thou shalt with patience see th' effect both sure and just:
6 Thy perfect life and godly name he will clear as the light,
So that the sun ev'n at noon-day shall not shine half so bright.

7 Be still therefore, and stedfastly on God see thou wait then,
Not shrinking for the prosp'rous state of lewd and wicked men.
8 Shake off despite, envy and hate let not thy anger rise,
That thou may'st not be drawn into some sinful enterprize.

9 For ev'ry wicked man will God most certainly destroy;
But such as trust in him are sure the land for to enjoy.
10 Wait but a while and thou shalt see no more the wicked train;
No, not so much as house or place, where once he did remain.

PART II.

11 But merciful and humble men enjoy shall sea and land:
In rest and peace they shall rejoice, for nought shall them withstand.
12 The lewd men and malicious do against the just conspire;
They gnash their teeth at him, as men who do his bane desire.

13 But while ungodly men thus think, the Lord laughs them to scorn;
For he doth see the time approach, when they shall sigh and mourn.
14 The wicked have their sword outdrawn, their bow is also bent,
To overthrow and kill the poor, whose life is innocent:

15 But the same sword shall pierce their heart, which was to kill the just;
So shall the bow in shivers break wherein they put their trust.
16 Doubtless the just man's poor estate is to be valu'd more
Than all the lewd and wicked man's rich pomp and heaped store.

17 For, tho' their power be most strong, God will it overthrow,
Where contrary he doth preserve the humble man and low.
18 He sees by his great providence the godly's upright way,
And will give them inheritance, which never shall decay.

19 Discouraged they shall not be when some are hard bestead;
When others shall be hunger-bit, they shall be clad and fed.
20 For whosoever wicked is and enemy to God,
Shall like the fat of lambs consume, or smoak that flies abroad.

PSALM XXXVIII.

PART III.

21 Behold the wicked borrows much, and payeth not again;
Whereas the just by lib'ral gifts the needy doth sustain.
22 For they whom God doth bless shall have the land for heritage,
And they whom he doth curse likewise shall perish in his rage.

23 The Lord the just man's steps doth guide, and all his ways doth bless,
To ev'ry thing he takes in hand he giveth good success:
24 Tho' he doth fall, yet he is sure not utterly to sink;
For God upholds him with his hand, and from him will not shrink.

25 I have been young, but now am old, and never yet saw I
The just man left, neither his seed reduc'd to beggary.
26 He gives always most lib'rally, and lends where there is need:
By which he doth from God secure a blessing to his seed.

27 Therefore flee vice and wickedness, and virtue do embrace:
So God shall grant thee long to have on earth a dwelling-place.
28 For God so loveth equity and shews to his such grace,
That he preserveth them, but doth cut off the wicked race:

29 Whereas the good and godly men inherit shall the land,
Having as lord all things therein in their own pow'r and hand.
30 The just man's mouth doth ever speak of matters wise and high,
His tongue doth talk of judgment and of truth and equity.

31 For in his heart the law of God doth evermore abide;
So that where-ever he doth go his foot shall never slide.
32 The wicked like a greedy wolf the just man doth beset,
By all means seeking him to kill, and take him in his net.

PART IV.

33 But tho' he fall into his hands, God will him succour send;
Tho' men against him sentence give, yet God will him defend.
34 Wait thou on God and keep his way, he shall preserve thee then;
The earth to rule, and thou shalt see destroy'd these wicked men.

35 The wicked have I seen most strong, and plac'd in high degree,
Spreading himself, and flourishing as doth the laurel-tree;
36 But suddenly he pass'd away, and lo, he was quite gone;
Then I him sought, but could not find the place where dwelt such one.

37 Mark and behold the upright man, how God doth him increase;
For the just man shall have at length great joy with rest and peace.
38 As for transgressors, woe to them, destroy'd they all shall be,
God will cut off their budding race and rich posterity.

39 But the salvation of the just doth come from God above,
Who in their trouble sends them aid of his mere grace and love.
40 God evermore delivers them from lewd men and unjust,
And still will save them whilst that they in him do put their trust.

PSALM XXXVIII. J. H.

1 PUT me not to rebuke, O Lord, in thy provoked ire,
And in thy wrath correct me not, I humbly thee desire,

2 Thy arrows do stick fast in me, thy hand doth press me sore,
And in my flesh no health at all appeareth any more:

3 And all this is by reason of thy wrath that I am in;
Nor any rest is in my bones by reason of my sin.
4 For lo my wicked doings, Lord, above my head are gone,
A greater load than I can bear they lie me sore upon:

5 My wounds do stink and are corrupt, and loathsome are to see;
Which all thro' my own foolishness doth happen unto me:
6 And I in careful wise am brought into such great distress,
That I go wailing all the day in doleful heaviness.

7 My loins are fill'd with sore disease, my flesh hath no whole part;
I feeble am and broken sore, and roar for grief of heart.
8 Thou know'st, Lord, my desire, my groans are open in thy sight;
My heart doth pant, my strength doth fail, my eyes have lost their light.

9 My lovers and my wonted friends stand looking on my woe,
My kinsmen they do far away from me depart also:
10 They that do seek my life lay snares, and they that go the way
To do me hurt, speak lies, and think on mischief all the day.

PART II.

11 But as a deaf man I became that cannot hear at all,
And as one dumb that opens not his mouth to speak withal.
12 For all my confidence, O Lord, I wholly place in thee;
Therefore, O Lord, who art my God, do thou give ear to me.

13 This do I crave, that they my foes triumph not over me;
For when my foot doth slip, then they rejoice my fall to see.
14 And I am ready for to halt, I cannot stand upright,
Also my grievous heaviness is ever in my sight.

15 For while that I my wickedness in humble wise confess,
And while I for my sinful deeds my sorrows do express,
16 My foes do still remain alive, and mighty are, I know,
And they that hate me wrongfully in number hugely grow.

17 They stand against me that my good with evil do repay,
Because that good and honest things I do pursue alway.
18 Forsake me not, O Lord my God; be thou not far away;
Make haste to help me, O my God, my safety and my stay.

PSALM XXXIX. J. H.

1 I SAID, I will look to my ways, for fear I should go wrong,
I will take heed all times that I offend not with my tongue;
2 As with a bit I will keep fast my mouth with force and might,
Not once to whisper all the while the wicked are in sight.

3 I held my tongue and spake no word, but kept me close and still,
Yea, from good talk I did refrain, but sore against my will:
4 My heart grew hot within my breast with musing, thought and doubt,
Which did increase and stir the fire, at last these words burst out;

5 Lord, number out my life and days, which yet I have not past:
So that I may be certify'd how long my life shall last.

6 For thou hast pointed out my life in length much like a span;
My age is nothing unto thee, so vain is every man!

7 Man walketh like a shade, and doth in vain himself annoy
In getting goods, and cannot tell who shall the same enjoy.
8 Therefore, O Lord, what wait I for? what help do I desire?
Truly my hope is ev'n in thee, I nothing else require.

PART II.

9 From all the sins that I have done, Lord, quit me out of hand,
And make me not a scorn to fools that nothing understand.
10 I was so dumb, that to complain no trouble could me move,
Because I knew it was thy work, my patience for to prove.

11 Lord, take from me thy scourge and plague, I cannot them withstand,
I faint and pine away for fear of thy most heavy hand.
12 When thou for sin dost man rebuke, he waxeth pale and wan,
As doth a cloth that moths have fret; so vain a thing is man!

13 Lord, hear my suit, and give good heed, regard my tears that fall:
I sojourn like a stranger here, as did my fathers all:
14 O spare a little, give me space my strength for to restore,
Before I go away from hence, and shall be seen no more.

PSALM XL. J. H.

1 I WAITED long and sought the Lord, and patiently did bear;
At length he did to me accord my voice and cry to hear:
2 He brought me from the dreadful pit, out of the mire and clay;
Upon a rock he set my feet, and he did guide my way:

3 To me he taught a psalm of praise, which I must shew abroad,
And sing new songs of thanks always unto the Lord our God.
4 When all the folk these things shall see, as people much afraid,
Then they unto the Lord will flee, and trust upon his aid.

5 Blessed is he whose hope and heart doth in the Lord remain,
That with the proud doth take no part, nor such as lies maintain.
6 For, Lord my God, thy wondrous deeds in greatness far do pass,
Thy favour towards us exceeds all things that ever was.

7 When I intend and do devise thy works abroad to show,
To such a reck'ning they do rise, thereof no end I know.
8 Burnt-off'rings thou delight'st not in, I know thy whole desire;
With sacrifice to purge his sin thou dost no man require.

9 Meat-offerings and sacrifice thou wouldst not have at all;
But thou, O Lord, hast open made my ears to hear withal.
10 But then, said I, behold and look, I come with heart most free,
For in the volume of the book thus it is said of me:

11 That I, O God, should do thy mind, which thing doth please me well,
For in my heart thy law I find fast placed there to dwell.
12 Thy righteousness and justice I in great assemblies tell;
Behold, my tongue no time doth cease, O Lord, thou knowest well.

PART II.

I have not hid within my breast thy goodness as by stealth;
But I declare and have exprest thy truth and saving health.
I kept not close thy loving mind, that no man it should know;
The trust that in thy truth I find to all the church I show.

5 Thy tender mercy, Lord, from me withdraw thou not away!
But let thy love and verity preserve me night and day.
6 For I with many troubles am encompassed about,
My sins so greatly do increase I cannot 'spy them out.

7 For why? in number they exceed the hairs upon my head,
My heart doth faint for very fear, that I am almost dead.
8 With speed send help and set me free, O Lord, I thee require;
Make haste with aid to succour me, O Lord, at my desire.

9 Confound them with rebuke and shame, that seek my soul to spill;
Drive back my foes, and them defame that wish me any ill.
0 For their ill fears do them descry that would deface my name,
Always at me they rail and cry, Fie on him, fie for shame!

1 Let them in thee have joy and wealth that seek to thee always,
That those that love thy saving health may say, To God be praise.
2 But as for me, I am but poor, opprest, and brought full low;
Yet thou, O Lord, wilt me restore to health, full well I know.

3 For why? thou art my hope and trust, my refuge, help and stay;
Wherefore, my God, as thou art just, with me no time delay.

PSALM XLI. T. S.

1 THE man is blest that doth provide for such as needy be;
For in the season perilous the Lord will set him free;
2 And he will keep him safe, and make him happy in the land,
And not deliver him into his enemies strong hand:

3 And from his bed of languishing the Lord will him restore:
For thou, O Lord, wilt turn to health his sickness and his sore.
4 Then in my sickness thus said I, Have mercy, Lord, on me,
And heal my soul, which grieved is that I offended thee.

5 My foes did wish me ill in heart, and thus of me did say,
When shall he die, that so his name may perish quite away?
6 And when they come to visit me, they ask if I do well;
But in their hearts they mischief hatch, and then abroad it tell.

7 All they that hate me do conspire against me craftily,
And still devise how to procure my hurt and misery.
8 So grievous sin hath brought him to this sickness, say they plain;
He is so low, that without doubt he cannot rise again.

9 The man also whom I did trust, with me did use deceit;
Who at my table did eat bread, the same for me laid wait.
10 Have mercy, Lord, on me therefore, and let me be preserv'd,
That I may render unto them the things they have deserv'd.

11 By this I know assuredly I am belov'd of thee,
Because my foes no power have to triumph over me:
12 But in my right thou hast me kept, and it maintained well;
And in thy presence place assign'd where I shall ever dwell.

13 The Lord, the God of Israel, be praised evermore;
Ev'n as be it, Lord, will I say, praise ye the Lord therefore.

PSALM XLII. J. H.

1 LIKE as the hart doth pant and bray the well-springs to obtain;
So doth my soul desire alway with thee, Lord, to remain.
2 My soul doth thirst, and would draw near, the living God of might;
Oh, when shall I come and appear in presence of his sight?

3 The tears all times are my repast which from my eyes do slide,
Whilst wicked men cry out so fast, where now is God thy guide?
4 Alas, what grief it is to think, the freedom once I had!
Therefore my soul, as at pit's brink, most heavy is and sad:

5 For I did march in good array with joyful company,
Unto the temple was our way to praise the Lord most high.
6 My soul, why art thou sad always, and frett'st thus in my breast?
Trust still in God, for him to praise I hold it always best:

7 By him I succour have at need against all pain and grief;
He is my God, who with all speed doth haste to send relief.
8 My soul is vexed in me, and therefore, O Lord, I will
Remember thee from Jordan's land and Hermon's little hill.

PART II.

9 One grief another in doth call, as clouds burst out their voice
The floods of evil that do fall run over me with noise.
10 Yet I by day felt his goodness and help at all essays,
Likewise at night I did not cease the living God to praise.

11 I am persuaded thus to say to him with reverence,
O Lord thou art my guide and stay, my rock and sure defence:
12 Why do I then in pensiveness hanging the head thus walk,
While that my enemies oppress and vex me with their talk?

13 For why? they pierce my inward parts with pains to be abhorr'd,
When they cry out with stubborn hearts, Where now is God thy Lord?
14 So soon, my soul, why dost thou faint with pain and grief opprest?
Why do sad thoughts without restraint thus rage within my breast?

15 Trust in the Lord thy God always, and thou the time shalt see,
To give him thanks with laud and praise, for health restor'd to thee.

PSALM XLIII. T. S.

1 JUDGE and defend my cause, O Lord, 'gainst them that evil be;
From wicked and deceitful men, O Lord, deliver me.
2 For of my strength thou art the God, why am I put from thee?
Why walk I heavily, whilst that my foe oppresseth me?

3 O Lord, send out thy light and truth, and lead me with thy grace,
Which may conduct me to thy hill, and to thy dwelling-place:

4 Then shall I to thy altar go, with joy to worship there,
And on my harp give thanks to thee, O God, my God most dear.

5 Why art thou then so sad, my soul, and frett'st thus in my breast?
Still trust in God, for him to praise I hold it always best.
6 By him I have deliverance from all my pain and grief:
He is my God, who doth always at need send me relief.

PSALM XLIV. T. S.

1 OUR ears have heard our fathers tell and rev'rently record
The wondrous works that thou hast done in ancient times, O Lord.
2 How thou didst drive the heathen out with a most powerful hand,
Planting our fathers in their place, and gav'st to them their land:

3 They conquer'd not by their own sword the land wherein they dwell;
But by thy hand, thy arm, and grace, because thou lov'dst them well.
4 Thou art my King, O God, who sav'st Jacob in sundry wise:
Led with thy pow'r we threw down such as did against us rise.

5 I trusted not in bow nor sword, they could not save me sound;
Thou kept'st us from our foes' great rage, and didst them all confound.
6 And still we boast of thee our God, and praise thy holy name;
Yet now thou go'st not with our host, but leavest us to shame.

7 Thou mad'st us flee before our foes, so were we overtrod;
They did us rob and spoil our goods, we were dispers'd abroad:
8 Thou hast us given to our foes, as sheep for to be slain;
Amongst the heathen every where we scatter'd do remain.

9 Thy people thou hast sold like slaves, and as a thing of nought;
For profit none thou hast thereby, no gain at all was sought,
10 And to our neighbours thou hast made of us a laughing stock.
And those that round about us dwell, at us do grin and mock.

PART II.

11 Thus we serve for no other use, but for a common talk;
They mock, they scorn, they shake their heads, wherever they do walk.
12 With shame and great confusion I afflicted am full sore;
Yea, so I blush, that all my face with red is cover'd o'er.

13 For why? we hear such sland'rous words such false reports and lies,
That death it is to see their wrongs, their threatnings and their cries.
14 For all this, we forgot not thee, nor yet thy cov'nant brake;
We turn'd not back our hearts from thee, nor yet thy paths forsake.

15 Yet thou hast trod us down in dust, where dens of dragons be,
And cover'd us with shade of death, and great adversity.
16 If we God's name forgotten have, and help of idols sought
Shall he not search and find it out? for he doth know our thought.

17 But 'tis for thy name's sake, O Lord, we always are slain thus,
As sheep into the shambles sent, ev'n so they deal with us.
18 Up, Lord, why sleepest thou? awake, for ever leave us not;
Why hidest thou thy countenance? our thrall thou hast forgot.

19 Ev'n to the dust our soul is brought, our troubles so increase:
Our belly cleaveth to the ground, our grief no time doth cease:

10 Rise up therefore for our defence, and help us, Lord, at need;
We, for thy goodness, thee beseech, to rescue us with speed.

PSALM XLV. J. H.

1 MY heart doth take in hand, some godly song to sing;
The praise that I shall shew therein, pertaineth to the king.
2 My tongue shall be as quick, his honour to indite,
As is the pen of any scribe, that useth fast to write.

3 O fairest of all men, thy lips with grace are pure;
For God hath blessed thee with gifts for ever to endure:
4 About thee gird thy sword, O prince of might eleft;
With honour, glory, and renown, thou art most richly deck'd:

5 Go forth with godly speed, with meekness, truth, and rig
And thy right hand shall thee instruct in works of dreadful might.
6 Thy arrows sharp and keen their hearts so sore shall sting
That they shall crouch and kneel to thee, yea, all thy foes, O King.

7 Thy royal seat, O Lord, for ever shall remain;
Because the sceptre of thy realm doth righteousness maintain.
8 Because thou lov'dst the right, and did'st the ill detest,
Therefore hath God anointed thee with joy above the rest.

9 With myrrh and savours sweet thy cloaths are all bespread,
When thou dost from thy palace pass, thereby to make thee glad.
10 Kings' daughters do attend in fine and rich array;
At thy right hand the Queen doth stand in gold and garments gay.

PART II.

11 O daughter, take good heed, incline and give good ear;
Thou must forget thy kindred all, and father's house most dear.
12 Then shall the king desire thy beauty more and more;
He is the Lord thy God, whom thou must worship and adore.

13 The daughters then of Tyre, with gifts full rich to see,
And all the wealthy of the land shall make their suit to thee
14 The daughter of the king is glorious to behold:
Within her closet she does sit all deck'd in beaten gold.

15 In robes with needle wrought, and every pleasant thing,
With virgins fair on her to wait, she cometh to the king.
16 Thus are they brought with joy and mirth on every side,
In to the palace of the king, and there they do abide.

17 Instead of fathers thou shalt children multiply,
Whom thou may'st princes make, to rule all lands successively.
18 Wherefore thy holy name all ages shall record,
The people shall give thanks to thee, for evermore, O Lord.

PSALM XLVI. J. H.

1 THE Lord is our defence and aid, the strength whereby we st
When we with woe are much dismay'd he is our help at hand.
2 Tho' the earth move, we will not fear, tho' mountains high and ste
Be thrust and hurled here and there within the sea so deep:

3 Nay, though the sea do rage so sore, that all the banks it spills,
And though it overflow the shore, and beat down mighty hills:
4 For one fair flood doth send abroad his pleasant streams apace,
To glad the city of our God, and wash his holy place.

5 In midst of her the Lord doth dwell, she never can decay,
All things against her that rebel the Lord will surely slay.
6 The heathen folk and kingdoms fear, the people make a noise,
The earth doth melt and disappear, when God puts forth his voice.

7 The Lord of hosts doth take our part, to us he hath an eye;
Our hope of health with all our heart on Jacob's God doth lie.
8 Come here, and see with mind and thought the working of our God,
What wonders he himself hath wrought in all the world abroad:

9 By him all wars are hush'd and gone, tho' countries did conspire,
Their bows and spears he brake each one, their chariots burnt with fire.
10 Be still therefore, and know that I am God, and therefore will
Among the heathen people be highly exalted still.

11 The Lord of hosts doth us defend, he is our strength and tow'r;
On Jacob's God we do depend, and on his mighty pow'r.

PSALM XLVII. J. H.

1 YE people all, with one accord clap hands, shout and rejoice,
Be glad and sing unto the Lord with sweet and pleasant voice;
2 For high the Lord and dreadful is, his wonders manifold,
A mighty king he is likewise in all the earth extol'd.

3 The people shall he make to be unto our bondage thrall,
And underneath our feet shall be the nations make to fall:
4 For us the heritage he chose which we possess alone,
The excellency of Jacob his well beloved one.

5 Our God ascended up on high with joy and pleasant noise,
The Lord goes up above the sky with trumpet's royal voice;
6 Sing praises to our God, sing praise, sing praises to our king:
For God is king of all the earth, all skilful praises sing.

7 God o'er the heathen reigns, and sits upon his holy throne;
The princes of the people have them joined every one
8 To Abraham's people; for our God, who is exalted high,
As with a buckler doth defend the earth continually.

PSALM XLVIII. J. H.

1 GREAT is the Lord, and with great praise to be advanced still
Within the city of our God, upon his holy hill.
2 Mount Sion is a pleasant place, it gladdeth all the land;
The city of the mighty King on her north-side doth stand:

3 Within the palaces thereof God is a refuge known;
For lo, the kings are gather'd, and together they are gone:
4 But when they did behold it so, they wondered, and they were
Astonish'd much, and suddenly were driven back with fear;

5 Great terror there on them did fall, for grief of heart they cry,
As doth a woman when she shall go travail speedily.

6 As thou with eastern winds the ships upon the sea doth break,
They were destroy'd, and ev'n as we have heard our fathers speak.

7 So in the city of the Lord we saw as it was told ;
Yea, in the city which our God for ever will uphold.
8 O Lord, we wait and do depend on thy good help and grace,
For which we do all times attend within thy holy place.

9 O Lord, according to thy name for ever is thy praise,
And thy right-hand, O Lord, is full of righteousness always.
10 For thy judgments let Sion mount be filled full with joys,
Also of Judah grant, O Lord, the daughters to rejoice.

11 Go, walk about all Sion hill, yea, round about her go,
And tell the towers that thereon are builded on a row ;
12 And mark ye well her bulwarks all, behold her towers there,
That ye may tell thereof to them that after shall be here.

13 For this most mighty God, our God for evermore is he,
And unto death we are resolv'd our guide he still shall be.

PSALM XLIX. J. H.

1 ALL people, hearken and give ear to that which I shall tell,
Both high and low, both rich and poor, that in the world do dwell :
2 For why? my mouth shall make discourse of many things most wise,
In understanding shall my heart its study exercise.

3 I will incline my ear to know the parable so dark,
And open all my doubtful speech in metre on my harp.
4 Wherefore should I affliction fear, or any careful toil ?
Or else my foes, which at my heels do press my life to spoil !

5 For as for such as riches have, wherein their trust is most,
And they who of their treasures great proudly do brag and boast :
6 There is not one of them that can his brother's life redeem,
Or give a ransom unto God sufficient in esteem :

7 It is too great a price to pay, none can thereto attain,
So that he might his life prolong, nor in the grave remain.
8 They see wise men as well as fools are subject to death's bands,
And being dead, strangers possess their houses, goods, and lands.

9 Their care is to build houses fair, and so determine sure
To make their names upon the earth for ever to endure.
10 Yet shall no man always enjoy high honour, wealth and rest ;
But must at length submit to death, as well as the brute beast.

PART II.

11 And tho' they find their foolish thoughts to be most lewd and vain,
Their children yet approve their talk, and in like sin remain.
12 As sheep into the fold are brought, they shall be laid in grave ;
Death shall them eat, and in that day the just shall lordship have.

13 Their beauty and their royal port shall fade and quite decay,
When from their house unto the pit with woe they pass away.
14 But God will surely me preserve from death and endless pain,
Because he will of his good grace my soul receive again.

15 If any man grow wondrous rich, be not afraid therefore,
Altho' the glory of his house increaseth more and more;
16 For when he dies, of all these things nothing shall he receive,
His glory will not follow him, his pomp will take its leave.

17 Yet in his life he counts himself the happiest under sun;
And others likewise flatter him, saying, All is well done.
18 But yet if he should live so long as did his fathers old,
Yet must he needs at length give place, and he brought to death's fold.

19 Man that in honour lives, and doth not understand, may be
Compar'd unto the very beasts that perish utterly.

PSALM L. W. W.

1 THE mighty God, th' Eternal hath thus spoke,
And all the world he will call and provoke;
Ev'n from the east, and so forth to the west,
Out of Sion, which place he liketh best,
God will appear in beauty most excellent,
Our God will come before long time be spent:

2 Devouring fire shall go before his face,
A tempest great shall round about him trace.
Then shall he call the earth and heavens bright
To judge his folk with equity and right;
Saying, Go to, and now my saints assemble;
My pact they keep, their gifts do not dissemble.

3 The heav'ns they shall declare his righteousness;
For God is judge of all things more or less.
Hear, my people, for I will now reveal;
List, Israel, I'll from thee nought conceal.
Thy God, the Lord am I, and will not blame thee
For not giving all sorts of off'rings to me:

4 I have no need to take of thee at all
Goats of thy fold, or calves out of thy stall:
For all the beasts are mine within the woods,
On Thousand hills cattle are mine own goods;
I know for mine all birds that are on mountains,
All beasts mine are which haunt the fields and fountains.

5 Were I hungry I would not thee it tell;
For all is mine that in the world doth dwell.
Eat I the flesh of great bulls or bullocks?
Or drink the blood of goats or of the flocks?
Offer to God praise and hearty thanksgiving,
And pay thy vows unto God ever-living.

6 Call upon me when troubled thou shalt be;
Then will I help and thou shalt honour me.
To the wicked thus saith th' eternal God,
Why dost thou preach my words and laws abroad,
Seeing thou hast them with thy mouth abus'd,
And hat'st to be by discipline reduc'd?

10 Make new my heart within my breast, and frame it to thy holy will,
And let thy spirit in me rest, which may my soul with comfort fill.

PART II.

11 Cast me not, Lord, out from thy sight, but speedily my torments end;
Take not from me thy holy spirit, which may from dangers me defend.
12 Restore me to those joys again, which I was wont in thee to find;
Let me thy free spirit retain, which unto thee may draw my mind.

13 Thus when I shall thy mercies know, I shall instruct others therein;
And men that are likewise brought low by my example, shall flee sin.
14 O God, that of my health art Lord, forgive me this my bloody vice;
My heart and tongue shall then accord to sing thy mercy and justice.

15 Touch thou my lips, my tongue untie, O Lord, I do thee humbly pray;
And then my mouth shall testify thy praise and wond'rous works alway.
16 And as for outward sacrifice, I would have offer'd many one;
But thou esteem'st them of no price, and therein pleasure takest none.

17 The heavy heart, the mind opprest, O Lord, thou never dost reject;
This sacrifice indeed is best, and that thou chiefly dost expect.
18 Lord, unto Sion turn thy face, pour out thy mercies on thy hill,
And on Jerusalem thy grace; build up the walls, and love it still.

19 Thou shalt accept then our off'rings of peace and righteousness alway;
Yea, calves and many other things upon thy altar we will lay.

ANOTHER OF THE SAME, BY J. H.

1 HAVE mercy on me, Lord, after thy great abounding grace,
After thy mercies multitude do thou my sins efface:
2 Yea, wash me clean from my offence and my iniquity;
For I do own my faults, and still my sin is in mine eye.

3 Against thee, thee alone, I have offended in this case,
And evil have I done before the presence of thy face;
4 That in the things which thou hast done upright thou may'st appear,
And when thou judgest, all may see that thou art very clear.

5 In wickedness I formed was, when I began to be;
My mother at the very first in sin conceived me:
6 But lo! truth in the inward parts is pleasant unto thee,
And secrets of thy wisdom thou revealed hast to me.

7 With hyssop, Lord, besprinkle me, I shall be cleansed so;
Yea, wash thou me, and then shall I be whiter than the snow
8 Of joy and gladness make thou me to hear the pleasant voice,
That so the bones which thou, O Lord, hast broken, may rejoice.

9 From the beholding of my sins, Lord, turn away thy face,
And all my deeds of wickedness do utterly efface:
10 O God, create in me a heart unspotted in thy sight;
Within my bowels, Lord, renew a firm and stable sp'rit:

11 Cast me not from thy sight, nor take thy spirit quite away;
The comfort of thy saving health, give me again, I pray:
12 With thy free spirit me support, then shall transgressors be,
By my instruction and advice, converted unto thee.

13 O God, that art God of my health, from blood deliver me,
That praises of thy righteousness my tongue may sing to thee;
14 My lips which yet fast closed be, do thou, O Lord, unloose;
The praises of thy Majesty my mouth shall then disclose.

15 I would have offer'd sacrifice, if that had pleased thee;
But pleased with burnt offerings I know thou wilt not be:
16 A spirit griev'd, is sacrifice delightful in thine eyes:
A broken and a contrite heart, Lord, thou wilt not despise.

17 In thy good-will, deal gently, Lord, with Sion, and withal
Grant that of thy Jerusalem uprear'd may be the wall;
18 Burnt-off'rings, gifts, and sacrifice of justice in that day
Thou shalt accept, and calves they shall upon thy altar lay.

PSALM LII. J. H.

1 WHY dost thou, tyrant, boast abroad thy wicked works to praise?
Dost thou not know there is a God, whose mercies last always?
2 Why doth thy mind yet still devise such wicked wiles to harp?
Thy tongue untrue in forging lies is like a razor sharp;

3 On mischief why sett'st thou thy mind, and wilt not walk upright?
Thou lovest more false tales to find, than bring the truth to light.
4 Thou dost delight in fraud and guile, in mischief, blood, and wrong,
Thy lips have learnt the flatt'ring style, O false deceitful tongue!

5 Therefore the Lord shall thee confound, and pluck thee from thy place,
Thy seed root out from off the ground, and utterly deface.
6 The just, when they behold thy fall, with fear will praise the Lord,
And in reproach of thee withal cry out with one accord;

7 Behold the man that did refuse the Lord for his defence,
But in his riches great did place his trust and confidence.
8 But I, as olive fresh and green shall spring and spread abroad,
Because my trust all times hath been in thee the living God.

9 For this therefore I will give praise to thee with heart and voice,
I will advance thy name always, wherein thy saints rejoice.

PSALM LIII. T. S.

1 THE foolish man within his heart blasphemously hath said,
There is not any God at all, why should we be afraid?
2 They are corrupt, and they also a heinous work have wrought,
Among them all there is not one of good that worketh aught.

3 The Lord look'd down from heav'n upon the sons of men below,
To see if any were that sought the living God to know;
4 Out of the way they all are gone, they all corrupted are,
There is not any that doth good, not one for God doth care.

5 Do not all wicked workers know, that they do feed upon
My people as they feed on bread? the Lord they call not on.
5 Ev'n there they were afraid, and stood with trembling all dismay'd,
When as there was no cause at all why they should be afraid:

7 For God his bones that thee besieg'd, hath scatter'd all abroad,
He hath confounded them, for they rejected are of God.
8 O Lord, give to thy people health, and thou, O Lord, fulfil
Thy promise made to Israel from out of Sion hill.

9 When God his people shall restore that once were captive led,
Then Jacob shall rejoice therein, and Israel be glad.

PSALM LIV. J. H.

1 GOD, save me for thy holy Name, and for thy goodness sake;
Unto the strength, Lord, of the same I do my cause betake.
2 Regard, O Lord, and give an ear to me when I do pray
Bow down thyself to me, and hear the words that I do say:

3 For strangers up against me rise, and tyrants vex me still,
Who have not God before their eyes, they seek my blood to spill.
4 But lo, my God doth give me aid, the Lord is nigh at hand;
With them by whom my soul is stay'd the Lord doth ever stand;

5 With plagues repay again all those for me that lie in wait,
And in thy truth destroy my foes with their own snare and bait.
6 An off'ring of free heart and will then I to thee shall make,
And praise thy Name, for therein still great comfort I do take.

7 Thou, Lord; at length hast set me free from them that craft conspire,
And now my eye with joy doth see on them my heart's desire.

PSALM LV. J H.

1 O GOD, give ear, and speedily hear me when I do pray,
And when to thee I call and cry hide not thyself away;
2 Take heed to me, grant my request, and answer me again;
With grief I pray, full sore opprest, sorrow doth me constrain.

3 Because my foes with threats and cries oppress me thro' despite,
And so the wicked sort likewise to vex me take delight.
4 For they in council do conspire to charge me with some ill,
And in their hasty wrath and ire they do pursue me still.

5 My heart doth faint for want of breath, it panteth in my breast;
With terror and the dread of death my soul is much opprest:
6 Such dreadful fear on me doth fall, that I therewith do quake:
Such horror overwhelmeth me, that I no shift can make.

7 Oh that I had wings like a dove! then would I swiftly flee
Away from hence unto a place where I at rest should be:
8 Lo, then I would go far away, to fly I would not cease,
And I would hide myself, and stay in some great wilderness;

9 I would be gone with speed and haste, and not abide behind,
Till I had safely over-past these blasts of boist'rous wind.
10 Divide them, Lord, and from them pull their false and double tongue;
For I have spy'd their city full of rapine, strife, and wrong.

11 Both day and night they go about within the city wall,
In midst of her is mischief wrought, and sorrow great withal;
12 Her inward parts are wicked plain, her deeds they are most vile,
And in her streets there doth remain nothing but fraud and guile.

PART II,

13 If that my foes did seek my shame, I might it well abide,
Because from all their check **and blame** somewhere I could me hide:
14 But thou it was, my fellow dear, who friendship didst pretend,
And didst my secret counsel hear as a familiar friend;

15 With whom I had delight to **talk** in secret and abroad;
And we together oft did walk unto the house of God.
16 Let death in haste upon them fall, and send **them** quick to hell;
For mischief doth abide in all the places where they dwell.

17 But I **unto** my God do cry, to **him for aid** I **flee;**
The Lord will **help** me speedily, and he will succour me.
18 At morning, **noon,** and ev'ning-tide unto the Lord I pray;
When I so constantly have cry'd, he did not say me nay.

19 To peace **he** shall restore me yet, tho' war be now at hand;
Altho' the number be full great that do against me stand.
20 The Lord that first and last doth **reign** both now and evermore,
Will hear when I to him complain, and punish them full sore.

21 For sure there is no hope that they to turn will once accord;
For why? they will **not** God obey, nor fear the living Lord.
22 Upon their friends they laid their hands, who were in cov'nant knit;
Of friendship to neglect the bands **they do not care one whit.**

23 While they have war within their hearts, as butter are their words;
And tho' they were as soft as oil, they cut as sharp as swords.
24 Cast thou thy care upon the **Lord,** and he shall nourish thee;
For in no wise will he accord the just in thrall to see.

25 But God shall cast them deep in pit who thirst for blood always;
He will no guileful man permit **to** live out half his days.
26 Though such be quite destroy'd and gone, on him is all my stay;
I will depend his grace upon with all my heart alway.

PSALM LVI. J. H.

1 HAVE mercy, Lord, on me, I pray, for man would me devour;
He fighteth with me day by day, and troubleth me each hour:
2 My foes do daily enterprize to swallow me outright;
To fight against me many rise, O thou most high of might.

3 When they would make me sore afraid with boasts and brags of pride,
I trust in thee alone for aid, by thee **I** will abide.
4 God's promise I do mind and praise, O Lord, I stick to thee;
I do not **care at all as·ays** **what** flesh can do to me.

5 What things I either did or spake they wrest them at their will,
And all the counsel that they take is how to work me ill:
6 They all consent themselves to hide, close watch for me to lay;
They spy my paths, and snares have try'd to take my life away.

7 Shall they escape, on mischief **set?** thou God, on them wilt frown;
For in thy wrath thou dost not let to throw whole kingdoms down.
8 Thou seest how oft they made me flee, and on my tears dost look;
Reverve them in a glass by thee, and write them in thy book.

9 When I do call upon thy name my foes away do start;
I well perceive it by the same that God doth take my part.
10 I glory in the word of God, to praise it I accord,
With joy I will declare abroad the promise of the Lord.

11 I trust in God the Lord, and say, as I before began,
The Lord he is my help and stay, I do not care for man.
12 I will perform with heart most free my vows to God always,
And I, O Lord, all times to thee will offer thanks and praise.

13 My soul from death thou dost defend and keep'st my feet upright,
That I before thee may ascend with such as live in light.

PSALM LVII. J. H.

1 TAKE pity for thy promise sake, have mercy, Lord, on me,
Because my soul doth her betake unto the help of thee:
2 Within the shadow of thy wings I set myself full fast,
Till mischief, malice, and like things be gone and over-past.

3 I call unto the God most high, to whom I stick and stand,
I mean the God that will stand by the cause I have in hand.
4 For he from heav'n hath sent his aid to save me from their spite,
That to devour me have assay'd, ev'n mercy, truth, and might.

5 I lead my life with lions fell all set on wrath and ire;
And with such wicked men I dwell who fret like flames of fire;
6 Their teeth are spears and arrows long, as sharp as I have seen,
They wound and cut with their quick tongue, like swords and weapons keen

7 Set up, and shew thyself, O God, above the heav'ns most bright,
Exalt thy praise on earth abroad, thy majesty and might.
8 They laid their net, and did prepare a privy cave and pit,
Wherein they thought my soul to snare, but are fall'n into it.

9 My heart is set to praise the Lord, in him to joy always:
My heart doth ever well accord to sing his laud and praise.
10 Awake, my joy, awake, I say, my lute, my harp, and string:
And I myself before the day will rise, rejoice and sing:

11 Among the people I will tell the goodness of my God,
And shew his praise that doth excel in heathen lands abroad.
12 His mercy doth extend as far as the heavens all are high,
His truth as high as any star that shineth in the sky.

13 Set forth, and shew thyself, O God, above the heav'ns most bright,
Exalt thyself on earth abroad, thy majesty and might.

PSALM LVIII. J. H.

1 YE rulers, that are put in trust to judge of wrong and right,
Be all your judgments true and just, regarding no man's might?
2 Nay, in your hearts ye daily muse in mischief to consent;
And where ye should true justice use, your hands to bribes are bent.

3 The wicked sort from their birth-day have erred on this wise,
And from their mothers' womb alway have used craft and lies:
4 In them the poison and the breath of serpents doth appear;
Yea, like the adder that is deaf, and fast doth stop her ear,

5 Because she will not hear the voice of one that charmeth well;
No, tho' he were the chief of choice, and therein did excel.
6 The teeth, O Lord, which fast are set in their mouth round about,
The lions' teeth that are so great do thou, O Lord, break out:

7 Let them consume away and waste as water runs forth right,
The shafts that they do shoot in haste let them be broke in flight;
8 As snails do waste within the shell, and unto slime do run,
As one before his time that fell, and never saw the sun:

9 Before the thorns that now are young as bushes big shall grow,
Thy storms of anger waxing strong shall take them e'er they know.
10 The just shall joy, it doth them good that God doth vengeance take;
And they shall wash their feet in blood of them that him forsake.

11 Then shall the world shew forth and tell that good men have reward,
And that a God on earth doth dwell, who justice doth regard.

PSALM LIX. J. H.

1 SEND aid, and save me from my foes, O Lord, I pray to thee;
Defend and keep me from all those that rise and strive with me.
2 O Lord, preserve me from those men whose doings are not good,
And set me sure and safe from them that thirst still after blood.

3 For lo, they wait my soul to take, they rage against me still;
Yea, for no fault that I did make, I never did them ill:
4 They run and do themselves prepare, when I no whit offend;
Arise, and save me from their snare, and see what they intend.

5 Arise, O God of Israel, smite ev'ry heathen land;
And pity none that do rebel, and in their mischief stand.
6 At night they run and seek about, like dogs they howl also,
And all the city quite throughout from place to place they go:

7 They speak of me with mouth alway, but in their lips are swords;
They have contriv'd my death, and say, there's none doth hear our words.
8 But, Lord, thou hast their ways espy'd, and thou shalt them disgrace;
The heathen folk thou dost deride, and mock them to their face.

9 The strength that does our foes withstand, O Lord, doth come from thee;
Thou art, O God, my help at hand, a fort and fence to me.
10 The Lord to me doth shew his grace in great abundance still,
That I may see my foes in case such as my heart doth will.

PART II.

11 Destroy them not at once, O Lord, lest it from mind do fall;
But with thy strength drive them abroad, and so consume them all.
12 For their ill words and lying tongue confound them in their pride,
Their wicked oaths with lies and wrong let all the world deride.

13 Consume them in thy wrath, O Lord, that nought of them remain;
That men may know thro'out the world that Jacob's God doth reign.
14 At ev'ning they return apace, as dogs they grin and cry;
Throughout the streets in ev'ry place they run about and spy:

15 They seek about for meat alway, but let them not be fed,
Nor find a house wherein they may be bold to put their head,

16 But I will shew thy strength abroad, thy goodness I will praise;
For thou art my defence and God in time of need always.
17 Thou art my strength, thou hast me stay'd, O Lord, I sing to thee;
Thou art my fort, my fence, and aid, a loving God to me

PSALM LX. J. H.

1 O LORD, thou didst us clean forsake, and scatter all abroad,
Such great displeasure thou didst take, return to us, O God.
2 Thy might did move the land so sore, that it in sunder brake?
The health, thereof, O Lord restore, for it doth bow and quake.

3 With heavy things thou plaguedst thus the people that are thine,
And thou hast given unto us a drink of deadly wine.
4 But yet to such as fear thy name a banner thou dost shew,
That they may triumph in the same, because thy word is true.

5 So that thy might may keep and save the folk that serveth thee,
That they thy help at hand may have, O Lord, grant this to me.
6 The Lord did speak from his own place, this was his joyful sound,
I will divide Sichem by pace, and mete out Succoth's ground.

7 Gilead is given to my hand, Manasseh's mine beside,
Ephraim the strength of all my land, my law doth Judah guide;
8 In Moab I will wash my feet, o'er Edom cast my shoe;
And thou, Philistia, ought'st to seek to me for favour too.

9 But who will bring me at this tide unto the city strong?
Or who to Edom will me guide, so that I go not wrong?
10 Lord, wilt not thou, who didst forsake thy folk, their land and coasts!
Our wars in hand thou wouldst not take, nor go forth with our hosts.

11 Give aid, O Lord, and us relieve from them that us disdain:
The help that hosts of men can give is all but weak and vain.
12 But thro' our God we shall have might to take great things in hand,
He will tread down, and put to flight all those that us withstand.

PSALM LXI. J. H.

1 REGARD, O Lord, for I complain and make my suit to thee;
Let not my words return in vain, but give an ear to me.
2 From out the coasts and utmost parts of all the earth, I cry,
In grief and anguish of my heart, to thee, O God most high.

3 Upon the rock of thy great pow'r my woeful mind repose;
Thou art my hope, my fort and tow'r, my fence against my foes.
4 Within thy tent I long to dwell, there ever to abide;
Under thy wings I know right well I shall me safely hide.

5 The Lord doth my desire regard, and doth fulfil the same;
With riches great will he reward all those that fear his name.
6 The king shall he in health maintain, and so prolong his days,
That he from age to age may reign with honour great always.

7 That he may have a dwelling-place before the Lord alway;
O let thy mercy, truth and grace defend him from decay:
8 And then, O Lord, I ever will sing praise unto thy name,
That all my vows I may fulfil, and daily pay the same.

PSALM LXII. J. H.

1 MY soul to God shall give good heed, and him alone attend,
Because my health and hope to speed doth whole on him depend,
2 For he alone is my defence, my rock, my health, and aid;
He is my stay, and no pretence shall make me much dismay'd.

3 O wicked folk! how long will ye use craft? sure ye must fall;
For as a rotten hedge ye be, and like a tott'ring wall.
4 Whom God doth love ye seek always to put him to the worse;
Ye love to lie, with mouth ye praise, and yet your heart doth curse.

5 Yet still my soul doth whole depend on God my chief desire;
From all ill fates to me defend none but him I require.
6 He is my rock, my fort and tow'r, my health is of his grace;
He doth support me, that no pow'r can move me out of place;

7 My glory and salvation doth on him alone depend;
He is my strength, my stay, my wealth, and still doth me defend.
8 O put your trust in him alway, ye folk, with one accord:
Pour out your hearts to him, and say, Our trust is in the Lord.

9 The sons of men deceitful are, on balance but a sleight,
With things most vain do them compare, for they can hold no weight.
10 Trust not in wrong and robbery, let vain delights be gone;
Tho' riches flow in suddenly, set not your hearts thereon.

11 The Lord long since one thing did tell which here to mind I call,
He spake it oft, I heard it well, that he alone doth all;
12 And that thou, Lord, art good and kind, thy mercy doth exceed;
So that all sorts with thee shall find according to their deed.

PSALM LXIII. T. S.

1 O GOD, my God, I early seek to come to thee in haste;
For why? my soul and body both do thirst of thee to taste:
2 And in this barren wilderness, where waters there are none;
My flesh is parch'd for thought of thee, for thee I wish alone;

3 That I might see yet once again thy glory, strength and might,
As I was wont it to behold within thy temple bright,
4 For why? thy mercies far surmount this life and wretched days;
My lips therefore shall give to thee due honour, laud and praise.

5 And whilst I live I will not fail to worship thee alway,
And in thy name I will lift up my hands when I do pray:
6 My soul is as with marrow fill'd, which is both fat and sweet;
My mouth therefore shall sing such songs as are for thee most meet.

7 When in my bed I think on thee, and in the wakeful night,
I under covert of thy wings rejoice with great delight:
8 My soul doth closely stick to thee thy right-hand is my pow'r,
And those that seek my soul to slay, death shall them soon devour;

9 The sword shall then devour each one, their carcasses shall feed
The hungry foxes which do run their prey to seek at need.
10 The king and all men shall rejoice that do profess God's word;
For liars' mouths shall then be stopp'd, and all their ways abhorr'd.

PSALM LXIV. J. H.

1 O LORD, unto my voice give ear, when I complain and pray,
And rid my life and soul from fear of foes that threat to slay:
2 Defend me from that sort of men who in deceit do lurk,
And from the frowning face of them who all ill-feats do work;

3 Who whet their tongues as we have seen men whet and sharp their swords,
And shoot abroad their arrows keen; I mean most bitter words:
4 They privily do shoot their shaft the upright man to hit;
The innocent do strike by craft they care or fear no whit.

5 A wicked work they have decreed, in council thus they cry,
To use deceit let us not dread, for none can it espy.
6 Which way to hurt they talk and muse all times within their heart
They all consult what feats to use, each doth invent his part.

7 But yet all this shall not prevail, when they think least thereon,
God with his dart shall sure assail, and wound them every one:
8 Their crafts and their ill tongues withal shall work themselves such blame
That they who then behold their fall shall wonder at the same:

9 And all that see shall know right well that God the thing hath wrought,
And praise his wond'rous works, and tell what he to pass hath brought.
10 Yet shall the just in God rejoice, still trusting in his might:
So shall they joy with mind and voice whose hearts are pure and right.

PSALM LXV. T. S.

1 THY praise alone, O Lord, doth reign in Sion, thine own hill,
Their vows to thee they do maintain, and promises fulfil:
2 For that thou dost their prayers still hear, and dost thereto agree,
The people all both far and near with trust shall come to thee.

3 Our wicked life so far exceeds, that we shall fall therein;
But, Lord, forgive our great misdeeds, and purge us from our sin.
4 The man is blest whom thou dost choose within thy courts to dwell,
Thy house and temple he shall use with pleasures that excel.

5 Of thy great justice hear, O God, our health of thee doth rise,
The hope of all the earth abroad, and the sea-coasts likewise.
6 With strength thou art beset about and compass'd with thy pow'r;
Thou mak'st the mountains strong and stout, to stand in ev'ry show'r:

7 The swelling seas thou dost asswage, making them very still;
Thou dost restrain the people's rage, and rule them at thy will.
8 The folk that dwell throughout the earth shall dread thy signs to see,
Morning and ev'ning with great mirth send praises up to thee.

9 When that the earth is chapt and dry, and thirsteth more and more,
Then with thy drops thou dost supply and much increase her store;
10 The flood of God doth overflow, and so doth cause to spring
The seed and corn which men do sow, for he doth guide the thing;

11 With rain thou dost her furrows fill, whereby her clods do fall;
Thy drops on her thou dost distil, and bless her fruit withal.
12 Thou deck'st the earth of thy good grace with fair and pleasant crop,
The clouds distil their dew apace, great plenty they do drop;

13 Whereby the desart shall begin full great increase to bring,
The little hills shall joy therein, much fruit in them shall spring;
14 In places plain the flocks shall feed, and cover all the earth;
The vales with corn shall so exceed, that they shall sing with mirth.

PSALM LXVI. T. S.

1 YE men on earth, in God rejoice, with praise set forth his Name,
Extol his might with heart and voice, give glory to the same.
2 How wonderful, O Lord, say ye, in all thy works thou art!
Thy foes for fear shall seek to thee full sore against their heart.

3 All men that dwell the earth throughout shall praise the Name of God,
The laud whereof the world about is shew'd and set abroad,
4 All folk, come forth, behold and see, what things the Lord hath wrought
Mark well the wond'rous works that be for man to pass hath brought:

5 He laid the sea like heaps on high, therein a way they had
On foot to pass, both fair and dry, whereof their hearts were glad.
6 His might doth rule the world alway, his eyes all things behold;
All such as will him disobey, by him shall be controul'd.

7 Ye people, give unto our God due laud and thanks always,
With joyful voice declare abroad and sing unto his praise,
8 Who doth endue our souls with life, and it preserve withal;
He stays our feet, so that no strife can make us slip or fall,

9 The Lord doth prove our deeds with fire, whether they will abide,
As workmen do when they desire to have their metals try'd.
10 Although thou dost us suffer long in prison to be cast,
And there with chains and fetters strong to lie in bondage fast;

PART II.

11 Although, I say, thou suffer men on us to ride and reign,
Tho' we thro' fire and water run with very grief and pain;
12 Yet sure thou dost of thy good grace dispose it to the best,
Bringing us out into a place to live in wealth and rest.

13 Unto thy house resort will I to offer and to pray,
And there I will myself apply my vows to thee to pay;
14 The vows that with my mouth I spake in all my grief and smart,
The vows, I say, which I did make in anguish of my heart.

15 Burnt off'rings I will give to thee of oxen fat and rams,
Yea, this my sacrifice shall be of bullocks, goats, and lambs.
16 Come forth and hearken here full soon, all ye that fear the Lord,
What he for my poor soul hath done to you I will record:

17 Full oft I call to mind his grace, this mouth to him doth cry;
And thou, my tongue, make speedy pace to praise him joyfully.
18 But if I feel my heart within in wicked works rejoice,
Or if I have delight in sin, God will not hear my voice.

19 But surely God my voice hath heard, and what I do require;
My prayer also he doth regard, and granteth my desire.
20 All praise to him that hath not put nor cast me out of mind,
Nor yet his mercy from me shut, which I do ever find.

PSALM LXVII. J. H.

1 HAVE mercy on us, Lord, and grant to us thy grace,
To shew to us do thou accord the brightness of thy face;
2 That all the earth may know the way to godly wealth,
And all the nations here below may see thy saving health.

3 Let all the world, O God, give praise unto thy Name,
And let the people all abroad extol and laud the same:
4 Throughout the world so wide let all rejoice with mirth,
For thou with truth and right dost guide the nations of the earth.

5 Let all the world, O God, give praise unto thy Name,
And let the people all abroad extol and laud the same:
6 Then shall the earth increase, great store of fruit shall fall;
And then our God, the God of peace, shall ever bless us all.

7 God shall us greatly bless, and then, both far and near,
The folk which all the earth possess of him shall stand in fear.

PSALM LXVIII. T. S.

1 LET God arise, and then his foes will turn themselves to flight,
His enemies for fear shall run, and scatter out of sight:
2 And as wax melts before the fire, and wind blows smoke away,
So in the presence of the Lord the wicked shall decay.

3 But righteous men before the Lord shall heartily rejoice,
They shall be glad and merry all, and cheerful in their voice.
4 Sing praise, sing praise unto the Lord, who rideth on the sky;
Extol the great Jehovah's Name, and him still magnify:

5 The same is he that is above within his holy place,
That father is of fatherless, and judge of widows' case;
6 Houses and issue both he gives unto the comfortless,
He bringeth bondmen out of thrall, and rebels to distress.

7 When thou didst march before thy folk th' Egyptians from among,
And brought'st them thro' the wilderness, which was both wide and long,
8 The earth did shake, the heav'ns did drop, great thunder-claps were heard,
Mount Sinai also moved was, when Israel's God appear'd:

9 Thy heritage with drops of rain abundantly was wash'd;
And if so be it barren was, by thee it was refresh'd;
10 Thy chosen flock doth there remain, thou hast prepar'd that place,
And for the poor thou dost provide of thine especial grace.

PART II.

11 God will give women causes just to magnify his Name,
When as his people triumphs make, and purchase mighty fame.
12 Puissant kings, for all their pow'r shall flee and take the foil,
And women which remain at home shall help to part the spoil.

13 And tho' ye were as black as pots, your hue shall pass the dove,
Whose wings and feathers seem to have silver and gold above.
14 When God shall triumph in this land o'er kings both high and low,
Then shall it be like Salmon hill, as white as is the snow.

15 Tho' Basan be a fruitful hill, and in height others pass,
Yet Sion, God's most holy hill, doth far excel in grace.
16 Why leap ye thus, ye hills most high, and thus in pride do swell?
The hill of Sion God doth love, and there will ever dwell.

17 God's army twenty thousand is of angels great and strong;
The Lord also in Sinai is present them among.
18 Thou didst, O Lord, ascend on high, and captive led'st them all,
Who in times past thy chosen flock in bondage did enthral.

19 Thou hast received gifts for men, ev'n for thine enemies,
Unto the end that God the Lord might dwell with them likewise.
20 Now praised be the Lord, for that he pours on us such grace;
From day to day he is the God both of our health and peace.

PART III.

21 He is the God from whom alone salvation we obtain,
He is the God by whom we 'scape all dangers, death, and pain;
22 And he shall wound the head of all his enemies also,
The hairy scalp of such as on in wickedness still go.

23 From Basan will I bring, said he, my people and my sheep,
And all my own, as I have done, from dangers of the deep;
24 And make them dip their feet in blood of those that hate my Name
The tongues of dogs they shall be red with licking of the same.

25 Thy goings they have seen, O God, unto their own disgrace,
How thou, my God and King, dost go within thy holy place;
26 The singers go before with joy, the minstrels make no stay,
And in the midst the damsels do with timbrels sweetly play.

27 Now in the congregations thou, O Israel, praise the Lord,
And Jacob's whole posterity, give thanks with one accord.
28 Their chief was little Benjamin, but Judah made their host,
With Zebulon and Nephthalim, who dwelt about their coast.

29 Thy God hath sent forth strength for thee, O God, make firm and sure,
The thing that thou hast wrought in us for ever to endure:
30 Then in thy temple gifts will we offer to thee, O Lord,
And in thy own Jerusalem praise thee with one accord.

PART IV.

31 Yea, and strange kings, by us subdu'd, shall do like in those days;
For unto thee they shall present their gifts of land and praise.
32 He shall destroy the spearmen's ranks, the calves and bulls of might,
And make them tribute pay, and daunt all such as love to fight.

33 Then shall the lords of Egypt come, and presents with them bring;
The Moors also stretch out their hands to God, their Lord and King.
34 Therefore, ye kingdoms of the earth, give praise unto the Lord;
Sing psalms to God with one consent, thereto let all accord.

35 For he doth ride, and ever did above the heav'ns most bright,
And by his fearful thunder-claps men may well know his might.
36 Therefore the strength of Israel ascribe to God on high,
Whose might and pow'r doth far extend above the cloudy sky.

37 O God, thy holiness and pow'r is dread for evermore:
The God of Israel gives us strength, therefore his Name adore.

PSALM LXIX. J. H.

1 SAVE me, O God, and that with speed, because the waters do
So very nigh my soul proceed, and enter there into;
2 I sink full deep in mire and clay, where I can feel no ground,
And in deep waters where I may most suddenly be drown'd.

3 With crying I am weary, lo, my throat is hoarse and dry,
My sight doth fail, looking also for help to God on high.
4 My guiltless soul for to oppress my foes with hate are led,
In number sure they are no less than hairs upon my head.

5 Tho' for no cause they vex me sore, they prosper and are glad;
They do compel me to restore the things I never had.
6 What I through my simplicity have done, Lord, thou canst tell,
And all my faults in privacy to thee are known full well.

7 O God of hosts, defend and stay all those that trust in thee,
Let no man shrink away for aught that happeneth unto me.
8 It is for thee and for thy sake that I do bear this blame;
In spite to thee they would me mak to hide my face for shame.

9 My mother's sons, my brethren all reject me with disgrace,
And as a stranger they me call, they will not know my face.
10 Unto thy house such zeal I bear, that it doth vex me much,
Their checks and taunts at thee to bear my very heart doth touch.

PART II.

11 Though I do fast my flesh to tame, yea, if I weep and moan,
I am reproached for the same by scorners every one.
12 If I for grief and pain of heart in sackcloth use to walk,
Reproachfully they it pervert, thereof they jest and talk.

13 Both high and low, and all the throng that sit within the gate,
They have me ever in their tongue, of me they talk and prate:
14 They that sit in the gate with spite against me all agree,
The drunkards that in wine delight do make their songs of me.

15 But unto thee, O Lord, I pray, that when it pleaseth thee,
For thy great truth thou wilt alway send down thy aid to me:
16 Pluck thou my feet out of the mire, from drowning do me keep,
From such as owe me wrath and ire, and from the waters deep;

17 Lest with the waves I should be drown'd, and depth my soul devour,
And lest the pit should me confound, and shut me in her pow'r.
18 O Lord of hosts, to me give ear, as thou art good and kind,
And as thy mercy is most dear, Lord, have me in thy mind;

19 And do not from thy servant hide, nor turn thy face away:
I am oppress'd on ev'ry side, in haste give ear, I pray.
20 O Lord, unto my soul draw nigh, the same with aid repose,
Because of their great tyranny acquit me from my foes.

PART III.

21 That I abide rebuke and shame thou know'st, and thou canst tell;
For those that seek and work the same thou seest them all full well.
22 When with reproach they break my heart, some help I fain would see,
But find no friends to ease my smart, not one to comfort me:

23 But in my meat they gave me gall, (too cruel for to think)
And gave me in my thirst withal strong vinegar to drink.
24 Lord, turn their table to a snare to take themselves therein,
And when they think full well to fare, then trap them in their gin:

25 And let their eyes be dark and blind, that they may nothing see;
Bow down their backs, and let them find themselves in thrall to be:
26 Pour out thy wrath as hot as fire, that it on them may fall,
Let thy displeasure in thine ire take hold upon them all:

27 As deserts dry their house disgrace, their seed do thou expel,
That none thereof possess their place, nor in their tents once dwell,
28 If thou dost strike the man to tame, on him they lay full sore,
And if that thou do wound the same, they seek to hurt him more.

29 Then let them heap up mischief still, since they are all pervert,
That of thy favour and good-will they never have a part:
30 And rase them clean out of thy book of life, of hope and trust,
That for their names they never look in number of the just.

PART IV.

31 Though I, O Lord, with pain and grief have been full sore oppress'd,
Thy help shall give me such relief that all shall be redress'd.
32 That I may give thy name the praise that doth to thee belong,
I will extol the same always with a thanksgiving song:

33 Which is more pleasant unto thee, (such mind thy grace hath born)
Than either ox or calf can be, that hath both hoof and horn,
34 When simple folk do this behold, it shall rejoice them sure;
And ye that seek the Lord, your life for ever shall endure.

35 For why? the Lord of hosts doth hear the poor when they complain,
His pris'ners are to him full dear, he doth them not disdain.
36 Wherefore the sky and earth below, the sea with flood and stream,
His praises shall declare and show, with all that live in them.

37 For sure our God will Sion save, and Judah's cities build;
Much folk possession there shall have, her streets shall all be fill'd:
38 His servants' seed shall keep the same all ages out of mind,
And there all they that love his name a dwelling-place shall find.

PSALM LXX. J. H.

1 O GOD, to me take heed, I help of thee require;
O Lord of hosts, with haste and speed help me, I thee desire:
2 With shame confound them all that seek my soul to spill,
Let them be turned back and fall that think and wish me ill.

3 Let them rewarded be with infamy and shame,
Who when harm happens unto me do triumph at the same;

4 But let them joyful be in thee, with joy and wealth,
Who only trust and seek to thee, and to thy saving health:

5 That they may say always, in mirth and one accord,
All glory, honour, laud, and praise be given to the Lord.
6 But I am weak and poor, come, Lord, thy aid I lack;
Thou art my stay and help, therefore make speed and be not slack.

PSALM LXXI. J. H.

1 MY Lord, my God, in all distress my hope is whole in thee;
Then let no shame my soul oppress, nor once take hold on me.
2 As thou art just, defend me, Lord, and rid me out of dread;
Give ear, and to my suit accord, and send me help at need.

3 Be thou my rock, to whom I may for aid all times resort:
Thy promise is to help alway, thou art my fence and fort.
4 Save me, my God, from wicked men, and from their strength and pow'r
From folk unjust, and also them that cruelly devour.

5 Thou art my stay whereon I rest, thou Lord of hosts, art he;
Ev'n from my youth I thought it best still to depend on thee.
6 Thou hast me kept ev'n from my birth, and I through thee was born;
Wherefore I will thee praise with mirth both ev'ning and at morn.

7 As to a monster seldom seen much folk about me throng;
But thou art new, and still hast been my fence and aid most strong.
8 Wherefore my mouth for ever shall be filled with thy praise,
Also my tongue shall never fail to honour thee always.

9 Reject me not, O Lord, I pray, when age my limbs doth take,
And when my strength doth waste away do not my soul forsake.
10 Among themselves my foes enquire to take me through deceit;
And they against me do conspire that for my soul lay wait.

PART II.

11 Lay hands upon him now, they said, for God from him is gone;
Dispatch him quite, for to his aid most sure there cometh none.
12 Do not withdraw thyself away, O Lord, when need shall be,
But that in time of grief I may have speedy help from thee.

13 With shame confound and overthrow all those that seek my life;
Suppress them with rebuke also that fain would work me strife.
14 But I will patiently abide thy help at all essays;
Still more and more each time and tide I will set forth thy praise:

15 My mouth thy justice shall record, that daily help doth send;
For thy great benefits, O Lord, no numbers have nor end.
16 Yet will I go and seek for one, with thy good help, O God,
The saving health of thee alone to shew and set abroad.

17 For of my mouth thou took'st the care, and dost instruct me still;
Therefore thy wonders to declare I have great mind and will.
18 And as in youth from wanton rage thou didst me keep and stay,
Forsake me not in my old age, and when my head is grey.

PART III.

19 That I thy strength and might may show to them that now be here,
And that our seed thy power may know hereafter many year.
20 O Lord, thy justice doth exceed, thy doings all may see;
Thy works are wonderful indeed, Oh, who is like to thee!

21 Thou mad'st me feel affliction sore, and yet thou didst me save;
Yea, thou didst help and me restore, and took'st me from the grave;
22 And thou my honour dost increase, my dignity maintain;
Yea, thou dost make all grief to cease, and comfort'st me again:

23 Therefore thy faithfulness to praise I will with viol sing;
My harp shall sound thy laud always, O Israel's holy King.
24 My mouth will joy with pleasant voice when I shall sing to thee,
Also my soul shall much rejoice, for thou hast set me free.

25 My tongue thy righteousness shall sound, I daily speak it will;
For grief and shame do them confound, that seek to work me ill.

PSALM LXXII. J. H.

1 LORD, give thy judgments to the king, therein instruct him well;
And with his son in every thing, Lord, let thy justice dwell;
2 That he may govern uprightly, and rule thy folk with right;
And so defend with equity the poor that have no might.

3 And let the mountains that are high unto thy folk give peace,
Let little hills also apply in justice to increase;
4 That he may help the weak and poor with aid, and make them strong,
And so destroy for evermore all those that do them wrong.

5 And then from age to age shall they regard and fear thy might,
So long as sun doth shine by day, the moon give light by night.
6 Lord, make the king unto the just like rain to fields new mown,
And like to drops that lay the dust, refreshing land new sown.

7 The just shall flourish in his days, and all shall be at peace,
Until the moon shall cease always to change, waste, or increase.
8 He shall be Lord, and have command from shore to shore throughout,
And from the floods within the land thro' all the earth about.

9 The people that in deserts dwell shall kneel to him full thick,
And all his foes that do rebel the earth and dust shall lick;
10 The lords of all the isles also great gifts to him shall bring,
Arabia and Saba's kings give many a costly thing.

PART II.

11 All kings shall seek with one accord in his good grace to stand
And all the people of the world obey at his command;
12 For he the needy sort doth save that unto him do call,
Also the simple folk that have no help of man at all.

13 He taketh pity on the poor that are with need opprest,
He doth preserve them evermore, and bring their souls to rest:
14 He shall redeem their souls from dread, from fraud, from wrong, and might
Also their blood that shall be shed is precious in his sight.

15 But he shall live, and they shall bring to him of Saba's gold,
He shall be honour'd as a king, and daily be extoll'd.
16 The mighty mountains of his land of corn shall bear such throng,
That it like cedar-trees shall stand in Libanus full long.

17 Their cities also well shall speed, the fruits thereof surpass;
In plenty it shall so exceed, and spring as green as grass.
18 For ever they shall praise his name, while that the sun is light,
And think them happy through the same, all folk shall bless his might.

19 Praise ye the Lord of hosts, and sing to Israel's God each one;
For he doth ev'ry wonderous thing, yea, he himself alone;
20 And blessed be his holy name all times eternally;
Let all the earth still praise the same, Amen, Amen, say I.

PSALM LXXIII. T. S.

1 TRULY the Lord is very good and kind to Israel,
And to all such as safely keep their conscience pure and well.
2 But as for me, I almost slip'd, my feet began to slide,
Before that I was well aware my steps did turn aside.

3 For when I saw such foolish men, I grudg'd with great disdain,
That wicked men all things should have without turmoil and pain:
4 They never suffer pains nor grief, as if death should them smite,
Their bodies are full stout and strong, and ever in good plight:

5 Always free from adversity and ev'ry sad event,
With other men they take no part of plague or punishment:
6 Therefore presumption doth embrace their necks as doth a chain,
They are ev'n wrapt as in a robe with rapine and disdain:

7 They are so fed, that ev'n with fat their eyes oftimes outstart,
And as for worldly goods, they have more than can wish their heart:
8 Their life is most licentious, and they boast much with their tongue
How they the poor and simple have oppressed with great wrong;

9 They set their mouth against the heav'ns, and do the Lord blaspheme,
They proudly boast of wordly things, no one they do esteem.
10 God's people often do turn back to see their prosp'rous state,
And almost drink the self-same cup, and talk at the same rate.

PART II.

11 How can it be that God, say they, should know or understand
Those worldly things, since wicked men be lords of sea and land?
12 For we may see how wicked men in riches still increase,
Rewarded well with worldly goods, and live in rest and peace.

13 Then why do I so carefully from wickedness refrain,
And wash my hands in innocence, and cleanse my heart in vain,
14 And suffer scourges ev'ry day, as subject to all blame,
And ev'ry morning from my youth sustain rebuke and shame?

15 Now I had almost said as they, misliking my estate;
But then I should thy children judge as most unfortunate.
16 Then I bethought me how I might this matter understand,
But yet the labour was too great for me to take in hand;

17 Until the time I went into thy holy place, and then
I understood right perfectly the end of all these men:
18 Namely, how that thou settest them upon a slipp'ry place,
And at thy pleasure and thy will thou dost them soon deface.

19 Then all men muse at that strange sight, to see how suddenly
They do consume, perish, and come to endless misery;
20 Much like a dream when one awakes, so shall their wealth decay,
Their famous names in all men's sight shall fail and pass away.

21 Yet thus my heart was grieved then, my mind was much opprest;
So simple and so ignorant, ev'n as it were a beast.
22 Nevertheless, by thy right-hand thou hold'st me always fast,
And with thy counsel shalt me guide to glory at the last.

23 What thing is there that I can wish but thee in heav'n above?
And in the earth there nothing is like thee that I can love.
24 My flesh and spirit both do fail, but God will me restore,
For of my heart he is the strength and portion evermore.

25 But lo, all such as thee forsake thou shalt destroy each one,
And those that trust in any thing saving in thee alone.
26 Therefore will I draw near to God, and ever with him dwell;
In God alone I put my trust, his wonders I will tell.

PSALM LXXIV. J. H.

1 WHY art thou, Lord, so long from us in all this danger deep?
Why doth thy anger kindle thus at thy own pasture sheep?
2 Lord, call thy people to thy thought which have been thine so long,
The which thou hast redeem'd and brought from bondage sore and strong;

3 Have mind therefore, and think upon, remember it full well,
The pleasant place, thy mount Sion, where thou wast wont to dwell;
4 Lift up thy feet and come in haste, and all thy foes deface,
Who now at pleasure rob and waste within thy holy place.

5 Amidst thy congregations all thy foes do roar, O God;
They set as signs on ev'ry wall banners displayed abroad:
6 As men with axes hew down trees that on the hills do grow,
So shine their bills and swords of these within thy temple now:

7 The ceiling fine and carved boards, with all the goodly stones,
With axes, hammers, bills, and swords, they beat them down at once;
8 Thy places they consume with flame, their rage doth so abound;
The house appointed to thy name they rase ev'n to the ground.

9 And thus they say within their heart, dispatch them out of hand:
Then burn they up in ev'ry part God's houses through the land.
10 Yet thou no sign of help dost send, our prophets all are gone,
To tell when this our plague shall end among us there is none.

11 How long, Lord, shall thy enemies thus boldly thee defame?
Shall they for evermore blaspheme thy great and holy name?
12 Why dost thou thy right hand withdraw from us so long away?
Out of thy bosom pluck it forth with speed thy foes to slay.

PART II.

13 O God, thou art our King and Lord, and evermore hast been;
Yea, thy good grace throughout the world for our great help is seen:
14 The seas, that are so deep and dead, thy might did make them dry,
And thou didst break the serpent's head, that he therein did die:

15 Yea, thou didst break the head so great of whales that are most fell,
And gav'st them to the folk to eat that in the deserts dwell.
16 Thou mad'st a spring with streams to rise from rocks both hard and high,
Thy mighty hand hath made likewise deep waters to be dry.

17 Both day and night also are thine, by thee they were begun:
And thou likewise prepared hast the light of moon and sun:
18 Thou didst appoint the ends and coasts of all the earth about,
Both summer heats and winter frosts thy hand hath found them out.

19 Think on, O Lord, no time forget, thy foes that thee defame,
And how the foolish folk are set to rail upon thy name:
20 Deliver not the soul, O Lord, of thy own turtle dove
Into their hands, but help afford the poor whom thou dost love.

21 Regard, O Lord, thy covenant, behold our misery;
All the dark places of the earth are full of cruelty;
22 Let not the simple man therefore be turned back with shame;
But let the needy evermore give praise unto thy name.

23 Arise, O Lord, and plead thy cause against thy enemies,
Who daily do reject thy laws, and them with scorn despise:
24 The voice forget not of thy foes, for the presumption high
Is more and more increas'd of those that hate thee spitefully.

PSALM LXXV. J. H.

1 TO thee, O God, will we give thanks, we will give thanks to thee,
Since thy name is so near, declare thy wondrous works will we.
2 I will uprightly judge, when get convenient time I may;
The earth is weak and all therein, but I her pillars stay.

3 I did to the mad people say, deal not so furiously,
And unto the ungodly ones, lift not your horns on high;
4 I said unto them, Set not up your raised horns on high,
And see that with stiff neck you do not speak presumptuously:

5 For neither from the eastern parts nor from the west likewise,
Nor from forsaken wilderness promotion doth arise;
6 But God, who rules both heav'n and earth, the righteous judge alone;
It's he that puts down one, and sets another on the throne:

7 For why? a cup of mighty wine is in the hand of God,
And all the mixture of the same himself will pour abroad;
8 As for the lees and filthy dregs that do remain of it,
The wicked of the earth shall drink and suck them ev'ry whit.

9 But I will talk of God alway, and his great name adore,
And will not cease to celebrate his praise for evermore;
10 In sunder break the horns of all ungodly men will I,
But then the horns of righteous men shall be exalted high.

PSALM LXXVI. J. H.

1 TO all that now in Judah dwell
the Lord is clearly known,
His name is great in Israel,
a people of his own;
2 At Salem he hath pitch'd his tent
to tarry there a space,
In Sion also he is bent
to fix his dwelling-place:

3 And there he brake both shaft and bow,
the sword, the spear, and shield,
His enemies did overthrow
in battle in the field.
4 Thou art more worthy honour, Lord,
more might in thee doth lie
Than in the strongest of the world
that rob on mountains high.

5 But now the proud are spoil'd thro' thee,
and they are fall'n asleep;
Thro' men of war no help can be,
themselves they could not keep.
6 At thy rebuke, O Jacob's God,
when thou didst them reprove,
As half asleep their chariots stood,
no horsemen once did move.

7 For thou art dreadful, Lord, indeed,
what man the courage hath
T' abide thy sight, and doth not dread
when thou art in thy wrath,
8 When thou dost make thy judgments heard
from heav'n unto the ground,
Then all the earth, full sore afraid,
in silence shall be found:

9 And when that thou, O God, dost stand
in judgment for to speak,
To save th' afflicted of the land,
that feeble are and weak,
10 The fury that in man doth reign
shall turn unto thy praise;
Hereafter, Lord, do thou restrain
their wrath and threats always.

11 Make vows and pay them to our God,
ye folk that nigh him be,
Bring gifts, all ye that dwell abroad,
for dreadful sure is he:
12 For he doth take both life and might
from princes great of birth;
And full of terror is his sight
to all the kings on earth.

PSALM LXXVII. J. H.

1 I WITH my voice to God did cry,
who lent a gracious ear;
My voice I lifted up on high,
and he my suit did hear;
2 In time of grief I sought to God,
by night no rest I took,
But stretch'd my hand to him abroad,
comfort my soul forsook.

3 When I to think on God intend,
my trouble then is more;
I spake, but could not make an end,
my breath was stopt so sore.
4 Thou dost mine eyes so hold from rest,
that I'm always awake:
With fear I am so sore opprest,
my speech doth me forsake:

5 The days of old in mind I cast,
and oft do think upon
The times and ages that are past
full many years agone:
6 By night my songs I call to mind,
once made thy praise to show,
And with my heart much talk I find,
my spirit search to know:

7 Will God, said I, at once for all
cast off his people thus,
So that henceforth no time he shall
be friendly unto us?
8 What, is his goodness quite decay'd,
and passed clean away?
Or is his promise now delay'd,
and doth his truth decay?

9 And will the Lord our God forget
his mercies manifold?
Or shall his wrath increase so hot,
his mercies be withheld?
10 At last, I said, this surely is
mine own infirmity;
But his right-hand can help all this,
and change it speedily,

PART II.

11 I will regard and think upon the working of the Lord,
And all his wonders past and gone I gladly will record,
12 Yea, all his words I will declare, and what he did devise;
To tell his facts I will not spare, and all his counsel wise.

13 Thy works, O Lord, are all upright, and holy all abroad;
What one hath strength to match the might of thee the Lord our God.
14 Thou art a God that dost forth show thy wonders ev'ry hour,
And so dost make the people know thy virtue and thy pow'r:

15 And thy own folk thou dost defend, with an out-stretched arm,
Those that from Jacob did descend, and Joseph's seed from harm.
16 The waters, Lord, perceived thee, the waters saw thee well;
And they for fear away did flee, the depths a trembling fell.

17 The clouds that were both thick and black did rain full plenteously,
The thunder in the air did crack, thy shafts abroad did fly;
18 Thy thunder in the air was heard, the lightnings from above
With flashes great made men afraid, the earth did quake and move:

19 Thy ways within the sea do lie, thy paths in waters deep;
Yet none can there thy steps espy, nor know thy paths to keep:
20 Thou ledd'st thy folk upon the land as sheep on ev'ry side,
By Moses and by Aaron's hand thou didst them safely guide.

PSALM LXXVIII. J. H.

1 ATTEND my people, to my law, and to my words incline;
My mouth shall speak strange parables, and sentences divine;
2 Which we ourselves have heard and learnt ev'n of our fathers old,
And which for our instruction them our fathers have us told:

3 Because we should not keep it close from them that after came,
Who should God's mighty power declare, and wond'rous works proclaim;
4 To Jacob he commandment gave how Israel should live,
Willing our fathers should the same unto their children give;

5 That they and their posterity that were not sprung up then,
Should have the knowledge of the law, and teach it their children:
6 That they might have the better hope in God that is above,
And not forget to keep his laws and his commands in love:

7 Not being as their fathers, who rebelled in God's sight,
And would not frame their wicked hearts to know their God aright;
8 How went the sons of Ephraim their neighbours for to spoil,
Shooting their darts in day of war, and yet receiv'd the foil?

9 For why? they did not keep with God the covenant that was made,
Nor yet would walk or lead their lives according as he said;
10 But put into oblivion his counsel and his will,
And all his works magnificent which he declared still.

PART II.

11 What wonders to our fore-fathers did he himself disclose,
In Egypt's land, within the field that call'd is Thaneos!

12 He did divide and part the sea, through which he made a way
For them to pass, and on a heap the waters made to stay;

13 He led them secret in a cloud by day, when it was bright,
And in the night when it was dark with fire he gave them light;
14 He clave the rocks in wilderness, and gave the people drink
As plentiful as when the deeps do flow up to the brink:

15 He drew forth rivers out of rocks, that were both dry and hard,
In such abundance that no floods to them might be compar'd.
16 Yet, for all this, against the Lord their sin they did increase,
And stirr'd up him who is most high to wrath in wilderness;

17 And in their hearts they tempted God like people of mistrust,
Requiring such a kind of meat as served to their lust:
18 Yea, they against him spake, and thus their boldness did express;
Can God prepare a table in this barren wilderness?

19 Indeed he smote the stony rock, and floods forthwith did flow,
But can he now give to his folk both bread and flesh also?
20 When God heard this, he waxed wroth with Jacob and his seed,
His indignation also did 'gainst Israel proceed.

PART III.

21 Because they did not faithfully believe, and hope that he
Could always help and succour them in their necessity;
22 Wherefore he did command the clouds, forthwith they brake in sunder,
And rain'd down manna for to eat, a food of mighty wonder;

23 When earthly men with angels' food did plentifully feast;
He made the east-wind blow away, and brought in the south-west:
24 He rain'd down flesh as thick as dust, and fowls as thick as sand,
Which he did cast amidst the place where all their tents did stand.

25 Then did they eat exceedingly, and all men had their fills:
Yet more and more they did desire to serve their lusts and wills:
26 But as the meat was in their mouths, his wrath upon them fell,
And slew the strength of all their youth, and choice of Israel.

27 Yet fell they to their wonted sin, and still they did him grieve;
For all the wonders that he wrought, they would not him believe:
28 Their days therefore he shorten'd, and did make their honour vain,
Their years did waste and pass away with terror and with pain:

29 But ever when he plagued them they sought him speedily,
Rememb'ring that he was their strength, their help and God most high:
30 Tho' with their mouths they nothing did but flatter with the Lord,
And with their tongues, and in their hearts, dissembled ev'ry word:

PART IV.

31 For why? their hearts were nothing bent to him, nor what he said,
Nor yet to keep or to perform the covenant he had made.
32 Yet was he still so merciful, when they deserv'd to die,
That he forgave them, and would not them utterly destroy.

33 Yea, many times he stay'd his wrath, and did not them surprise,
And would not suffer that his whole displeasure should arise;

34 Considering they were but **flesh,** or like to wind and rain,
Passing away that never doth return and come again.

35 How often in the wilderness did they the Lord provoke!
How they **did** move and stir him **up** to plague them with his stroke!
36 Yet did they turn again to sin, and tempt him very soon,
Prescribing to the mighty God what things they would have done:

37 Not thinking of his mighty hand, nor of the day when he
Deliver'd them out of the hand of the fierce enemy;
38 Nor how he wrought his miracles (as they themselves beheld)
In Egypt, and the wonders that he did in Zoan field:

39 Nor how he turned by his pow'r their waters into blood,
That no man might receive his drink at river or at flood;
40 Nor how he sent them swarms of flies, which did them sore annoy,
And fill'd their country full of frogs, which did their land destroy.

PART V.

41 Nor how he did their fruits unto the caterpillar give,
And of the labour of their hands locusts did them deprive:
42 With hail-stones he destroy'd their **vines,** so that they all were lost,
And likewise **all their sycamores,** he did consume with frost:

43 With hail-stones also once again the Lord their cattle smote,
And all their flocks and herds **likewise** with thunder-bolts full hot:
44 **He cast** upon them his fierce wrath, and indgnation sore,
Amongst them evil angels sent, which troubled them yet more.

45 **Then to** his wrath he made a way, and spared not the least,
But **gave unto the** pestilence the man as well as beast:
46 He smote **also** all the first-born that up in Egypt came,
And all the chief of men and beasts within the tents of Ham:

47 But as for his own people, he **did them** preserve and keep,
And carried **them** through wilderness, **ev'n** like a flock of sheep:
48 Without **all fear,** both safe and **sound,** **he** brought them out of thrall;
Whereas **their foes** with rage of seas were overwhelmed all;

49 And brought them out into the coasts of his own holy land,
Ev'n to the mount **which he had got** **by his** strong arm and hand:
50 And there cast out **the heathen folk,** and did their land divide,
And in their tents he **set the tribes** of Israel to abide.

51 **Yet, for** all this, the God **most high** they mov'd and tempted still,
And **would** not keep his testament, nor yet obey his will;
52 **But as** their fathers turned back, ev'n so they went astray,
Much like a bow that would **not bend,** but slip and start away;

PART VI.

53 And **griev'd** him with their hill altars, with offerings and fire,
And **with their** idols grievously provoked him to ire.
54 For which his wrath began again to kindle in his breast,
The wickedness **of Israel** he **did so** much detest:

55 The tabernacle **he** forsook of **Silo,** where he was
Right conversant with earthly men, ev'n as his dwelling-place.

56 Then suffer'd he his might and pow'r in bondage for to be,
And gave the honour of his ark unto the enemy:

57 And did commit them to the sword, wroth with his heritage;
Their young men were consum'd with fire, maids had no marriage:
58 And with the sword the priests also did perish every one,
Nor was a widow left alive their death for to bemoan.

59 Then did the Lord awake as one whom sleep could not confine,
And like a mighty giant that refreshed is with wine;
60 With em'rods in the hinder parts his enemies he smote,
And put them unto such a shame as should not be forgot:

61 The tent and tabernacle he of Joseph did refuse,
Also the tribe of Ephraim he would in no wise chuse;
62 But he the tribe of Judah chose, that he therein might dwell,
Ev'n the most noble mount Sion, which he did love so well:

63 And there he did his temple build, both sumptuously and sure,
Like as the earth, which he hath made for ever to endure.
64 Then chose he David him to serve, his people for to keep,
Whom he took up and brought away ev'n from the folds of sheep:

65 From following the ewes with young the Lord did him advance,
To feed his people Israel, and his inheritance.
66 Thus David with a faithful heart his flock and charge did feed,
And prudently with all his pow'r did govern them indeed.

PSALM LXXIX. J. H.

1 O GOD the Gentiles do invade thy heritage to spoil;
Jerusalem a heap is made, thy temple they defile;
2 The bodies of thy saints most dear abroad to birds they cast,
The flesh of them that do thee fear the beasts devour and waste.

3 Their blood throughout Jerusalem as waters spilt they have,
So that there is not one of them to lay their dead in grave.
4 Thus are we made a laughing-stock almost the world throughout,
The enemies at us do mock who dwell our coasts about.

5 How long, O Lord, wilt thou retain thy anger and thy rage?
And shall thy wrath and jealousy not any more asswage?
6 Upon those people pour the same, who did thee never know,
The realms which call not on thy name consume and overthrow:

7 For they have got the upper hand, and Jacob's seed destroy'd,
His habitation and his land they have laid waste and void.
8 Bear not in mind our former faults, with speed some pity show;
And aid us, Lord, in our assaults, for we are weak and low.

PART II.

9 O God, that giv'st all health and grace, on us declare the same,
Weigh not our works, our sins efface, for honour of thy name.
10 Why should the wicked thus alway to us as people dumb,
In thy reproach rejoice and say, where is their God become?

11 Requite, O Lord, as thou seest good before our eyes in sight
Of all these folk thy servants' blood, which they spilt in despight;

12 Receive into thy sight in haste the clamours, grief and wrong,
Of such as are in prison cast, and bound in irons strong:

13 Thy force and strength to celebrate, Lord, set them out of band,
Who unto death are destinate, and in their foes' strong hand;
14 The nations which have been so bold, as to blaspheme thy name,
Into their laps do thou sev'n-fold repay again the same.

15 So we thy flock and pasture-sheep will praise thee evermore,
And teach all ages how to keep for thee like praise in store.

PSALM LXXX. J. H.

1 THOU Shepherd, that dost Israel keep, give ear, and take good heed,
Who leadest Joseph like a sheep, and dost him watch and feed;
2 And thou, O Lord, whose seat is set on cherubim most bright,
Shew forth thyself, and do not let, send down thy beams of light:

3 Before Ephraim and Benjamin, Manasses in likewise,
To shew thy power do thou begin, come help us, Lord, arise;
4 Direct our hearts by thy good grace, convert us unto thee,
Shew us the brightness of thy face, and then full safe are we.

5 Lord God of hosts of Israel, how long wilt thou delay,
And 'gainst thy folk in anger swell, and wilt not hear them pray?
6 Thou dost them feed with sorrows deep, their bread with grief they eat,
And drink the tears that they do weep, in measure full and great.

7 Thou hast us made a very strife to those that dwell about,
Which much doth please our enemies, they laugh and jest it out.
8 O take us, Lord, unto thy grace, convert our hearts to thee;
Shew forth to us thy joyful face, and we full safe shall be.

9 From Egypt, where it grew not well, thou brought'st a vine full dear
The heathen folk thou didst expel, and thou didst plant it there:
10 Thou didst prepare for it a place, and set its roots so fast,
That it did grow and spring apace, and fill'd the land at last:

PART II.

11 The hills were covered round about with shade that from it came,
Also the cedars strong and stout with branches of the same.
12 Why then didst thou her walls destroy? her hedge pluck'd up thou hast
That all the folk that pass thereby, the same do spoil and waste:

13 The boar out of the wood so wild doth dig and root it out,
The furious beasts out of the field devour it all about.
14 O Lord of hosts, return again, from heav'n do thou look down,
Behold, and with thy help sustain thy vineyard overthrown:

15 Thy pleasant vine, thy Israel, which thy right hand hath set,
The same which thou didst love so well, O Lord, do not forget;
16 They lop and cut it off apace, they burn it down with fire;
And through the frowning of thy face we perish in thine ire.

17 Let thy right hand be with him now, whom thou hast kept so long,
And with the son of man, whom thou to thee hast made so strong:
18 And so, when thou hast set us free and saved us from shame,
Then will we never fall from thee, but call upon thy name.

19 O Lord of hosts, through thy good grace convert us unto thee;
Behold us with a pleasant face, and then full safe are we.

PSALM LXXXI. J. H.

1 BE light and glad, in God rejoice, who is our strength and stay;
Be joyful and lift up your voice to Jacob's God alway:
2 Prepare your instruments most meet some joyful psalm to sing,
Strike up with harp and lute so sweet on every pleasant string:

3 Blow as it were in the new moon with trumpets of the best,
As it is used to be done at any solemn feast:
4 For this is unto Israel a statute, which was made
By Jacob's God, and must full well be evermore obey'd;

5 This clause with Joseph was decreed, when he from Egypt came,
That as a witness all his seed should still observe the same.
6 When God himself had so prepar'd to bring him from that land,
Whereas the speech that he had heard he did not understand;

7 I from his shoulder took, saith he, the burden clean away,
And from the furnace set him free from burning brick of clay;
8 When thou in grief didst cry and call I help'd thee speedily;
And I did answer thee withal in thunder from on high:

9 Yea, at the waters of discord I did thee tempt and prove,
Where thou the anger of the Lord with murmuring didst move.
10 Hear, O my people Israel, what I do promise thee,
Regard and mark my words full well, if thou wilt cleave to me.

PART II.

11 Thou shalt no god in thee reserve of any land abroad,
And in no wise bow to or serve a strange and foreign god;
12 I am the Lord thy God, and I from Egypt set thee free;
Then ask of me abundantly, and I will give it thee.

13 But yet my people would not hear my voice when that I spake,
And Israel would not obey, but did me quite forsake:
14 Then did I leave them to their will, in hardness of their heart,
To walk in their own counsels still themselves they did pervert,

15 O that my people would have heard the words that I did say;
And Israel with due regard had walked in my way;
16 I should have soon destroy'd their foes, and brought them down full low,
And turn'd my hand against all those that sought their overthrow;

17 And they that at the Lord did rage as lyars shall be found;
But for his folk, their time and age should with great joys be crown'd:
18 I would have fed them with the crop and finest of the wheat,
And made the rock with honey drop, that they their fills might eat.

PSALM LXXXII. J. H.

1 AMONG the princes, men of might, the Lord himself doth stand,
To plead the cause of truth and right with judges of the land.
2 How long, saith he, will ye proceed false judgments to award?
Why have ye partially agreed the wicked to regard?

3 Whereas of right ye should defend the fatherless and weak;
And when the poor man doth contend, in judgment justly speak.
4 If ye be wise, defend the cause of poor men in their right,
And rid the needy from the claws of tyrants force and might.

5 They will not learn nor understand, but still in darkness go;
All the foundations of the land are out of course also.
6 I had decreed assuredly as gods to take you all;
Children also of the most high, for love I did you call;
7 But notwithstanding ye shall die as men, and so decay;
O tyrants, you destroy will I, and pluck you quite away.
8 Up, Lord, and let thy strength be known, and judge the world with might,
For why? all nations are thy own, to take them as thy right.

PSALM LXXXIII. J. H.

1 DO not, O God, refrain thy tongue, in silence do not stay;
With-hold not, Lord, thyself so long, and make no more delay.
2 For why? behold thy foes, and see how they do rage and cry;
And those that bear a hate to thee hold up their heads on high:

3 Against thy folk they use deceit, and craftily enquire;
For thine elect to lie in wait in council they conspire.
4 Come on, say they, let us expel and pluck this folk away,
So that the name of Israel may utterly decay.

5 They all conspire within their heart how they may thee withstand,
Against the Lord to take a part they are in league and band:
6 The tents of all the Edomites, the Ismaelites likewise,
The Hagarens and Moabites their plots do still devise;

7 Gebal and Ammon do likewise with Amalek conspire,
The Philistines against thee rise, with them that dwell at Tyre;
8 Assur is also join'd to them in their conspiracy,
And is become a fence and aid to Lot's posterity.

9 As thou didst to the Midianites, so serve them, Lord, each one;
To Jabin and to Sisera, beside the brook Kison;
10 Whom thou in Endor didst destroy, and waste them thro' thy might,
That they like dung on earth did lie, and that in open sight.

PART II.

11 Make them now and their lords appear like Zeb and Oreb then;
As Zeba and Zalmunna were, the kings of Midian;
12 Who said, let us throughout the land, in all the coasts abroad,
Possess and take into our hand the fair houses of God.

13 Turn them, O God, with storms so fast as wheels that have no stay,
Or like the chaff, which men do cast with wind to fly away;
14 Like as the fire with rage and fume the mighty forest spills,
And as the flame doth quite consume the mountains and the hills;

15 So let the tempest of thy wrath upon their necks be laid,
And of thy wind and stormy breath, Lord, make them all afraid.
16 Lord, bring them all, I thee desire, to such rebuke and shame,
That it may cause them to enquire, and learn to seek thy name:

17 And let them daily more and more to shame and slander fall,
And in rebuke and obloquy confound and seek them all;
18 That they may know and understand, thou art the God most high,
And that thou dost with mighty hand the world rule constantly.

PSALM LXXXIV. J. H.

1 HOW pleasant is thy dwelling-place, O Lord of hosts, to me?
The tabernacles of thy grace, how pleasant, Lord, they be?
2 My soul doth long full sore to go into thy courts abroad,
My heart and flesh cry out also for thee the living God.

3 The sparrows find a room to rest, and save themselves from wrong,
The swallow also hath a nest wherein to keep her young:
4 These birds full nigh thy altar may have place to sit and sing,
O Lord of hosts, thou art alway my only God and King.

5 O they be blessed that may dwell within thine house always!
For they all times thy facts do tell, and ever give thee praise:
6 Yea, happy sure likewise are they, whose stay and strength thou art,
Who to thine house do mind the way, and seek it in their heart.

7 As they go through the vale of tears they dig up fountains still;
That as a spring it all appears, and thou their pits dost fill.
8 From strength to strength they go full fast, no faintness there shall be;
And so the God of gods at last in Sion they do see.

9 O Lord of hosts, to me give heed, and hearken to my cry,
And let it through thine ears proceed, O Jacob's God most high.
10 O God our shield, of thy good grace regard, and so draw near,
Regard, O Lord, behold the face of thine Anointed dear:

11 For why? within thy courts one day is better to abide,
Than other where to keep or stay a thousand days beside.
12 Much rather had I keep a door within the house of God,
Than in the tents of wickedness to settle my abode.

13 For God the Lord, light and defence, will grace and worship give,
And no good thing will he withhold, from them that purely live.
14 O Lord of hosts, that man is blest, and happy sure is he,
That is persuaded in his breast to trust all times in thee.

PSALM LXXXV. J. H.

1 THOU hast been merciful indeed, O Lord, unto thy land;
For thou restored'st Jacob's seed from thraldom by strong hand:
2 The wicked ways that they were in thou didst them clean remit;
And thou didst hide thy people's sin, full close thou cover'dst it:

3 And thou thy anger didst aswage, that all thy wrath was gone;
And so didst turn thee from thy rage, with them to be at one.
4 O God our help, do thou convert thy people unto thee,
Put all thy wrath from us apart, and angry cease to be.

5 Shall thy fierce anger never end, but still be pour'd on us?
And shall thy wrath itself extend unto all ages thus?
6 Wilt thou not rather turn again, and quicken us, that we
And all thy folk that yet remain may glad and joyful be?

7 O Lord, on us do thou declare thy goodness to our wealth;
Shew forth to us, and do not spare thy aid and saving health.
8 I'll hear what God the Lord doth say, to his he speaketh peace,
And to his saints, that never they return to foolishness.

9 For why? his help is still at hand to such as do him fear,
Whereby great glory in our land shall dwell and flourish there,
10 For truth and mercy there shall meet in one to take their place,
And peace shall justice with kiss greet, and there they shall embrace.

11 Truth from the earth shall spring apace, and flourish pleasantly;
So righteousness shall shew her face, and look from heav'n most high:
12 Yea, God himself doth take in hand to give us each good thing,
And through the coasts of all the land the earth her fruit shall bring.

13 Before his face shall justice go, like to a guide or stay,
He shall direct his steps also, and keep them in the way.

PSALM LXXXVI. J. H.

1 LORD, bow thy ear to my request, and hear me speedily;
For with great pain and grief opprest, full poor and weak am I:
2 Preserve my soul, because my ways and doings holy be;
And save thy servant, O my God, that puts his trust in thee.

3 Thy mercy upon me express, and me defend alway,
For through the day I do not cease to thee, O Lord, to pray.
4 Comfort thy servant's soul, I pray, that now with pain is pin'd;
For unto thee I do alway lift up my soul and mind,

5 For thou art good and bountiful, thy gifts of grace are free,
Also thy mercy plentiful to all that call on thee.
6 O Lord, likewise when I do pray, regard and give an ear,
Mark well the words that I do say, all my petitions hear.

7 In time when trouble doth me move to thee I do complain;
For why? I know and well do prove thou answer'st me again,
8 Among the gods, O Lord is none with thee to be compar'd;
And none can do as thou hast done, the like has not been heard.

PART II.

9 The Gentiles and the people all whom thou didst make and frame,
Before thy face on knees shall fall, and glorify thy name,
10 For why? thou art so much of might, all power is thy own,
Thou workest wonders still in sight; for thou art God alone.

11 O teach me, Lord, thy way, and I shall in thy truth proceed;
O join my heart to thee so nigh that I thy name may dread.
12 To thee will I give thanks and praise, O Lord, with all my heart,
And glorify thy name always, because my God thou art.

13 For why? thy mercy shew'd to me is great and doth excel;
Thou sett'st my soul at liberty out from the lowest hell.
14 O Lord, the proud against me rise, and heaps of men of might;
They seek my soul, and in no wise will have thee in their sight.

15 Thou, Lord, art merciful and kind, but very slow to wrath;
Thy goodness is full great, I find, thy truth no measure hath;

16 O turn to me, and mercy show, thy strength to me apply;
O help and save thy servant now, thy handmaid's son am I:

17 On me some sign of favour show, that all my foes may see
And be asham'd, because that thou dost help and comfort me.

PSALM LXXXVII. J. H.

1 THAT city shall full well endure her ground-work still doth stay
Upon the holy hills full sure, it can no time decay.
2 God loves the gates of Sion best, his grace doth there abide,
He loves them more than all the rest of Jacob's ten's beside.

3 Full glorious things reported be in Sion and abroad;
Great things, I say, are said of thee, thou city of our God.
4 On Rahab I will cast an eye, and bear in mind the same;
To Babylon also apply, and them that know thy name.

5 Lo, Palestine, and Tyre also, with Ethiope likewise:
A people old, full long ago, were born and there did rise.
6 Of Sion they shall say abroad, that divers men of fame
Have there sprung up, and the high God hath founded fast the same.

7 In their records to them it shall by him be made appear,
Of Sion, that the chief of all had his beginning there.
8 The trumpeters with such as sing there in great plenty be:
My fountains and my pleasant springs are all contain'd in thee.

PSALM LXXXVIII. J. H.

1 LORD God of health, the hope and stay thou art alone to me,
I call and cry throughout the day, and all the night to thee.
2 O let my prayer with speed ascend unto thy sight on high,
Incline thine ear, O Lord, attend, and hearken to my cry.

3 For why? with woe my heart is fill'd, and doth in trouble dwel
My life and breath doth almost yield, and draweth nigh to hell.
4 I am esteem'd as one of them that in the pit do fall,
And made as one among those men that have no strength at all;

5 As one among the dead, and free, from things that here remain;
It were more ease for me to be with them the which are slain;
6 As those that lie in grave, I say, whom thou hast clean forgot,
The which thy hand hath cut away, and thou regard'st them not:

7 Yea like to one shut up full sure within the lowest pit,
In darksome place and all obscure, and in the depth of it.
8 Thy anger and thy wrath likewise full sore on me do lie,
And all thy storms against me rise, my soul to vex and try.

9 Thou putt'st my friends far off from me, and mak'st them hate me sore,
I am shut up in prison fast, and can come forth no more:
10 My sight doth fail, through grief and woe, I call to thee, O God,
Throughout the day my hands also to thee I stretch abroad.

PART II.

11 Dost thou unto the dead declare thy wondrous works of fame?
Shall dead to life again repair, and praise thee for the same?

12 Or shall thy loving-kindness, Lord, be shewed in the grave?
Or shall with them that are destroy'd thy truth her honour have?

13 Shall they that lie in dark full low see all thy wonders great?
Or there shall they thy justice know, where men all thing forget?
14 But I, O Lord, to thee alway do cry and call apace,
My pray'r also ere it be day shall come before thy face.

15 Why dost thou, Lord, abhor my soul in grief that seeketh thee?
And now, O Lord, why dost thou hide thy face away from me?
16 I am afflicted, dying still from youth many a year,
Thy terrors which do work me ill with troubled mind I bear:

17 The furies of thy wrathful rage full sore upon me lie,
Thy terrors they do not asswage, but press me heavily;
18 All day they compass me about, as water at the tide,
And all at once with streams full great beset me on each side.

19 Thou settest far from me my friends and lovers every one;
Yea, and my old acquaintance all out of my sight are gone.

PSALM LXXXIX. J. H.

1 TO sing the mercies of the Lord my tongue shall never spare;
My mouth from age to age accord thy truth for to declare.
2 For I have said that mercy shall for evermore endure,
Thy faithfulness in the heav'ns all is 'stablsh'd firm and sure.

3 With mine elect, saith God, have I a faithful cov'nant made
And sworn to David solemnly, having to him thus said,
4 Thy seed for ever I will stay, and 'stablish it full fast,
And still uphold thy throne alway from age to age to last.

5 The heav'ns do shew with joy and mirth thy wond'rous works, O Lord;
Thy saints within the church on earth thy faith and truth record.
6 Who with the Lord is equal then in all the clouds abroad?
Among the sons of gods and men what one is like our God?

7 God in th' assembly of the saints is greatly to be dread,
And over all that dwell about in rev'rence to be had.
8 Lord God of hosts, in all the world what one is like to thee?
On every side, most mighty Lord, thy truth is seen to be.

9 The rage and fury of the sea thou rulest at thy will,
And when the waves thereof arise, thou mak'st them calm and still:
10 And Egypt, Lord, thou hast subdu'd, thou hast destroy'd it quite;
Thy foes thou closely hast pursu'd, and scatter'd thro' thy might.

PART II.

11 The heav'ns are thine, and still have been, likewise the earth and land,
The world and all that is therein thou foundest with thy hand:
12 Both north and south, with east and west, thyself didst make and frame;
Both Tabor mount, and Hermon hill rejoice, and praise thy name.

13 Thy arm is strong and full of power, all might therein doth lie,
The strength of thy right hand each hour thou liftest up on high;
14 In righteousness and equity thou hast thy seat and place;
Mercy and truth are still with thee, and go before thy face.

15 That folk is blest that knoweth right the joyful sound, O God;
For in the favour of thy sight they walk full safe abroad;
16 And in thy name throughout the day they greatly do rejoice,
And through thy righteousness have they a pleasant fame and noise.

17 For why? their glory, strength, and aid, in thee alone doth lie;
And thy goodness which hath us staid, shall lift our horn on high.
18 Our strength that doth defend us well the Lord to us doth bring;
The Holy One of Israel he is our guide and king.

19 Sometimes thy will to holy men in visions thou didst show,
And thus didst say unto them then thy mind to make them know,
20 A man of might I have erect your King and guide to be,
And set him up whom I elect among the folk to me.

PART III.

21 My servant David I appoint to rule my people well,
And with my holy oil anoint him king of Israel.
22 For why? my hand is ready still with him for to remain,
And with my arm I also will him strengthen and sustain:

23 The enemies shall not oppress, they shall not him devour,
Nor shall the sons of wickedness on him have any pow'r:
24 His foes likewise I will destroy before his face in sight,
Those that him hate I will annoy, and strike them with my might:

25 My truth and mercy shall likewise upon him ever lie,
And in my name his horn shall rise, and be exalted high:
26 His kingdom I will set to be upon the sea and land;
Also the running floods shall he embrace with his right hand:

27 He shall depend with all his heart on me, and thus shall say,
My Father and my God thou art, my rock, my health, and stay:
28 As my first-born I him will count of all on earth that springs:
His might and honour shall surmount above all earthly kings.

29 My mercy shall be with him still, as I myself have told,
My faithful cov'nant to fulfil my promise I will hold:
30 Also his seed I will sustain for ever strong and sure;
So that his seat shall still remain, while heav'n and earth endure.

PART IV.

31 But if his sons forsake my law, and so begin to swerve,
And of my judgments have no awe, and will not them observe:
32 Or if they do not use aright my laws for them prepar'd;
But set all my commandments light, and will not them regard;

33 Then with the rod I will begin their doings to amend,
And so will scourge them for their sin, whenever they offend.
34 But yet my mercy and goodness I will not take away
From him, nor let my faithfulness in any wise decay:

35 But sure my cov'nant I will hold with all that I have spoke:
No word the which my lips have told shall alter or be broke.
36 Once sware I by my holiness and that perform will I;
With David I will promise keep, to him I will not lye:

37 His seed for evermore shall reign, also his throne of might,
As doth the sun it shall remain for ever in my sight:
38 And as the moon within the sky for ever standeth fast,
A faithful witness from on high; so shall his kingdom last.

39 But, Lord, thou dost him now reject, and put him in great fear;
Yea, thou art wroth with thine elect, thy own anointed dear:
40 The cov'nant with thy servant made thou hast quite overthrown,
And down upon the ground hast laid and cast his royal crown:

PART V.

41 His hedges thou hast overthrown, his walls destroy'd quite round,
All his strong holds hast beaten down, and levell'd with the ground:
42 That he is sore destroy'd and torn of comers-by throughout,
And so is made a mock and scorn to all that dwell about:

43 Thou their right hand hast arm'd with pow'r, that him so sore annoy;
And all his foes that him devour, lo, thou hast made to joy.
44 His sword's edge thou dost take away that should his foes withstand;
To him in war no victory thou giv'st, nor upper hand:

45 His glory thou dost also waste, his throne, his joy and mirth
By thee is overthrown and cast full low upon the earth:
46 Thou hast cut off, and made full short his youth and joyful days,
And rais'd of him an ill report, to his shame and dispraise.

47 How long away from me therefore, for ever wilt thou turn?
And shall thine anger evermore like fire consume and burn?
48 O call to mind, remember then, my time consumeth fast:
Why hast thou made the sons of men as things in vain to waste?

49 What man is he that liveth, and death never thinks to see?
Or from the grave's devouring hand shall he his soul set free?
50 Where is, O Lord, thy great goodness so oft declar'd before,
Which by thy truth and uprightness to David thou hast swore?

51 The great rebukes to mind I call that on thy servants lie,
The railings of the people all, borne in my breast have I.
52 Wherewith, O Lord, thine enemies blasphemed have thy Name;
The steps of thine anointed one they cease not to defame.

53 All praise be given unto thee, O God the Lord most high,
From this time forth for evermore, Amen, amen, say I.

PSALM XC. J. H.

1 THOU, Lord, hast been our sure defence, our place of ease and rest,
In all times past, yea, so long since as cannot be exprest.
2 Before was made mountain or hill, the earth and world abroad,
From age to age, and always still for ever thou art God.

3 Thou grindest men through grief and pain to dust or clay, and then
Thou unto them dost say again, return ye sons of men.
4 The lasting of a thousand years, what is it in thy sight?
As yesterday it doth appear, or as a watch by night.

5 So soon as thou dost scatter them, then is their life and trade
Ev'n as a sleep, or like the grass, whose beauty soon doth fade:

6 Which in the morning shines full bright, but fadeth suddenly,
And is cut down before the night, all wither'd, dead, and dry.

7 For through thy anger we consume, our might is much decay'd,
And of thy fervent wrath, O Lord, we are full sore afraid.
8 The wicked works that we have wrought thou sett'st before thy eye,
Our privy faults, yea all our thoughts thy countenance doth spy.

9 For though thy wrath our days do waste, thereof doth nought remain:
Our years consume as doth a blast, and are not call'd again.
10 The time of our abode on earth is threescore years and ten;
But if we come to fourscore years, our life is grievous then:

PART II.

11 For of this time the strength and chief we dote so much upon,
Is nothing else but pain and grief, and we as blasts are gone.
12 What man doth know what power and what might thy anger hath?
Or in his heart who doth thee fear according to thy wrath?

13 Instruct us, Lord, to know and try how long our days remain;
That so we may our hearts apply true wisdom to attain.
14 Return, O Lord, how long wilt thou in thy great wrath proceed?
Shew favour to thy servants now, and help them at their need.

15 Refresh us with thy mercy soon, then shall we joyful be,
All times so long as life doth last in heart rejoice will we.
16 As thou hast plagued us before, now also make us glad,
And for the years wherein full sore affliction we have had.

17 O let thy work and pow'r appear, and on thy servants light,
And shew unto thy children dear thy glory and thy might:
18 Lord, let thy grace and glory stand on us thy servants thus;
Confirm the works we take in hand, and prosper them to us.

PSALM XCI. J. H.

1 HE that within the secret place of God most high doth dwell,
Under the shadow of his grace he shall be safe and well.
2 Thou art my hope and my strong hold, I to the Lord will say,
My God he is, in him will I my whole affiance stay.

3 He shall defend thee from the snare, the which the hunter laid,
And from the deadly plague and care whereof thou art afraid:
4 And with his wings shall cover thee and keep thee safely there;
His faith and truth thy fence shall be as sure as shield and spear.

5 So that thou never shalt have cause to fear or be affright,
For all the shafts that fly by day, or terrors of the night;
6 Nor of the plague that privily doth walk in darkness fast,
Nor yet of that which doth destroy, and at noon-day doth waste.

7 Yea, at thy side as thou dost stand, a thousand dead shall be;
Ten thousand more at thy right hand, and yet shalt thou be free.
8 But thou shalt see it for thy part, thy eyes shall well regard,
According unto their desert the wicked have reward.

9 For why? O Lord, I only rest and fix my hope on thee;
In the most high I put my trust, my sure defence is he.

10 No evil shalt thou need to fear, with thee it shall go well;
No plague shall ever once come near the house where thou dost dwell:

11 For why? unto his angels all with charge commanded he,
That still in all thy ways they shall preserve and prosper thee;
12 And in their hands shall bear thee up, still waiting thee upon,
Lest that thy foot should happen for to dash against a stone.

13 Upon the lion thou shalt go, the adder fell and long;
On the young lions tread also, with dragons stout and strong.
14 Because he sets his love on me, I'll save him by my might,
And him advance, because that he doth know my Name aright.

15 When he for help to me doth cry, an answer I will give;
And from his grief take him will I in glory for to live.
16 With length of days and years I will him fully satisfy,
And also my salvation still shew him assuredly.

PSALM XCII. J. H.

1 IT is a thing both good and meet to praise the highest Lord,
And to thy Name, O thou most High, to sing with one accord:
2 To shew the kindness of the Lord, before the day be light,
And to declare his truth abroad, when it doth draw to night;

3 On a ten-stringed instrument, on lute and harp so sweet,
With all the mirth you can invent of instruments most meet.
4 For thou hast made me to rejoice in things so wrought by thee,
That I have joy in heart and voice thy handy-works to see.

5 O Lord, how glorious and how great are thy works round about?
So deeply are thy counsels set, that none can find them out:
6 The man unwise cannot tell how this work to pass to bring,
And fools also are most unfit to understand this thing.

7 When as the wicked at their will like grass do spring full fast,
And when they flourish in their ill, they suddenly shall waste.
8 But thou art mighty, Lord most high, and thou dost reign therefore
In glory and great majesty, both now and evermore.

9 Behold, O Lord, thy enemies shall be destroy'd alway,
And all that work iniquity shall perish and decay.
10 But thou, like as an unicorn, shalt lift my horn on high;
With fresh and new prepared oil anointed king am I;

11 And of my foes before my eyes shall see the fall and shame,
Of all that do against me rise my ears shall hear the same.
12 The righteous flourish shall on high, as palm-trees bud and blow,
And as the cedars multiply In Libanus that grow.

13 For they are planted in the place and dwelling of our God;
Within his courts they spring apace, and flourish all abroad:
14 And in their age much fruit shall bring, most pleasant to be seen,
And also shall both bud and spring, with boughs and branches green;

15 To shew that God is good and just, and upright in his will:
He is my rock, my hope and trust, in him there is no ill.

PSALM XCIII. J. H.

1 THE Lord doth reign, and cloathed is with majesty most bright,
And to declare his strength likewise hath girt himself with might.
2 The Lord also the earth hath made, and shaped it most sure,
No might can make it move nor fade, at stay it doth endure.

3 Before the world was made or wrought, thy seat was set before;
Beyond all time that can be thought thou hast been evermore.
4 The floods, O Lord, the floods do rise, they roar and make a noise,
The floods, I say, did enterprise, and lifted up their voice.

5 Yea, though the storms arise in sight, though seas do rage and swell,
The Lord is strong and more of might; for he on high doth dwell.
6 O Lord, thy testimonies great are very sure: therefore
Doth holiness become thy seat and house for evermore.

PSALM XCIV. J. H.

1 O LORD, thou dost revenge all wrong, vengeance belongs to thee:
Since then it doth to thee belong, declare that all may see.
2 Set forth thyself, for thou of right the earth dost judge and guide;
Reward the proud and men of might according to their pride.

3 How long shall wicked men bear sway with lifting up their voice?
Shall proud and wicked men alway thus triumph and rejoice?
4 How long shall they with brags burst out and proudly talk their fill?
Shall they rejoice that be so stout, whose works are ever ill?

5 Thy flock, O Lord, thine heritage they spoil and vex full sore,
Against thy people they do rage still daily more and more.
6 The widows which are comfortless, and strangers they destroy;
They slay the children fatherless, and none doth put them by.

7 And when they take these things in hand, this talk they have of thee,
Can Jacob's God this understand? tush, no; he cannot see.
8 O folk unwise, and people rude, some knowledge now discern,
Ye fools among the multitude at length begin to learn.

9 The Lord who made the ear of man, he needs of right must hear;
He made the eye, all things must then before his sight appear;
10 The Lord doth all the world correct, and make them understand:
Shall he not then your deeds detect? how can ye 'scape his hand?

PART II.

11 The Lord doth know the heart of man, and sees the same full plain,
And he his very thoughts doth span, and findeth them but vain.
12 But, Lord, that man is happy sure, whom thou dost keep in awe,
And through correction doth procure to teach him in thy law:

13 Whereby he shall in quiet rest in time of trouble sit,
When wicked men shall be supprest, and fall into the pit.
14 For sure the Lord will not refuse his people for to take,
His heritage whom he did chuse he will no time forsake;

15 Until that judgment be decreed to justice to convert,
That all may follow her with speed that are of upright heart.

16 But who upon my part will stand against the cursed train?
Or who shall rid me from their hand that wicked works maintain?

17 Except the Lord had been my aid, my enemies to quell,
My soul and life had now been laid almost as low as hell.
18 When I did say, My foot doth slide: before that I could call,
Thy mercy, Lord, most ready was to save me from the fall:

19 When with myself I mused much, and could no comfort find,
Then, Lord, thy goodness did me touch, and that did ease my mind.
20 Wilt thou accustom, Lord, thyself with wicked men to sit,
Who with pretence, instead of law, much mischief do commit?

21 For they consult against the life of righteous men and good,
And in their counsels they are rife to shed the guiltless blood.
22 But yet the Lord is unto me a sure and strong defence;
To him I flee, because he is my strength and confidence:

23 And he shall cause their mischiefs all themselves for to annoy;
And in their malice they shall fall; our God shall them destroy.

PSALM XCV. J. H.

1 O COME, let us lift up our voice, and sing unto the Lord,
In him our rock of health rejoice let us with one accord:
2 Yea, let us come before his face to give him thanks and praise
In singing Psalms unto his grace let us be glad always.

3 For why? the Lord he is no doubt a great and mighty God,
A King above all gods throughout, in all the world abroad.
4 The secrets of the earth so deep, and corners of the land,
The tops of hills that are most steep, he holds them in his hand:

5 The sea and waters all are his, for he the same hath wrought,
The earth and all that therein is his hand hath made of nought.
6 Come let us bow and praise the Lord, before him let us fall,
And kneel to him with one accord, for he hath made us all.

7 For why? he is the Lord our God, for us he doth provide;
We are his flock, he doth us feed, his sheep, and he our guide.
8 To-day if ye his voice will hear, then harden not your heart,
As ye with grudging many a year provok'd him in desart:

9 Whereas your fathers tempted me, my power for to prove;
My wondrous works when they did see, yet still they would me move.
10 Twice twenty years they did me grieve, which caused me to say,
They err in heart, nor will believe, they have not known my way.

11 Wherefore I sware when that my wrath was kindled in my breast,
That they should never tread the path to enter in my rest.

PSALM XCVI. J. H.

1 SING ye with praise unto the Lord new songs with joy and mirth,
Sing unto him with one accord, all people on the earth:
2 Yea, sing unto the Lord alway, praise ye his holy Name,
Declare and shew from day to day salvation by the same.

3 Among the heathen all declare his honour round about,
To shew his wonders do not spare in all the world throughout.

4 For why? the Lord is great in might, and worthy of all praise,
And he is to be fear'd of right above all gods always.

5 For all the gods of heathen folk are idols that will fade,
Whereas our God, he is the Lord that heav'n and earth hath made.
6 All praise and honour also dwell ever before his face:
Both pow'r and might likewise excel within his holy place.

7 Ascribe unto the Lord therefore all men with one accord,
All might and worship evermore ascribe unto the Lord:
8 Ascribe unto the Lord also the glory of his Name,
Into his courts with presents go, and offer there the same.

PART II.

9 Fall down and worship ye the Lord within his temple bright,
Let all the people of the world be fearful at his sight.
10 Tell all the world, be not afraid, the Lord doth reign above,
Yea, he the earth so fast hath stay'd, that it can never move:

11 And that it is the Lord alone that rules with princely might,
To judge the nations every one with equity and right.
12 The heav'ns shall joyfully begin, the earth likewise rejoice,
The sea with all that is therein shall shout and make a noise.

13 The fields shall joy, and every thing that springeth on the earth,
The wood and every tree shall sing with gladness and with mirth;
14 Before the presence of the Lord, and coming of his might,
When he shall come to judge the world, and rule his folk with right.

PSALM XCVII.

1 THE Lord doth reign, for which the earth may sing with pleasant voice,
The isles also with joyful mirth may triumph and rejoice.
2 Both clouds and darkness likewise swell, and round about him beat,
Yea, right and justice ever dwell and bide about his seat:

3 Yea, fire and heat at once do run, and go before his face,
Which all his enemies shall burn abroad in every place.
4 His lightnings great full bright did blaze, and to the world appear,
Whereat the earth did look and gaze with dread and deadly fear:

5 The hills like wax did melt in sight and presence of the Lord,
They fled before that ruler's might, who guideth all the world.
6 The heav'ns likewise declare and show his justice forth abroad,
That all the world may see and know the glory of our God.

7 Confusion sure shall come to such as worship idols vain,
Also to those that glory much dumb pictures to maintain.
8 For all the idols of the world, which they their gods do call,
Shall feel the power of the Lord, and down before him fall.

9 With joy shall Sion hear this thing, and Judah shall rejoice;
For at thy judgments they shall sing with a most cheerful voice.
10 For thou, O Lord, art set on high in all the earth abroad,
And art exalted wondrously above each other god.

11 All ye that love the Lord in heart hate all things that are ill,
For he doth keep the souls of his from such as would them spill,
12 And light doth spring up to the just, with pleasure for his part,
Gladness and joy likewise to them that are of upright heart.

13 Ye righteous in the Lord rejoice his holiness proclaim,
And thankfully with heart and voice be mindful of the same.

PSALM XCVIII. J. H.

1 O SING ye now unto the Lord a new and pleasant song,
For he hath wrought throughout the world his wonders great and strong
2 With his right hand full worthily he does his foes devour,
And gets himself the victory with his own arm and pow'r.

3 The Lord doth make the people know his saving health and might,
And also doth his justice show in all the heathens' sight.
4 His grace and truth to Israel in mind he doth record,
And all the earth hath seen right well the goodness of the Lord.

5 Be glad in him with joyful voice, all people on the earth,
Give thanks to God, sing and rejoice to him with joy and mirth;
6 Upon the harp unto him sing, give thanks to him always,
Rejoice before the Lord our King, with trumpets sound his praise.

7 Yea, let the sea with all therein for joy both roar and swell;
The earth likewise let it begin, with all that therein dwell.
8 And let the floods rejoice their fills, and clap their hands apace;
Yea, let the mountains and the hills triumph before his face.

9 For he shall come to judge and try the world and every wight,
And rule the people mightily, with justice and with right.

PSALM XCIX. J. H.

1 THE Lord doth reign, although at it the people rage full sore:
Yea, on the cherubims doth sit, though all the world do roar;
2 The Lord that doth in Sion dwell is high and wondrous great,
Above all folk he doth excel, and he aloft is set.

3 Let all men praise thy mighty name, for it is fearful sure,
And let them magnify the same, that holy is and pure.
4 The princely power of our king doth judgment love and right;
Thou rightly rulest every thing in Jacob thro' thy might.

5 To praise the Lord our God devise, all honour to him shew:
And at his footstool worship him that holy is and true.
6 Moses, Aaron, and Samuel as priests on him did call;
When they did pray he heard them well, and gave them answer all:

7 Within the cloud to them he spake, then did they labour still
To keep such laws as he did make, according to his will.
8 O Lord our God, thou didst them hear, and answer'dst them again;
But their inventions punishedst, which foolish were and vain.

9 O praise our God and Lord therefore upon his holy hill:
For why? our God whom we adore is the most holy still

PSALM C. J. H.

1 ALL people that on earth do dwell, sing to the Lord with cheerful voice
Him serve with fear, his praise forth tell, come ye before him and rejoice.
2 The Lord ye know is God indeed, without our aid he did us make,
We are his flock, he doth us feed, and for his sheep he doth us take.

3 O enter then his gates with praise, approach with joy his courts unto,
Praise, laud, and bless his name always, for it is seemly so to do.
4 For why? the Lord our God is good, his mercy is for ever sure,
His truth at all times firmly stood, and shall from age to age endure.

ANOTHER OF THE SAME, BY J. H.

1 IN God the Lord be glad and light, praise him throughout the earth;
Serve him and come before his sight with singing and with mirth.
2 Know that the Lord our God he is, he did us make and keep,
Not we ourselves, for we are his own flock and pasture sheep.

3 O go into his gates always, give thanks within the same,
Within his courts set forth his praise, and laud his holy name.
4 For why? the goodness of the Lord for evermore doth reign,
From age to age throughout the world his truth doth still remain.

PSALM CI. J. H.

1 I MERCY will and judgment sing, O Lord God, unto thee,
O let me understand the ways that good and holy be.
2 Within my house I daily will walk with an heart upright,
And I no kind of wicked thing will set before my sight.

3 I hate their works that fall away, they shall not cleave to me;
From me shall go the froward heart, no evil will I see.
4 Him I'll destroy that slandereth his neighbour privily;
The lofty heart I will not bear, nor him that looketh high.

5 My eyes shall be on them within the land that faithful be;
In perfect way who walketh, shall be servant unto me:
6 I will no guileful person have within my house to dwell,
And in my presence he shall not remain that lies doth tell.

7 Betimes I will destroy ev'n all the wicked of the land,
That I may from God's city cut the wicked workers' hand.

PSALM CII. J. H.

1 HEAR thou my prayer, O Lord, and let my cry come unto thee,
In time of trouble do not hide thy face away from me:
2 Incline thine ear to me, make haste to hear me when I call;
For as the smoke doth fade, so do my days consume and fall:

3 And as on earth my bones are burnt, my heart is smitten dead,
And withers like the grass, that I forget to eat my bread.
4 By reason of my groaning voice my bones cleave to my skin;
As pelican in wilderness, such case now am I in.

5 And as an owl in desert is, lo, I am such a one:
I watch, and as a sparrow on the house-top am alone:

6 For daily in reproachful wise my foes they do me scorn;
And them that mad upon me are, against me they have sworn.

7 Surely with ashes as with bread my hunger I have fill'd,
And mingled have my drink with tears, that from my eyes distill'd,
8 Because of thy displeasure, Lord, thy wrath and great disdain:
For thou hast set me up on high, and cast me down again.

9 The days wherein I pass my life are like the fleeting shade;
And I am wither'd like the grass, that soon away doth fade,
10 But thou, O Lord, for ever dost remain in steady place,
And thy remembrance ever doth abide from race to race.

PART II.

11 Thou wilt arise, and mercy thou to Sion wilt extend,
The time of mercy, now the time foreset is come to end:
12 For in the very stones thereof thy servants do delight,
And on the dust thereof they have compassion in their sight.

13 Then shall the heathen people fear the Lord's most holy name,
And all the kings on earth shall dread his glory and his fame.
14 Then when the Lord the mighty God again shall Sion rear,
And then when he most nobly in his glory shall appear;

15 To prayer of the poor destitute when he himself shall bend,
When he shall not disdain unto their suits for to attend;
16 This shall be written for the age that after shall succeed:
The people that are yet unborn the Lord's renown shall spread.

17 From his high sanctuary he hath looked down below,
And out of heav'n most high he hath beheld the earth also:
18 That of the mourning captive he might hear the woeful cry,
And that he might deliver those that were condemn'd to die:

19 That they in Sion may declare the Lord's most holy name,
And in Jerusalem set forth the praises of the same;
20 Then when the people of the land and kingdoms with accord,
Shall be assembled to perform their service to the Lord.

PART III.

21 My former force of strength he hath abated in the way,
And shorter he did cut my days, thus I therefore did say,
22 My God, in midst of all my days now take me not away;
Thy years endure eternally, and never to decay;

23 Thou the foundations of the earth before all time hast laid;
The heav'ns also, they are the work which thy own hands have made,
24 They all shall perish and decay, but thou remainest still;
And they shall all in time wax old ev'n as a garment will:

25 Thou as a vesture shalt them change, and changed shall they be,
But thou dost still abide the same, thy years do never flee.
26 The children of thy servants shall continue and endure,
And in thy sight their happy seed for ever shall stand sure.

PSALM CIII.

PSALM CIII. T. S.

1 MY soul, give praise unto the Lord, my spirit do the same;
And all the secrets of my heart, praise ye his holy name;
2 Praise thou the Lord, my soul, who hath to thee been very kind,
And suffer not his benefits to slip out of thy mind:

3 That gave thee pardon for thy faults, and thee restor'd again
From all thy weak and frail disease, and heal'd thee of thy pain;
4 That did redeem thy life from death, from which thou could'st not flee;
His mercy and compassion both he did extend to thee;

5 That fill'd with goodness thy desire, and did thy youth prolong,
Like as the eagle casts her bill, again becoming young.
6 The Lord with justice doth repay all such as are opprest,
So that their sufferings and wrongs are turned to the best.

7 His ways and his commandments all to Moses he did show;
His counsels and his valiant acts the Israelites did know.
8 The Lord is kind and merciful, when sinners do him grieve,
The slowest to conceive a wrath, and readiest to forgive:

9 He will not always chiding be, though we be full of strife;
Nor keep our faults in memory, for all our sinful life:
10 According to our sins also he doth us not regard,
And after our iniquities he doth us not reward:

11 But as the space is wondrous great 'twixt earth and heav'n above;
So is his goodness much more large to them that do him love.
12 He doth remove our sins from us, and our offences all,
As far as is the sun-rising full distant from his fall.

PART II.

13 Behold, what pity parents do unto their children bear,
Like pity beareth God to such as worship him in fear.
14 The Lord that made us knows our shape, our mould and fashion just,
How weak and frail our nature is, and that we are but dust:

15 And how the time of mortal men is like the withering hay,
Or like the flow'r right fair in field, that fadeth soon away;
16 Whose gloss and beauty stormy winds do utterly deface,
And make that after their assaults such blossoms have no place:

17 But yet the goodness of the Lord with his shall ever stand;
Their children's children do receive his righteousness at hand:
18 I mean who keep his covenant with all their whole desire,
And not forget to do the thing that he doth them require.

19 The heav'ns most high are made the seat and footstool of the Lord;
And by his pow'r imperial he governs all the world.
20 Ye angels that are great in pow'r, praise ye and bless the Lord,
Who to obey and do his will immediately accord;

21 Ye noble hosts and ministers, cease not to praise him still,
Who ready are to execute his pleasure and his will:
22 Yea, all his works in ev'ry place praise ye his holy name:
My thankful heart, my mind and soul, praise ye also the same.

PSALM CIV.

PSALM CIV. W. K.

1 MY soul, praise the **Lord,** speak good of his name;
O Lord our great **God,** how dost thou appear?
So passing in glory, that great is thy fame,
Honour and Majesty **in thee shine** most clear.

2 With light as a robe thou hast thyself clad,
Whereby all the earth thy greatness may see;
The heav'ns in such sort thou also hast spread,
That they to a curtain compared may be.

3 **His** chamber-beams lie in the clouds full sure,
Which as his chariots are made him to bear:
And there with much swiftness his course doth endure,
Upon the wings riding of winds in the air.

4 He maketh his spirits as heralds to go,
And lightnings to serve we see also prest;
His will to accomplish they run to and fro,
To save or consume things as seemeth him best.

5 He groundeth the earth so firmly and fast,
That it once to move none shall have such pow'r:
The deep a fair cov'ring for it made thou hast,
Which by its own nature the hills would devour.

6 But at thy rebuke the waters do flee,
And so give due place thy word to obey:
At thy voice of thunder so fearful they be,
That in their great raging they haste soon away.

7 The mountains full high they then up ascend,
If thou do but speak, thy word they fulfil;
So likewise the valleys most quickly descend,
Where thou them appointest remain do they still:

8 Their bounds thou hast set how far they shall run,
So that in their rage **not** that pass they can:
For God hath appointed they shall not return
The earth to destroy more which made was for man.

PART II.

9 He sendeth the springs to strong streams or lakes,
Which run do full swift among the huge hills;
Where both the wild asses their thirst often slake,
And beasts of the mountains thereof drink their fills.

10 By these pleasant springs and rivers most clear,
The fowls of the air abide shall and dwell,
Who moved by nature **to** hop here and there,
Among the green branches their songs shall excel.

11 The mountains to moist the clouds he doth use;
The earth with his works is wholly replete.
So as the brute cattle he doth not refuse,
But grass doth provide them, and herb for man's meat.

12 Yea, bread, wine, and oil, he made for man's sake,
His face to refresh, and heart to make strong.
The cedars of Liban the great Lord did make,
Which trees he doth nourish, that grow up so long.

13 In these may birds build, and all make their nests;
In fir-trees the storks remain and abide:
The high hills are succours for wild goats to rest,
Also the rock stony for conies to hide.

14 The moon then is set her seasons to run,
The day from the night thereby to discern;
And by the descending also of the sun,
The cold from heat alway thereby we do learn.

15 When darkness doth come by God's will and pow'r,
Then creep forth do all the beasts of the wood;
The lions range roaring their prey to devour:
But yet 'tis thou, Lord, who givest them food.

16 As soon as the sun is up, they retire,
To couch in their dens then are they full fain;
That man to his work may, as right doth require,
Till night come and call him to take rest again.

PART III.

17 How sundry, O Lord, are all thy works found?
With wisdom full great they are indeed wrought;
So that the whole world of thy praise doth sound,
And as for thy riches, they pass all men's thought:

18 So in the great sea which is large and broad,
Where creeping things swarm and beasts of each sort;
There mighty ships sail, and some lie at rode,
The whale huge and monstrous there also doth sport.

19 All things on thee wait, thou dost them relieve,
And thou in due time full well dost them feed:
Now when it doth please thee the same for to give,
They gather full gladly those things which they need.

20 Thou open'st thy hand, and they find such grace,
That they with good things are filled we see:
But sore they are troubled if thou hide thy face,
For if thou their breath take vile dust then they be.

21 Again, when thy spirit from thee doth proceed,
All things to appoint, and what shall ensue;
Then are they created as thou hast decreed,
And dost by thy goodness the dry earth renew.

22 The praise of the Lord for ever shall last,
Who may in his works by right well rejoice:
His look can the earth make to tremble full fast,
And likewise the mountains to smoke at his voice.

23 To this Lord and God will I sing always;
So long as I live my God praise will I:

Then am I most certain my words shall him please;
I will rejoice in him, to him I will cry.

24 The sinners, O Lord, consume in thine ire,
Also the perverse, them root out with shame;
But as for my soul now, let it still desire,
And say with the faithful, praise ye the Lord's name.

PSALM CV. N.

1 GIVE praises unto God the Lord, and call upon his name,
Among the people all declare his works to spread his fame:
2 Sing joyfully unto the Lord, yea, sing unto him praise;
And talk of all his wondrous works that he hath wrought always.

3 In honour of his holy name rejoice with one accord,
And let the heart also be glad of them that seek the Lord.
4 Seek ye the Lord, and seek the strength of his eternal might,
Yea, seek his face incessantly, and presence of his sight.

5 The wondrous works which he hath done, keep still in mindful heart;
Let not the judgments of his mouth out of your mind depart.
6 Ye that of faithful Abraham his servant are the seed,
Ye his elect, the children that of Jacob do proceed.

7 For why? 'tis he alone that is the mighty Lord our God,
And his most righteous judgments are in all the earth abroad.
8 His promise and his covenant which he hath made to his,
He hath remember'd evermore to thousands of degrees.

PART II.

9 The covenant which he hath made with Abraham long ago,
And faithful oath which he hath sworn to Isaac also:
10 And did appoint it for a law, that Jacob should obey,
And for eternal covenant to Israel alway.

11 When thus he said, Lo, I to you all Canaan land will give,
The lot of your inheritance, wherein your seed shall live:
12 Although their number at that time did very small appear;
Yea, very small, and in the land they then but strangers were;

13 While yet they went from land to land without a sure abode;
And while from sundry kingdoms they did wander all abroad.
14 Yet wrong at no oppressor's hands he suffer'd them to take;
But even great and mighty kings reproved for their sake.

15 And thus he said, Touch ye not them that mine anointed be,
Nor do the prophets any harm that do pertain to me,
16 He call'd a dearth upon the land, of bread destroy'd the store;
But yet against the time of need did send a man before;

PART III.

17 Ev'n Joseph, who had once been sold to live a slave in woe;
Whose feet they hurt in stocks, whose soul the iron pierc'd into:
18 Until the time came when his cause was known apparently,
The mighty word of God the Lord his innocence did try.

9 The king sent and deliver'd him from prison where he was,
The ruler of the people then did freely let him pass;
10 And over all his house he made him lord, to bear the sway,
And of his substance made him have the rule and all the stay:

11 That he might to his will instruct the princes of the land,
And wisdom teach his senators rightly to understand.
12 Then into the Egyptian land came Israel also,
And Jacob in the land of Ham did sojourn to and fro.

13 His people he exceedingly in numbers made to grow,
And stronger than their enemies who sought their overthrow;
14 Whose heart he turned, that with hate they did his people treat;
And did his servants wrongfully abuse with base deceit.

PART IV.

15 His faithful servant Moses then, and Aaron whom he chose,
He did command to go to them his message to disclose.
16 His wonderful and mighty signs among them they did show,
And wonders in the land of Ham then did they work also:

17 Darkness he sent and made it dark instead of brighter day;
And his commission and his word they did not disobey:
18 He turn'd their waters into blood, their fish also did slay;
Their land brought frogs ev'n in the place where their king Pharaoh lay:

19 He spake, and at his voice there came great swarms of noisome flies;
And all the quarters of their land were fill'd with crawling lice;
30 He gave them cold and stony hail instead of milder rain;
And fiery flames within their land he sent unto their pain:

31 He smote their vines and all the trees whereon the figs did grow;
And all the trees within their coasts also did overthrow:
32 He spake, then caterpillars did and grasshoppers abound,
Eating the grass in all their land and fruit of all their ground:

PART V.

33 The first-begotten in their land, with death did likewise smite,
Yea, the beginning and first-fruit of all their strength and might;
34 With gold and silver caused his from Egypt's land to pass,
And in the number of their tribes no feeble one there was.

35 Egypt was glad and joyful then when they did thence depart;
For terror and the fear of them was fall'n upon their heart;
36 To shroud them from the parching heat a cloud he did display;
And fire he sent to give them light, when night had hid the day.

37 They asked, and he called quails to rain at their request,
And fully with the bread of heav'n their hunger he represt;
38 He opened the stony rock, and waters gushed out:
Also the dry and parched ground like rivers ran about.

39 For of his holy cov'nant he was mindful evermore,
Which to his servant Abraham he plighted long before.
40 He brought his people forth with mirth, and his elect with joy,
Out of the cruel land where they had liv'd in great annoy.

42 Full oftentimes from thrall had he deliver'd them before;
But they rebell'd against him, and provok'd him evermore.

43 Therefore they by their wickedness were brought full low to lie:
Yet when he saw them in distress, he heark'ned to their cry;
44 He call'd to mind his covenant, which he to them had swore,
And by his mercies' multitude repented him therefore:

45 And favour he them made to find before the sight of those
That led them captive from their land, though they had been their foes.
46 Save us, O Lord, that art our God, we do thee humbly pray,
And from among the heathen folk, Lord, gather us away;

47 That we may triumph and rejoice in thy most holy Name,
That we may glory in thy praise, and sounding of thy fame.
48 The Lord the God of Israel be blessed evermore:
Let all the people say, Amen, praise ye the Lord therefore.

PSALM CVII. W. K.

1 GIVE thanks unto the Lord our God, for very kind is he;
And that his mercy hath no end all mortal men may see,
2 Such as the Lord redeemed hath with thanks shall praise his name
And shew how they from foes were freed, and how he wrought the same.

3 He gather'd them forth of the lands that lay so far about;
From east to west, from north to south his hand did find them out.
4 They wander'd in the wilderness, and strayed from the way,
Finding no city where to dwell, that might serve for their stay:

5 Whose thirst and hunger was so great within those deserts void,
That faintness them assaulted, and their souls greatly annoy'd.
6 Then did they cry in their distress unto the Lord for aid,
Who did remove their troublous state, according as they pray'd:

7 And by the way which was most right he led them like a guide;
That they might to their city go, and safely there abide.
8 Let men therefore before the Lord confess his goodness then,
And shew the wonders that he doth before the sons of men.

9 For he their empty souls sustain'd, whom thirst had made to faint;
Their hungry souls with goodness fed, and heard their sad complaint.
10 Such as do dwell in darkness deep, where they on death do wait,
Fast bound to bear such grievous pains, as iron chains do threat;

PART II.

11 Because against the words of God they proudly did rebel,
Esteeming light his counsels high, which do so far excel.
12 But when he humbled them full low, they then fell down with grief;
And none was found that could them help, or give them some relief.

13 Then did they cry in their distress unto the Lord for aid,
Who did remove their troublous state, according as they pray'd;
14 For he from darkness brought them out, and from death's dreadful shade
Bursting with force the iron bands which them before did lade.

15 Let men therefore before the Lord confess his goodness then,
And shew the wonders that he doth before the sons of men.

16 For he threw down the gates of brass with strong and mighty hand,
The iron bars in sunder brake, nothing could him withstand.

17 The foolish folk great plagues do feel by reason of their sin,
And for the great transgressions which they still continue in.
18 Their soul abhorr'd all sorts of meat, no relish they could have;
By which means they were almost brought unto the very grave.

19 Then did they cry in their distress unto the Lord for aid,
Who did remove their troublous state according as they pray'd:
20 For then he sent to them his word, which health did soon restore,
And brought them from those dangers deep, wherein they were before.

PART III.

21 Let men therefore before the Lord confess his goodness then,
And shew the wonders that he doth before the sons of men;
22 And let them offer sacrifice: to him most thankfully,
And speak of all his wond'rous works with gladness and with joy.

23 Such as in ships and brittle barks into the seas descend;
Their merchandise through fearful floods to compass and to end;
24 These men are forced to behold the Lord's works what they be,
And in the dreadful deep the same most marvellous they see.

25 For at his word the stormy wind ariseth in a rage.
And stirreth up the surges so that nought can them assuage,
26 Then are they lifted up so high the clouds they seem to gain,
And plunging down the depth, until their souls consume with pain:

27 And like a drunkard, to and fro now here, now there they reel,
As men who had their reason lost, and had no sense to feel.
28 Then did they cry in their distress unto the Lord for aid,
Who did remove their troubled state, according as they pray'd;

29 For with his word the Lord doth make the sturdy storms to cease,
So that the waves from their great rage are brought to rest and peace.
30 Then are they glad when rest is come, which they so much did crave,
And to the hav'n by him are brought, which they so fain would have.

PART IV.

31 Let men therefore before the Lord confess his goodness then,
And shew the wonders that he doth before the sons of men.
32 Let them in presence of the folk with praise extol his name,
And where the elders use to sit, there let them do the same.

33 The wilderness he often makes with waters to abound,
And water-springs he often turns to dry and parched ground;
34 A fruitful land with pleasures deck'd full barren doth he make,
When on their sins that dwell therein he doth just vengeance take.

35 Again the wilderness full rude he maketh fruit to bear,
With pleasant springs of water clear, though none before were there.
36 Wherein such hungry souls are set as he hath freely chose,
That they a city may them build to dwell in safe from foes;

37 That they may sow their pleasant land, and vineyards also plant,
To yield them fruits of such increase that they may have no want.
38 They multiply exceedingly, the Lord doth bless them so,
Who also maketh the brute beasts in numbers great to grow.

39 But when the faithful are brought low by the oppressors stout,
Diminishing through many plagues that compass them about;
40 Then doth he princes bring to shame, which did them sore oppress,
And likewise caused them to err when in the wilderness.

41 But yet the poor he raiseth up out of his troubles deep,
And often doth his train augment, like to a flock of sheep.
42 The righteous shall behold this sight, and also much rejoice;
Whereas the wicked and perverse with grief shall stop their voice.

43 But who is wise, that now full well he may these things record?
For certainly such shall perceive the kindness of the Lord.

PSALM CVIII. J. H.

1 O GOD, my heart prepared is, my tongue is likewise so;
I will advance my voice and song, that I thy praise may show.
2 Awake, my viol and my harp sweet melody to make,
And in the morning I myself right early will awake.

3 By me among the people, Lord, still praised shalt thou be,
And I among the heathen folk will praises sing to thee:
4 Because thy mercy doth ascend above the heav'ns most high:
Also thy truth doth reach the clouds within the lofty sky.

5 Above the starry heavens high exalt thyself, O God,
Display likewise upon the earth thy glory all abroad;
6 That thy beloved also may be set at liberty;
Help, O my God, with thy right-hand, and hear me speedily.

7 God in his holiness hath spoke, wherefore my joys abound,
Sichem I will divide, and mete the vale of Succoth's ground
8 And Gilead shall be my own, Manasses mine shall be,
My head-strength Ephraim, and law shall Judah give to me.

9 Moab my wash-pot is, my shoe o'er Edom I will throw,
Upon the land of Palestine in triumph I will go.
10 Who to the city strong shall be leader and guide to me?
Also by whom to Edom's land conveyed shall I be?

11 Is it not thou, O Lord, who late hast us forsaken quite:
And wilt not thou, Lord, also go forth with our hosts to fight?
12 Give us, O Lord, thy saving aid, when troubles do assail;
For all the help of man is vain, and can no whit avail.

13 Through God we shall do valiant acts, and worthy of renown;
He shall subdue our enemies, yea, he shall tread them down.

PSALM CIX. N.

1 IN speechless silence do not hold, O God, thy tongue always,
Ev'n thou, O Lord, because thou art the God of all my praise.
The wicked and the guileful mouths on me disclosed be,
And they with false and lying tongue have spoken unto me.

3 They did beset me round about with words of hateful spite,
Without all cause of my desert against me they did fight.
4 For my good-will they were my foes, then I began to pray;
My good with ill, my friendliness with hate they did repay.

5 Set thou the wicked over him, to have the upper hand,
At his right-hand, Lord, suffer thou his hateful foe to stand.
6 When he is judged, let him then condemned be therein,
And let the prayer that he doth make be turned into sin:

7 Few be his days, his charge also let thou another take,
His children let be fatherless, his wife a widow make:
8 His offspring let be vagabonds, and ever beg their bread,
In places desolate and waste let them seek to be fed:

9 Let covetous extortioners get all his goods in store,
And let the stranger spoil the fruit of all his toil before:
10 Let there be none to pity him, let there be none at all
That on his children fatherless will let their mercy fall:

PART II.

11 Let his posterity be quite destroy'd and never breed,
Their name out-blotted in the age that after shall succeed:
12 Let not his father's wickedness from God's remembrance fall,
And never let his mother's sin be done away at all.

13 But in the presence of the Lord let them for ever stay,
That from the earth their memory he may cut clean away;
14 Since mercy he forgot to shew, but did pursue with spite
The troubled man, and sought to slay the woeful-hearted wight.

15 As he did cursing love, it shall happen unto him so;
And as he did not blessing love, far from him it shall go.
16 As he with cursing clad himself so it like water shall
Enter his bowels, and like oil into his bones shall fall.

17 Ev'n as a garment let it be to cover him withal,
And as a girdle wherewith he always be girded shall.
18 Let this be the reward from God of him that is my foe,
Yea, and of those that evil speak against my soul also.

19 But thou, O Lord, that art my God, deal graciously with me;
Deliver me for thy name's sake, for great thy mercies be;
20 Because in depth of great distress I needy am and poor,
Also within my pained breast my heart is wounded sore.

PART III.

21 Ev'n so do I depart away, as doth declining shade,
And as the grasshopper, so I am shaken off and fade,
22 With fasting long from needful food my knees enfeebled are,
And all the fatness of my flesh is gone with grief and care:

23 And I also a vile reproach to them am made to be,
And they that did upon me look did shake their heads at me.
24 Help me therefore, O God, I pray, my aid and succour be,
According to thy mercies great save and deliver me.

25 And they shall know thereby, that this is thy most mighty hand,
And that 'tis thou that hast it done they well shall understand.
26 Although they curse with spite, yet thou shalt bless with loving voice:
When they rise up, and come to shame, thy servant shall rejoice.

27 Let them with shame be cloathed all that are mine enemies,
And with confusion as a cloak be covered likewise.
28 But greatly I will with my mouth give thanks unto the Lord,
And I among the multitude his praises will record.

29 For he with help at his right hand will stand the poor man by,
To save him from the man that would condemn his soul to die.

PSALM CX. N.

1 THE Lord did say unto my Lord, sit thou on my right hand,
Till I have made thy foes a stool whereon thy feet shall stand,
2 The Lord shall out of Sion send the sceptre of thy might;
Amidst thy mortal foes be thou the ruler in their sight.

3 And in the day on which thy reign and power they shall see,
Then free-will offerings shall all the people give to thee:
4 Yea, with an holy worshipping then shall they offer all;
Thy birth-dew is the dew that doth from womb of morning fall.

5 The Lord hath sworn, and never will repent what he doth say,
By th' order of Melchisedech thou art a priest alway.
6 The Lord thy God on thy right hand that standeth for thy stay,
Shall wound for thee the stately kings in that his wrathful day.

7 The heathen he shall judge, and fill the place with bodies dead,
And over divers countries shall in sunder smite the head.
8 And he shall drink out of the brook that runneth in the way,
Wherefore he shall lift up on high his royal head that day.

PSALM CXI. N.

1 WITH heart I do accord to praise and laud the Lord,
In presence of the just; for great his works are found,
To search them such are bound as do him love and trust.

2 His works are glorious, and righteousness to us,
It ever doth endure: his wondrous works he would
We still remember should; his mercy is full sure.

3 Such as to him bear love, a portion fair above
He hath up for them laid; for this they shall well find,
He will them have in mind, and keep them as he said.

4 For he did not disdain his works to shew them plain,
By lightnings and by thunders; when he the heathen's land
Did give into their hand, where they beheld his wonders.

5 Of all his works ensu'th both judgment, right and truth,
Whereto his statutes tend; they are decreed sure
For ever to endure, on which we may depend.

6 Redemption great he gave his people for to save,
It also hath appear'd; his promise doth not fail,
But evermore prevail; his holy name be fear'd.

7 Whoso with heart full fain true wisdom would attain,
The Lord fear and obey; such as his laws do keep
Shall knowledge have full deep; his praise shall last alway.

PSALM CXII. W. K.

1 THE man is blest that God doth fear, and that his law doth love indeed;
His seed on earth God will uprear, and bless such as from him proceed;
His house with riches he will fill, his righteousness endure shall still.

2 Unto the righteous doth arise in trouble, joy, in darkness light:
Compassion great is in his eyes, and mercy always in his sight.
Yea, pity moveth him to lend, he doth with judgment things expend.

3 And surely he shall never fail, for in remembrance had is he;
Nor tidings ill his mind assail, who in the Lord sore hope doth see;
His heart is firm, his fear is past, for he shall see his foes down cast.

4 He did well for the poor provide, his righteousness doth still remain;
And his estate with praise abide, which wicked men behold with pain;
Yea, gnash their teeth thereat shall they, and so consume and melt away.

PSALM CXIII. W. K.

1 YE children which do serve the Lord, praise ye his name with one accord;
Yea, blessed be always his name, who from the rising of the sun,
Till it return where it begun, is to be praised with great fame.

The Lord all people doth surmount, as for his glory we may count,
Above the heavens high to be. With God the Lord who can compare
Whose dwellings in the heavens are? of such great pow'r and force is he.

2 He doth abase himself we know, things to behold on earth below,
And also in the heav'n above: The needy out of dust to draw,
Also the poor which help none saw, his only mercy did him move;

And so did set him up on high, with princes of great dignity,
That rule his people with great fame. The barren he doth make to bear,
And with great joy her fruit doth rear; therefore praise ye his holy name.

PSALM CXIV. W. W.

1 WHEN Israel by God's command from Pharaoh's land was bent,
And Jacob's house the strangers left, and in the same train went:
2 In Judah God his glory shew'd, his holiness most bright:
So did the Israelites declare his kingdom, pow'r, and might.

3 The sea saw it and suddenly as all amaz'd did fly,
The roaring streams of Jordan's flood gave back immediately.
4 As rams afraid, the mountains skip'd, their strength did them forsake;
And as the silly trembling lambs their tops did beat and shake.

5 What ailed thee, O sea, that thou, so suddenly didst fly?
Ye rolling waves of Jordan's flood, why turn'd ye so swiftly?
6 Ye mountains, ev'n as rams afraid, why did your strength so shake?
Why did your tops as trembling lambs quiver with fear and quake?

7 O earth, confess thy Sovereign **Lord**, and dread his mighty hand,
Before the face of Jacob's God fear ye both sea and land.
8 I mean the God, who from hard rocks causeth floods to appear,
And from the stony flint doth **send** fountains of water clear.

PSALM CXV. N.

1 NOT unto us, Lord, not to us, but to thy name give praise:
Both for thy mercy and thy truth that are in thee always.
2 Why shall the heathen scorners say, where is their God become?
Our God he is in heav'n, and what he will'd, that he hath done.

3 Their idols silver are and gold, work of men's hands they be;
They have a mouth, but do not speak, and eyes but do not see:
4 And they have ears join'd to their heads, but do not hear at all;
Noses also they formed have, but not to smell withal:

5 And hands they have, but handle not, and feet, **but** cannot walk:
A throat they have, yet through the same they do not speak or talk.
6 They and their makers are alike, and those whose trust they be:
O Israel, trust thou in the Lord, thy help and shield is he.

7 O Aaron's house, trust in the Lord, that still defendeth thee;
Ye that do fear him, trust in him, your sure defence is he.
8 The Lord of us hath mindful been, and will us bless also,
On Israel and Aaron's house his blessings will bestow.

9 They that be fearers of the Lord he sure will bless them all,
Yea, he will bless them ev'ry one, ev'n both the great and small.
10 To you alway the living Lord will multiply his grace,
And also to the children that shall follow of your race.

11 Ye are the blessed of the Lord, even of the Lord most high,
Who both the heav'n and earth did make, and fix immoveably.
12 The heav'ns above the highest heav'n belong unto the Lord;
The earth unto the sons of men he gave of free accord.

13 They that be dead do not with praise set forth the Lord's renown,
Nor any that into the place of silence do go down:
14 But we will praise the Lord our God henceforth for evermore;
He only worthy is of **praise**, praise ye the Lord therefore.

PSALM CXVI. N.

1 I LOVE the Lord, because the voice of my prayer heard hath he,
I'll ever call on him, because he bow'd his ear to me.
2 Ev'n when the snares of cruel death about beset me round,
When pains of hell me caught, and when I woe and sorrow found:

3 Upon the name of God the Lord then did I call and say,
Deliver thou my soul, O Lord, I do thee humbly pray.
4 The Lord is very merciful, and just he is also,
And in our God compassion doth most plentifully flow.

5 The Lord in safety doth preserve all those that simple be,
I was in woeful misery, and he deliver'd me.
6 And now my soul, since thou art safe, return unto thy rest,
For largely unto thee the Lord his bounty hath exprest,

7 Because thou hast delivered my soul from deadly thrall,
My moisten'd eyes from mournful tears, my sliding feet from fall;
8 Before the Lord I in the land of life will walk therefore:
I did believe, therefore I spake, but I was troubled sore.

PART II.

9 I said in my distress and fear, that all men liars be:
What shall I pay the Lord for all his benefits to me?
10 The wholesome cup of saving health I thankfully will take,
And on the name of God will call, when I my prayers do make.

11 I to the Lord will pay my vows with joy and great delight,
Now at this very present time in all his people's sight.
12 Right dear and precious in his sight he always doth esteem
The death of all his holy ones, whatever men do deem.

13 Thy servant, Lord, thy servant, lo, I do myself confess,
Son of thy handmaid, thou hast broke the bonds of my distress.
14 Therefore I'll offer up to thee a sacrifice of praise:
And I will call upon the name of God the Lord always?

15 I to the Lord will pay my vows with joy and great delight,
Now at this very present time in all his people's sight:
16 Yea, in the courts of God's own house, and in the midst of thee,
O thou Jerusalem: therefore the Lord our God praise ye.

PSALM CXVII. N.

1 O ALL ye nations of the world, praise ye the Lord always,
And all ye people every where set forth his noble praise;
2 For great his kindness is to us, his truth doth not decay;
Wherefore praise ye the Lord our God, praise ye the Lord alway.

PSALM CXVIII. N.

1 O GIVE ye thanks to God the Lord, for very kind is he,
Because his mercy doth endure to all eternity.
2 Le Israel confess that his mercy doth ever dure,
Let Aaron's house likewise confess, his mercy is most sure;

3 Let all that fear the Lord our God, ev'n now confess and say,
The mercy of the Lord our God endureth still alway.
4 In trouble and in heaviness, unto the Lord I cry'd,
Who lovingly heard me at large, my suit was not deny'd.

5 The Lord himself is on my side, I will not stand in doubt,
Nor fear what man can do to me, when God stands me about.
6 The Lord doth take my part with them that help to succour me,
Therefore I shall see my desire upon my enemy.

7 Better it is to trust in God, than in man's mortal seed;
Or to put confidence in kings or princes in our need.
8 All nations have inclosed me, and compassed me round:
But in the name of God shall I my enemies confound,

9 They kept me in on every side, and did me quite surround;
But in the Lord's most mighty name I cast them to the ground.

10 They came about me all like bees, but in the Lord's great name
I quench'd their thorns that were on fire, and did destroy the same.

PART II.

11 They did with force thrust sore at me that I indeed might fall,
But through the Lord I found such help as did them vanquish all.
12 The Lord is my defence and strength, my joy, my mirth, and song,
And is become to me indeed a Saviour great and strong.

13 The right hand of the Lord our God doth bring to pass great things,
He causeth voice of joy and health in righteous men's dwellings.
14 The right hand of the Lord doth bring most mighty things to pass,
His hand hath the preeminence, his force is as it was.

15 I shall not die, but ever live, to utter and declare
The mighty power of the Lord, his works and what they are.
16 The Lord himself hath chastened and hath corrected me,
But not me given over yet to death, as you may see.

17 Set open unto me the gates of truth and righteousness,
That I may enter into them his praise for to express.
18 This is the gate of God the Lord, which open shall be set,
That good and righteous men always may enter into it.

PART III.

19 I will give thanks to thee, O Lord, and ever will praise thee,
Who hast me heard, and art become a Saviour unto me.
20 The stone which formerly among the builders was refus'd
Is now become the corner-stone, and chiefly to be us'd.

21 This was the mighty work of God, it was the Lord's own fact;
And it is wondrous to behold that great and noble act.
22 This is the joyful day indeed, which God himself hath wrought,
Let us be glad and joy therein in heart, in mind and thought.

23 Now help us, Lord, and prosper us, we wish with one accord:
Blessed is he that comes to us in the name of the Lord.
24 God is the Lord that shews us light, bind ye therefore with cord
Your sacrifice to the altar, and give thanks to the Lord.

25 Thou art my God, I will confess, and render thanks to thee;
Thou art my God, and I will praise thy mercy towards me.
26 O give ye thanks to God the Lord, for very kind is he,
Because his mercy doth endure to all eternity.

PSALM CXIX. W. W.

ALEPH.

1 BLESSED are they that perfect are, and pure in mind and heart;
Whose lives and conversations do from God's laws ne'er depart.
2 Blessed are they that give themselves his statutes to observe,
Seeking the Lord with all their heart, and never from him swerve.

3 Doubtless such men go not astray, nor do a wicked thing,
But stedfastly walk in his way without any wand'ring.
'Tis thy commandment and thy will, that with attentive heed
4 Thy precepts, which are most divine, we learn and keep indeed.

5 O would to God it might thee please, my ways so to direct,
That I might always keep thy laws, and never them reject!
6 So shall I not ashamed be, whilst I thus set my eyes,
And bend my mind always to muse on thy decrees most wise.

7 Then will I praise with upright heart, and magnify thy name,
When I shall learn thy judgments just, and also prove the same.
8 And wholly will I give myself to keep thy laws most right;
Forsake me not for ever, Lord, but shew thy grace and might.

BETH.

9 By what means may a young man best his life learn to amend?
If that he mark and keep thy word, and therein his time spend.
10 Unfeignedly I have thee sought, and thus seeking abide:
O never suffer me, O Lord, from thy commands to slide.

11 Within my heart and secret thoughts thy words I have hid still,
That I might not at any time offend thy holy will.
12 We magnify thy name, O Lord, and praise thee evermore;
Thy statutes of most worthy fame, O Lord, teach me, therefore.

13 My lips have never ceas'd to preach and publish day and night
The judgments all which did proceed from thy mouth full of might.
14 Thy testimonies and thy ways much more my heart rejoice,
Than all the treasures of the earth, which worldlings make their choice.

15 Upon thy precepts I will muse, and thereto frame my talk;
As at a mark, so will I aim how I thy ways may walk.
16 My only joy shall be so fixt, and on thy laws so set,
That nothing shall me so far blind, that I thy words forget.

GIMEL.

17 Grant to thy servant now such grace, as may my life prolong;
Thy holy word then will I keep both in my heart and tongue.
18 My eyes which are dim and shut up, so open and make bright,
That of thy law and wondrous works I may have the clear sight.

19 I am a stranger on the earth, wand'ring now here, now there,
Thy words therefore to me disclose, my footsteps for to clear.
20 My soul is ravish'd with desire, and never is at rest,
But seeks to know thy judgments high, and what may please thee best.

21 The proud and the malicious men thou dost destroy each one,
And cursed are such as do not thy laws attend upon.
22 Lord, turn from me rebuke and shame which wicked men conspire,
For I have kept thy covenants with zeal as hot as fire.

23 The princes great in council sat, and did against me speak;
But then thy servant thought how he thy statutes might not break.
24 For why? thy cov'nants are the joy and solace of my heart,
They are my faithful counsellors, from them I'll not depart.

DALETH.

25 Alas, I am as brought to grave, and almost turn'd to dust;
Therefore restore my life again, as thy promise is just.

26 My ways when I acknowledged with mercy thou didst hear;
Hear now also, and me instruct thy laws to love and fear.

27 Make me, O Lord, to understand thy precepts evermore,
Then on thy works I'll meditate, and lay them up in store.
28 My soul I feel so sore oppress'd, that it doth melt for grief,
According to thy word therefore haste, Lord, to send relief.

29 From lying and deceitful lips let thy grace me defend,
And that I may learn thee to love, thy holy law me send.
30 The way of truth both straight and sure, I chosen have and found;
Before me I thy judgments set, which keep me safe and sound.

31 Since then, O Lord, I readily thy covenants embrace,
Let me therefore have no rebuke, nor check, in any case.
32 Then will I run most joyfully where thy word doth me call,
When thou enlarged hast my heart, and rid me out of thrall.

HE.

33 Instruct me, Lord, in the right way of thy statutes divine,
And them to keep unto the end my heart I will incline.
34 Grant me the knowledge of thy law, and I shall it obey;
With heart and mind and all my might I will it keep alway.

35 In the right paths of thy commands guide me, Lord, I require;
No other pleasure do I wish, no greater thing desire.
36 Incline my heart thy laws to keep, and cov'nants to embrace,
And from all filthy avarice, Lord, shield me with thy grace.

37 From vain desires and worldly lusts turn back my eyes and sight,
And with thy spirit strengthen me to walk thy ways aright.
38 Confirm thy gracious promise, Lord, which thou hast made to me,
Who am thy servant, and do love, and nothing fear but thee.

39 Reproach and shame, which I do fear, from me, O Lord, expel;
For thou dost judge with equity, and therein dost excel.
40 Behold my heart's desire is bent thy laws to keep alway:
O strengthen me so with thy grace, that it perform I may.

VAU.

41 Thy mercies great and manifold let me obtain, O Lord,
Thy saving health let me enjoy, according to thy word.
42 So shall I stop the sland'rous mouths of lewd men and unjust,
For in thy faithful word is all my confidence and trust.

43 The word of truth within my mouth let evermore be prest,
For in thy judgments wonderful my hope doth always rest.
44 And whilst that breath within me doth this mortal life preserve,
Yea, till this world shall be dissolv'd, thy law will I observe.

45 So walk will I as set at large from dread and danger free,
Because I study how to keep thy precepts faithfully.
46 Thy noble acts I will describe as things of most great fame,
Ev'n before kings I will them blaze, and shrink no whit for shame.

47 I will rejoice then to obey thy just commands and will,
Which evermore I've loved best, and so will love them still.

48 My hands I will lift to thy laws which I have dearly sought,
And practise thy commandments all in word, in deed, and thought.

ZAIN.

49 Thy promise which thou mad'st to me remember, Lord, I pray;
For therein have I put my trust and confidence alway.
50 It is my comfort and my joy, when troubles me assail;
For were my life not by thy word, it suddenly would fail.

51 The proud and such as God contemn still make of me a scorn;
Yet will I not thy law forsake, as if I were forlorn:
52 But call to mind, Lord, thy great works shew'd to our fathers old,
Whereby I feel my joy surmount my grief an hundred fold.

53 Horror hath taken hold on me, because the wicked do
Forsake thy righteous law, and will have no regard thereto.
54 But as for me, I fram'd my songs thy statutes to exalt,
When I among the strangers dwelt, and grief did me assault.

55 I thought upon thy Name, O Lord, by night when others sleep;
Thy law also I kept always, and ever will it keep.
56 This grace I did obtain, because thy covenants most dear
I did embrace and also keep with reverence and fear.

CHETH.

57 O God, who art my part and lot, my comfort and my stay,
I have decreed and promised thy laws to keep alway.
58 With my whole heart I humbly su'd, in presence of thy face,
As thou therefore hast promised, Lord, grant to me thy grace.

59 My life I have examined, and try'd my secret heart,
Which to thy statutes caused me my feet straight to convert.
60 I did not stay nor linger long, as they that slothful are,
But hastily thy laws to keep I did myself prepare.

61 The cruel bands of wicked men have made of me their prey;
Yet would I not thy law forget, nor from thee go astray.
62 Thy righteous laws and judgments are so very great and high,
That ev'n at midnight I will rise thy name to magnify.

63 I am companion of all them who fear thee in their heart;
O therefore grant I never may from thy commandments start.
64 Thy mercies, Lord, most plenteously the earth throughout do fill:
O teach me how I may obey thy statutes and thy will.

TETH.

65 According to thy promise, Lord, so hast thou with me dealt,
For of thy grace in sundry sorts have I thy servant felt.
66 Teach me to judge always aright, and give me knowledge sure;
For stedfastly I do believe thy precepts are most pure.

67 Before that I afflicted was I err'd and went astray;
But now I keep thy holy word, and make it all my stay.
68 Thou art both good and gracious, Lord, and in thy gifts most free,
Thy ordinances how to keep therefore, O Lord, teach me.

69 The proud and the ungodly have against me forg'd a lie;
Yet thy commandments still observe with all my heart will I.
70 Their hearts are ev'n like unto brawn, which is exceeding fat:
But in thy law do I delight, and nothing seek but that.

71 O happy time, may I well say, when thou didst me correct,
That I thereby might learn thy laws, and never them reject.
72 So that thy word and law to me is dearer manifold,
Than gold and silver in great sums, or aught that can be told.

JOD.

73 Thy hands have made and fashion'd me, thy creature, Lord, am I;
Make me to understand thy law, and keep it faithfully.
74 So they that fear thee shall rejoice whenever they me see,
Because I've learned by thy word to put my trust in thee.

75 I know, O Lord, thy judgments all most just and righteous be,
And that in very faithfulness thou hast afflicted me.
76 Now of thy goodness I thee pray some comfort to me send,
And as thou hast me hitherto, O Lord, still me defend.

77 Thy tender mercies pour on me, then shall I surely live,
For joy and consolation both thy law to me doth give.
78 Confound the proud who do me seek perversely to destroy;
But as for me, thy laws to know I will myself employ.

79 Whoso with rev'rence do thee fear, to me let them retire;
And such as know thy covenants, and them alone desire.
80 My heart without all wavering let on thy laws be bent,
That no confusion come to me, nor any discontent.

CAPH.

81 My soul doth faint, and ceaseth not thy saving health to crave;
And for thy word's sake still I trust my heart's desire to have.
82 My eyes do fail with looking for thy word, and thus I say,
Oh when wilt thou me comfort, Lord? why dost thou thus delay?

83 Like as a bottle in the smoke, so am I parch'd and dry'd;
Yet will I not out of my heart let thy commandments slide.
84 How long, O Lord, shall I yet live before I see the hour,
That on my foes which me torment thy vengeance thou wilt pour?

85 Presumptuous men have digged pits, thinking to make me sure:
Thus quite contrary to thy law, my hurt they do procure.
86 But thy commandments are all true, and causeless they me grieve;
To thee therefore I do complain, that thou may'st me relieve.

87 Almost they had me clean destroy'd and brought me quite to groun[d]
Yet by thy statutes I abode, and therein succour found.
88 Restore me, Lord, again to life, thy mercies do excel;
And so shall I thy statutes keep, till death my life expel.

LAMED.

89 In heav'n, O Lord, where thou dost dwell thy word is 'stablish'd sure,
And shall to all eternity fast settled there endure.

90 From age to age thy truth abides, as doth the earth witness;
Whose ground-work thou hast laid so sure, as no tongue can express.

91 Ev'n to this day we may well see how thou dost them preserve
According to thy ordinance, for all things do thee serve.
92 Had it not been that in thy law my soul hath comfort sought,
Long time e'er now in my distress I had been brought to nought.

93 Therefore will I thy precepts keep in memory full fast,
Because that thou by them, O Lord, my life restored hast.
94 No man to me can title make, for I am only thine;
Save me, therefore, for to thy laws my ears and heart incline.

95 The wicked men that seek my bane for me do lie in wait;
But I will meditate upon thy testimonies great;
96 For nothing in this world I see which hath at length no end;
But thy commandments and thy word beyond all time extend.

MEM.

97 What great desire and fervent love unto thy law I bear!
On it my daily study is, that so I may thee fear.
98 Thy word hath taught me to exceed in wisdom all my foes:
For they are ever with me, and do give me sweet repose.

99 My teachers, who did me instruct, in knowledge I excel;
Because I do thy statutes keep, and them to others tell.
100 In wisdom I do far surpass the ancient men also;
And that because I keep thy laws, and so resolve to do.

101 My feet I have refrain'd likewise from ev'ry evil way;
That so I might thy word observe and keep without delay.
102 I have not from thy judgments swerv'd nor shrunk, as thou canst tell;
Because thou hast me taught thereby to live godly and well.

103 O Lord, how sweet unto my taste I find thy word alway!
Doubtless no honey in my mouth doth taste so sweet as they.
104 Thy laws have me such wisdom learn'd, that I do hate therefore
All wicked and ungodly ways, and will do evermore.

NUN.

105 Ev'n as a lantern to my feet, so doth thy word shine bright,
And to my paths where I do go it is a flaming light.
106 I have both sworn and will perform in truth and faithfulness,
That I will keep thy judgments just, and them in life express.

107 Affliction hath me sore opprest, and brought me to death's door;
O Lord, as thou hast promised, so me to life restore.
108 The free-will off'rings of my mouth, which I to thee do give,
Accept, and teach me how I may after thy judgments live.

109 My soul is ever in my hand, great dangers me assail;
Yet do I not thy law forget, nor it to keep will fail.
110 Although the wicked laid their nets to make of me a prey,
Yet from thy precepts did I not once swerve or go astray.

111 Thy law, O Lord, I taken have my heritage to be:
Because such great delight and joy it doth afford to me.

PSALM CXIX.

155 As for the wicked, they are far from saving health and grace:
Because the way thy laws to know they enter not the trace.
156 Great are thy mercies, Lord, I grant, what tongue can them explain?
According to thy judgments good let me my life obtain.

157 Though many men did trouble me and persecute me sore,
Yet from thy laws I never shrunk, nor went aside therefore.
158 The great trangressors I behold, which is a grief to me;
Because they do not keep thy word, nor ever seek to thee.

159 Behold how I do love thy laws with a most upright heart,
Then quicken me, O Lord, for thou most good and gracious art.
160 Thy word from the beginning hath been ever true and just,
Thy righteous judgments ev'ry one always continue must.

SCHIN.

161 Princes have persecuted me without a cause, but saw
It was in vain, for of thy word my heart did stand in awe.
162 And surely of thy word I was more joyful and more glad,
Than he that of rich spoils and rey great store and plenty had.

163 But as for lies and falsities, them I hate and detest;
Because thy holy law I do above all things love best.
164 Seven times a day I praise thee, Lord, singing with heart and voice;
Because thy righteous judgments do greatly my heart rejoice.

165 Great peace and rest shall all such have as do thy statutes love;
No danger shall their quiet state impair or once remove.
166 My only health and comfort, Lord, I look for at thy hand:
And therefore have I done those things which thou didst me command.

167 Thy laws have been my exercise, which my soul most desir'd;
So much to them my love was bent, that nought else I requir'd.
168 Thy statutes and commandments I have kept with heart upright;
For all my doings and my ways are present in thy sight.

TAU.

169 O Lord, let my complaint and cry before thy face appear,
And as thou hast me promise made, so teach me thee to fear.
170 O let my supplication, Lord, have free access to thee;
And let me be delivered, as thou hast promis'd me.

171 Then shall my lips thy praises speak after most ample sort,
When thou thy statutes hast me taught, wherein stands my comfort.
172 My tongue shall freely preach thy word, and evermore confess,
Thy famous acts and noble laws are truth and righteousness.

173 Stretch out thy hand, I thee beseech, and speedily me save;
For thy commandments to observe chosen, O Lord, I have.
174 Of thee alone, Lord, I crave health, for other I know none;
And in thy law to meditate I do delight alone.

175 Grant me therefore long days to live thy name to magnify,
And of thy judgments wonderful let me the favour try.
176 For I was lost and went astray ev'n like a wand'ring sheep:
O seek me, for I have not fail'd thy statutes for to keep.

PSALM CXX. T. S.

1 IN trouble and in thrall unto the Lord I call,
And he doth me comfort; deliver me, I pray,
From lying lips alway, and tongues of false report.

2 What 'vantage or what thing gett'st thou thus for to sting,
Thou false and flatt'ring liar? Thy tongue doth hurt, it's seen,
No less than arrows keen, or hot consuming fire.

3 Alas; that I am fain in those tents to remain,
Which Kedar are by name; by whom the flock elect,
And all of Isaac's sect, are put to open shame.

4 With them that peace do hate I came to meditate,
And set a quiet life: but when my mind was told,
Causeless I was controul'd by them that loved strife.

PSALM CXXI. W. W.

1 I LIFT my eyes to Sion hill, from whence I do attend,
Till succour God me send: The mighty God me succour will,
Which heav'n and earth did frame, and all things therein name.

2 Thy foot from slip he will preserve, and will thee safely keep;
For he doth never sleep; Lo, him that Israel doth conserve
Sleep never can surprize, nor slumber close his eyes.

3 The Lord thy keeper is alway, on thy right-hand is he
A shade to cover thee: The sun shall not thee parch by day,
Nor moon, scarce half so bright, with cold thee hurt by night.

4 The Lord will keep thee from distress, and will thy life sure save;
Yea, thou shalt also have In all thy business good success:
When thou go'st in or out he'll compass thee about.

PSALM CXXII. W. K.

1 I DID in heart rejoice to hear the people's voice,
In offering so willingly: For let us up, say they,
And in the Lord's house pray: thus spake the folk with amity.

2 Our feet that wander'd wide shall in thy gates abide,
O thou Jerusalem full fair, which art so seemly set
Much like a city neat, whither the people do repair:

3 The tribes with one accord to give thanks to the Lord
Are thither bent their way to take: so God before did tell
That there his Israel their prayers should together make.

4 For there are thrones erect, and that for this respect,
To set forth justice orderly: which thrones right to maintain,
To David's house remain, his folk to judge with equity.

5 To pray let us not cease for Jerusalem's peace!
Thy friends God keep in amity! peace be thy walls about;
And prosper thee throughout thy palaces continually.

6 For my friends' sake will I with that prosperity
May evermore abide in thee; God's house doth me allure
Thy wealth for to procure, so much as lies in me.

PSALM CXXIII. T. S.

1 O THOU that in the heav'ns dost dwell, I lift my eyes to thee;
Ev'n as a servant lifeth his, his master's hand to see:
2 As handmaids watch their mistress' hand, some grace for to atchieve,
So we behold the Lord our God, till he do us forgive.

3 O grant to us compassion, Lord, and mercy in thy sight,
For we are fill'd and overcome with hatred and despite.
4 Our minds are fill'd with great rebuke, the rich and worldly wise
Do make of us their mocking-stocks, the proud do us despise.

PSALM CXXIV. W. W.

1 NOW Israel may say, and that truly,
If that the Lord had not our cause maintain'd,
If that the Lord had not our right sustain'd,
When all the world against us furiously
Made their uproars, and said we should all die:

2 Then long ago they had devour'd us all,
And swallow'd quick, for aught that we could deem;
Such was their rage, as we might well esteem;
And as the floods with mighty force do fall,
So had they now our lives ev'n brought to thrall.

3 The raging streams, most proud in roaring noise,
Had long ago o'erwhelm'd us in the deep:
Praised be God which doth us safely keep
From bloody teeth and their most cruel voice,
Who as a prey to eat us would rejoice.

4 Ev'n as a bird from fowler's gin or pen
Escapes away, right so it fares with us:
Broke are the nets, and we escaped thus.
God who made heav'n and earth is our help then,
His name hath sav'd us from these wicked men.

PSALM CXXV. W. K.

1 SUCH as in God the Lord do trust, as Sion mount shall firmly stand,
And be removed at no hand: the Lord will count them right and just
So that they shall be sure for ever to endure.

2 As many mountains huge and great Jerusalem about do close,
So will the Lord do unto those who on his godly will do wait:
Such are to him so dear they never need to fear.

3 For though the righteous try doth he by making wicked men his rod,
Lest they thro' grief forsake their God, it shall not always their lot be,
Give, Lord, to us thy light, whose hearts are true and right:

4 But as for such as turn aside by crooked ways which they out-sought
The Lord will surely bring to nought; with workers vile they shall abide;
But peace with Israel for evermore shall dwell.

PSALM CXXV, CXXVI, CXXVII.

ANOTHER OF THE SAME, BY W. W.

1 THOSE that do place their confidence upon the Lord our God only,
And flee to him for their defence in all their need and misery,
Their faith is sure still to endure, grounded on Christ the corner-stone;
Mov'd with no ill, but standeth still stedfast like to the mount Sion.

2 And as about Jerusalem the mighty hills do it compass,
So that no foes can come to them to hurt that town in any case;
So God indeed in ev'ry need, his faithful people doth defend,
Standing them by assuredly from this time forth world without end.

3 Right wise and good is our Lord God, and will not suffer certainly
The sinner's and ungodly's rod to rest upon his family,
Lest they also from God should stray, falling to sin and wickedness:
O Lord, defend both night and day thy little flock, and them still bless.

4 O Lord, do good to Christians all that stedfast in thy word abide:
But such as from the Lord do fall and to false doctrine daily slide,
Them will the Lord scatter abroad, with hypocrites thrown down to hell;
God will them send pains without end; but, Lord, grant peace to Israel.

PSALM CXXVI. W. W.

1 WHEN that the Lord again his Sion had forth brought
From bondage great and also servitude extreme,
His work was such as did surmount man's heart and thought,
So that we were much like to them that use to dream:
Our mouths were all with laughter filled then,
Also our tongues did shew us joyful men.

2 The heathen folk were forced then this to confess,
How that the Lord for them also great things had done:
But much more we, and therefore can confess no less;
Wherefore to joy we have good cause, as we begun.
O Lord, go forth, thou canst our bondage end,
Who to deserts dost flowing rivers send.

3 Full true it is, that they which sow in tears indeed,
A time will come when they shall reap in mirth and joy.
They went and wept in bearing of their precious seed,
For that their foes full oftentimes did them annoy;
But their return they joyfully shall see,
Their sheaves bring home, and not impaired be.

PSALM CXXVII. W. W.

1 EXCEPT the Lord the house doth make and thereunto doth set his hand,
What men do build, it cannot stand: likewise in vain men undertake
Cities and holds to watch and ward, except the Lord be their safe-guard.

2 Tho' in the morn ye rise early, and so at night go late to bed,
Eating with carefulness your bread, your labour is but vanity:
But they whom God doth love and keep enjoy all things with quiet sleep.

3 Therefore mark well, when you do see that men have heirs t'enjoy their land,
It is the gift of God's own hand: for God doth multiply to thee
Of his great liberality the blessing of posterity.

4 And when the children come to age, they grow in strength and activeness,
In person and in comeliness: so that a shaft shot with courage
Of one that hath a most strong arm flies not so swift nor does like harm.

5 Oh well is he that hath his quiver furnish'd with such artillery:
For when in peril he shall be, such one shall never quake or shiver,
When he doth plead before the judge against his foes that bear him grudge.

PSALM CXXVIII. T. S.

1 BLESSED art thou that fearest God, and walkest in his ways;
For of thy labour thou shalt eat, happy shall be thy days.
2 Like fruitful vines on thy house side so doth thy wife spring out;
Thy children stand like olive-plants thy table round about.

3 Thus art thou blest that fearest God, and he shall let thee see
The promised Jerusalem, and her felicity.
4 Thou shalt thy children's children see to thy great joys' encrease,
And likewise grace on Israel, prosperity and peace.

PSALM CXXIX. N.

1 OFT they, now Israel may say, me from my youth assail'd;
Oft they assail'd me from my youth, yet never have prevail'd.
2 Upon my back the ploughers plough'd, and furrows long did cast:
The righteous Lord hath cut the cords of wicked men at last.

3 They that hate me shall be asham'd, and turned back also,
And made as grass upon the house, which withers ere it grow:
4 Whereof the mower cannot find enough to fill his hand.
Nor can he fill his lap that goes to glean upon the land,

5 Now passers by pray God on them to let his blessing fall;
Nor say, We bless you in his name who is Lord over all.

PSALM CXXX. W. W.

1 LORD, unto thee I make my moan, when dangers me oppress;
I call, I sigh, complain and groan, trusting to find release.
2 Hearken, O Lord, to my request, unto my suit incline,
And let thine ears, O Lord, be prest to hear this prayer of mine.

3 O Lord our God, if thou survey our sins, and them peruse,
Who shall escape? or who dare say, I can myself excuse?
4 But thou art merciful and free, and boundless in thy grace,
That we might always careful be to fear before thy face.

5 In God the Lord I put my trust, my soul waits on his will;
His promise is for ever just, and I hope therein still.
6 My soul to God hath great regard, wishing for him alway:
Much more than they that watch and ward to see the dawning day.

7 O Israel, trust in the Lord, with him there mercy is,
And he doth plenteously afford redemption unto his.
8 Even he it is that Israel shall, through his abundant grace,
Redeem from his offence, all, and wholly them deface.

PSALM CXXXI. N.

1 O LORD, I am not puft in mind, I have no scornful eye,
I do not exercise myself in things that be too high:
2 But as a child that weaned is ev'n from his mother's breast,
So have I, Lord, behav'd myself in silence and in rest.

3 O Israel, trust in the Lord, let him be all thy stay
From this time forth for evermore, from age to age alway.

PSALM CXXXII. N.

1 REMEMBER David's troubles, Lord, how unto thee he swore,
And vow'd a vow to Jacob's God, to keep for evermore:
2 I will not come within my house, nor climb up to my bed,
Nor let my temples take their rest, nor eyes within my head;

3 Till I have found out for the Lord a place to sit thereon,
An house for Jacob's God to be an habitation.
4 We heard of it at Ephrata, there did we hear this sound,
And in the fields and forests there these voices first were found:

5 We will essay and go into his tabernacle there,
Before his footstool to fall down, and worship him in fear,
6 Arise, O Lord, arise, I pray, into the resting place,
Thou and the ark of thy great strength, the presence of thy grace.

7 Let all thy priests be clothed, Lord, with truth and righteousness,
Let all thy saints with songs of praise their joyfulness express.
8 And for thy servant David's sake refuse not, Lord, I pray,
The face of thy anointed, and turn not from him away.

PART II.

9 The Lord to David swore in truth, and will not shrink from it,
The fruit that from thy loins proceed upon thy seat shall sit:
10 And if thy sons my laws will keep, that I shall learn each one,
Then shall their sons for ever sit upon thy princely throne.

11 The Lord himself hath Sion chose, and loves therein to dwell,
Saying, This is my resting place, I love and like it well;
12 And I will bless with great increase her victuals ev'ry where,
And also satisfy with bread the needy that be there:

13 With my salvation I will clothe her priests for evermore,
And all her saints likewise shall sing and shout for joy therefore.
14 There will I surely make the horn of David for to bud;
For there I have ordain'd for him a lantern bright and good.

15 As for his foes, I will them clothe with shame for evermore;
But I will cause his crown to shine more fresh than heretofore.

PSALM CXXXIII. W. W.

1 O WHAT a happy thing it is, and joyful for to see,
Brethren to dwell together in friendship and unity!
2 It's like the precious ointment that was pour'd on Aaron's head,
Which from his beard down to the skirts of his rich garments spread.

3 And as the lower ground doth drink the dew of Hermon hill,
And Sion with his silver drops the fields with fruit doth fill;
4 Ev'n so the Lord doth pour on them his blessings manifold,
Whose hearts and minds sincerely do this knot fast keep and hold.

PSALM CXXXIV. W. W.

1 BEHOLD, and have regard, ye servants of the Lord,
Who in his house by night do watch, praise him with one accord.
2 Lift up your hands on high unto his holy place,
And give the Lord his praises due, his benefits embrace.

3 For why? the Lord our God, who heav'n and earth did frame,
Doth Sion bless, and will preserve for evermore the same.

PSALM CXXXV. N.

1 O PRAISE the Lord, praise ye his name, praise him with one accord;
O praise him still, all ye that be the servants of the Lord.
2 O praise him, ye that stand and be in the house of the Lord,
Ye of his court and of his house praise him with one accord.

3 Praise ye the Lord, for he is good, sing praises to his name;
It is a good and pleasant thing always to do the same.
4 For why? the Lord hath Jacob chose his very own, ye see;
So hath he chosen Israel his treasure for to be.

5 For this I know, and am right sure, the Lord is very great;
He is indeed above all gods most easy to intreat.
6 For whatsoever pleased him, all that full well he wrought
In heav'n, in earth, and in the sea, which he hath made of nought.

7 He lifts the clouds above the earth, he lightnings makes and rain;
He bringeth forth the winds also, and nothing made in vain.
8 He smote the first-born of each thing in Egypt that took rest,
He spared there no thing living, the man, nor yet the beast.

9 He did likewise shew wonders great on their inhabitants,
Upon king Pharaoh, and also on his severe servants.
10 He smote then many nations, and did great and wondrous things
He likewise slew the mightiest and chiefest of their kings:

11 Sehon king of the Amorites, and Og king of Basan,
He slew also the kingdoms all that were of Canaan;
12 And gave their land to Israel an heritage to be,
To Israel his people, and to their posterity.

PART II.

13 Thy name shall still endure, and thy memorial likewise,
Throughout all generations that are now, or shall arise.
14 The Lord most surely will avenge his people all with speed:
And to his servants he will shew favour in time of need.

15 The idols of the heathen which are in the coasts and lands,
Of silver and of gold they be, the work ev'n of men's hands.
16 They have their mouths, but cannot speak, and eyes that have no sight:
And they have ears, but nothing hear, their mouths are breathless qu

17 Wherefore all they are like to them that so do set them forth,
And likewise those that in them trust, or think they be aught worth.
18 O all ye house of Israel, see that ye praise the Lord;
And ye that be of Aaron's house, praise him with one accord:

19 And ye that be of Levi's house, praise ye likewise the Lord,
All ye that stand in awe of him, praise him with one accord.
20 And out of Sion sound his praise, the great praise of the Lord,
Who dwelleth in Jerusalem, praise him with one accord.

PSALM CXXXVI. N.

1 PRAISE ye the Lord, for he is good, for his mercy endureth for ever:
2 Give praise unto the God of gods; for his mercy, &c
3 Give praise unto the Lord of lords; for his mercy, &c.
4 Who only doth great wondrous works; for his mercy, &c.

5 Who by his wisdom made the heav'ns; for his mercy, &c.
6 Who on the waters stretch'd the earth; for his mercy, &c.
7 Who made great lights to shine abroad; for his mercy, &c.
8 The sun to rule the lightsome day; for his mercy, &c.

9 The moon and stars to rule the night; for his mercy, &c.
10 Who Egypt smote with their first-born; for his mercy, &c.
11 And Israel brought out from thence; for his mercy, &c.
12 With mighty hand and out-stretch'd arm; for his mercy, &c.

13 Who cut the Red-sea in two parts; for his mercy, &c.
14 And Israel made to pass through; for his mercy, &c.
15 And drowned Pharaoh and his host; for his mercy, &c.
16 Through wilderness his people led: for his mercy, &c.

17 Who did smite great and noble kings; for his mercy, &c.
18 Yea, and also slew mighty kings: for his mercy, &c.
19 Sehon king of the Amorites; for his mercy, &c.
20 And Og the king of Basan land; for his mercy, &c.

21 And gave their land for heritage; for his mercy, &c.
22 Even to his servant Israel; for his mercy, &c.
23 Remembering us in low estate; for his mercy, &c.
24 And from oppressors rescu'd us; for his mercy, &c.

25 Who giveth food unto all flesh: for his mercy, &c.
26 Praise ye the Lord of heav'n above; for his mercy, &c.
27 Give thanks unto the Lord of lords; for his mercy endureth for ever.

ANOTHER OF THE SAME, BY T. C.

1 O PRAISE the Lord benign, whose mercy ne'er decays;
Give thanks and praises sing to God of gods always;
For certainly his mercies dure
Both firm and sure eternally.
2 The Lord of lords praise ye, whose mercies ever dure
Great wonders only he doth by his power sure:
For certainly, &c.

3 Which God omnipotent by his great wisdom he
The heav'n and firmament did frame, as we may see:
For certainly, &c.
4 Yea, he the heavy charge of all the earth did lay
Upon the waters large, remaining to this day:
For certainly, &c.

5 Great lights he made, for why? his mercy lasts always;
The sun most gloriously to rule the lightsome day:
For certainly, &c.
6 Also the moon so clear, which shineth in our sight,
And stars that do appear to guide the darksome night:
For certainly &c.

7 With grievous plagues and sore all Egypt smote he then,
The first-born, less or more, he slew of beasts and men:
For certainly, &c.
8 And from amidst their land his Israel forth brought,
Which he with mighty hand and out-stretch'd arm hath wrought:
For certainly, &c.

9 The sea he cut in two, which stood up like a wall,
And made it through to go his chosen children all:
For certainly, &c.
10 But overwhelmed then the haughty king Pharaoh,
With his huge host of men and chariots also:
For certainly, &c.

11 Who led through wilderness his people safe and sound:
And for his love endless great kings he brought to ground:
For certainly, &c.
12 And with puissant hand slew kings of mighty fame,
As of the Amorites' land Sehon the king by name:
For certainly, &c.

13 And Og, the giant large, of Basan king also,
Whose land for heritage he gave his people to:
For certainly, &c.
14 Even unto Israel his servant dear, I say,
That he therein might dwell, and there abide alway:
For certainly, &c.

15 Who us remember'd when in our most low degree,
And from oppressors then in safety set us free:
For certainly, &c.
16 Who doth all flesh with food abundantly supply;
Wherefore let God most good be prais'd incessantly:
For certainly his mercies dure
Both firm and sure eternally.

PSALM CXXXVII. W. W.

1 WHEN we did sit in Babylon, the rivers round about,
Then in remembrance of Sion, the tears for grief burst out.
2 We hang'd our harps and instruments the willow trees upon:
For in that place men for their use had planted many a one.

3 Then they to whom we pris'ners were said to us tauntingly,
Now let us hear your Hebrew songs and pleasant melody.
4 Alas, said we, who can once frame his heavy heart to sing
The praises of our loving God, thus under a strange king?

5 But yet if I Jerusalem out of my heart let slide,
Then let my fingers quite forget the warbling harp to guide:
6 And let my tongue within my mouth be ty'd for ever fast,
If I rejoice before I see thy full deliv'rance past.

7 Therefore, O Lord, remember now the cursed noise and cry
That Edom's sons against us made, when they ras'd our city.
8 Remember, Lord, their cruel words, when with a mighty sound
They cried, Down, yea, down with it unto the very ground.

9 E'en so shalt thou, O Babylon, at length to dust be brought;
And happy shall that man be call'd that our revenge hath wrought:
10 Yea, blessed shall that man be call'd, that takes thy little ones
And dasheth them in pieces small against the very stones.

PSALM CXXXVIII. N.

1 THEE will I praise with my whole heart, my Lord my God, always;
E'en in the presence of the gods I will advance thy praise.
2 Towards thy holy temple I will look, and worship thee:
And praised in my thankful mouth thy holy Name shall be;

3 Ev'n for thy loving-kindness sake, and for thy truth withal:
For thou thy Name hast by thy word advanced over all.
4 When I did call thou heardest me, and thou hast made also
The power of increased strength within my soul to grow.

5 Yea, all the kings on earth shall give praise unto thee, O Lord:
For they of thy most holy mouth have heard the mighty word.
6 They of the ways of God the Lord in singing shall repeat;
Because the glory of the Lord is so exceeding great.

7 The Lord is high, but yet he doth the lowly man respect;
The proud he knows far off, and them with scorn he doth reject.
8 Although in midst of trouble I do walk, yet shall I stand
Reviv'd by thee; for thou, O Lord, wilt stretch out thy right-hand,

9 Upon the wrath of all my foes, and saved shall I be
By thy right-hand; the Lord God will perform his work to me.
10 Thy mercies last for evermore, Lord, do me not forsake;
Forsake me not, who am the work which thy own hand did make.

PSALM CXXXIX. N.

1 O LORD, thou hast me try'd and known, my sitting down dost know,
My rising up and thoughts far off thou understand'st also.
2 My path, yea, and my bed likewise thou art about always,
And by familiar custom art acquainted with my ways.

3 No word is in my tongue, O Lord, that is not known to thee;
Thou hast beset me round about, and laid thy hand on me.
4 Such knowledge is too wonderful, and past my skill to gain
It is so high that I unto the same cannot attain.

5 From thy all-seeing spirit then, Lord, whither shall I go?
Or whither shall I fly away from thy presence also?
6 For if to heav'n I do climb up, lo! thou art present there:
In hell if I lie down below, ev'n there thou dost appear.

7 Yea, let me take the morning's wing, and let me go and dwell
Ev'n in the very utmost parts, where flowing seas do swell:
8 Yet, certainly there also shall thy hand me lead and guide,
And thy right-hand shall hold me fast, and make me to abide.

9 Or if I say the darkness shall shroud me quite from thy sight,
Ev'n then the night that is most dark about me shall be light.
10 The darkness hideth not from thee, but night doth shine as day;
To thee the darkness and the light are both alike alway.

PART II.

11 For thou possessed has my reins, and thou didst cover me
Within my mother's womb, when I was there enclos'd by thee
12 Thee will I praise, made fearfully and wond'rously I am;
Thy works are marvellous, right well my soul doth know the same.

13 My bones they are not hid from thee, altho' in secret place
I have been made, and in the earth beneath I shaped was.
14 When I was formless, then thy eye saw me; for in thy book
Were all my members written, and nought after fashion took.

15 The thoughts therefore of thee, O God, how dear are they to me!
And of them all, how very great the endless numbers be;
16 If I should count them, lo, their sum more than the sand would be;
And whensoever I awake I present am with thee.

17 The wicked and ungodly thou most certainly will slay,
Therefore now, all ye bloody men, depart from me away.
18 These are the men, O Lord, who speak most wickedly of thee,
And take thy Name in vain, because thy enemies they be.

19 Hate I not them that hate thee, Lord, and that in earnest wise
Am I not grieved with all those that up against thee rise?
20 I hate them with a perfect hate, ev'n as my utter foes:
Try me, O God, and know my heart, my thoughts pvove and disclose.

21 Consider, Lord, if wickedness in me there any be;
And in thy way, O God, my guide, for ever lead thou me.

PSALM CXL. N.

1 LORD, save me from the evil man, and from his pride and spight,
And from all those who do in violence delight:
2 Who evermore on me make war; their tongues, lo, they have whet
Like serpents; underneath their lips is adders' poison set.

3 Keep me, O Lord, from wicked hands, preserve me to abide
Free from the cruel man that means to cause my steps to slide.
4 The proud have laid a snare for me, and they have spread a net
With cords in my path-way, and gins for me also have set.

6 Therefore I said unto the Lord, thou art my God alone,
Hear me, therefore, O hear the voice wherewith I pray and moan.

6 O Lord my God, thou only art the strength that saveth me;
My head in day of battle hath been cover'd still by thee.

7 Let not, O Lord, the wicked have the end of his desire,
Perform not his ill thought, lest he with pride be set on fire.
8 Of them that compass me about, the chiefest of them all,
Lord, let the mischief of their lips upon their own heads fall.

9 Let coals fall on them, let them be cast in consuming flame,
And in deep pit, that never they may rise out of the same.
10 For no backbiters shall on earth be set in stable plight;
And evil to destruction still shall hunt the cruel wight.

11 I know the Lord th' afflicted will revenge, and judge the poor:
The just shall praise thy name, and shall dwell with thee evermore.

PSALM CXLI. N,

1 O LORD, upon thee do I call, then haste thee unto me,
And hearken thou unto my voice when I do cry to thee.
2 As incense let my prayers still be directed in thy eyes,
And the uplifting of my hands as evening sacrifice.

3 For guiding of my mouth, O Lord, set thou a watch before,
And also of my moving lips, O Lord, keep thou the door.
4 That I should wicked works commit, incline thou not my heart;
With ill men of their delicates, Lord, let me eat no part.

5 But let the righteous smite me, Lord, for that is good for me;
Let him reprove me, and the same a precious oil shall be:
6 Such smiting shall not break my head, the time shall shortly fall,
When I shall in their misery make prayers for them all.

7 And when in stony places down their judges shall be cast,
Then shall they hear my words, because they have a pleasant taste.
8 Our bones about the pit's mouth are all scattered and found;
As when one breaketh and doth hew the wood upon the ground.

9 But, O my Lord and God, my eyes do look up unto thee;
In thee is all my trust, let not my soul forsaken be:
10 Keep and preserve me from the snare which they for me have laid,
And from the gins of wicked men, whereof I am afraid.

11 The wicked into their own nets together let them fall,
While I do by thy help escape the danger of them all.

PSALM CXLII. N

1 UNTO the Lord God with my voice I did send out my cry,
And with my strained voice unto the Lord God prayed I:
2 My meditation in his sight to pour I did not spare,
And in the presence of the Lord my trouble did declare.

3 Altho' perplexed was my soul, my path was known to thee;
In way where I did walk a snare they slily laid for me.
4 I look'd and view'd on my right-hand, but none there would me know:
All refuge failed me, and for my soul none care did show.

5 Then cried I to thee and said, O Lord, my hope thou art,
And in the land of the living my portion and my part.
6 Hear now my cry, for I am brought full low, deliver me
From them that do me persecute, for me too strong they be:

7 That I may praise thy name, my soul from prison, Lord, bring out:
When thou art good to me, the just shall compass me about.

PSALM CXLIII. N.

1 LORD, hear my pray'r and my complaint which I do make to thee,
And in thy native truth, and in thy justice answer me.
2 In judgment with thy servant, Lord, O enter not at all:
For justify'd be in thy sight not one that liveth shall.

3 The enemy pursu'd my soul, my life to ground hath thrown,
And laid me in the dark like them that are to grave gone down:
4 Therefore my spirit in me is in great perplexity,
My heart within me is also afflicted grievously.

5 Yet I record time past, and on thy works I meditate,
Yea, I do muse upon the works that thy hands have create.
6 To thee, O Lord my God, do I stretch forth my craving hand;
My soul desireth after thee as do the thirsty lands.

7 Hear me with speed, my spirit fails, hide not thy face, lest I
Be like to them that in the pit sink down, and there do lie.
8 Let me thy loving-kindness in the morning hear and know:
For in thee is my trust, shew me the way that I should go.

9 For unto thee I lift my soul, O Lord, deliver me
From all mine enemies, for I have hid myself with thee.
10 Teach me to do my will, for thou, thou art my God alway,
Let thy good spirit to the land of mercy me convey.

11 For thy name's sake with quick'ning grace alive do thou me make,
And out of trouble bring my soul, even for thy justice sake;
12 And of thy mercy slay my foes, let them destroyed be
That do oppress my soul, for I a servant am to thee.

PSALM CXLIV. N.

1 BLEST be the Lord my strength, that doth instruct my hands to fight,
The Lord that doth my fingers frame to battle by his might.
2 He is my hope, my fort, and tow'r, deliverer and shield;
In him I trust, my people he subdues to me to yield.

3 O Lord, what thing is man, that him thou dost so highly prize!
Or son of man, that upon him thou thinkest in such wise!
4 Man is but like to vanity, so pass his days to end,
As fleeting shade. Bow down, O Lord, the heavens, and thence descend;

5 The mountains touch, and they shall smoke, cast forth thy light'nings' flame,
And scatter them; thy arrows shoot, consume them with the same.
6 Send down thy hand from heav'n above, O Lord, deliver me,
Take me from waters great, from hand of strangers set me free;

7 Whose subtil mouth of vanity with flatt'ring words doth treat,
And their right-hand is a right-hand of falshood and deceit.

8 A new song will I sing to thee, O God the Lord most high,
And on a ten-string'd lute also praise thee most joyfully.

9 Even he it is that only gives deliverance to kings;
Unto his servant David help from hurtful sword he brings;
10 From strangers hand me save and shield, whose mouth talks vanity,
And their right-hand is a right-hand of guile and subtilty.

11 That so our sons may be as plants which growing youth doth rear,
Our daughters as carv'd corner-stones, like to a palace fair;
12 Our garners full and plenty may of sundry sorts be found;
Our sheep bring thousands, in our streets ten thousands may abound.

13 Our oxen be to labour strong, that none may us invade;
No goings out there be, nor cries within our streets be made.
14 The people happy are that with such blessings great are stor'd;
Yea, blessed all the people are, whose God is God the Lord.

PSALM CXLV. N.

1 THEE will I laud, my God and King, and bless thy name alway;
For ever will I praise the same, and bless thee day by day.
2 Great is the Lord, most worthy praise, his greatness none can reach;
From race to race they shall thy works praise, and thy power preach.

3 I of thy glorious majesty the beauty will record,
And meditate upon thy works most wonderful, O Lord:
4 And they shall of thy pow'r, and of thy fearful acts declare,
And I to publish all abroad thy greatness will not spare:

5 And they into the mention shall break of thy goodness great,
And I aloud thy righteousness in singing will repeat.
6 The Lord our God most gracious is and merciful also,
Of great abounding mercy, and to anger he is slow.

7 Yea good to all; and all his works his mercy doth exceed;
Lo, all thy works do praise thee, Lord, and honour thee indeed.
8 Thy saints do bless thee, and they do thy kingdom's glory show,
And blaze thy pow'r to cause, the sons of men the same to know.

PART II.

11 And of thy kingdom's majesty do spread the glorious praise;
12 Thy kingdom, Lord, a kingdom is that doth endure always:
13 And thy dominion through each age endures without decay:
The Lord upholdeth them that fall, their sliding he doth stay.

15 The eyes of all do wait on thee, thou dost them all relieve,
And thou to each sufficing food in season due dost give:
16 Thou openest thy plenteous hand, and bounteously dost fill
All things whatever that do live with gifts of thy good will.

17 The Lord is just in all his ways, his works are holy all,
18 And he is near all those that do in truth upon him call:
19 He the desires of all them that fear him will fulfil,
And he will hear them when they cry, and save them all he will.

15 The Lord preserves all those to him that bear a loving heart;
But he all them that wicked are will utterly subvert.
16 My thankful mouth shall gladly speak the praises of the Lord:
All flesh to praise his holy name for ever shall accord.

PSALM CXLVI. J. H.

1 MY soul, praise thou the Lord always, my God I will confess;
While breath and life prolong my days, my tongue no time shall cease.
2 Trust not in worldly princes then, though they abound in wealth;
Nor in the sons of mortal men, in whom there is no health

3 For why; their breath doth soon depart, to earth anon they fall,
And then the counsels of their heart decay and perish all.
4 Blessed and happy are all they whom Jacob's God doth aid,
And he whose hope doth not decay, but on the Lord is staid:

5 Who made the earth and waters deep, the heav'ns most high withal;
Who doth his word and promise keep in truth and ever shall.
6 With right always doth he proceed for such as suffer wrong,
The poor and hungry he doth feed, and loose the fetters strong:

7 The Lord doth send the blind their sight, the lame to limbs restore;
He loveth all that are upright, and just men evermore:
8 He doth defend the fatherless, and strangers sad in heart,
He frees the widow from distress, and ill men's ways subvert.

9 The Lord thy God eternally, O Sion, still shall reign,
In time of all posterity for ever to remain.

PSALM CXLVII. N.

1 PRAISE ye the Lord, for it is good unto our God to sing;
For it is pleasant, and to praise it is a comely thing.
2 The Lord his own Jerusalem he buildeth up alone,
And the dispers'd of Israel doth gather into one:

3 He heals the broken in their heart, their sores up doth he bind,
He counts the number of the stars, and names them in their kind;
4 Great is the Lord, great is his pow'r, his wisdom infinite;
The Lord relieves the meek, and throws to ground the wicked wight.

5 Sing unto God the Lord with praise, unto the Lord rejoice,
And to our God upon the harp advance your singing voice.
6 He covers heav'n with clouds, and for the earth prepareth rain,
And on the mountains he doth make the grass to grow again:

7 He gives to beasts their food, and to young ravens when they cry;
His pleasure not in strength of horse, nor in man's legs doth lie:
8 But in all those that do him fear the Lord hath his delight,
And such as do attend upon his mercies shining light.

PART II.

9 O praise the Lord, Jerusalem, thy God, O Sion, praise;
For he the bars hath forged strong wherewith thy gates he stays:
10 Thy children in thee he hath blest, and in thy borders he
Doth settle peace, and with the flour of wheat he filleth thee:

11 And his command likewise upon the earth he sendeth **on**
Also his word with speedy course doth swiftly run about:
12 He giveth snow like wool, and frost like ashes scatters wide,
Like morsels casts his ice: the cold thereof who can abide?

13 He sendeth forth his mighty **word** and melteth them again;
His wind he makes to blow, and **then** the waters flow amain.
14 The doctrine of his holy word to Jacob he doth show,
His statutes and his judgments he gives Israel to know.

15 With any nation hath he not so dealt, nor have they known
His secret judgments: ye therefore, praise ye the Lord alone.

PSALM CXLVIII. J. H.

1 GIVE laud unto the Lord, from heav'n that is so high;
Praise him in deed and word, above the starry sky:
And also ye, his angels all,
Armies royal, praise joyfully:

2 Praise him both moon and sun, which are so clear and bright;
The same of you be done, ye glittering stars of light.
And ye no less ye heavens fair,
Clouds of the air, his praise express:

3 For at his word they were all formed as **we see,**
At his voice did appear all things in their degree,
Which he set fast; to them he made
A law and trade always to last.

4 Extol and praise God's name **on** earth, ye dragons fell;
All deeps, do ye the same, for it becomes ye well,
The same do ye, fire, hail, ice, snow,
And storms that blow at his decree:

5 The hills and mountains all and trees that fruitful are,
The cedars great and tall, his worthy praise declare;
Beasts and cattle, **yea,** birds of wing,
And worms creeping, **that** on earth dwell:

6 All kings both great and small, with all their pompous train,
Princes and judges all that in the world remain,
Exalt his name; young men and maids,
Old men and babes, do ye the same.

7 For his name **shall** we prove to be most excellent,
Whose praise is far above the earth and firmament:
For sure he shall exalt with bliss
The horn of his, and help them all.

8 His saints all shall forth tell **his praise and** worthiness,
The sons of Israel, each one both more and less:
And also they that with good will
His words fulfil, and him obey.

PSALM CXLIX. N.

1 SING ye unto the Lord our God a new rejoicing song,
And let the praise of him be heard his holy saints among.

2 Let Israel rejoice in God, and praises to him sing,
And let the seed of Sion be most joyful in their king:

3 Let them sound praise with voice of lute unto his holy name,
And with the timbrel and the harp sing praises to the same.
4 For why? the Lord his pleasure all hath in his people set,
And by deliv'rance he will raise the meek to glory great.

5 With glory and with honour now let all his saints rejoice,
Aloud upon their beds also advance their singing voice.
6 And in their mouths let be the high praises of God the Lord,
And in their hands likewise a sharp and a two-edged sword:

7 To plague the heathen, and correct the people with their hands;
To bind their stately kings in chains, their lords in iron bands;
8 To execute on them the doom that written was before:
This honour all his saints shall have; praise ye the Lord therefore.

PSALM CL. N.

1 YIELD unto God the mighty Lord praise in his holiness,
And in the firmament of his great pow'r praise him no less.
2 Advance his name, and praise him in his mighty acts always!
According to his excellence and greatness give him praise.

3 His praises with the princely noise of sounding trumpets blow;
Praise him upon the viol, and upon the harp also:
4 Praise him with timbrel and with flute, organs and virginals,
With sounding cymbals praise ye him, praise him with loud cymbals.

5 Whatever hath the benefit of breathing, praise the Lord;
To praise his great and holy name agree with one accord.

THE END OF THE PSALMS.

VENI CREATOR.

1 COME Holy Ghost, eternal God, proceeding from above,
Both from the Father and the Son, the God of peace and love;
2 Visit our minds, and into us thy heavenly grace inspire;
That truth and godliness we may pursue with full desire.

3 Thou art the very Comforter in all grief and distress;
The heavenly gift of God most high, which no tongue can express;
4 The fountain and the living spring of joy celestial;
The fire so bright, the love so sweet, and unction spiritual.

5 Thou in thy gifts art manifold, whereby Christ's Church doth stand;
In faithful hearts writing thy law, the finger of God's hand.
6 According to thy promise made, thou givest speech with grace,
That through thy help God's praises may resound in ev'ry place.

7 O Holy Ghost, into our souls send down thy heav'nly light;
Inflame our hearts with fervent love to serve God day and night.
8 Our weakness strengthen and confirm, which feeble is and frail,
That neither devil, world, nor flesh against us may prevail.

9 Our enemies put far from us, and help us to obtain
Peace in our hearts with God and man, the best and truest gain:
10 And grant, O Lord, that thou being our leader and our guide,
We may escape the snares of sin, and never from thee slide.

11 Such measures of thy pow'rful grace grant, Lord, to us, we pray;
That thou may'st be our Comforter at the last dreadful day.
12 Of strife and all dissention, Lord, do thou dissolve the bands,
And knit the knots of peace and love throughout all Christian lands.

13 Grant us the grace that we may know the Father of all might:
That we of his beloved Son may gain the blissful sight;
14 And that we may with perfect faith always acknowledge thee
The Spirit of Father and of Son, one God in persons three.

15 To God the Father laud and praise, and to his blessed Son,
And to the Holy Spirit of grace, co-equal three in one.
16 And pray we that our only Lord would please his Spirit to send
On all that shall profess his Name, from hence to the world's end. Amen.

THE LORD'S PRAYER, OR PATER-NOSTER.

1 OUR Father which in heaven art, Lord, Hallowed be thy Name;
Thy kingdom come. Thy will be done in earth, even as the same
2 In heaven is. Give us, O Lord, our daily bread this day.
As we forgive our debtors, so forgive our debts we pray.

3 Into temptation lead us not, from evil keep us free,
For kingdom, power, and glory is thine to eternity.

A Thanksgiving after the Receiving of the Lord's Supper.

1 THE Lord be thanked for his gifts and mercies evermore,
That he doth shew unto his saints; to him be laud therefore.
2 Our tongues cannot so praise the Lord as he doth right deserve;
Our hearts cannot of him so think as he doth us preserve:

3 His benefits they be so great to us who are but sin,
That at our hands a recompence he cannot hope to win.

4 O sinful man, that thou should'st have such mercies of the Lord,
Who dost deserve most worthily of him to be abhorr'd!

5 Nought else but sin and wretchedness dost rest within our hearts,
And stubbornly against the Lord we daily act our parts.
6 The sun that in the firmament is set for us a light,
Doth shew itself more clear and pure than we be in his sight.

7 The heav'n above and all therein more holy are than we;
They serve the Lord in their estate, each one in his degree:
8 They do not strive for mastership, nor light their office set;
But serve the Lord and do his will, there's nothing can them let.

9 Also the earth and all therein of God doth stand in awe,
Observing the Creator's will, by skilful nature's law.
10 The sea and all that is therein doth bend when God doth beck,
Spirits beneath do tremble all, and fear his wrathful check.

11 But we, alas! for whom all these were made them for to rule,
Do not so know or love the Lord as doth the ox or mule.
12 A law he gave us for to know what was his holy will;
He would us good, but we would not avoid the thing that's ill.

13 Not one of us that seeketh out the Lord of life to please,
Nor doth the thing that might us lead to Christ and quiet ease.
14 Thus are we all his enemies, we can it not deny;
And be again of his good-will would not that we should die.

15 Therefore when remedy was none to bring us unto life,
The Son of God our flesh did take to end our mortal strife.
16 And all the law of God the Lord he fully did obey,
And for our sins upon the cross, his blood our debts did pay.

17 And that we never should forget what good for us he wrought,
A sign he left our eyes to tell that he our bodies bought.
18 In bread and wine here visible unto thy eyes and taste,
His mercies great thou may'st record, if that his grace thou hast.

19 As once the corn did live and grow, and was cut down with scythe,
And threshed out with many stripes, out of his husk to drive;
20 And as the mill with violence did tear it out so small,
And made it like to earthly dust, not sparing it at all;

21 And as the oven with fire hot doth close it up with hea
And all this done, as I have said, that it should be our meat;
22 So was the Lord in his ripe age cut down by cruel death;
His soul he gave in torments great and yielded up his breath.

23 Because that he to us might be an everlasting bread;
With such reproach and troubles great on earth his life he led.
24 And as the grapes in pleasant time are pressed very sore,
And plucked down when they be ripe, and let to grow no more;

25 Because the juice that in them is as comfortable drink
We might receive, and joyful be when sorrows make us shrink;
26 So was the blood of Christ press'd out, also with nails and spear:
The juice thereof doth save all those that rightly do him fear.

27 And as the corns by unity into one loaf are knit,
So is the Lord and his whole Church, though he in heaven do sit.
28 As many grapes make but one wine, so should we be but one
In faith and love in Christ above, and into Christ alone.

29 Leading a life without all strife, in quiet, rest, and peace:
From envy and from malice both our hearts and tongues shall cease.
30 Which if we do, then we shall show that we his chosen be:
By faith in him to lead a life as always willed he.

31 And that we may so do indeed, God send us all his grace:
Then after death we shall be sure with him to have a place.

THE HUMBLE SUIT OF A SINNER.

1 O LORD, on whom I do depend, behold my careful heart;
And when thy will and pleasure is release me of my smart.
2 Thou see'st my sorrows what they are, my grief is known to thee;
And there is none that can remove or take the same from me,

3 But only thou, whose aid I crave, whose mercy still is prest
To ease all those that come to thee for succour and for rest.
4 And since thou see'st my restless eyes, my tears and grievous groan,
Attend unto my suit, O Lord, mark my complaint and moan.

5 For sin hath so inclosed me and compass'd me about,
That I am without remedy, if mercy help not out;
6 For mortal man cannot release or mitigate my pain,
But only Christ, my Lord and God, who for my sins was slain;

7 Whose bloody wounds are yet to see, though not with mortal eye;
Yet do thy saints behold them all, and so I trust shall I.
8 Tho' sin doth hinder me awhile, when thou shalt see it good,
I shall enjoy the sight of him who shed for me his blood.

9 And as thy angels and thy saints do now behold the same,
So trust I to possess that place, with them to praise thy Name.
10 But whilst I here live in this vale where sinners do frequent,
Assist me ever with thy grace my sins still to lament:

11 Lest that I tread the sinners' path, and give them my consent
To dwell with them in wickedness, whereto my nature's bent.
12 Only thy grace must be my stay, let that with me remain;
For if I fall, then of my self I cannot rise again.

13 Wherefore this is yet once again my suit and my request,
To grant me pardon for my sin, that I in thee may rest:
14 Then shall my heart and tongue also be instruments of praise,
And in thy church and house of saints sing psalms to thee always.

THE LAMENTATION OF A SINNER.

1 O LORD, turn not thy face away from him that lies prostrate,
Lamenting sore his sinful life, before thy mercy gate;
2 Which thou dost open wide to those that do lament their sin:
O shut it not against me, Lord, but let me enter in.

3 Call me not to a strict account how I have lived here:
For then I know right well, O Lord, most vile I shall appear.

4 I need not to confess my life, for surely thou canst tell
What I have been, and what I am, thou knowest very well.

5 O Lord, thou know'st what things be past, also the things that be:
Thou know'st also what is to come; nothing is hid from thee.
6 Before the heav'ns and earth were made thou knew'st what things were then
As all things else that have been done among the sons of men:

7 And can the things that I have done be hidden from thee then?
No, no, thou know'st them all, O Lord, where they were done, and when
8 Wherefore with tears I come to thee to beg and to intreat,
Ev'n as a child that hath done ill, and feareth to be beat.

9 So come I to the throne of grace, where mercy doth abound,
Desiring mercy for my sins, to heal my deadly wound.
10 O Lord, I need not to repeat what I do beg or crave:
For thou dost know, before I ask, the thing that I would have.

11 Mercy, good Lord, mercy I ask, this is the total sum;
For mercy, Lord, is all my suit, O let thy mercy come.

GLORIA PATRI.

COMMON MEASURE.

TO Father, Son, and Holy Ghost, immortal glory be;
As was, and is, and shall be still, to all eternity.

ANOTHER.

To Father, Son, and Holy Ghost, all glory be therefore;
As in beginning was, is now, and shall be evermore.

AS THE HUNDRED PSALM.

To Father, Son, and Holy Ghost, all praise and glory be therefore:
As in beginning was, is now, and so shall be for evermore

ANOTHER.

To Father, Son, and Holy Ghost, the God whom Earth and Heav'n adore,
Be glory, as it was of old, is now and shall be evermore.

AS THE HUNDRED AND FOURTH PSALM.

By Angels in Heaven of ev'ry degree,
And Saints upon earth, all praise be addrest
To God in Three Persons, one God ever blest;
As it has been, now is, and always shall be.

AS VENI CREATOR.

All glory to the Trinity that is of mighties most,
To God the living Father, and the Son and Holy Ghost:
As it hath been in all the time that hath been heretofore,
As it is now, and so shall be henceforth for evermore.

THE END.

A COMPANION

TO

THE ALTAR.

Companion to the Altar;

SHEWING

THE NATURE AND NECESSITY

OF A

SACRAMENTAL PREPARATION,

In Order to our worthy receiving

THE HOLY COMMUNION:

TO WHICH ARE ADDED,

PRAYERS AND MEDITATIONS.

London:

PRINTED BY JOHN JARVIS, 1791.

Price One Shilling.

PREFACE.

THE usual reason which men assign for their not coming so often to the holy Sacrament as they would do, is their fear of eating and drinking unworthily, and consequently of incurring their own damnation thereby. The design then of this short discourse is, to shew what that Sacramental Preparation is, which is absolutely necessary to qualify men for a worthy participation of the Lord's Supper, that so men may come without the least fear of eating and drinking damnation to themselves; For which purpose, no rule, no instruction can be more safe, easy, and instructive than that of our Church Catechism; which is here endeavoured to be explained and accommodated for the use and benefit of the meanest capacity.

The concluding part of this discourse contains *Prayers* and *Meditations* preparative to a Sacramental Preparation; and though they be few in number, yet it is hoped they will fully answer all those several parts of a Communicant's Duty, according to that rule and standard which our Church has fixed for our Guide and Companion to the Holy Altar. By the addition of those Psalms and Proper Lessons annexed to each particular Prayer and Meditation, the Communicant may enlarge his devotions to what degree or length he pleaseth.

TO

THE ALTAR.

ALL those blessings which we now enjoy, and hope hereafter to receive from Almighty God, are purchased for us, and must be obtained through the merits and intercession of the holy Jesus, who has "instituted and ordained holy mysteries, as pledges of his love, and for a continual remembrance of his death and passion, to our great and endless comfort." *Luke* xxii. 19. 1 *Cor.* xi. 14. But then we must remember, that these benefits and blessings, which the Son of God has purchased for us, are no where promised but upon condition that we ourselves are first duly qualified for them. The sacrament of the Lord's Supper is a solemn ratification of our baptismal covenant; wherein God, for his part, hath faithfully promised "pardon and remission of sins to all true penitents;" and we, for our parts, are therein solemnly bound to be faithful and obedient unto him, 2 *Tim.* ii. 19. Before then we can promise to ourselves any benefit or advantage from the participation of this solemn rite and covenant between God and us, we must endeavour (what in us lies) to possess our souls with all those divine qualifications which this sacrament of the Lord's Supper requires, to render us worthy partakers thereof.

And what those are, it is the design of this discourse to enquire; wherein I shall endeavour to shew what that *preparation* of heart and mind is, which must dispose us for a worthy participation of the blessed sacrament: And herein I hope to remove all those fears and scruples which arise in our minds, about "eating and drinking unworthily, and of incurring our "own damnation thereby," as groundless and unwarrantable; and to do this, I shall take occasion to explain that part of our Church Catechism, designedly intended for our instruction, with relation to this duty of a sacramental preparation: namely,

Q. "What is required of them who come to the Lord's "Supper?"

A. "To examine themselves whether they repent them truly of their former sins, stedfastly purposing to lead a new life, "have a lively faith in God's mercy through Christ, with a "thankful remembrance of his death, and to be in charity "with all men." This is that sacramental preparation which our Church (in as few words as is possible) hath provided for our companion or guide to the holy altar. The duty then of a devout communicant consisteth in these six following particulars: 1. Self-examination; *to examine themselves.* 2. Repentance twards God; *whether they repent them truly of their former sins.* 3. Holy purposes or resolutions of a new life; *stedfastly purposing to lead a new life.* 4. Faith in God's mercy through Christ; *to have a lively faith,* &c. 5. A thankful remembrance of his death. 6. and lastly, Unfeigned love or charity for all mankind; *and to be in charity with all men.*

The first part then of a communicant's duty is self-examination: a duty not only enjoined by human authority, but likewise commanded by St. Paul; *But let a man examine himself, and so let him eat of that bread and drink of that cup,* 1 Cor. xi. 28; intimating, that no man should presume to eat of that bread and drink of that cup without a previous preparation, if he mean to escape that same judgment or condemnation which these *Corinthians* brought upon themselves for their irreverent, sinful, and disorderly behaviour at this sacrament; and this was the occasion of St. Paul's caution and reproof: *He that eateth and drinketh unworthily,* says the apostle, *eateth and drinketh damnation* to himself, not discerning the Lord's body,* ver. 29.

But that our preparation may be so well performed by us as to prevent the like danger, let us, as the wise men adviseth, *remember the end, and we shall never do amiss,* Eccl. vii. 16. First then, That we may come to this heavenly feast holy, and adorned with the wedding garment, *Matth.* xxii. 11, we must search our hearts, and examine our consciences, not only till we see our sins, but until we hate them; and instead of those filthy rags of

---

* This word, "Damnation," does not signify "eternal condemnation;" but on the contrary, some temporal punishment or judgment (as you have it in the margin of your bible) such as sickness or death, with which the city of Corinth was afflicted, for their great abuse and profanation of this solemn institution; so that the sins here reproved (namely, gluttony, drunkenness, and fashion, ver. 18, 21, 22.) and the damnation here threatened, hath no relation to us, unless it could be proved, that any of us were ever guilty of the same wickedness with these Corinthians; which I believe no man ever was, or would be suffered to approach the Lord's Table after such a disorderly manner as they did, if men were so lewd and profane.

our righteousness, we must adorn our minds with pure and pious dispositions; *even that clean linen, the righteousness of the saints*, Rev. xix. 8. With these ornaments are holy souls fitted for the society of that celestial company which are to be met with at this solemnity. 2dly, Another end or design of this strict preparation is, that we may be accepted by God as worthy communicants; that *He who knoweth the secrets of all our hearts, neither is there any creature that is not manifest in his sight, but all things are naked and open unto the eyes of him with whom we have to do*, Jer. xvii. 10, Heb. iv. 13, may approve of the sincerity of our repentance; and the King who comes in to view the guests, *Matth.* xxii. 11, may (though strictly speaking we are not so) count us worthy of his favour and countenance. And how to attain so great a blessing, these following instructions will help and assist us.

Repentance.

First, We are directed to *repent us truly of all our former sins.* This is that preparation which Christ himself requires of us, *Matth.* iii. 2, 3. A duty, you know, which our sinful lives make always necessary for our consideration, if ever we expect eternal happiness hereafter, Luke xiii. 3. But more especially the dignity of this sacrament requires, that it should be inquired into with more than ordinary care and circumspection, because, without sincere repentance, we cannot expect any benefit or advantage from the death and passion of Christ, which in this sacrament we commemorate, and have the merits of it conveyed to us by this sacred memorial. Supposing then, that this is sufficient to convince you of the necessity and importance of this duty, that upon it depends our welcome unto this heavenly feast, unto which we are called; I proceed now, in the second place, to inform you, That if our repentance or return to God be real and sincere, it will produce these following *good effects* in us.

The Nature of a true Repentance.

First, "A sense, a sorrow, and confession of all our former "sins. Secondly, A stedfast purpose or resolu-"tion to lead a new life." These are the genuine fruits of a true repentance, and must always accompany our return to God, if we hope to have it effectual to our salvation. And,

The Ten Commandments.

First, We must labour to get a *sense* or *sight* of all our former sins and wickedness; this will readily present itself to us, by comparing our lives and actions by the rule or standard of God's Word, which must make the measure of our * examination. St. *Paul* shews us,

* See the Daily Self-Examinant: or, An Earnest Persuasive to the Duty of Self-Examination, &c. By R. Warren, D. D.

Rom. iii. 20, that by the law is the knowledge of sin; and our own experience will convince us, that there is no way more likely to discover our iniquities, and to humble ourselves for them, than a serious application of God's Word to our crooked paths: And this duty of self-examination is never more properly applied to, than when we intend to receive the Holy Communion; for unless we see the number, and apprehend the heinousness of our offences, and fear the vengeance due unto us for them, we are altogether unfit for the commemoration of his death, *who died for our sins, and rose again for our justification.* It is the sense and sight of sin, that must shew us the need and necessity of a glorious Redeemer, and what obligations we are under to bless and praise God for our salvation by his Son Jesus Christ. Of such great use and advantage is this duty of self-examination, at all times, that *Pythagoras*, in those *golden verses* which go under his name, particularly recommends the same to his scholars. "Every night before they slept, he enjoins "them to examine themselves what good they had done, and "wherein they had transgressed. Run over these things, *said* "*he:* and if you have done any evil, be troubled; if good, re-"joice." This course, if daily followed as suggested by *Hierocles*, his commentator, perfects the divine image in those that use it. ---*Plutarch*, *Epictetus*, *Seneca*, and the emperor *Marcus Antoninus*, agree in recommending the same practice by their own example, but especially holy *David*; *I thought on my ways, and turned my feet unto thy testimonies*, Psalm cxix. 59. And this method, no doubt, is an admirable means to improve us in virtue, and the most effectual way to keep our consciences awake, and to make us stand in awe of ourselves, and afraid to sin, when we know beforehand that we must give so severe an account to ourselves of every action. And when we are employing our minds in this duty of self-examination, before the communion, or at any other time, we must discharge it as impartially as is possible for us, judging as severely of our own actions, as we would do of our greatest and worst enemy; or, otherwise we shall but flatter and deceive ourselves, in a matter of the greatest weight and importance, namely, the knowing the state and condition of our souls: But if our inquiries are just and true, we shall then plainly discover wherein, and how often we have gone astray and done amiss. We shall, by the faithful discharge of this duty, bring to light "all our ungodly, unjust, and uncharitable actions; all our vain "and filthy speeches; all our wanton, proud, and covetous "thoughts." Such a strict and impartial examination will discover to us that accursed thing, *Sin*, Deut. vii. 26. which has defiled our nature, made God our enemy, and will exclude us the kingdom of heaven, if not repented of, 1 *Cor.* vi. 9, 10. But by such a severe scrutiny as this, we shall soon perceive the number of our transgressions, what vile wretches and grievous offenders we are, how often we have broken our most serious vows and resolutions, especially after the receiving the holy sacrament, and in times of sickness and distress: such a sight, and such a prospect of misery as this, should excite in us a hearty trouble and sorrow for sin; especially if we cast an eye upon the final issue and consequence of it, with respect to the world to come. *Upon the ungodly*, says holy *David*, *God will rain snares, fire and brimstone, storm and tempest; this shall be their portion to drink*, Psalm xi. 7. *Great plagues remain for the ungodly: indignation and wrath, tribulation and anguish, upon every soul of man that doth evil*, Rom. ii. 8, 9. *The wicked shall be turned into Hell, and all the people that forget God.* These, and many other such-like texts of Scripture, may give us some idea or notion of the deplorable condition of the wicked in a future state, and of God's hatred against sin. And is not this then, without multiplying arguments, sufficient to affect us with great grief and sorrow, when we consider that so long as we live in a vicious course, so long are we exposed to all those plagues and torments which God hath in store for wicked men, and will most certainly be their lot and portion, if not prevented by a timely repentance?

Contrition.

The Second part of a true repentance is *Contrition*, or a sorrowful bewailing of our own sinfulness, in thought, word, and deed. When we call to mind the sins and follies of our past lives, and the dangers we are like to fall into, surely we cannot be otherwise affected, than sensibly grieved with the thoughts and apprehensions of our present and approaching misery. The sorrows of *David*, and the repentance of *Peter*, 2 Sam. xii. Luke xxii. shewed themselves in floods of tears, and were too great to be confined within: But our hearts are generally so hard and unrelenting, that we sin against God, and lose our own souls without so much as a sigh or a tear. I know that the tempers of people are different; some can shed tears upon every slight occasion; and others cannot weep, though their hearts are ready to break for grief: and therefore we are not to judge of the sincerity of our own or other people's repentance by such signs and tokens; nor are tears always necessary to repentance, though they very well become us; and the least we can do when we have done amiss, is to be sorry for it, and to condemn our folly, and to be full of indignation and displeasure against ourselves. *I will declare mine iniquity*, saith holy *David*, *and be sorry for my sin*, Psalm xxxviii. 18. especially if we have been very wicked, and have multiplied our transgressions, and have continued long in an evil course, have neglected God, and have forgotten him days without number; then the measure of our sorrow must bear some proportion to the degrees of our sins: if they have been as *scarlet* and *crimson*, Isaiah i. 18; that is, of a deeper dye than ordinary, then our sorrow must be as deep as our guilt: if not so great, we ought to shew so much trouble and contrition of spirit, as to produce in us a penitential confession of all our former sins:

Confession of Sins.

Which is the Third property of a sincere repentance? *I will acknowledge my sin unto thee*, says holy *David*, *and mine unrighteousness have I not hid. I said, I will confess my sins unto the Lord, and so thou forgavest the iniquity of my sin*, Psalm xxxii. 5. Which confession of sins must not be in general terms only, that we are sinners with the rest of mankind, but it must be a special declaration to God of all our most heinous sins in *thought*, *word*, and *deed*, with all their several aggravations, laying open our sores to our heavenly physician; and this we must do to shew that we condemn all our former evil and vicious courses, with a full purpose and resolution of mind (by God's Assistance) never to do the like again. Unless this be done, our sorrow for sin, and the confession of our wickedness, can never profit us in the sight of God, if it be not joined with a firm resolution of leading a new life:

A new Life.

Which is the Fourth and most essential part of a sincere repentance, and the only condition of finding mercy with God? *He that covereth his sins shall not prosper; but whoso confesseth and forsaketh them, shall have mercy*, Prov. xxviii. 13. *Let the wicked man forsake his ways, and the unrighteous man his thoughts, and let him return unto the Lord, and he will have mercy upon him, and to our God, and he will abundantly pardon*, Isaiah lv. 7. *I tell you nay*, saith Christ, *but except ye repent ye shall all likewise perish*, Luke xiii. 3. *Repent ye therefore, and be converted, that your sins may be blotted out*, Acts iii. 19. Those preceding parts of repentance beforementioned, are only preparative to this; that which must complete and finish the work of a new convert is, to become *a new creature*, "to turn from our evil ways, and to break off our sins by righteousness." This certainly must be the desire and intention of all communicants, if they hope or expect any benefit or advantage from this solemn rite or covenant; for he that comes with a design or intention of continuing his former sins, comes somewhat like unto Judas, that came and received, and at the same time continued his resolution of betraying his master.

That which makes a man absolutely unfit to receive the holy sacrament, is the living in the constant and habitual practice of any known sin, without the least desire or intention of repentance or amendment. Such a man's approach to the holy table, no doubt, is to " eat and drink his own damnation," since it is a plain mocking of God, and a great contempt and abuse of his divine authority. We must therefore (by the help and assistance of God's grace) " resolve to lead a new life, following the commandments of God," or otherwise our former examinations will appear but slight and superficial, our sight and sense of sin trivial and indifferent, our sorrow and contrition of spirit forced and hypocritical, and our confessions odious and formal. Therefore examine well the sincerity of your repentance and resolutions, that you neither deceive God nor yourselves: Him you cannot, because he is *a searcher of the heart, and a discerner of the thoughts*; nor will he accept of any thing which is not hearty and unfeigned.

No absolute obedience expected after the holy Sacrament.

Not that we are to suppose that this sacrament to the Lord's supper doth require perfect obedience in all our addresses to the holy altar, or that none must come but such as are in a sinless state of perfection: No: this were impossible, because *there is no man which liveth and sinneth not*; *for who can say, I have made my heart clean, I am pure from my sin?* The sacrament of the Lord's supper is not a converting, but a confirming ordinance, intended to preserve and increase that spiritual *life* and *grace* which we receive at our baptism: so that when we come to the holy communion, we come thither for fresh supplies of grace and goodness, " for the " strengthening and refreshing of our souls in all holiness and " virtue." As our natural bodies are fed and nourished with those elements of bread and wine, the same effect is wrought in the soul, in the inward man, by these holy mysteries, as in the outward man by bread and wine; bread being the staff of life, and wine the most sovereign cordial (when taken in due proportion) to chear and rejoice the heart. And thus our souls, by this sacrament, are fortified and strengthened with grace, wisdom, courage, and all other spiritual gifts, to keep us through faith unto salvation. Both the comfort and benefit of it are great; the comfort of it, because it does not only represent to us the exceeding love of our Saviour, in giving his body to be broken, and his blood to be shed for us; but it likewise seals to us all those blessings and benefits which are purchased and procured for us by his death and passion; namely, the pardon of sin, and power against it. The benefit of frequent communion is also of great advantage, because hereby we are confirmed in all grace, and goodness, and our resolutions to live in obedience and conformity to God's laws are strengthened; and the grace of God's holy spirit, to do his will, is hereby conveyed to us: it is the sovereign remedy against all temptations, by mortifying our passions, and by spiritualizing our affections: in a word, it is the likeliest method to make our bodies the temples of the holy ghost, and to prepare our souls for the enjoyment of God to all eternity.

Relapses after Receiving, not dangerous.

And if at any time, through ignorance, surprise, or the violence of any other temptation, we shall fall into those very sins which we have repented of, and vowed against when we were at the last sacrament, yet these relapses should not make us afraid of coming again, since we have always the benefit of repentance allowed us; if after a relapse we repent, and renew our resolutions with a hearty grief and contrition of spirit, we are made whole as before. *If the wicked*, saith God, *will turn from all his sins that he hath committed; all his transgressions that he hath committed, they shall not be mentioned unto him*, Ezek. xviii. 21, 22. *Sin no more*, says our Saviour to the woman taken in adultery, *and I will not condemn thee*, John viii. 11. It is not the commission of this or that great sin that will utterly exclude us from God's mercy and forgiveness, for then, indeed, no person could escape damnation, because *there is not a just man upon earth that doth good, and sinneth not*, Eccles. vii. 20. But it is our living and dying without repentance and amendment, that brings God's wrath and vengeance upon us. His mercies are not limited; he will not only pardon us once or twice, but always upon our repentance and return to him. No time, no age, or season, does he except against; but *whenever the wicked man turneth away from his wickedness that he hath committed, and doth that which is lawful and right, he shall save his soul alive*, Ezek. xvii. 27. Neither is there any sin, though never so vile and heinous in its own nature, but shall be remitted and forgiven, unless it be that against the Holy Ghost. *All manner of sins and blasphemies shall be forgiven unto men, but the blasphemy against the Holy Ghost shall not be forgiven*, Matth. xii. 31, 32. And consequently this sin of eating and drinking unworthily, in the worst sense, cannot be a damning sin, because God in the Gospel (for Christ's sake) hath promised to forgive all our sin, upon our repentance, and therefore this of unworthy receiving among the rest.

Some people, I remember, have been very much concerned and discomposed at their devotions, upon the repetition of some few expressions contained in the last exhortation to the Communion; namely, " Of being guilty of the body and blood of

"Christ our Saviour;---of eating and drinking our own damnation---not considering the Lord's body;----kindling God's wrath against us;---provoking him to plague us with divers diseases, and sundry kinds of death." These are hard sayings, and some of them too hard to be understood; but however they are all avoided and escaped by coming worthily, that is, with *faith* and *repentance*: Therefore let not these terrible expressions trouble you, or detain you from the holy Communion: repent and believe, and you are safe and secure from falling into any of these dangers, which these sentences may seem to threaten you with. So that the want of preparation, as some men have alledged, and in the sense they generally take it, can never be a sufficient plea or pretence for their not coming to the holy Communion; because, after our best and strictest endeavours to prepare ourselves, we profess (before God and the congregation) "That we do not come to this heavenly table trusting in our own righteousness, but in his manifold and great mercies." By these we are invited to come; and to the mercy of God (through Christ) all of us must flee, and take sanctuary in; who has promised that *he will in no wise cast out those who come unto him*, John vi. 37. *A broken and a contrite heart, O God, thou wilt not despise*, Psalm li. 17. There is nothing dreadful in this sacrament, but to the wilful, impenitent, and persevering sinner, whose condition is dreadful, and every page in Scripture is terrible against such, whether they come, or not; but to the penitent and humble soul, nothing is dismal or affrighting in this holy feast; for there is none condemned for unworthy receiving, but such who deserve it for continuing in their iniquities; and this impenitence renders even their prayers an "abomination unto the Lord." Though they never partake of the body and blood of Christ, they are in equal danger with those who eat and drink unworthily; nay, I might say, in greater; because the latter use the means in obedience to our Saviour's command; and the former wilfully neglect that which would prevent their damnation, if rightly considered, and timely applied to. The surest way, I say, to prevent our damnation is, to receive the sacrament more frequently than men usually do, that by a constant participation of this spiritual food, of the living Bread which comes down from heaven, their souls may be nourished in all goodness, and new supplies of God's grace and Holy Spirit may be continually derived to them, for the purifying of their hearts, and to enable them to run the ways of God's Commandments with more constancy and delight than they did before. So that the true consequence of eating and drinking unworthily should rather excite our care and diligence in this duty, than delude us with false reasonings, to such a neglect as will certainly increase our damnation; it being certain that God will never cast any man into eternal flames for striving to do his duty as well as he can. *If there be first a willing mind*, saith the Apostle, *it is accepted according to that a man hath, and not according to that he hath not*, 2 Cor. viii. 12. Neither ought we to think so unworthily of the Son of God, who came into the world *to save sinners*, that he would institute this ordinance to be a snare to entangle our souls with. It was not ordained for angels, or for glorified saints, but for humble and penitent sinners, to bring them home to God, it being a seal of their pardon, and a refreshing declaration of our heavenly Father's readiness to forgive the chiefest of sinners for Jesus's sake; who graciously calls upon all who are *wearied and oppressed with the guilt and burden of their sins to come to him, and he will refresh them*, Matth. xi. 28: *Christ came not to call the righteous, but sinners to repentance*, Matth. ix. 13; and consequently such as account themselves most unworthy, are those very persons whom Christ doth here call and invite to this sacrament, when deeply sensible of their unworthiness. Were we not sinners, were we not *conceived and born in sin*, we should not need such means and instruments of grace as sacraments are: but "being by nature born in sin, and the children of wrath, "we are hereby made the children of grace, and inheritors of "the kingdom of heaven." *They that are whole*, saith Christ, *have no need of a physician, but they that are sick.* This being the case of all mankind with respect to their spiritual life; there is no other way to free ourselves from this death of sin, but by speedily applying ourselves to our heavenly Physician, *who came into the world to seek and to save those that are lost*, and ready to perish; and the very sense of our own unworthiness is, of all other arguments, the best qualification to recommend us to God's favour and mercy, since we know that *he resisteth the proud* [and presumptuous sinner] but never denies his grace and favour to the humble and meek. As often then as we come to the holy Communion with such an honest and true heart, as to exercise our "repentance towards God, our faith and hope of "his mercy, through Christ, for the forgiveness of our sins, and "our love and charity for all mankind;" such a temper and resolution of mind as this, will doubtless render us worthy partakers of these holy mysteries, and prevent us "eating and "drinking damnation to ourselves." Nay, I further add, that any person thus disposed or qualified may come (if it should be required) at an hour's warning, as safely as he may come to Church and say his prayers, or hear a sermon. The dueness of preparation doth not so much depend upon our setting aside so many extraordinary days for the forcing ourselves into a religious posture of mind, as upon the plain natural frame and disposition of our souls, as they constantly stand inclined to virtue and goodness through the general course of our lives. From whence I infer, that a multitude of business, or a man's being deeply engaged in the public affairs of this world, cannot be any just plea or pretence for his not coming to the holy Communion; because all business is consistent with the duties of religion, provided we govern ours affairs by Christian principles: For though such men have not leisure for so much actual preparation, yet they may have that habitual preparation, upon which the great stress ought to be laid in this matter: Nay, even the conscientious discharge of a man's duty in his business, may be one of the best qualifications to recommend him to God: since every man serves God when he follows his calling with diligence, and observes justice and honesty in all his dealings: and consequently, the greater danger and temptation he is exposed to through the multiplicity of business, the more need hath he of God's grace and assistance, which are abundantly communicated to us in this holy ordinance: So that men of business, if they have any serious thoughts of another world, ought more especially to lay hold on such opportunities which secure the salvation of their souls; for as they who have leisure ought to receive constantly, as the best improvement of their time, so they that are engaged in many wordly affairs, ought to come the oftener to the holy Communion, and learn how to sanctify their employments. But to proceed:

Men of great Business, either public or private, are not thereby excused from frequent Communion.

The other branch of a communicant's duty is, to "examine "whether he hath a lively faith in God's mercy "through Christ." *Examine yourselves, whether ye be in the faith*, 2 Cor. xiii. 5; this sacrament of the Lord's Supper being only appointed for such believers as own their baptism, and profess the faith of Christ crucified, and understand the fundamental articles of the Christian religion, contained in the Apostles' Creed, and also the end and design of this holy institution. The benefits of our Saviour's death and passion in this sacrament are indeed freely offered unto all, but only effectually to believers. *As many as received him, to them gave he power to become the sons of God, even to them that believe in his Name*, John i. 12. *And this is life eternal, that they might know thee, the only true God, and Jesus Christ, whom thou hast sent*, John vii. 3. All that Christ hath done and suffered for us men and our salvation, can never profit us, unless we have *faith* to believe it,

A lively Faith in God's Mercy.

That which must render the benefits and blessing of the gospel effectual to our salvation is, our *faith* in Christ. *Verily I say unto you*, saith our Saviour, *he that heareth my words, and believeth on him that sent me, hath everlasting life, and shall not come into condemnation, but is passed from death unto life*, John v. 24. The ancient Churches accounted those only *faithful* that had received the Lord's Supper: and the *Germans* allowed none to come unto their sacrifices who had lost their shields; nor does our own Church allow that any of us should come to this Christian sacrifice without the shield of faith. "Draw near with faith (says the priest) and "take this holy sacrament to your comfort." And this faith hath God's mercy, through Christ, for its object, as the fountain and foundation of all those infinite blessings and comforts which we gain by his manifestation in the flesh. And if we inquire into the cause and reason of so much mercy and goodness to mankind, no other can be given but, *The riches of his mercy*, Eph. ii. 4. And if we further inquire, how this mercy becomes ours, the answer is plain---It was through Christ; by whom all the blessings of this life, and those of a better, are purchased for us, and must be obtained through the merits and intercession of the holy Jesus: By him we were redeemed; *and according to the riches of his grace we have obtained remission of our sins; and through him at last we shall be glorified.*

A thankful Remembrance of his Death.

And to this *faith* we must join "a thankful remembrance of "his death, and of those benefits which we re-"ceive thereby." *Our gracious and merciful Lord*, saith holy David, *hath so done his marvellous works, that they ought to be had in remembrance*, Psalm cxi. 4. But especially this work of our redemption by Jesus Christ, which to forget were an ingratitude baser and viler than ever heathens, or publicans, the very worst of people among the Jews, were known to be guilty of towards their benefactors, Matth. v. 46. *Herein is love, not that we loved God, but that he loved us, and sent his Son to be the propitiation for our sins*, 1 *John* iv. 10. This is a mercy far above all other mercies; nay, it is even this which sweetens all other mercies to us. Had there been no redemption, our creation had only made us capable of endless torments; and it had been better for us never to have been born, than to be born to inevitable ruin; which must have been our lot and portion, had not "the "Son of God, by his one oblation of himself, once offered upon "the cross, made a full, perfect, and sufficient sacrifice and satis-"faction to God for the sins of the whole world." The consequences of this redemption are so infinitely great and valuable, that it as much surpasses our understanding as it does our merits. ---We are to declare and publish to all the world what God hath done to save mankind from that damnation which they had deserved, and restore us again to that happiness and glory which we could never expect or hope to enjoy, had not Christ died for us. *O come hither and hearken, all ye that fear God, and I will tell you what he hath done for my soul*, Psalm lxvi. 16. *Praise the Lord, O my soul, and all that is within me; praise his holy name: praise the Lord, O my soul, and forget not all his benefits; who forgiveth all thy sins, and healeth all thy infirmities; who saveth thy life from destruction, and crowneth thee with mercy and loving-kindness*, Psalm ciii. 1, 2, 3, 4. With what joy and thankfulness then should every good Christian commemorate this exceeding love of God, in the salvation of sinners by Jesus Christ! This was the proper end and design of this institution, to perpetuate this wonderful love of Christ in laying down his life for us. *Do this in remembrance of me*, saith our Saviour a little before his crucifixion; which being a solemn command of "our Master and only Saviour thus dying for us," we cannot refuse obedience hereunto, without being guilty of the most horrible ingratitude and contempt of his divine authority. He hath appointed it for a solemn commemoration of his great love to us, in laying down his life for us men, and for our salvation; and therefore he commands us to do it *in remembrance of him*: And St. *Paul* tells us, that *as often as we eat this bread and drink this cup, we do shew forth the Lord's death till he come.* As for those men then amongst us who profess themselves Christians, and hope for salvation by Jesus Christ, not to pay obedience to this command, is a downright affront to his sacred majesty; and he may justly upbraid us Christians, as he did once the Jews, *Why call ye me, Lord, Lord, and do not the things which I say?* How unworthy are we of that salvation which he hath wrought for us, if we deny him so small a favour, such a reasonable request, as to commemorate his death and bitter passion once a month, or at least thrice a year, "who "did humble himself even to the death of the cross for us mi-"serable sinners; who lay in darkness, and in the shadow of "death, that he might make us the children of God, and exalt "us to everlasting life." In this sacrament of the Lord's Supper we have the pardon and remission of all our sins, the grace and assistance of God's holy Spirit, and the hopes of eternal life and happiness, freely offered unto us: And therefore had we no love, no regard, or reverence, to the dying words of our crucified Saviour, yet surely the consideration of our own present and future advan-

Our Obligations to a frequent Communion.

Men's own Interest should oblige them to a constant Communion, because of its great Benefits.

tage might prevail with us to be more frequent at the Lord's table than we usually are.

Hitherto a communicant hath been directed to set his heart right towards God: but this is not all; he must proceed farther, and inquire how it stands towards his neighbour; since we are expressly forbidden, *Matth.* v. 23, 24, to offer up any gift or oblation unto God, if our hearts are leavened with malice, hatred, or revenge. *If thou bring thy gift unto the altar, and there rememberest that thy brother hath aught against thee, leave there thy gift before the altar, and go thy way, first be reconciled to thy brother, and then come and offer thy gift.* Here you see that Christ prefers *mercy* before *sacrifice.* And it is generally agreed on by the antient fathers, that these words of our Saviour do directly point at this sacrament, on purpose to oblige all communicants to forgive all manner of injuries, "before they presume to eat of that bread, or to drink of that cup." And it is expressly said, *Matth.* vi. 14, 15, that our prayers are not accepted, nor our pardon sealed in heaven, until such time as we *forgive men their trespasses*; and to be sure we can never be welcome or worthy guests at this heavenly feast, where Jesus the Saviour of penitents and the Prince of peace is spiritually present, unless our repentance reconcile us to God, and our charity, to all mankind.

And to be in Charity with all Men.

Forgiving of Injuries expected from a Communicant.

And this charity of the heart, in forgiving injuries, must likewise shew itself by the hand, in relieving the wants and necessities of the poor. We read, that when this sacrament was administered in the Apostles' days, large collections of monies were then gathered for the maintenance of the poor clergy and laity, *Acts* ii. 44, 45, 46, and 1 *Cor.* xvi. 1. And *Theodoret* observes, that *Theodosius* the Emperor, when his time came to offer, arose and presented his oblations with his own hands. It was not determined how much every man should give, but all men were exhorted and enjoined to offer something, according to their ability; which if any neglected, the Fathers censured them as unworthy communicants: and to be sure, nothing within our power can so effectually recommend our prayers and devotions as this of charity; it being well observed, *Matth.* vi. that our Saviour hath inclosed *alms* between *prayer* and *fasting*, and therefore they are called its two wings, without which it will never fly so high as the throne of God. While *Cornelius* was fasting and praying, we read, that an angel from heaven was dispatched to him with this happy message: *Thy prayers and thine alms are come up for a memorial before God,* Acts x. 4. *He that hath pity upon the poor lendeth unto*

Charity to the poor.

the Lord; and that which he hath given will he pay him again, Prov. xix. 17. *Charge them that are rich in this world—that they be rich in good works, ready to distribute, willing to communicate, laying up in store for themselves a good foundation against the time to come, that they may lay hold on eternal life,* 1 Tim. vi. 17, 18, 19. *Do ye not know, that they who minister about holy things live of the sacrifice, and they who wait at the altar are partakers with the altar? Even so hath the Lord also ordained, that they who preach the Gospel should live of the Gospel,* 1 Cor. ix. 13, 14. *If we have sown unto you spiritual things, is it a great matter if we shall reap your worldly things?* Ver. 11. But we may justly complain with *Basil*, that we know some who will "fast and pray, "sigh and groan, yea, and do all acts of religion "which cost them nothing, but will not give one farthing to "the poor: What benefit is there (saith he) of all the rest of "their devotions?"

Basil. Homil. in Matth. xix.

And when the communicant has thus far advanced towards the altar, in his *examination, repentance,* &c. he must not forget another excellent preparative belonging to this duty of communicating worthily; which although it be not mentioned in our Church Catechism, yet it is always implied as a necessary part of our sacramental preparation; that is, *Prayer*, private and public; a duty upon which all our present and future blessings depend, *Matth.* vii. 7, 8. and 21, 22. And so near a relation hath this duty of prayer with this sacrament, that all those blessings therein contained and promised, are only in return to our prayers: and no doubt but that man who makes a conscientious practice of this duty, in his closet and at the Church, can never be unprepared for this sacrament, nor want a title to God's peculiar favour and blessing: *For the eyes of the Lord are over the righteous, and his ears are open unto their prayers,* 1 Pet. iii. 12. The constant exercise of *prayer* is the best method to get the mastery over our evil inclinations and corrupt affections, and to overcome our vicious habits: It preserves a lively sense of God and religion in our minds, and fortifies us against those temptations that assault us; it spiritualizes our nature, raiseth our souls above this world; and supports us under the troubles and calamities of this life, by sanctifying such afflictions; it leads us gradually to the perfection of a Christian life; and preserves that union between God and our souls which feeds our spiritual life with grace and goodness; without it we in vain pretend to discharge those Christian duties incumbent on us, or to prosper in our temporal affairs, which must have God's blessing to crown them with success.— And as prayer in general has these great blessings and advantages

Prayer.

Public Prayers recommended.

attending it; so give me leave to suggest to you under this head, that those public prayers and devotions which we offer unto God in our Churches, are not only more acceptable to him, but also much more edifying and advantageous to ourselves: They cannot but be more acceptable to God, because thereby his honour and glory are much more considerably advanced and maintained in the world, than by our private devotions: By these outward *signs* and *tokens*, we publicly declare to all the world that inward regard and esteem which we have for his divine perfections and goodness; hereby we *let our light so shine before men, that they may see our good works, and glorify our Father which is in heaven*, Matt. v. 16.---There is no duty in scripture more frequently commanded, none more earnestly pressed upon us, than this of public prayer. We have the example of all good men in all ages for it, and of Christ himself, who was daily in the temple and in the synagogues, and, no question, frequented those places at the usual hours of prayer, because then he had the fairest opportunity, from those public assemblies, to instruct, and to exhort to *faith* and *repentance*. 2dly, We may expect greater blessings and success to our requests and desires, when we join in the public prayers of our church, than from private, because our Saviour has in a special manner promised to such assemblies his immediate presence, that *where two or three are gathered together in his name, there will he be in the midst of them*; which he hath no where said of private prayer, though both are very good, nay, both are absolutely necessary for the beginning and ending of a christian life; and it is a very bad sign of some evil principle or other, for any man to be much a stranger to the house of prayer, which is one of the greatest blessings and privileges (if we know how to value the same) that we can have in this world, and has always been accounted such among all wise and good men. It is certain that the *Turks*, whom we call infidels, go to their public devotions five times every day; and shall not they rise in judgment against us Christians, who cannot afford to go once or twice a day to God's house, when we have both leisure and opportunity? If men shall be judged for every idle word, to be sure they shall not pass unpunished for all the neglects and omissions of their duty of this nature. But to proceed:

To this duty of *fervent prayer*, the communicant should spend some portion of time in reading and meditation, to raise his soul into a devout and heavenly temper; the proper office of reading, is to gain spiritual food and sustenance; and of meditation, to digest it. Those divine

Reading and Meditation.

subjects most proper for our serious contemplation on this solemn occasion, I think, are "our Saviour's sermon on the "mount: the love of God in the salvation of sinners, through "Jesus Christ; repentance, faith, charity, * Death and judgment; the happy condition of a future state of blessedness, "and the miserable condition of the damned in hell." These, and the like, as they offer themselves unto you, should be meditated upon, until some sorrow of mind, some ardor of devotion, some act of faith, some flame of love and charity, arise in your souls.

Thus have I briefly represented to you both the nature and necessity of a *sacramental preparation*, which in great measure contains the whole duty of a christian's life; namely, "repentance "towards God, faith towards our Lord Jesus Christ, and charity "towards our neighbour:" And I also hope, whosoever among us will but endeavour to prepare themselves for the holy communion, according to the formentioned directions, may (by the help of God) upon all occasions come to the Lord's table, without the least fear or danger of "eating and drinking damnation "to themselves."

And now some people may censure this discourse, as giving too great liberty and encouragement to approach the Lord's table with less preparation than otherwise men would venture to do; but I know no ground or reason for any such suggestion, if they impartially consider the excellence and perfection of that guide and companion I have followed throughout the whole: and to represent this duty of frequent communion otherewise than what the church requires, is an injury both to God and to ourselves: and I dare affirm, that no part of divine worship has suffered more on this account, than that of the holy communion; thousands of people not daring, in all their life-time (tho' very good livers) to partake of the Lord's supper, for fear of eating and drinking their own damnation.

The Church Catechism.

---

* See Mr. Norris's "effectual remedy against the fear of death."

PRAYERS AND MEDITATIONS

PREPARATIVE TO

A SACRAMENTAL PREPARATION,

ACCORDING TO WHAT THE CHURCH OF ENGLAND REQUIRES FROM HER COMMUNICANTS.

¶ *A Prayer to God for his gracious assistance and direction in our Sacramental Preparation.*

HOLY, holy, holy Lord God of Sabaoth, heaven and earth are full of thy majesty and of thy glory: I, the unworthiest of all creatures do here, in all humility of soul and body, prostrate myself before thee, acknowledging my own weakness and insufficiency to do any thing that is good or well pleasing in thy sight: and therefore humbly implore the special influence of thy grace and holy Spirit, to further these my endeavours for a worthy participation of the holy communion of the body and blood of Christ, which he has commanded me to do in remembrance of him, and of those benefits which we receive thereby. Teach me, O Lord, the right way, and lead me in the paths of holy preparation, that I may be received as a worthy and welcome guest at this thy heavenly table. Possess my mind with a true sense of the greatness of this mystery, and the excellency of thy mercy in preparing this table for our spiritual food: inspire my soul with pure and pious dispositions; and, instead of those filthy rags of my righteousness, clothe me with the righteousness of the saints, that my heart may be a clean, though homely receptacle for my Saviour, and one day fitted for the blessed society of saints and angels in heaven, through Jesus Christ our Lord. *Amen.*

Our Father, &c. See *Psalm* xxiii. xxvi. cxi.

A Prayer for the gift and grace of Repentance.

ALMIGHTY and eternal Lord God, *who art of purer eyes than to behold iniquity, and hast more especially enjoined all those who compass thine altar, to wash their hands in innocency,* vouchsafe me unfeigned repentance for my past sins, a hearty sorrow and contrition of spirit to lament my sinfulness, and most firm and stedfast purposes to lead a new life. It is the voice of thy wondrous goodness and mercy, that if *the wicked shall forsake his ways, and the unrighteous man his thoughts, thou wilt have mercy upon him, and abundantly pardon him.* O let thy goodness (whereof I have had so great a share, and plentiful experience) *lead me to repentance not to be repented of*, that I may be a fit guest at thy Son's Table. "Have mercy upon me, O Lord, and according to the "multitude of thy tender mercies, blot out all my transgressions "for thy mercy's sake in Christ Jesus, the Son of thy love, "whom thou hast sent forth to be the propitiation for our sins." Grant this, O merciful Father, for the sake of my blessed Saviour and Redeemer. *Amen.*

See *Psalm* vi. xxv. xxxii. xxxviii.

A Prayer before Self-examination.

O LORD, thou that art the *searcher of all our hearts and a discerner of the very thoughts, and in whose sight all things are naked and open*, be pleased to impart a ray of thy heavenly light, to discover all the sins and infirmities of my past life, and whatsoever else thou knowest wherein I have done amiss, that henceforward no secret sin may lie undiscovered and corrupted in my soul; that by examining my life and conversation by thy law, the rule and measure of my duty, I may understand the true state and condition of my soul, and from a just sense and sight of all my transgressions, through the assistance of thy grace and heavenly benediction, I may be enabled to reform my life, and to turn my feet unto thy testimonies; so faithfully to search and examine my own conscience, that I may come holy and clean to the heavenly feast, and be received as a worthy partaker of that holy table which thou hast called me to. Grant this for thy mercy's sake in Christ Jesus. *Amen.*

See *Psalm* cxxxix.

Brief Heads of Self-Examination upon each Commandment.

COMMANDMENT I.

THOUGH I have not atheistically denied the being of a God, or wickedly renounced him by apostacy, yet have I not loved, desired and delighted in other things more than in God? Or, have I not feared men, and dreaded the displeasure of the world, more than of God? Or, have I not trusted in men, and relied upon the world, more than upon God? Have I not despaired of God's mercy? Or, by presuming too much upon it, encouraged myself in sin? Have I not been unthankful for mercies received? Or, have I not ascribed the glory and honour of what I now enjoy, to myself more than to God? (Say) *God be merciful to me a sinner*, or, *lay not this* (or *these*) *sins to my charge.* [Repeat the same at the end of every commandment.]

II.

Though I have not worshipped God by images, yet have I not entertained gross and false conceptions of him? Or, have I not wilfully omitted coming to church, or to the public prayers, when I had no just occasion to hinder me? Or, have I not rudely, irreverently, or wantonly behaved myself during the time of divine service? Or, have I not wilfully refused to come to the Lord's Supper, when I have been called to it? Or, have I not rashly and unadvisedly received the sacrament without due preparation? Or, have I not broken my vows and resolutions which I then made?

III.

If I have not openly blasphemed the name of God, yet have I not lightly or irreverently spoken of him? Or, have I not profanely jested upon, or abused his holy places or persons, or any thing else dedicated to his service? Or, have I not taken God's Name in vain, by common swearing and cursing? Or, have I not taken false and unlawful oaths? Or, have I not broken my own vows and resolutions, especially my baptismal?

IV.

Have I not neglected the worship of God on his sabbaths? Have I not spent part thereof in vain sports, idle discourses, visits, and many other unnecessary affairs? Or, have I not suffered others to profane the sabbath, when it was in my power to restrain them from so doing?

V.

Have I not been stubborn, irreverent, and undutiful towards my parents, rejecting their counsels, despising their government, and coveting their estates before their death? Or, have I contributed towards their necessities when they were in want, and I had it in my power to help them? Or, have I not been disloyal to my prince, stubborn and unfaithful to my master, refractory and unthankful to my minister, peevish and unkind to my friend and companion?

VI.

If I have not actually taken away the life of any person, yet have I not made my neighbour's life grievous by oppression, rage, and violence against him? Or, have I not by fighting or quarrelling wounded his person? Or, have I not tempted him, by any other vice or intemperance, to destroy his health, and so shorten his days? Or, have I not by false or contumelious speeches wounded his good name and reputation? Or, have I not, by my own luxury and intemperance in eating and drinking, been accessary to my own death?

VII.

If I have escaped the grosser acts of adultery and fornication, yet have I not conceived lust in mine heart, and neglected the means to preserve my own and others' chastity? Or, have I not by gluttony and drunkenness, or by any impure thoughts or words, defiled my soul? Or, have I not accustomed myself to filthy talking, jesting, and immodest garbs, and unchaste behaviour in common conversation?

VIII.

If I have not been guilty of common and public stealing, yet have I been true and just in all my dealings? Or, have I not contracted debts when I was conscious to myself that I was not able to pay, or make restitution? Or, have I not wasted my own or others' estates by riotous living? Or, have I not by violence and oppression exacted of my inferiors, or by unlawful usury taken advantage of their necessities.

IX.

If I have not before the magistrates sworn falsely against any man, yet have I not accustomed myself to lying and slandering? Or, have I not accused my neighbour unjustly? Or, have I not concealed the truth of another, when justice and charity obliged me to give evidence of it? Or, have I not unjustly sought to uphold my own credit, or to blast any other person's?

X.

Have I not secretly complained against the providence of God, as if others had too much, and I too little? Or, have I not by unlawful means endeavoured to deprive others of their goods and property? Or, have I laboured truly and faithfully to get my own living, and been content with that state of life unto which it hath pleased God to call me?

A penitential Confession of Sins; with an humble Supplication for Mercy and Forgiveness.

ALMIGHTY and everlasting God, who hatest nothing that thou hast made, and dost forgive the sins of all them that are penitent; create and make in me a new and contrite heart, that I worthily lamenting my sins, and acknowledging my wretchedness, may obtain of thee, the God of all mercy, perfect remission and forgiveness, through Jesus Christ our Lord. *Amen.*

Here call to mind all your most grievous sins.

See *Psalm* ii. vi. xxxii. xxxviii.

An Act of Contrition.

FATHER, *I have sinned against heaven, and before thee, and am no more worthy to be called thy son. Woe is me, O Lord, who was conceived and born in sin:* the thoughts of my heart were inclined unto evil from my youth. Woe is me, that I have sinned against thee, my Creator and kind Benefactor! Lord, I have done evil continually in thy sight, and my life hath been little else than one continual course of impiety, unthankfulness, and of unworthy returns for all thy goodness and loving-kindness to me. Woe is me, that I should thus requite the Lord! O that my head were waters, and mine eyes a fountain of tears, that I might weep day and night for my sin! O gracious Lord, look on me as thou didst on the Apostle St. *Peter*, and let thy compassionate look so pierce my stony heart, that I may weep bitterly for my sins, and may have that *godly sorrow which worketh repentance unto salvatian not to be repented of*, for Jesus's sake! *Amen.*

See *Psalm* xxv. xxxii. xxxviii.

A Resolution to lead a new Life.

AND now, O Lord, I do not only with great shame, and confusion of face, confess and bewail the sinfulness and vanity of my own life; but I do stedfastly resolve and purpose (through the assistance of thy grace and holy Spirit directing me) to "renounce the devil and all his works, the pomps and vanities of this wicked world, and all the sinful lusts of the flesh." Be pleased, O Lord, to strengthen and confirm all these good resolutions in me. And I heartily thank thee, O heavenly Father, for calling me to this state of salvation through Jesus Christ my Saviour, *who died for my sins, and rose again for my justification*; and I humbly beseech thee, for his sake, to give me grace to continue in the same unto my life's end. *Amen.*

See *Psalm* i. xxiii. xxiv. xxv. cxix. cxxvi.

A Prayer for Faith in God's Mercy through Christ.

ALMIGHTY God, our heavenly Father, who, for the greater confirmation of our faith and confidence in thy mercy, hast in thy holy gospel declared, that *whosoever believeth in thy Son Jesus Christ shall not perish, but have everlasting life*; and that *this is life eternal, to know* thee, the *only true God, and Jesus Christ, whom thou sent:* Increase this knowledge, and confirm this faith in me evermore. O let me not rest in a dead faith; but that I may have such a lively faith as will shew itself by love and good works; such a victorious faith which may enable me to overcome the world, and conform me to the image of thy Son Jesus Christ, in whom I believe! O grant me such a due sense of thy infinite mercy, shewed to mankind in so much misery, as may never depart out of my mind.

I stedfastly believe, O blessed Jesus, that thou didst suffer upon the cross to save me, and all the world, from the guilt and punishment of our sins. O give me that grace, that I may die to sin, and rise again unto righteousness! Accept my imperfect sorrow, repentance, faith, and weak resolutions; and let thy precious merits, O my crucified Saviour, supply all my wants and imperfections! Thou hast said, *Come unto me, all ye that labour, and are weary and heavy laden, and I will refresh you.* O blessed Jesus, I come unto thee in all humility, and deeply sensible of my great unworthiness; O do thou bear this burden of sin for me, and refresh me with comfortable hopes of thy mercy and forgiveness, and the truth of thy salvation, O gracious Lord! to whom, with the Father and the Holy Ghost, be all honour and glory for ever. *Amen.* See *Psalm* xix. lvii. *Eph.* ii, 6, 11.

A thankful Remembrance of the Death of Christ.

"ALMIGHTY God, our heavenly Father, who of thy tender "mercy didst give thine only Son Jesus Christ to suffer "death upon the cross for our redemption, and hast instituted "and ordained holy mysteries as pledges of his death and pas"sion, to our great and endless comfort:" Behold, I do most affectionately, and with all the powers of my soul and body, return my most hearty praise and thanksgiving for thy great mercy and tender compassion to me and all mankind, in sending thy only Son into the world to redeem us from sin and misery, and by his meritorious death and passion, to purchase for us eternal life. Grant, O Lord, that I may always most gratefully remember this exceeding love of my only Saviour Jesus Christ, thus dying for me; and work in me in all such holy and heavenly affections, as may dispose my heart to be a worthy guest at thy holy table, prepared for the continual remembrance of the sacrifice of the death of Christ, and of those benefits which we receive thereby. *Praise the Lord, O my soul, and forget not all his benefits; who forgiveth all thy sins, and healeth all thine infirmities; who saveth thy life from destruction, and crowneth thee with mercy and loving-kindness.* See *Psalm* ciii. 2, 3, 4.

A Prayer for the Grace of Charity.

"O LORD, who hast taught us that all our doings without "charity are nothing worth; send thy Holy Ghost, and "pour into my heart that most excellent gift of charity, the "very bond of peace, and of all virtues; without which, who-"soever liveth is counted dead before thee;" more especially when I am going to commemorate the unspeakable love of my blessed Saviour in dying for me, let not my heart be destitute of love towards my brethren; extend thy mercy and forgiveness unto all mine enemies, persecutors, and slanderers, and turn their hearts; which I as sincerely beg for them, as I hope for mercy and forgiveness at thy hands. Possess me with kindness and good-will for all mankind, that my faith may work by love, and dispose my heart according to my ability, to administer towards the wants and necessities of those who are any-wise afflicted or distressed in mind, body, or estate, and to do unto all men as I would they should do unto me; and give me that charity which covereth a multitude of sins, that, by doing good for evil, all men may know that I am thy disciple. Grant this for Jesus's sake. Amen.

See *Psalm* xv. cxxxiii. xli. cxii. *Matth.* xxv. 34, 41. *Matth.* xviii. 21. 1 *Cor.* xiii.

A Prayer the Morning you intend to communicate.

O MOST gracious and eternal Lord God, who hast called all such as are weary and heavy laden to come unto thee by faith and repentance, and thou wilt refresh them; in affiance on this thy gracious invitation I will come to thy heavenly table, not trusting in my own righteousness, but in thy manifold and great mercies; and although I am not worthy so much as to gather up the crumbs that fall from thy table, yet, since it is thy property always to have mercy, I will not despair of a kind reception: Forgive my want of a due preparation, and accept of my sincere desire to perform an acceptable service unto thee: Clothe me with the wedding garment, even the graces of the Gospel, and then I am sure I shall be a welcome guest at thy table, when I shall come thither in the likeness of thy Son Jesus Christ, in whom thou art well pleased. Possess my soul with a lively faith, profound humility, filial obedience, inflamed affection, and universal charity, that so I may become a worthy partaker of these holy mysteries, to thy great and endless comfort. .Grant this, O heavenly Father, if it be thy blessed will, through Jesus Christ. Amen. *Our Father, &c.*

See Psalm xxiii. xxv. xxvi.

A short Prayer before the Minister begins the Communion Service.

IN the multitude of thy tender mercies, O Lord God, do I now approach thine altar; O pardon my sins, and look not upon my unworthiness, (for I am a sinful creature, O Lord) but upon those motives which drew me hither, even my own miseries, and thy tender mercies: therefore help me to supply in humility what I want in worthiness: and let my bended knees and contrite heart shew, that I durst not have adventured hither, had not thy mercy held out the golden sceptre, and said, *Come unto me, all ye that labour and are heavy laden, and I will refresh you.*

¶ *Then shall the Priest return to the Lord's Table and begin the Offertory, saying one or more of these Sentences following, as he thinketh most convenient in his discretion.*

LET your light so shine before men, that they may see your good works, and glorify your Father which is in heaven. St. *Matth.* v. 16.

Lay not up for yourselves treasures upon earth, where moth and rust doth corrupt, and where thieves break through and steal: But lay up for yourselves treasures in heaven, where neither moth nor rust doth corrupt, and where thieves do not break through nor steal. St. *Matth.* vi. 19, 20.

Whatsoever ye would that men should do unto you, even so do unto them: For this is the law and the prophets. St. *Matth.* vii. 12.

Not every one that saith unto me, Lord, Lord, shall enter into the kingdom of heaven; but he that doeth the will of my Father, which is in heaven. St. *Matth.* vii. 12.

Zacchens stood forth and said unto the Lord, Behold, Lord, the half of my goods I give to the poor; and if I have done any wrong to any man, I restore him four-fold. St. *Luke* xix. 8.

Who goeth a warfare at any time at his own cost? Who planteth a vineyard and eateth not of the fruit thereof? Or who feedeth a flock, and eateth not of the milk of the flock? 1 *Cor.* ix. 7.

If we have sown unto you spiritual things, is it a great matter if we shall reap your worldly things? 1 *Cor.* ix. 11.

Do ye not know, that they who minister about holy things live of the sacrifice? and they who wait at the altar are partakers with the altar? Even so hath the Lord also ordained, that they who preach the gospel should live of the Gospel. 1 *Cor.* ix. 13, 14.

He that soweth little shall reap little: and he that soweth plenteously shall reap plenteously. Let every man do according as he is disposed in his heart: not grudgingly, or of necessity: For God loveth a cheerful giver. 2 *Cor.* ix. 6, 7.

Let him that is taught in the Word minister unto him that teacheth in all good things. Be not deceived, God is not mocked: for whatsoever a man soweth, that shall he reap. *Gal.* vi. 6, 7.

While we have time, let us do good unto all men; and specially unto them that are of the houshold of faith. *Gal.* vi. 10.

Godliness is great riches, if a man be content with that he hath: for we brought nothing into the world, neither may we carry any thing out. 1 *Tim.* vi. 6, 7.

Charge them who are rich in this world, that they may be ready to give, and glad to distribute; laying up in store for themselves a good foundation against the time to come, that they may attain eternal life. 1 *Tim.* vi. 17, 18, 19.

God is not unrighteous, that he will forget your works and labour, that proceedeth of love; which love ye have shewed for his Name's sake, who have ministered unto the saints, and yet do minister. *Heb.* vi. 10.

To do good, and to distribute, forget not: for with such sacrifices God is well pleased. *Heb.* xiii. 16.

Whoso hath this world's good, and seeth his brother have need, and shutteth up his compassion from him, how dwelleth the love of God in him? 1 St. *John* iii. 17.

Give alms of thy goods, and never turn thy face from any poor man; and then the face of the Lord shall not be turned away from thee. *Tob.* iv. 7.

Be merciful after thy power. If thou hast much, give plenteously: if thou hast little, do thy diligence gladly to give of that little: for so gatherest thou thyself a good reward in the day of necessity. *Tob.* iv. 8, 9.

He that hath pity upon the poor lendeth unto the Lord: and look, what he layeth out, it shall be paid him again. *Prov.* xix. 17.

Blessed be the man that provideth for the sick and needy: the Lord shall deliver him in the time of trouble. *Psalm* xli. 1.

¶ *Whilst these Sentences are in reading, the Deacons, Church-wardens, or other fit Person appointed for that purpose, shall receive the* **Alms** *for the Poor, and other Devotions of the People, in a decent Bason to be provided by the Parish for that Purpose, and reverently bring it to the Priest, who shall humbly present and place* **it** *upon the holy Table.*

At giving your Alms.

O LORD, who didst not despise the widow's mite, accept of this free-will offering of my hands, as an acknowledgment of thy right to all I enjoy, and towards the relief of any of thy poor members.

¶ *A Prayer to be said at going to the Altar, if Time will admit.*

O LORD, look down in mercy upon thy poor servant, who with great humility doth now approach thy holy table; O vouchsafe to grant me whatsoever thou seest wanting to fit me for thy divine acceptance, and for a worthy receiving of this blessed sacrament. Give me repentance unto life, not to be repented of; endue me with a lively faith, a perfect love of thee, and an universal charity and good-will to all mankind; that, thou pitying my weaknesses and forgiving my infirmities, I may worthily receive these pledges of thy divine love, to my support and comfort in this life, and my eternal happiness in that which is to come. *Amen.*

¶ *I would advise my devout Communicant, by all means, to read over these Prayers after receiving the Bread and Cup, and after drinking, if Time will admit; which will be the Case in a Number of Communicants.*

When you receive the Bread.

LORD, I am not worthy of the crumbs which fall from thy table, and yet thou givest unto me the bread of life. O let this divine food instil into my weak and languishing soul new supplies of grace, new life, new love, new vigour, and new resolutions, that I may never again faint nor tire in my duty.

Before receiving the Cup.

WHAT reward shall I give unto the Lord for all the benefits that he hath done unto me? I will receive the cup of salvation, and call upon the Name of the Lord. Grant, O merciful God, that this cup, which I am now about to receive, may be filled with thy mercy, and be unto me the cup of eternal blessing. Sprinkle me with the blood of the ever blessed

Jesus, that my soul being cleansed from all its corruptions, it may be ever precious in thy sight, O Lord, my strength, and my Redeemer!

After drinking.

BLESSED be God, the Father of our Lord Jesus Christ, for his unspeakable gift, in whom we have redemption through his blood, even the forgiveness of sins. Lord, I have done as thou hast commanded me, O let me find the great benefit of this divine institution. Pour down thy grace upon me, direct my paths, and enable me, by the strength of this divine food, to persevere in the practice of a holy and religious life, even to the last moment of my days. *Amen.*

¶ *And when there is a Communion, the Priest shall then place upon the Table so much Bread and Wine as he shall think sufficient. After which done, the Priest shall say,*

Let us pray for the whole State of Christ's Church militant here in Earth.

ALMIGHTY and everliving God, who, by thy holy Apostle hast taught us to make prayers and supplications, and to give thanks for all men; we humbly beseech thee most mercifully [* *to accept our alms and oblations, and*] to receive these our prayers which we offer unto thy divine Majesty, beseeching thee to inspire continually the universal Church with the spirit of truth, unity, and concord: And grant that all they that do confess thy holy Name, may agree in the truth of thy holy Word, and live in unity and godly love. We beseech thee also to save and defend all Christian kings, princes, and governors; and especially thy servant *GEORGE* our king, that under him we may be godly and quietly governed: And grant unto his whole council, and to all that are put in authority under him, that they may truly and indifferently minister justice, to the punishment of wickedness and vice, and to the maintenance of thy true religion and virtue. Give grace, O heavenly Father, to all bishops and curates, that they may, both by their life and doctrine, set forth thy true and lively Word, and rightly and duly administer thy holy sacraments. And to all thy people give thy heavenly grace; and especially to this congregation here present; that with meek heart and due reverence they may hear and receive thy holy Word; truly serving thee in holiness and righteousness all the days of their life. And we most humbly beseech thee of thy goodness, O

* If there be no Alms or Oblations, then shall the words ("to accept our Alms and Oblations") be left out.

Lord, to comfort and succour all them who in this transitory life are in trouble, sorrow, need, sickness, or any other adversity. And we also bless thy holy Name for all thy servants departed this life in thy faith and fear; beseeching thee to give us grace so to follow their good examples, that with them we may be partakers of thy heavenly kingdom. Grant this, O Father, for Jesus Christ's sake, our only Mediator and Advocate. *Amen.*

¶ *At the Time of the Celebration of the Communion, the Communicants being conveniently placed for the Receiving of the holy Sacrament, the Priest shall say this Exhortation:*

DEARLY beloved in the Lord, ye that mind to come to the Holy Communion of the body and blood of our Saviour Christ, must consider how Saint Paul exhorteth all persons diligently to try and examine themselves, before they presume to eat of that bread and drink of that cup. For as the benefit is great, if with a true penitent heart and lively faith we receive that holy sacrament (for then we spiritually eat the flesh of Christ, and drink his blood; then we dwell in Christ, and Christ in us; we are one with Christ, and Christ with us) so is the danger great, if we receive the same unworthily. For then we are guilty of the body and blood of Christ our Saviour; we eat and drink our damnation, not considering the Lord's body: we kindle God's wrath against us; we provoke him to plague us with divers diseases, and sundry kinds of death. Judge therefore yourselves, brethren, that ye be not judged of the Lord; repent ye truly for your sins past; have a lively and stedfast faith in Christ our Saviour; amend your lives, and be in perfect charity with all men; so shall ye be meet partakers of those holy mysteries. And above all things, ye must give most humble and hearty thanks to God the Father, the Son, and the Holy Ghost, for the redemption of the world by the death and passion of our Saviour Christ, both God and Man; who did humble himself even to the death upon the cross for us miserable sinners; who lay in darkness and the shadow of death, that he might make us the children of God, and exalt us to everlasting life. And to the end that we should always remember the exceeding great love of our Master and only Saviour, Jesus Christ, thus dying for us, and the innumerable benefits which by his precious blood-shedding he hath obtained to us; he hath instituted and ordained holy mysteries, as pledges of his love, and for a continual remembrance of his death, to our great and endless comfort. To him therefore, with the Father and the Holy Ghost, let us give (as we are most bounden) continual thanks; submitting ourselves wholly to his holy will and pleasure, and studying to serve him in true holiness and righteousness all the days of our life. *Amen.*

¶ *Then shall the Priest say to them that come to receive the Holy Communion,*

YE that do truly and earnestly repent you of your sins, and are in love and charity with your neighbours, and intend to lead a new life, following the commandments of God, and walking from henceforth in his holy ways, draw near with faith, and take this holy sacrament to your comfort; and make your humble confession to Almighty God, meekly kneeling upon your knees.

¶ *Then shall this general Confession be made, in the Name of all those that are minded to receive the Holy Communion, by one of the Ministers, both he and all the People kneeling humbly upon their Knees, and saying,*

ALMIGHTY God, Father of our Lord Jesus Christ, Maker of all things, Judge of all men, we acknowledge and bewail our manifold sins and wickedness, which we from time to time most grievously have committed, by thought, word, and deed, against thy divine Majesty, provoking most justly thy wrath and indignation against us. We do earnestly repent, and are heartily sorry for these our misdoings; the remembrance of them is grievous unto us; the burden of them is intolerable. Have mercy upon us, have mercy upon us, most merciful Father; for thy Son, our Lord, Jesus Christ's sake, forgive us all that is past; and grant that we may ever hereafter serve and please thee in newness of life, to the honour and glory of thy Name, through Jesus Christ our Lord. *Amen.*

¶ *Then shall the Priest (or the Bishop, being present) stand up, and turning himself to the People, pronounce this Absolution.*

ALMIGHTY God, our heavenly Father, who of his great mercy hath promised forgiveness of sins to all them that with hearty repentance and true faith turn unto him; have mercy upon you, pardon and deliver you from all your sins, confirm and strengthen you in all goodness, and bring you to everlasting life, through Jesus Christ our Lord. *Amen.*

¶ *Then shall the Priest say,*

Hear what comfortable words our Saviour Christ saith unto all that truly turn to him.

COME unto me, all ye that travel, and are heavy laden, and I will refresh you. St. *Matth.* xi. 28.

So God loved the world, that he gave his only begotten Son, to the end that all that believe in him should not perish, but have everlasting life. St. *John* iii. 16.

Hear also what Saint Paul saith.

This is a true saying, and worthy of all men to be received, That Jesus Christ came into the world to save sinners.—— 1 *Tim.* i. 15.

Hear also what Saint John saith.

If any man sin, we have an advocate with the Father, Jesus Christ the righteous; and he is the propitiation for our sins. 1 St. *John*, ii. 1, 2.

¶ *After which the Priest shall proceed, saying,*

Lift up your hearts.
Answ. We lift them up unto the Lord.
Priest. Let us give thanks unto our Lord God.
Answ. It is meet and right so to do.

¶ *Then shall the Priest turn to the Lord's Table, and say,*

IT is very meet, right, and our bounden duty, that we should at all times, and in all places, give thanks unto thee, O Lord, Holy * Father, Almighty Everlasting God.

¶ *Here shall follow the proper Preface according to the time, if there be any specially appointed, or else immediately shall follow,*

THEREFORE with angels and archangels, and with all the company of heaven, we laud and magnify thy glorious Name; evermore praising thee, and saying, Holy, holy, holy Lord God of hosts, heaven and earth are full of thy glory: glory be to thee, O Lord most high. Amen.

¶ *Proper Prefaces.*

¶ *Upon Christmas-day, and seven days after.*

BECAUSE thou didst give Jesus Christ thine only Son to be born as at this time for us: who, by the operation of the Holy Ghost, was made very man of the substance of the Virgin Mary his Mother, and that without spot of sin, to make us clean from all sin. Therefore with angels, &c.

* These words [Holy Father] must be omitted on Trinity Sunday.

¶ *Upon Easter-day, and seven days after.*

BUT chiefly are we bound to praise thee for the glorious resurrection of thy Son Jesus Christ our Lord: for he is the very Paschal Lamb, which was offered for us, and hath taken away the sin of the world; who by his death hath destroyed death, and by his rising to life again hath restored us to everlasting life. Therefore with angels, &c.

¶ *Upon Ascension-day, and seven days after.*

THROUGH thy most dearly beloved Son Jesus Christ our Lord: who after his most glorious resurrection manifestly appeared to all his Apostles, and in their sight ascended up into heaven, to prepare a place for us; that where he is, thither we might also ascend, and reign with him in glory. Therefore with angels, &c.

¶ *Upon Whitsunday, and six days after.*

THROUGH Jesus Christ our Lord; according to whose most true promise, the Holy Ghost came down as at this time from heaven with a sudden great sound, as it had been a mighty wind, in the likeness of fiery tongues, lighting upon the Apostles, to teach them and to lead them to all truth; giving them both the gift of divers languages, and also boldness with fervent zeal constantly to preach the gospel unto all nations; whereby we have been brought out of darkness and error, into the clear light and true knowledge of thee, and of thy Son Jesus Christ. Therefore with angels, &c.

¶ *Upon the feast of Trinity only,*

WHO art one God, one Lord: not one only person, but three persons in one substance. For that which we believe of the glory of the Father, the same we believe of the Son, and of the Holy Ghost, without any difference or inequality. Therefore with angels, &c.

¶ *After each of which Prefaces, shall immediately be sung or said,*

THEREFORE with angels and archangels, and with all the company of heaven, we laud and magnify thy glorious name; evermore praising thee, and saying, Holy, holy, holy Lord God of hosts, heaven and earth are full of thy glory: Glory be to thee, O Lord most high. Amen.

¶ *Then shall the Priest, kneeling down at the Lord's Table, say, in the Name of all them that shall receive the Communion, this Prayer following:*

WE do not presume to come to this thy table, O merciful Lord, trusting in our own righteousness, but in thy manifold and great mercies: We are not worthy so much as to gather up the crumbs under thy table. But thou art the same Lord; whose property is always to have mercy; grant us therefore, gracious Lord, so to eat the flesh of thy dear Son Jesus Christ, and to drink his blood, that our sinful bodies may be made clean by his body, and our souls washed through his most precious blood, and that we may ever more dwell in him, and he in us. Amen.

¶ *When the Priest, standing before the Table, hath so ordered the Bread and Wine, that he may with the more readiness and decency break the Bread before the People, and take the Cup into his hands, he shall say the Prayer of Consecration as followeth.*

ALMIGHTY God, our heavenly Father, who of thy tender mercy didst give thine only Son Jesus Christ to suffer death upon the Cross for our redemption; who made there (by his own oblation of himself once offered) a full, perfect, and sufficient sacrifice, oblation, and satisfaction for the sins of the whole world; and did institute, and in his holy Gospel command us to continue a perpetual memory of that his precious death, until his coming again; Hear us, O merciful Father, we most humbly beseech thee: and grant that we receiving these thy creatures of Bread and Wine, according to thy Son our Saviour Jesus Christ's holy institution, in remembrance of his death and passion, may be partakers of his most blessed Body and Blood: Who in the same night that he was betrayed * took bread; and when he had given thanks, † he brake it; and gave it to his disciples, saying, Take, eat, ‡ this is my body which is given for you; do this in remembrance of me. Likewise after Supper § he took the cup; and when he had given thanks, he gave it to them, saying, Drink ye all of this, for this ‖ is my Blood of the New Testament, which is shed for you, and for many, for the remission of sins: Do this, as oft as ye shall drink it, in remembrance of me. Amen.

* Here the Priest is to take the paten into his hands;

† And here to break the bread;

‡ And here to lay his hand upon all the bread.

§ Here he is to take the cup into his hand;

‖ And here to lay his hand upon every vessel (be it chalice or flagon) in which there is any wine to be Consecrated.

¶ *Then shall the Minister first receive the Communion in both kinds himself, and then proceed to deliver the same to the Bishops, Priests, and Deacons, in like manner, (if any be present) and after that to the people also in order, into their hands, all meekly kneeling. And when he delivereth the bread to any one, he shall say,*

THE body of our Lord Jesus Christ, which was given for thee, preserve thy body and soul unto everlasting life. Take, and eat this in remembrance that Christ died for thee, and feed on him in thy heart by faith with thanksgiving.

¶ *And the Minister that delivereth the Cup to any one, shall say,*

THE blood of our Lord Jesus Christ, which was shed for thee, preserve thy body and soul unto everlasting life.--- Drink this in remembrance that Christ's blood was shed for thee, and be thankful.

¶ *Then shall the Priest say the Lord's Prayer, the people repeating after him every petition.*

OUR Father which art in heaven, hallowed be thy Name; thy kingdom come; thy will be done in earth, as it is in heaven: give us this day our daily bread; and forgive us our trespasses, as we forgive them that trespass against us; and lead us not into temptation, but deliver us from evil: for thine is the kingdom, and the power, and the glory, for ever and ever. Amen.

¶ *After shall be said as followeth.*

O LORD and heavenly Father, we thy humble servants entirely desire thy fatherly goodness, mercifully to accept this our sacrifice of praise and thanksgiving; most humbly beseeching thee to grant, that by the merits and death of thy Son Jesus Christ, and through faith in his blood, we and all thy whole church may obtain remission of our sins, and all other benefits of his passion. And here we offer and present unto thee, O Lord, ourselves, our souls and bodies, to be a reasonable, holy, and lively sacrifice unto thee; humbly beseeching thee, that all we who are partakers of this holy communion, may be fulfilled with thy grace and heavenly benediction. And although we be unworthy through our manifold sins, to offer unto thee any sacrifice, yet we beseech thee to accept this our bounden duty and service; not weighing our merits, but pardoning our offences, through Jesus Christ our Lord; by whom, and with whom, in the unity of the Holy Ghost, all honour and glory be unto thee, O Father Almighty, world without end. *Amen.*

¶ *Or this:*

ALMIGHTY and everlasting God, we most heartily thank thee, for that thou dost vouchsafe to feed us, who have duly received these holy mysteries, with the spiritual food of the most precious body and blood of thy Son our Saviour Jesus Christ; and dost assure us thereby of thy favour and goodness towards us; and that we are very members incorporate in the mystical body of thy Son, which is the blessed company of all faithful people: and are also heirs through hope of thy everlasting kingdom, by the merits of the most precious death and passion of thy dear Son. And we most humbly beseech thee, O heavenly Father, so to assist us with thy grace, that we may continue in that holy fellowship, and do all such good works as thou hast prepared for us to walk in, through Jesus Christ our Lord; to whom, with thee and the Holy Ghost, be all honour and glory, world without end. *Amen.*

¶ *Then shall be said or sung,*

GLORY be to God on high, and in earth peace, good-will towards men. We praise thee, we bless thee, we worship thee, we glorify thee, we give thanks to thee for thy great glory, O Lord God, heavenly King, God the Father Almighty.

O Lord, the only begotten Son Jesu Christ; O Lord God, Lamb of God, Son of the Father, that takest away the sins of the world, have mercy upon us: Thou that takest away the sins of the world, have mercy upon us: Thou that takest away the sins of the world, receive our prayer: Thou that sittest at the right hand of God the Father, have mercy upon us.

For thou only art holy; thou only art the Lord; thou only, O Christ, with the Holy Ghost, art most high in the glory of God the Father. *Amen.*

¶ *Then the Priest (or Bishop, if he be present) shall let them depart with this Blessing:*

THE peace of God, which passeth all understanding, keep your hearts and minds in the knowledge and love of God, and of his Son Jesus Christ our Lord; and the blessing of God Almighty, the Father, the Son, and the Holy Ghost, be amongst you, and remain with you always. *Amen.*

¶ *Collects to be said after the Offertory, when there is no Communion, every such day one or more; and the same may be said also as often as occasion shall serve, after the Collects either of Morning or Evening Prayer, Communion, or Litany, by the Discretion of the Minister.*

ASSIST us mercifully, O Lord, in these our supplications and prayers, and dispose the ways of thy servants towards the attainment of everlasting salvation; that, among all the changes and chances of this mortal life, they may ever be defended by thy most gracious and ready help, through Jesus Christ our Lord. *Amen.*

O ALMIGHTY Lord, and everlasting God, vouchsafe, we beseech thee to direct, sanctify, and govern both our hearts and bodies in the ways of thy laws, and in the works of thy commandments; that through thy most mighty protection, both here and ever, we may be preserved in body and soul, through our Lord and Saviour Jesus Christ. *Amen.*

GRANT, we beseech thee, Almighty God, that the words which we have heard this day with our outward ears may, through thy grace, be so grafted inwardly in our hearts, that they may bring forth in us the fruit of good living, to the honour and praise of thy Name, through Jesus Christ our Lord. *Amen.*

PREVENT us, O Lord, in all our doings with thy most gracious favour, and further us with thy continual help; that in all our works begun, continued, and ended in thee, we may glorify thy holy Name, and finally by thy mercy obtain everlasting life, through Jesus Christ our Lord. *Amen.*

ALMIGHTY God, the Fountain of all wisdom, who knowest our necessities before we ask, and our ignorance in asking, we beseech thee to have compassion upon our infirmities; and those things which for our unworthiness we dare not, and for our blindness we cannot ask, vouchsafe to give us, for the worthiness of thy Son Jesus Christ our Lord. *Amen.*

ALMIGHTY God, who hast promised to hear the petitions of them that ask in thy Son's name: we beseech thee mercifully to incline thine ears to us that have made now our prayers and supplications unto thee; and grant that those things which we have faithfully asked according to thy will, may effectually be obtained to the relief of our necessity, and to the setting forth of thy glory, through Jesus Christ our Lord. *Amen.*

When you retire from the Altar.

'BLESS the Lord, O my soul: and all that is within me, 'bless his holy Name; bless the Lord, O my soul, and 'forget not all his benefits; who forgiveth all thine iniquities, 'and healeth all thy diseases; who redeemeth thy life from 'destruction, and crowneth thee with loving-kindness and tender 'mercies.' O let that heavenly food, which thou hast so lately fed me with, transfuse new life and new vigour into my soul, and into the souls of all those who have been partakers with me of this holy Communion, that our faith, hope, and charity may daily increase, and that we may all grow in grace, and in the knowledge of our Lord and Saviour Jesus Christ. *Amen* and *Amen.*

See *Psalm* viii. xxiii. lxvi. ciii.

PRAYERS AND MEDITATIONS

Which may be joined to the former, where the Communions are large.

Aspirations for a devout Communicant.

ENLIGHTEN, O Lord, the eyes of my understanding with the light of faith and wisdom, that I may ever look on thee, my Redeemer, as the *way*, the *truth*, and the *life*, which leadeth unto eternal life.---What am I, Lord, and what is my Father's house, that thou shouldest thus follow me with thy blessings? I was created by thee, and for thee; and mayest thou ever be the comfort of my soul. Good Jesus, my hope, and only refuge, I here render thee hearty thanks for all thy sufferings, and I beg that I may find shelter in thy wounds against all enemies, ghostly and bodily: imprint the memory of them fast in my heart, that I may love thee, and in all my sufferings never want thy divine assistance, or forget what thou hast suffered for me. Take from me all self-love, and give me perfect love for thee, that I may now be more faithful in my duty; and let nothing for the future put me out of my way: O that I could ever remember thee, think of thee, and delight in thee alone, and love thee only, who hast loved us, and washed us with thy most precious blood from the guilt of our sins. O that my senses may ever be shut against all vanity and sin, that my mind being free from all fruitless solicitude and fear, I may fix my heart there where true joys are only to be found! From henceforth I will seek unto thee, my only God; my affections and desires shall be fixed on thee; *in whose presence there is fulness of joy, and at whose right hand there are pleasures for evermore.*---My will I now resign into thy hands, desiring that thy will may be mine, both now and for ever. Be thou my Instructor and Director in all things, that I may never do or speak, desire or think, any thing but what is according to thy good will.

2 I AM thy servant, O Lord: O give me understanding according to thy word, that I may learn thy commandments, and lay aside all interest beside that of heaven. O sweet Jesus, Fountain of all goodness, guide my feet in thy paths, and teach me to do thy will: Disengage my heart from all unprofitable solicitude and vain desires: and though I live here upon earth, yet raise my affections to things above. How sweet, O Lord, is

thy Spirit! how pleasant to my lips are the words of thy mouth! O that I could ever be mindful of them, to fulfil thy laws! Make me to die daily to the world and all its vanities, and let the greatness of thy love make all that is earthly appear as nothing to me. Protect me against mine enemies; and in all dangers appear in my defence; make haste to help me, O Lord; and say unto my soul, *I am thy salvation.* Remember thou art my Redeemer, and have compassion on my poor distressed soul; clothe it with all virtue, and feed it with thy grace; for it belongs to thee to take care of those whom thou hast redeemed. In thee I live, sweet Jesus; for thy sake, I desire to die; both living and dying I will ever profess that thou art good, and that thy mercy endures for ever.

3 O THAT I could now give thee, O Lord, all that praise, glory, and honour, with which the angels and blessed spirits glorify thee in heaven! But because I am unable to do this, accept at least this my desire and good-will. Deliver me, O God, from every thing that is contrary to thy will; and be pleased so to dispose of my soul, as may be for thy glory and honour. I surrender myself into thy hands, and entirely resolve to submit to that state of life thou hast pleased to appoint me; and if it be more for thy honour that I suffer, I cheerfully accept it; *not my will, but thine be done.* Let nothing be now my comfort but thou, Lord Jesu, and nothing afflict me but my sins, and whatever else is displeasing to thy divine Majesty. O blessed Jesus, life eternal, by whom I live, and without whom I die, grant that I may now be united to thee, and that in the embraces of thy holy love and divine will, I may rest for ever. When shall I see thee, O sweet Saviour; when shall I appear before thy face; when shall I see thee in the land of the living? Till then I sigh, and bewail my banishment, desiring to be dissolved, and to be with Christ.

If these Ejaculations are not sufficient until the Post-Communion begins, you may enlarge them by reading more or less of these following Places in Scripture.

For Grace to love God's Law. Psalm xix. cxix.
For a Holy Life. Psalm lxxxv.
For Salvation and eternal Joy. Psalm xvi. xxiv.
For assurance of God's Care and Protection. Psalm xxxvii.
For the Comfort of God's Holy Spirit. Psalm xxxiv.
For the Grace of Humility. Psalm cxxxi.
For Devotion in Religion. Psalm xxvii.
Thanksgiving for God's mercies. Psalm ciii. cxxxvi. cxxxviii.

For Pardon of Sins. Psalm lxxxv. cvi. cxviii.
For Redemption by Christ. Psalm xcviii. cxviii.

An Act of Thankfulness and Resolution before the Post-Communion begins.

P*RAISE the Lord, O my soul; and all that is within me, bless his holy Name*; for now I find the mercy, the peace, the comfort, and the grace which flows from this fountain of spiritual communion with Christ: let the world know what he hath done for my soul; he hath rescued me, and many of these my poor brethren, from the nethermost hell: Wherefore I will love thee, O holy Jesus, more than I can express, and live and die in that most holy religion which thou hast revealed to me. O let me never pollute that body, or defile that soul, which the Saviour of the world delights to dwell in. O let no oaths or lyings, backbitings or slanderings, profane those lips, no obscenity or intemperance pollute that mouth through which these holy symbols have so lately passed: For which fresh instance of thy mercy and goodness I will praise thy holy name, beseeching thee to keep me in this temper and resolution of mind until *death is swallowed up in victory. Amen.*

A Prayer against evil and perplexing Thoughts.

G*O not far from me, O Lord my God; make haste to help me*; for corrupt imaginations are perpetually rising in my breast, and innumerable fears and sorrows close me in on every side. Be pleased, O gracious Lord, in this perplexity, to refresh my soul with some speedy comfort. Scatter and disperse all these dark and sinful thoughts which haunt my soul, by shedding abroad the light of thy grace in my heart; for in the extremity of this my grief, this is my only hope and comfort, that I can take sanctuary in thy goodness; repose my confidence, and cast all my care and burden on thee, who never failest them that call upon thee: Give me patience under these adversities, and a happy issue out of all these afflictions, both of body and mind. *Turn thee unto me, and have mercy upon me, for I am desolate and in misery: The sorrows of my heart are enlarged: O bring thou me out of all my troubles: Look upon my adversity and misery, and forgive me all my sins. O keep my soul and deliver me: Let me not be confounded, for I have put my trust in thee*, through Jesus Christ our Lord. *Amen.*

See *Psalm* vi. xxxiv. xlii. xliii. cii.

Upon Christmas-day, *and seven days after, you may add these to your other Devotions.*

I DESIRE, O Lord, to bless and praise thine infinite goodness, who didst take compassion upon mankind in their greatest misery, and hast provided so admirable a remedy, by sending thy only begotten Son to recover our corrupt and degenerate nature, and, by the purity of his doctrine, the example of his life, and the sacrifice of his death, to purchase eternal happiness for us. Grant, O Lord, that, through the assistance of thy grace and heavenly benediction, I may daily comply with those great things which thou hast done and designed for my salvation. Possess my soul with purity and piety, and all other Christian graces and virtues; that, living soberly, righteously, and godly in this present world, I may hereafter dwell with thee, O Father of mercies, and God of all comforts, in those mansions of bliss and glory which thou hast prepared for them that love thee. *Amen.*

See *Psalm* xix. xliv. lxxxix.

Easter-day, *and seven days after.*

BLESSED Jesus, who hast triumphed over the powers of darkness, and conquered hell and the grave, and who, by thy glorious resurrection, hast made known the power of thy divinity, and proved thyself the true Messias, keep me stedfast in this faith; and grant that all the actions of my life may testify the reality and sincerity of my belief, by a suitable conversation; that I may rise from the death of sin unto the life of righteousness; that as I am buried with thee by baptism, I may henceforth mortify all my corrupt lusts and affections, and daily proceed in all virtue and godliness of living, that, departing this life in thy faith and fear, I may have perfect consummation and bliss, both in body and soul, in thy eternal everlasting kingdom, who livest and reignest with the Father and the Holy Ghost, one God world without end. *Amen.*

See *Psalm* ii. lvii. cxi.

Whitsunday, *and six days after.*

O LORD my God, who by thy Son, our Saviour, Jesus Christ, hast promised the assistance of thy Holy Spirit to all that ask it of thee, I beseech thee always to direct my ways and actions, the thoughts and intentions of my heart, by the light of thy Holy Spirit. Let him be unto me a Spirit of sanctification, to purify my corrupt nature; a Spirit of counsel in all my difficulties; of direction, in all my doubts, fears, and scruples; of courage, in all my dangers; of constancy and consolation to me, under all my persecutions and sufferings, especially in time of sickness, and at the hour of death; that, being governed and guided by his divine influence and direction, I may pass through all the changes and chances of this mortal life, till he brings me to everlasting life, there to reign with the ever-blessed and glorious Trinity, world without end. *Amen.*

See *Psalm* xxxiv. xlii. xliii. li.

Trinity-Sunday.

GLORY be to thee, O God the Father, for creating me after thine own image, capable of loving thee, and enjoying thee eternally; for recovering me from a state of sin and misery, when I had lost and undone myself.---Glory be to thee, O God the Son, for undertaking the wonderful work of man's redemption, for rescuing me from the slavery of sin, and the dominion of Satan; for the accomplishing of which miraculous work of our salvation, thou didst descend from heaven, and didst put on the form of a servant, live a miserable life, and die a painful and accursed death.---Glory be to thee, O God the Holy Ghost, for those miraculous gifts and graces thou didst bestow upon the Apostles, and for those ordinary gifts whereby sincere Christians in all ages are enabled to work out their salvation; for thy preventing and restraining grace; for the subduing our understanding and affections to the obedience of faith and godliness; for inspiring us with good thoughts, and kindling good desires in our souls; for assisting us in all the methods of procuring eternal happiness.---Blessing and honour, thanksgiving and praise, more than I can express or conceive, be unto thee, O Father, Son, and Holy Ghost, for ever and ever. *Amen.*

See *Psalm* ii. xlvii. lxxii. cx.

After the Blessing, namely, *The Peace of God.*

GRANT, O Lord, that we, and all thy faithful servants, who have this day been made partakers of the holy sacrament, may obtain remission of our sins, and be confirmed in piety towards God, and in charity towards our neighbour, and may be delivered from the power and temptations of Satan, and, being filled with thy Spirit, may become worthy members of Christ's holy Church, and at last inherit eternal life, through the same our Lord Jesus Christ. *Amen.*

A Thanksgiving after the Sacrament, to be said at Home.

THOU, O my God, hast comforted my soul, thou hast strengthened and refreshed me with thy blessings, and rejoiced my heart with the tokens of thy love. How transporting are thy comforts, and how ravishing the effects of thy goodness towards them that fear thee! Thou hast treated a vile sinner at thy own table, and fed me with the bread that came down from heaven.---In what am I better than those to whom thou dost not grant this favour? It is not for my merits; but because thou wilt be glorified in doing good to the most unworthy, thou hast this day made me a happy example of this thy free grace and bounty. Grant me this favour also, O my God, that through the whole course of my life I may give thee praise and glory; that the due sense of thy mercies may make me unfeignedly thankful; and that my thankfulness may appear in a care to walk before thee in holiness, sobriety, and righteousness all the days of my life.

A Prayer in private, after receiving the Holy Communion.

O HOW plentiful is thy goodness, which thou hast laid up for them that fear thee, which thou hast prepared for them that put their trust in thy mercy, even before the sons of men! I praise and magnify thy great and glorious Name, O Lord, for all those manifold mercies and comforts which thou hast bestowed upon me ever since I was born. O Lord God, thou hast been my trust from my youth; by thee have I been holden up from the womb; my praise shall continually be of thee: But above all, blessed, and for ever blessed, be thy holy Name, for the manifestation of thy Son Jesus Christ, the fountain and foundation of all our happiness, and for feeding me this day (who am unworthy of the least of thy mercies) with the spiritual food of his most precious body and blood, to my great and endless comfort. Enable me, O Lord, through thy gracious assistance, to perform the conditions of that sacramental covenant which I have this day so solemnly renewed and confirmed in thy presence, and at thy table, that through the strength and power of that heavenly food I have there been partaker of, I may daily grow in grace, and in the knowledge of Christ Jesus, and abound in every good word and work. And subdue in me all those inordinate lusts and corrupt affections which war against my soul; purify my mind from all evil thoughts, bad intentions, and evil designs; and suffer not pride, vain-glory, self-love, malice, hatred, or revenge, or any other evil whatsoever, to reign in my mortal body; but do thou keep it for ever in the purpose of my heart, faithfully to fulfil these my baptismal vows and resolutions, which I have now again renewed at thy holy table; that, by persevering in all virtue and holiness of life, I may at length be an inheritor of that infinite happiness and glory which thou hast promised by Christ our Lord. *Amen.*

A Prayer in private for the grace of Perseverance.

HEAR, most merciful Saviour, I humbly beseech thee, and let thy grace be ever assistant to all the endeavours and designs of thy weak and unworthy servant. I am not able of myself to do or think any thing that is good or well-pleasing in thy sight. O let thy Holy Spirit continually guard me against those numerous temptations which so strongly encounter me. Fix my inconstant mind, that I may not be led away with the errors of the wicked, and fall from my own stedfastness, but that I may persevere in good works unto the end. Moderate my affections and desires, and confine them only to such objects as are well-pleasing in thy sight. Let thy will be the sole guide and measure of mine, that all my hopes and wishes may center in thee alone, and nothing may ever appear desirable to me, in comparison of a pure heart and peaceable conscience:---*Teach me thy way, O Lord, and I will walk in thy truth: O knit my heart unto thee, that I may fear thy Name.* Make me to love thee (as I ought) above all things, and let the interest of thy honour and glory be always dearer to me than gold or silver, or any other temporal advantage; for thou, O Lord, art my portion, thou art my only rest, in thee alone is fulness of joy and true satisfaction, and without thee is misery and torment. O Grant me this blessed retreat, this happy security, and then I shall find rest unto my soul, both here and hereafter. *Amen.*

See *Psalm* lxxxvi. cxix.

MORNING PRAYER.

PONDER my words, O Lord; consider my meditation: my voice shalt thou hear betimes, O Lord; early in the morning will I direct my prayer unto thee, and will look up, Psalm v. 1, 3. Almighty God, who dwellest in the highest heavens, yet vouchsafest do regard the lowest creature here upon earth, I humbly adore thy sacred majesty, and with all the powers of my soul and body to exalt and praise thy holy Name, for all the mercies and comforts of this life, and for the hopes and assurance of a better; for protecting me from the evils and dangers of the night past, and for bringing me safe to the light of a new day; continue this thy mercy and goodness to me; and as thou hast awakened my body from sleep, to raise my soul from the death of sin unto a life of righteousness. Deliver me, O God, from the evils of this day, and guide my feet in the paths of peace and holiness, and strengthen my resolutions to embrace all opportunities of doing good, and carefully to avoid all occasions of evil, especially those sins * which by nature and inclination I am most likely to fall into: and when through frailty, or the violence of any other temptation, I fall from my duty, do thou in mercy restore me again with a double portion of thy grace and holy Spirit, to maintain a more vigorous defence against Satan and his devices. Shower down thy graces and blessings upon all my relations, [*on my father and mother, on my brethren and sisters*] on all my friends, and give thy holy angels charge over them, to protect them from all sin and danger. Make me diligent in the duties of my calling, and that in all the changes and chances of this life, I may absolutely submit to thy divine providence. Let thy blessings be upon my actions, and let thy wisdom direct my intentions, that so the whole course of my life, and the principal designs of my heart, may be ordered by thy governance to do always that is righteous in thy sight, through Jesus Christ our Lord. *Amen.*

* Here name such sins as you are most afraid of.

See *Psalm* iv. xvi. xxiii. lxxxvi.

When you go out of your Chamber.

THE blessing of God descend upon me and all belonging to me, and dwell in my heart for evermore; and bless my going out and my coming in, now and for ever. *Amen.*

EVENING PRAYER.

LET my prayer, O Lord, be set forth as incense, and the lifting up of my hands be as an evening sacrifice, Psalm cxli. 2. O Lord our heavenly Father, Almighty and Everlasting God, whose glory the heaven of heavens cannot contain, look down from the throne of thy Majesty, and behold thy unworthy servant, prostrate at the foot of thy mercy-seat, humbly confessing unto thee the vanity and sinfulness of my whole life, especially the omissions of my duty and commissions of sin * this day, wherewith I have so lately offended thine infinite Majesty and goodness, and so grievously wounded my own soul: of these and all other my transgressions I most earnestly repent, and am heartily sorry for these

* Here name particular sins and failings of the day.

my misdoings; the remembrance of them is grievous unto me, the burden of them is intolerable: have mercy upon me, most merciful Father; for thy Son Jesus Christ's sake forgive me all that is past, and accept of these my prayers and supplications, through the merits and mediation of the same our mediator and redeemer. And although I am unworthy, through my manifold sins and iniquities, to offer unto thee any sacrifice of praise and thanksgiving, yet I beseech thee to accept of this my bounden duty, with my unfeigned thanks for all thy goodness and loving-kindness to me and all mankind † purely proceeding from thy bounty, and wholly intended for my good, and particularly for preserving me this day in the midst of so many dangers incident to my condition, and from so many calamities as are due to my sins. Thou art my creator, O my God, and protector; thou art the ultimate end of my being, and supreme perfection of my nature; under the shadow of thy wings is perpetual repose, and from the light of thy countenance flows eternal joy and felicity: to whom be glory and honour, world without end. Amen.

† Here name particular blessings and mercies.

And thou, O Lord, by whom kings reign, and princes decree justice, bless our most gracious Sovereign Lord King *George*, our gracious Queen *Charlotte*, his Royal Highness the Prince of *Wales*, and all the Royal Family: all my relations, friends, and kind benefactors *; let thy providence succour them and theirs from all evil and danger, and do thou reward them sevenfold into their bosom for all the good they have done or said of me. Be pleased likewise, O Lord, (in whose hands are the issues of life and death) to succour, help, and comfort all that are in danger, necessity and tribulation, all that labour under any bodily pain, sickness, or temptation *, or are disturbed in mind; relieve such according to their several necessities, giving them patience under their sufferings, and a happy issue out of all their afflictions. Subdue in me the evil spirit of wrath and revenge, and dispose my heart patiently to bear reproaches and wrongs, and to be ready not only to forgive, but also to do good for evil, that all men may know that I am Christ's disciple. And finally, O Lord, since thou hast ordained the day to labour in, and the night to take our rest, as I praise thee for the mercies of the day, so I humbly beg the continuance of thy gracious protection over me this night. Let thy holy angels pitch their tents, about my bed, that being safely delivered from all perils and dangers of this night, and comfortably refreshed with moderate

* Here name particular persons.

* Especially those for whom our prayers are desired.

sleep, I may be enabled to discharge the duties of my calling, and faithfully to persevere in holiness and pureness of living all the days of my life, to thy honour and glory, through our only mediator and advocate, Jesus Christ our Lord. *Amen. Our Father, &c.*

When you lie down in your bed.

I WILL lay me down in peace, and take my rest, for it is thou Lord only, that makest me to dwell in safety; and into thy hands I recommend my spirit, my soul and my body, for thou hast redeemed me, O Lord, thou God of truth.

THE END.

www.ingramcontent.com/pod-product-compliance
Lightning Source LLC
Chambersburg PA
CBHW031347070726
47496CB00017B/1821
9783744784887